> ## "Nolo's home page is worth bookmarking."
> —WALL STREET JOURNAL

LEGAL INFORMATION ONLINE ANYTIME

24 hours a day

www.nolo.com

AT THE NOLO.COM SELF-HELP LAW CENTER ON THE WEB, YOU'LL FIND

- Nolo's comprehensive Legal Encyclopedia, with links to other online resources
- SharkTalk: Everybody's Legal Dictionary
- Auntie Nolo—if you've got questions, Auntie's got answers
- Update information on Nolo books and software
- The Law Store—over 250 self-help legal products including:
     Downloadable Software, Books, Form Kits and E-Guides
- Discounts and other good deals, plus our hilarious Shark Talk game
- Our ever-popular lawyer jokes
- NoloBriefs.com, our monthly email newsletter

Quality LAW BOOKS & SOFTWARE FOR NON-LAWYERS

Nolo.com legal books and software are consistently first-rate because:

- A dozen in-house Nolo legal editors, working with highly skilled authors, ensure that our products are accurate, up-to-date and easy to use.
- We know our books get better when we listen to what our customers tell us. (Yes, we really do want to hear from you—please fill out and return the card at the back of this book.)
- We are maniacal about updating every book and software program to keep up with changes in the law.
- Our commitment to a more democratic legal system informs all of our work.

KEEPING CURRENT

We update our books regularly to reflect changes in the law and in legal procedures. Use our

SPECIAL UPGRADE OFFER

to stay up-to-date. See the back of this book for details.

DETROIT COLLEGE OF LAW

AN IMPORTANT MESSAGE TO OUR READERS

This product provides information and general advice about the law. But laws and procedures change frequently, and they can be interpreted differently by different people. For specific advice geared to your specific situation, consult an expert. No book, software or other published material is a substitute for personalized advice from a knowledgable lawyer licensed to practice law in your state.

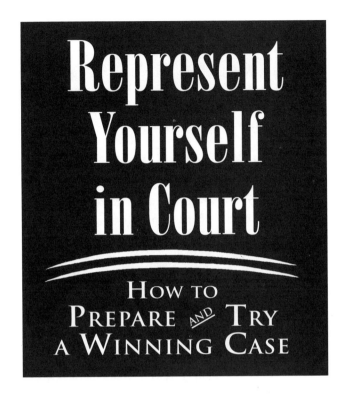

Represent Yourself in Court

How to Prepare and Try a Winning Case

BY ATTORNEYS PAUL BERGMAN
& SARA J. BERMAN-BARRETT

EDITED BY ATTORNEYS MARY RANDOLPH
& RALPH WARNER

COVER ILLUSTRATION BY BUD PEEN

CARTOONS BY MIKE TWOHY

nolo.com
LAW FOR ALL

KEEPING UP-TO-DATE

To keep its books up to date, Nolo issues new printings and new editions periodically. New printings reflect minor legal changes and technical corrections. New editions contain major legal changes, major text additions or major reorganizations. To find out if a later printing or edition of any Nolo book is available, call Nolo at 510-549-1976 or check our website at www.nolo.com.

To stay current, follow the "Update" service our website at www.nolo.com. In another effort to help you use Nolo's latest materials, we offer a 35% discount off the purchase of the new edition of your Nolo book when you turn in the cover of an earlier edition. (See the "Special Upgrade Offer" in the back of the book.)

This book was last revised in: JANUARY 1998

Second Edition	January 1998
Cover Illustration	Bud Peen
Cartoons	Mike Twohy
Book Design	Terri Hearsh
Production	Susan Putney
Proofreading	Ely Newman
Index	Jean Mann
Printing	Bertelsmann Industry Services, Inc.

Bergman, Paul, 1943—
   Represent yourself in court : how to prepare and try a winning case / by Paul Bergman & Sara J. Berman-Barrett ; edited by Mary Randolph & Ralph Warner. -- 2nd ed.
      p.   cm.
   Includes index.
   ISBN 0-87337-402-9
   1. Pro se representation--United States--Popular works.
I. Berman-Barrett, Sara J., 1964-   II. Randolph, Mary. III. Warner, Ralph E. IV. Title.
KF8841.B47   1997
347.73'504--dc21

                                      97-14437
                                        CIP

Quantity sales: For information on bulk purchases or corporate premium sales, please contact the Special Sales department. For academic sales or textbook adoptions, ask for Academic Sales. 800-955-4775, Nolo.com, 950 Parker St., Berkeley, CA, 94710.

DEDICATIONS

To Andrea and David,
and to all our readers whose active and knowledgeable participation in courtrooms across the country will improve the American system of justice.

ACKNOWLEDGMENTS

For the second edition, we gratefully acknowledge the assistance of Gordon Griller and Bob James of the Self-Service Center (Superior Court of Arizona), divorce lawyer and mediator Heidi Tuffias and two wonderful student researchers, Julie Drew and Elaine Draper.

TABLE OF CONTENTS

4 INVESTIGATING YOUR CASE

5 SETTLEMENT

6 PRE-TRIAL HEARINGS AND MOTIONS

7 WHAT YOU NEED TO PROVE AT TRIAL: THE PLAINTIFF'S PERSPECTIVE

8 WHAT YOU NEED TO PROVE AT TRIAL: THE DEFENDANT'S PERSPECTIVE

9 SELECTING THE DECISION-MAKER

10 OPENING STATEMENT

11 DIRECT EXAMINATION

12 CROSS-EXAMINATION

13 CLOSING ARGUMENT

17 ORGANIZING A TRIAL NOTEBOOK

18 EXPERT WITNESSES

19 WHEN YOUR TRIAL ENDS: JUDGMENTS & APPEALS

1

GOING IT ALONE IN COURT

This book provides the information you need to prepare for trial and represent yourself in court.

Whether you are a plaintiff (meaning that you have filed a lawsuit yourself) or a defendant (meaning that you have been sued), or whether you find yourself in state or federal court, understanding the procedures and techniques described in the book will help you present a persuasive, legally proper case.

If you had your "druthers," you might prefer to turn your case over to a trial attorney, who is trained to gather and present evidence in court. But a modern-day reality is that in many common situations it doesn't make economic sense to hire a lawyer. Perhaps you find yourself in a situation like one of these:

- You injured your back when you slipped on loose carpeting in an office building.

- You own a small manufacturing business and have sued a supplier for delivering faulty raw material.

- Your landlord has sued to evict you from your apartment, and you claim that the eviction is unlawful.

- You have filed a claim against your ex-spouse seeking increased child support.

- You are a building contractor who has been sued by a homeowner for using building materials other than those specified in a remodeling contract, and you claim that at the request of the homeowner you agreed to modify the contract after work was begun.

- Money that was left to you in trust by your parents has been depleted by improper investments made by the trust company having control of the trust assets.

In any of these instances (and many more), if you can't resolve your dispute in a friendly way, you may have to go to court to protect your rights.

Unfortunately, with fees charged by lawyers commonly running in excess of $150 an hour, it may not make economic sense for you to hire a lawyer. Even if you win and are able to collect what the other side owes you, the lawyer's fees may devour much of your gain. As a result, representing yourself in court or dropping your claim or defense altogether may be your only realistic alternatives.

A. THE SCOPE OF THIS BOOK

This book concentrates on rules and techniques for preparing and trying a civil case, including how to handle a case in family court (see Sidebar). You will learn how to figure out what evidence you need to gather to present a legally solid case, whether you are a plaintiff or a defendant. Among other things, you will also learn:

- how to prepare the initial pleadings (usually a complaint or an answer) that get a civil case underway (see Chapter 3)

- how to investigate your case, using both informal methods and formal "discovery" (see Chapter 4)

- how to try to settle your case without going to trial (see Chapter 5)

- how to select a jury if you are involved in a jury trial (see Chapter 9)

- how to present your own testimony and conduct "direct examination" of your witnesses and "cross-examination" of your adversary's witnesses (see Chapters 11 and 12)

- how to apply rules of evidence so that a judge will accept your admissible evidence and exclude your adversary's improper evidence (see Chapter 15)

- how to locate, hire and effectively use expert witnesses (see Chapter 18)

- how to present a persuasive opening statement and closing argument (see Chapters 10 and 13)

- how to comply with courtroom procedural rules, such as those governing where and when to sit and stand (see Chapter 2), how to handle "exhibits" (tangible objects like photographs and receipts) (see Chapter 14), and how to address the judge and opposing counsel (see Chapters 2 and 16)

The book guides you step by step through every phase of a civil trial, and each step is illustrated with sample dialogue.

Unless you are in court regularly, you may be uncertain about how a case proceeds from initial filing through trial. Therefore, this book also provides you with background information about what you can expect to see and what you need to do when you enter a courthouse and the courtroom in which your case will be heard. You will learn about where to file your court papers, how to subpoena witnesses (order witnesses to come to court and testify), the functions of a Clerk's Office and of a courtroom clerk and the powers and duties of all the personnel who typically carry out courthouse business, including bailiffs, court reporters, interpreters, attorneys, jurors and, of course, judges.

CIVIL VS. CRIMINAL CASES

This book covers only civil cases, which arise when private citizens (including corporations and other associations) sue each other. Criminal trials, by contrast, occur when a state or the federal government seeks to punish someone for violating a criminal law. The major differences are:

- **The Result:** Civil cases typically involve money paid by one party to the other; criminal cases may result in fines paid to the government and imprisonment.

- **The Burden of Proof:** In most civil cases, a plaintiff wins by convincing a judge or jury by a "preponderance of evidence" that her claim is true. In criminal cases the prosecution must prove a defendant's guilt "beyond a reasonable doubt."

- **The Right to a Jury Trial:** You are entitled to a jury in all criminal cases, but not in all civil cases. For example, you are entitled to a jury trial in personal injury cases, but not in child custody and spousal support cases. Also, most states require unanimous jury verdicts in criminal trials, but agreement by only three-fourths of the jurors in a civil case.

Finally, we devote a separate chapter (Chapter 20, Represent Yourself in Divorce and Family Court) to cases involving divorce and related family law matters, such as spousal abuse, child custody and support and spousal support. One reason for treating family law separately is that at least one spouse self-represents in a majority of divorce matters, and the percentage of cases with at least one self-represented litigant continues to increase. (See Sidebar for more reasons.)

FAMILY COURT CASES

Family court proceedings differ in substantial ways from regular civil court proceedings. Many issues are resolved in short hearings rather than at trial, judges alone decide family law matters (without a jury), mediation is used more frequently in family law cases and family law matters tend to be ongoing—they do not end after trial like most regular civil cases. For these reasons, family court will be handled in a separate chapter—Chapter 20, Represent Yourself in Divorce and Family Court. If you are getting divorced, need child support or alimony, seek a change in child custody or visitation rights, or need protection from an abusive spouse, please skip to Chapter 20 and read it first. Then you may refer back to specific sections as needed.

B. CAN YOU REALLY REPRESENT YOURSELF?

Unless your case is unusually complex, the answer is yes—a resounding yes. You may not have all the legal training of a lawyer, but you do not need to go to law school to have common sense, to learn how to ask intelligible questions or to recognize what makes people and information believable. In the words of Oliver Wendell Holmes, one of the country's most revered United States Supreme Court justices, "The life of the law has not been logic, it has been experience." As these words suggest, your everyday life experience is the foundation of most of what you need to know in order to present a coherent, convincing case. Besides, as former Supreme Court Chief Justice Warren Burger was fond of pointing out, many lawyers are not such hotshots; they often come to court ill-prepared and lacking professional skills.

Nor need you be intimidated by the difficulty of the law or legal reasoning. Your trial will probably be concerned with facts, not abstract legal issues. For the most part, you can look up the law you need to know. (See Chapter 22, Legal Research.) It turns out that legal reasoning is no different from everyday rational thinking. Forget the silly notion that you have to act or sound like an experienced lawyer to be successful in court. Both lawyers and non-lawyers with extremely varied personal styles can succeed in court. The admonition to "be yourself" is as appropriate inside the courtroom as outside.

Finally, no matter how many times you read this book and how carefully you prepare, you will probably feel anxious when you represent yourself in court, especially if your opponent has a lawyer. Perhaps it will help you to realize that you aren't alone. Many professionals feel anxiety—particularly before a first performance—whether they are lawyers about to begin a trial, teachers about to teach a class or actors about to perform on stage. So take a deep breath and gather up your courage. As long as you combine your common sense with the principles and techniques described in this book, and are not afraid to ask a court clerk, a law librarian, an attorney or even the judge for help if you become confused, you should be able to represent yourself competently and effectively.

C. COPING WITH BEING A "STRANGER IN A STRANGE LAND"

Courts are public institutions belonging to the people, and you have the right to represent yourself there. However, courts are also bureaucratic institutions with very heavy caseloads. Historically, filing clerks, courtroom clerks, court reporters and even judges have usually preferred to deal with lawyers rather than with people who represent themselves. (When you represent yourself, you may find yourself referred to as a "pro per" or "pro se" litigant—Latin abbreviations favored by judges and lawyers.) Although the increasing number of people representing themselves is beginning to change these attitudes in some places, many court personnel believe (often mistakenly) that because lawyers know how the system works, the court personnel can do their work more quickly and easily when they work with lawyers than when they work with pro pers.

So even if it seems highly unfair, do not be surprised if you encounter initial hostility from court personnel. In your eyes, you are an individual seeking justice and doing what you have a right to do. But to the people who work in courthouses every day, you may be perceived as someone who will make their jobs more difficult. Instead of helping you, they may even attempt to put obstacles in your path, hoping that you will get discouraged and go away.

Knowing ahead of time that you may encounter a hostile attitude is the best weapon against it. Read and study this book and other legal resources, many of which are available free in your local library. Learn how to prepare and present a persuasive case and follow correct clerk's office and courtroom procedures. If you believe that court personnel at any level are being rude to you, be courteous and professional in return, even as you insist upon fair treatment. By knowing and following court rules and courtroom techniques, you can often earn the respect of the judge and the others who work in the courtroom, and as a result you may well find that they will go out of their way to help you.

D. USING A LAWYER AS A "SELF-HELP LAW COACH"

Even if it does not make economic sense for you to turn your entire case over to an attorney, you may want to hire one on an hourly basis as a legal coach, to give you occasional advice. Your legal coach may simplify your legal research, suggest evidence you should look for to prove your legal claims, explain a confusing rule of evidence, inform you of time deadlines, provide help with courtroom procedures that are peculiar to your local court system and not covered in this book, or suggest ways of making your arguments more persuasive.

Attorneys have traditionally either assumed overall responsibility for a client's case or declined representation. However, due to a combination of the economics and time demands of a modern law practice and increased competition from paralegals (trained attorney assistants), accountants and other professionals, it is likely that many attorneys will agree to act as a legal coach.

Throughout the book, as we explain the process of preparing for and conducting a trial, we suggest situations in which you may want to look to a legal coach for assistance. But don't consult a coach until you read through the entire book. You may find that this book either answers many of the questions you would pay a lawyer to answer or points you in the direction in which you will be able to easily find the answer on your own. (For detailed advice about hiring and working with a legal coach, see Chapter 21, Getting Help from Attorneys: Hiring a Legal Coach.)

WORKING WITH AN ATTORNEY WHO IS REPRESENTING YOU

This book can be of assistance to you even if you are represented by an attorney in the traditional fashion. Your case belongs to you, not to your lawyer. A good lawyer will be able to do a better job of representing you if you are informed and knowledgeable about the trial process and can participate in making critical decisions.

E. HOW TO USE THIS BOOK

This book is very different from other books written for non-lawyers. It does not focus on any single area of the law or type of legal problem, but serves as a guide to courtroom self-representation in any kind of case. Because of the book's unique nature, you may find the following comments and suggestions helpful.

1. If Time Permits, Read Through the Book in Its Entirety

This book is designed both to increase your overall understanding of the litigation process and to provide detailed advice about each stage of trial. So,

unless you are already in the midst of trial and need to refer to a particular chapter immediately, begin preparing to represent yourself by reading through the book as a whole. As you become familiar with the litigation process, you will understand the significance of procedures and techniques that may initially seem peculiar or unnecessary.

LEARNING THE LINGO

There's no way to avoid it: If you represent yourself in court, you're going to run into a lot of unfamiliar legal terminology. This book tries to translate the most common jargon into plain English. For quick reference, check the Glossary at the back of the book.

---

2. Use This Book in Conjunction with Your Court System's Rules

This book can guide you through nearly every kind of trial in every court system (state or federal), because the litigation process is remarkably uniform throughout all of them. In part, this is because federal courts and most state courts share a "common law" heritage—a way of trying cases that came over from England and developed along with the country. And in part, it is because many local procedures are consistent with national legal codes (sets of rules and regulations). For example, the Federal Rules of Evidence govern the introduction of evidence in federal court trials. But around 40 states also use the Federal Rules in their trials. And even those states that have not formally adopted the Federal Rules have evidence rules that are remarkably similar to them. This means that, for the most part, trials are conducted in the same way nationwide. Because of this basic uniformity, the book frequently refers you to specific rules which, even if they differ somewhat from your state's rules, should help you undexrstand the procedures that will be followed in your case.

However, this book cannot serve as a complete guide to all the rules you need to know. For one thing, the exact rule in your court system may be somewhat different from the example we give. In that event, knowing of a specific federal or another state's rule can help you locate the rule in your state. (Chapter 22, Legal Research, will help you do this.) For another, each court system has procedural rules which, though important, cannot be covered in this book. For example, local court rules set time limits for filing various kinds of documents and page limits on the length of those documents. You will have to learn and comply with these local requirements.

That means that whenever you are concerned about a specific rule of evidence or procedure, you should always read your court system's specific provision. In general, the rule books you will need to have handy are these:

- **Your state's "Rules of Evidence."** These rules define the evidence you and your adversary are allowed to introduce for the consideration of a judge or jury. Evidence rules may be collected in an "Evidence Code" or a particular "chapter" or "title" of your state's laws, or they may be included in a larger collection of laws called "Rules of Civil Procedure."

- **Your state's "Rules of Court."** These are rules that set the procedures and deadlines that the courts in a state must follow. Generally, states have separate sets of rules for different kinds of courts. For example, a state may have one set of

rules for its "Municipal Courts" (courts that try cases involving limited amounts of money), another for its "Superior Courts" (courts that try cases involving higher amounts of money) and still others for its "Appellate Courts" (courts that review the decisions of Municipal and Superior courts). All the rules may, however, be published in a single book. Some states also have separate sets of rules for specialized courts, such as Family Law Courts, which hear cases involving divorce, child custody and child support, and Probate Courts, which hear cases involving wills and trusts.

- **Your specific court's "Local Court Rules."** These rules define the rules for a specific courthouse, and generally allocate business between different courtrooms, specify where to file documents, set rules of courtroom behavior and the like.

STATES ORGANIZE THEIR TRIAL COURTS DIFFERENTLY

Some states have just one kind of trial court, which hears all sorts of cases. In Illinois, for example, "circuit courts" hear all kinds of disputes. But in California, cases that involve less than a certain dollar amount must be tried in Municipal Court, while larger cases go to "Superior Courts."

Books containing all of these rules should be available in a public law library. You may also want to purchase these books separately from the Clerk's Office (in the courthouse) or from a legal bookstore, so that you can have them close at hand for reference as you read through this book and go to court.

⚠️ **You must learn the court rules.** Even though you are not a lawyer, judges will expect you to know and follow all court rules. If you miss a deadline, use the wrong kind of paper or violate some other rule, you will suffer the consequences even though you are a pro per litigant.

For instance, assume that you want to ask for a jury trial and that your local rule requires that a jury trial request must be made 30 days after the initial pleadings are filed. If you miss that deadline, you will not have a jury trial unless you go through a laborious process to request an extension of time to file your demand and the judge is willing to make an exception (don't count on it!).

3. Make a Trial Notebook

We strongly recommend that you prepare a "trial notebook." A trial notebook is a series of outlines covering such matters as what you must prove (or, if you are a defendant, disprove), the evidence you have available to prove (or disprove) those matters, the topics you intend to cover on direct and cross-examination, a list of the names, addresses and telephone numbers of your witnesses, and the exhibits you plan to introduce into evidence. The notebook serves as your courtroom manager, because you can refer to it to make sure that you do not overlook evidence you planned to offer or an argument you intended to make.

As you read through the chapters describing the various stages of a trial, you will find specific sections indicating how to prepare an outline for inclusion in your trial notebook. A separate chapter (Chapter 17, Organizing a Trial Notebook) pulls together suggestions from earlier chapters and describes how to organize a trial notebook.

F. TRY TO SETTLE YOUR CASE

Over 90% of all lawsuits filed are resolved without a trial. If you can arrive at a fair resolution with your adversary without going to trial, you can save yourself time and money. By showing you how to prove and disprove legal claims, this book can help you arrive at a fair resolution of your dispute using settlement procedures.

There are also many alternatives to trials that are gaining in popularity. If you become involved in one or more of them, you can still use this book to understand and prepare your arguments.

Here are the typical non-trial situations you may find yourself in.

1. Hearings

Depending on the kind of dispute you're involved in, you may find yourself in a hearing rather than a trial. For example, you'll probably have a hearing if you are seeking an increase or a decrease in spousal or child support following your divorce, or if you need to prove how much money you are entitled to after a defendant has failed to answer your complaint. A court hearing is usually a short and narrowly defined proceeding in which you are not entitled to a jury. A judge conducts the hearing and makes a ruling. The other party to the dispute may not even be present in court. However, this book's advice is as pertinent to hearings as it is to trials. Many of the courtroom procedures and rules of evidence are exactly the same in a hearing as in a trial. And you still must offer evidence in a way that persuades the judge or hearing officer to rule in your favor.

2. Arbitration

Arbitration is an alternative to trial that is often perceived to be quicker and less costly than a trial. In arbitration, a privately agreed-to arbitrator, not a judge, rules on the case. There is no jury, pre-hearing procedures are more informal and the arbitrator is not strictly bound by rules of evidence. Arbitrators generally charge by either the full or half day; you and your adversary split the arbitrator's fee.

If you have a legal dispute, you may well find yourself involved in an arbitration rather than a trial. One reason is that in many states, judges have the power in certain kinds of cases to order you and your adversary to arbitrate a dispute. A second reason is that even though you didn't realize it, you may have signed an agreement that provides for binding arbitration of all disputes arising under the agreement. For example, if you are an investor who believes a brokerage house violated securities laws while handling your account, a condominium owner who has made a complaint against your condominium association for unreasonably restricting your right to remodel your unit, or a businessperson who wants to sue for breach of a written contract, you may have agreed in writing (in the broker's agreement, the condominium association's set of rules or the business contract) to arbitrate all disputes.

Though arbitration proceedings are generally more informal than trials, most of the principles described in this book also apply to arbitration. As

in a trial, you and your adversary present evidence to the arbitrator through your own testimony and the testimony of witnesses. Like a judge, an arbitrator evaluates the credibility and legal significance of evidence in order to decide whether you win or lose the case.

Also, because most arbitrators are lawyers, their actions tend to be strongly influenced by their legal training. The rules and procedures they follow generally closely resemble those used by judges in trials.

RESOURCES ON ARBITRATION

Arbitration Strategy and Technique, 3d ed., by Craig Peterson (Michie Co.), a comprehensive discussion of arbitration of legal disputes.

Settle It Out of Court: How to Resolve Business and Personal Disputes Using Mediation, Arbitration and Negotiation, by Thomas Crowley (John Wiley & Sons), a comprehensive guide that includes strategies for selecting arbitrators and mediators.

Alternative Dispute Resolution: Panacea or Anathema, by Harry T. Edwards, 99 Harvard Law Review 668 (1986), an analysis of the advantages and disadvantages of arbitration and other dispute resolution procedures.

Dispute Resolution, by Goldberg, Sander & Rogers (Little Brown & Co.), a textbook setting forth arbitration principles and methods.

3. Mediation

Another popular method of resolving disputes outside of court is mediation, which is generally more informal and less costly than arbitration. Mediation is a voluntary process in which you meet with your adversary in the company of a third person, the mediator. The mediator, who has no power to impose a solution, usually tries to facilitate settlement by clarifying each party's position, encouraging cooperation and suggesting possible solutions. Professional mediators charge for their services, typically by the hour. Normally, the parties split the mediator's fee.

Even though mediation may be informal, to use it to arrive at an acceptable solution you will probably need to demonstrate both to your adversary and to yourself that you have strong evidence to support your legal position, and that the evidence is admissible in court should mediation fail. Otherwise, you may make an unwise and unfair settlement just because you are afraid to go to trial. And just as in a trial, this book will help you represent your position effectively during mediation.

RESOURCES ON MEDIATION

How to Mediate Your Dispute, by Peter Lovenheim (Nolo Press).

Mediation: A Comprehensive Guide to Resolving Conflicts Without Litigation, by Folberg & Taylor (Jossey-Bass).

Mediation Processes: Practical Strategies for Resolving Conflict, by Christopher Moore (Jossey-Bass).

A Student's Guide to Mediation, by Rogers & Salem (Matthew Bender).

A Guide to Divorce Mediation, by Gary J. Friedman (Workman).

4. Negotiation

The most ancient way to settle a dispute is negotiation, in which you sit down with your adversary and try to resolve your differences. Whether or not your case goes to trial, you will almost certainly find yourself negotiating some or all of the issues that are important to you.

Against this background, it doesn't normally make sense to interpret your adversary's offer to "talk settlement" as a sign of weakness. Nor should you be reluctant to be the one to suggest a negotiated settlement. In fact, judges, arbitrators and mediators routinely urge adversaries to explore settlement even if previous attempts have failed. It's a wise person who never closes the door to a reasonable settlement.

RESOURCES ON NEGOTIATION

Effective Legal Negotiation and Settlement, by Charles Craver (Michie).

Effective Approaches to Settlement: A Handbook for Lawyers and Judges, by Wayne Brazil (Prentice Hall).

Getting to Yes, by Roger Fisher and William Ury (Houghton Mifflin) (the Bible on positional bargaining).

Joy of Settlement: The Family Lawyer's Guide to Effective Negotiation and Settlement Strategies, by Greg Herman, ed. (ABA). ■

2

THE COURTHOUSE AND THE COURTROOM

Representing yourself in court can be like traveling to a different country. Courtrooms, like nations, have unique rules and customs and even a somewhat different language. Just as with traveling, a successful courtroom experience depends on knowing where you want to go, what the rules are during your journey and what to expect when you get to your destination.

If you think of this book as your access guide to trial, this chapter is the part that explains the duties and functions of various people you are likely to encounter, the "lay of the land," customs and etiquette of the natives and tips for dealing with them.

A. AN OVERVIEW OF DIFFERENT COURTS

Federal courts decide cases involving federal laws or the U.S. Constitution, and cases where the parties are from different states and the amount of money in dispute is more than $75,000. In the federal system, there are three levels of courts:

- District courts, where most trials occur

- Courts of Appeal, which hear appeals from the district courts

- The United States Supreme Court (the highest of the federal courts), which hears appeals in a few cases of its choosing.

There are also some specialized courts within the federal court system, such as tax and bankruptcy courts.

State courts decide all the matters that are not covered in federal courts. State courts handle disputes involving state constitutions and state laws covering a wide variety of subjects, such as contracts, personal injuries and family law. In some situations, either a state or a federal court can hear a case.

State court systems have a variety of different names for their courts. Many (but not all) states have two or more kinds of trial courts. The lowest level courts are often called small claims, municipal, city, justice or traffic court—all of which have fairly tight limits on the types of cases they can hear. The next level of trial courts typically handles larger civil cases, serious criminal cases and most divorce and other domestic cases. In addition, some states have specialized courts that handle only very limited types of cases, such as juvenile or probate; these may be divisions of the general trial court.

The next level of court, in most states, is courts of appeal, which can review trial court decisions. And last is the highest state court, often called the supreme court (in New York, called the Appellate

Division). State supreme courts, like the U.S. Supreme Court, generally choose what cases they will hear from among the many requests they receive. They choose cases that deal with important legal issues, such as those affecting the legal weight and significance of future cases and the constitutionality of laws.

To appeal a case means to go to an appellate court and ask that it review and overturn the lower court's decision. Usually, you can appeal only if you think the trial court made a mistake about the law that affected the outcome of your case. You cannot appeal just because you don't think a judge or a jury made the correct decision. A trial court is often called the "finder of fact," and its factual conclusions are almost always binding on an appellate court. (See Chapter 19, When Your Trial Ends: Judgments and Appeals.)

RESOURCES ON COURTS

For more information, you may want to look at a book on the United States legal system, such as *Law and the Courts: A Handbook about United States Law and Procedures*, by the American Bar Association Public Education Division (ABA).

B. A TYPICAL COURTHOUSE

Before looking inside a courtroom, let's consider the courthouse as a whole. A courthouse is, in essence, a public office building for judges and their support personnel. Different courts are often located in different buildings; for example, the criminal court may be in a different building from the civil court.

THE COURTHOUSE AND THE COURTROOM

Inside the main entrance to a courthouse, you will often find a directory that lists particular courtrooms or offices. To locate the room you need, however, you may have to ask a guard, since courthouse directories tend not to be user-friendly. They may, for example, refer to courtrooms as "departments." They usually don't list helpful information such as where you must go to file legal papers or get information, and they often don't say where places like the cafeteria or law library are located. This is because it is assumed that lawyers—the courthouse's main clientele—know such things already.

BEEFED-UP SECURITY

As you enter some courthouses or courtrooms, especially in larger metropolitan communities, you may have to pass through a metal detector. Like airports, courthouses are now concerned about people bringing weapons in the building. There may also be a guard on duty.

You may feel a little lost or intimidated, especially on your first trip to court. The corridors—full of busy lawyers dragging huge briefcases, jurors roaming in bunches and the occasional armed guard standing by—can be rather imposing. It may help to know that you are not the only one who feels out of place. Since little effort is expended to orient the newcomer, new lawyers often get lost too. Of course, this lack of even minimal hospitality tends to hit pro pers like you harder.

It may help to remember the foreign country analogy; think of this as a very strange land where the people have a different culture and language. Learn their ways by putting aside any shyness you feel and asking for help as soon as you need it. If you don't get understandable answers, just keep asking. The courthouse is a public building, supported by your tax dollars; you not only have the right to be there but also to ask as many questions as you want.

Try not to get frustrated or angry. At times, court personnel can appear hostile even when they don't mean to be, simply because they are busy and usually overworked. Also, too often they assume that everyone who appears in court is experienced, and they don't take the little bit of extra time necessary to orient pro pers. With some patience, you will learn your way around the courthouse, and soon enough you may look so much like you know where you are going that people start asking you for help!

1. The Clerk's Office

One of the most important offices in the courthouse is the Clerk's Office. It's often located on the first or main floor. Typically, the Clerk's Office is where documents relating to all the cases pending or decided in a courthouse are filed and stored. If one building houses two or more courts, such as small claims court and civil court or federal district court and bankruptcy court, each court will have its own Clerk's Office. That's because each court has its own filing and record-keeping procedure. You'll have to locate the Clerk's Office for the court hearing your case.

⚠️ **Don't confuse the Clerk's Office and a judge's clerk.** Each judge (or courtroom) usually has an assistant called a "clerk." And that clerk may even have an office. But that is not the same as the central Clerk's Office in the courthouse, where documents are filed and stored. You will likely have to consult both the general Clerk's Office and your judge's clerk, as your case progresses. The duties of a judge's courtroom clerk are discussed in Section C, below.

WAITING ON LINE AT THE CLERK'S OFFICE

At many Clerk's Offices, as at the Post Office or bank, you'll probably file papers and talk to clerks over a counter or through a window. And, also as at the Post Office, there may be bureaucratic details like rigid hours and different windows for different services. For example, even if you've been waiting patiently in line, the Clerk's Office may close at lunch time, or you may belatedly learn that you waited in the criminal instead of the civil clerk's line. To avoid such problems, call ahead for information about hours and the specific procedures you must follow to file papers for your civil case.

Once you get to the front of the line, rule one is to be polite. The Clerk's Office personnel can help or hinder you, so it pays to try to get them on your side. Understand, however, that some clerks are prejudiced against pro pers. (A few even post signs warning you not to ask questions because they don't practice law.) So if you run into someone who is hostile, you must remain firm and not become intimidated. You are entitled to the procedural information you need, provided in language that you can understand. If you don't get it, ask to see the supervising clerk.

You will need to go to the Clerk's Office when you file legal papers in your case. You may also deal with the Clerk's Office to check court rules and procedures throughout your case. For example, you will go to the Clerk's Office if you need to file documents such as a pre-trial motion (a request for a court order, discussed in Chapter 6, Pre-Trial Hearings and Motions) or to get a subpoena (court order to appear in court). You can also review documents in the court file, a master file that typically includes all documents filed by you, your opponent or issued by the judge.

2. The Law Library

Many courthouses contain law libraries that are open to the public. The first day you go to the courthouse, it may be a good idea to locate the law library, find out its hours and walk through to take a look. You will learn more about using the law library in Chapter 22, Legal Research, but the more comfortable you are there, the more user-friendly it will be.

Often, several courthouses rely on one central library, and a few states don't provide courthouse libraries at all. If you need to consult some legal research materials and your courthouse doesn't have a public law library, ask someone at the Clerk's Office or an attorney you pass in the hallway where the nearest public law library is located. It may, for example, be at a nearby law school.

3. Courtrooms

The most important part of the courthouse is its courtrooms. We'll explore the inside of a typical courtroom in detail in Section D, below, but first a few words about the outside. Judges usually have their own regular courtrooms where they hold trials and other public hearings, and the judge's name and a number are usually posted on or next to the courtroom door.

Most courts prepare a calendar each day, listing the scheduled court hearings, and post it on or near the front door of the courtroom. And calendars for all courtrooms are usually posted in the Clerk's Office. Since a judge may be assigned to different courtrooms on different days or other calendaring changes may occur, it is good practice to verify the time and place of your court hearing both at the Clerk's Office and the courtroom.

A courtroom by another name is still a courtroom. The word "courtroom" may not appear on either posted calendars or the courtroom doors. Some courts use other words, such as "department." For example, you may see a sign like this outside a courtroom: DEPARTMENT 1 - JUDGE SUZANNE KAY.

Almost all trials are public, so unless there is a sign to the contrary, it's fine to walk into a courtroom, sit in the spectator section and observe. Always enter quietly so as not to disturb ongoing court proceedings.

4. Other Offices

Courthouses contain offices for court personnel, from judges to secretaries. They may also house the offices of local officials, such as the city or county attorney and public defender, and law enforcement officers, such as the sheriff or marshal. Courthouses sometimes contain office space for legal newspa-pers (newspapers that feature articles about current cases and advertisements for lawyers, legal secretaries, court reporters and other legal services). You may not need to deal with any of these offices personally.

Don't forget to eat. It's hard to function on an empty stomach, so you may want to ask if the courthouse has a snack bar or cafeteria. Many do, but the location is often so obscure that you wouldn't find it on your own.

C. THE COURTROOM PLAYERS

Who will you find in a typical courtroom? What are their roles? You need to understand, if only to know whom to approach for advice when you have questions.

1. The Judge

The judge is the man or woman, usually wearing a black robe, who sits on a raised platform at the front of the courtroom and presides over pre-trial hearings and trials. As their principal duties, judges:

- conduct hearings for and make rulings on pre-trial motions and discovery disputes

- preside over pre-trial conferences and facilitate settlement conferences

- control the trial of your case, subject to legal rules of evidence and procedure

- make legal rulings, such as deciding whether a particular piece of evidence can be presented in court or whether it must be excluded (not considered in evaluating the case)

- decide who wins and loses, and how much the loser must pay in damages, when there is no jury, and

- instruct the jury as to the law it must follow in rendering its verdict, in jury trials.

A judge by any other name is still a judge. The words "court," "bench," "magistrate," "commissioner" and "justice" are sometimes interchanged with the word "judge." ("Justice" typically refers to a judge on the highest appeals court in a state or in the United States Supreme Court.) So if the judge asks you to "approach the bench," that means the judge wants you to step up close so she can talk to you and your opponent privately. You'll refer to the judge as "Your Honor" or "the court." For example, you might say, "I ask that the court [meaning the judge] instruct Ms. Loretta Charles, a witness the defendant intends to have testify later on today, to leave the courtroom immediately."

Some judges hear criminal matters, others conduct only civil (non-criminal) proceedings, still others hear only cases involving juveniles. Judges' powers depend on the courts in which they preside. For instance, judges in small claims courts usually have power only to grant a limited sum of money damages, often between $2,500 and $5,000.

Judges in appeals courts do not conduct trials at all, but review decisions of trial courts. (See Chapter 19, When Your Trial Ends: Judgments and Appeals.) In large communities, where there are many judges, some judges may conduct hearings on pre-trial concerns but not the trials themselves. (See Chapter 6, Pre-Trial Hearings and Motions.) It follows that a different judge may be assigned to your case during different parts of the litigation process. For example, one judge may rule on your opponent's pre-trial motion to dismiss the case, another may conduct settlement negotiations, and still another may preside over the trial. (For information on how to challenge a judge—have the judge removed from your case—see Chapter 9, Selecting the Decision-Maker.)

Cases are also sometimes decided by someone known as a "judge pro tem" (short for the Latin, "judge pro tempore"). Generally, a judge pro tem is a practicing lawyer who is appointed to serve as a temporary judge. You almost always have a right not to accept a judge pro tem and to insist on a regular judge. However, if you exercise this right, your case may be delayed. If you agree to have your case heard by a judge pro tem, the pro tem has all the powers of a regularly appointed judge.

In some courtrooms, the judge is called a commissioner or magistrate. A commissioner or magistrate, typically an employee of the court system, is appointed to act as a judge and hear cases relating to a particular subject matter or in a particular court, such as city, municipal, small claims or traffic court. U.S. Magistrates are appointed by judges of federal district courts (federal trial courts); they hear pre-trial matters in civil and criminal cases and conduct some trials. Sometimes, the magistrate will hear a case (if the parties agree), and make a recommendation to the district court for a particular ruling; the district court judge signs the actual court order.

2.   The Judge's Court Clerk

The judge's clerk (also called the court clerk or the judge's court clerk) is a member of the court clerk's staff who works for a particular judge. The judge's clerk has many duties, including preparing and maintaining the judge's calendar (often called the "docket"), which, like an appointment calendar, lists the dates and times for trials and other matters. The judge's clerk normally sits at a desk in front of the judge's bench. Either the clerk or the bailiff (see Section 4, below) will check you in when you arrive in the courtroom.

The judge's clerk also retrieves case files, which are maintained and stored in the main Clerk's Office. Your case file consists of the papers, briefs, pleadings and other documents having to do with your case that have been filed—that is, delivered to the court's custody to be stored as permanent public records.

During trial, the judge's clerk keeps custody of exhibits, administers oaths to witnesses, jurors and interpreters, and generally helps the judge move cases along. If there are papers you must present to the judge during a court proceeding, you may be directed to hand them to the court clerk (or sometimes the bailiff), who will then pass them on to the judge or file them in the court file. For example, you may need to show the clerk a copy of a subpoena that you served on a witness who did not appear.

When a judge makes a final decision or issues an interim order (decision on an issue that arises before the close of the case), the judge's clerk typically prepares the order for the judge to sign, although some judges request attorneys or pro pers to prepare the orders.

GETTING ADVICE FROM CLERKS

Generally, you are not supposed to discuss the merits of your case with any court personnel without the other side present (called an "ex parte" contact). And clerks cannot give legal advice. However, you may ask commonplace procedural questions of the judge's clerk or law clerk, such as how you might get an extension ("continuance") for a court deadline you will not be able to meet. The judge's clerks (both the court clerk and law clerk) can also be a very valuable resource for routine questions about local court rules and special procedures unique to your judge. For example, a judge may want an extra copy (called a "courtesy copy") of pleadings you file with the main Clerk's Office to be sent directly to her courtroom.

If you are concerned that your question may be improper, try explaining the general idea of what you want to ask before you proceed with the full question. The most important thing to remember is to be especially polite to the judge's clerk and law clerk. They work with the judge on a daily basis, and they will not hesitate to tell the judge when someone has been rude to them.

3.   Law Clerks

Many judges, especially in federal and higher level state courts, have law clerks. Law clerks are often recent law school graduates. To assist their judge, law clerks:

- research the legal issues presented by the parties

- assist the judge with legal questions that arise before and sometimes during trials, and

- help draft the written orders or opinions judges sometimes produce to explain their rulings.

4.   The Bailiff

The bailiff, often classified as a peace officer and commonly dressed in uniform and armed, is an official of the court. As part of a wide range of duties, the bailiff:

- maintains order and decorum in the courtroom—for example, by removing disruptive spectators from the courtroom

- takes charge of juries

- escorts witnesses into and out of the courtroom, and

- hands exhibits to witnesses who are testifying, unless the court clerk does this.

5.   The Court Reporter

In most courts, a person called a court reporter records every word that is said during any official ("on the record") proceeding in the courtroom. During the proceeding, the reporter will read back testimony of a witness or a statement of a lawyer or pro per, upon request of the judge. If you want something read back for your own or the jury's benefit, you must ask the judge for permission to have the court reporter read it back.

In a few courts, such as small claims and some lower-level state trial courts, a court reporter is used only if the parties request one. And some courts now record proceedings with tape recorders. Someone (often a clerk) still runs the tape recorder, so that statements can be played back at the judge's request.

💡 **Speak clearly for court reporters and tape recorders.** When you're in court, stand tall and speak up so that a tape recorder or court reporter can correctly record your statements. Speak directly into the microphone if one is provided. Have your witnesses speak up too. And avoid interrupting, except when it is essential, such as in order to make objections. (See Chapter 16, Making and Responding to Objections.) It's difficult for a court reporter, and sometimes for a judge or jury, to sort out what's said when two or more people talk at once.

Court reporters will prepare a transcript booklet of what was said at a particular court session, upon the request of a party or the judge. It is often necessary to get a transcript if you plan to appeal. (See Chapter 19, When Your Trial Ends: Judgments and Appeals.) Court reporters typically charge by the page to prepare transcripts. Depending on the length of the hearing, they can be costly—several hundred dollars for just a few hours of court time.

6. Interpreters

Interpreters translate for witnesses and parties who have difficulty speaking or understanding English. Interpreters are sworn to interpret accurately. Parties typically pay for interpreters in civil cases—a one-day trial may cost between $150 and $300 for a common language such as Spanish, and as much as three or four times that for a less-common language. In most cases you cannot bring in just anyone (such as a friend or relative), even if that person would be well qualified to interpret. So, if you or a witness need an interpreter, ask the Clerk's Office, your judge's court clerk or your legal coach how to arrange for a court-certified interpreter.

7. Jurors

Jurors are people drawn from the area in which the court is located, to evaluate evidence and render verdicts in both criminal and civil cases. Typically called to be available for a couple of weeks at a time, potential jurors may never actually serve on a trial either because they are never needed or because the judge or a party dismisses them.

When jurors do serve on civil trials, their job is to decide whether claims are factually valid, and, if money is awarded, how much the winning party should receive. In limited situations, judges can overturn a jury's verdict or modify the amount of damages the jury awarded. (See Chapter 19, When Your Trial Ends: Judgments and Appeals.)

In typical civil jury trials, there are between six and 12 jurors and a few alternates, in case a juror gets sick or is unable to finish the trial. In contrast to criminal cases, which often require a unanimous jury, most states allow civil cases to be decided when three-fourths of the jurors agree.

Many cases do not come before juries; they are handled by judges alone. In a few situations, you are not allowed a jury; for example, judges alone handle many family law, bankruptcy and pre-trial matters. For some types of cases, in which a jury trial is an option, neither you nor your adversary will want a jury. (See Chapter 9, Selecting the Decision-Maker.)

8. Parties

Parties are the people or organizations (such as businesses or nonprofit groups) in whose names a case is brought (usually called "plaintiffs") or defended (usually called "defendants"). Cases can involve multiple defendants and sometimes multiple plaintiffs. As a pro per (sometimes called "pro se") you are a party who is representing yourself.

9. Witnesses

Two kinds of witnesses may appear at a trial: ordinary witnesses and expert witnesses.

a. Ordinary Witnesses

Witnesses testify under oath to information they know through personal knowledge. In the language of the courtroom, they may testify only to things they have perceived with their own senses, meaning what they have personally seen, heard, smelled, tasted or touched. For example, a bystander at a car accident may come into court and, when asked what she saw, say, "I saw the red car go through the stop sign and hit the blue car." However, if the owner of the blue car went home after the accident and told his neighbor (who did not witness the accident) all about it, the neighbor could not testify about how the accident actually occurred. The reason is that the neighbor did not perceive the accident.

Except for reimbursement of the costs of coming to court (a limited allowance for things like mileage to and from the courthouse), ordinary witnesses cannot be paid to testify. You can obtain a subpoena (court order) to compel a witness to come to court and testify, but typically only if the witness lives or works relatively near the courthouse—in some courts, within 100 miles. (For more details on subpoenas, see Chapter 11, Direct Examination.)

b.   Expert Witnesses

After a judge rules that a witness is qualified as an expert, that person can testify based on her special knowledge or training. Experts are not just medical doctors or rocket scientists, but also people such as auto mechanics, building contractors and computer programmers.

Experts testify under oath either about what they have personally seen or heard (like ordinary witnesses) or, more commonly, give their opinions about what conclusions should be drawn from testimony given by non-expert witnesses.

Unlike other witnesses, experts can be and almost always are paid for their time in preparing for and giving testimony, in addition to reimbursement for costs of coming to court. (See Chapter 18, Expert Witnesses.)

10. Attorneys

Attorneys—also called counsel, counselors or lawyers—speak and act on behalf of parties. Attorneys generally handle most aspects of a case for the parties they represent. For example, during trial attorneys may:

- question witnesses to bring out testimony that helps the client's case or refutes the opposing party's evidence (see Chapters 11 and 12 on Direct and Cross-Examination)

- object to improper testimony, exhibits or arguments of the opposing party (see Chapter 16, Making and Responding to Objections), and

- argue to the judge or jury how the facts and law show that her client should win the case (see Chapter 13, Closing Argument).

Attorneys also perform many out-of-court functions, such as conducting legal research, advising clients on strategy, drafting legal documents and negotiating settlements on behalf of their clients. Attorneys also sign and arrange for documents to be filed with the court and served (delivered) to the other party and witnesses on behalf of their clients.

In some courts, attorneys may be asked to draft court orders after a judge has made a ruling. This may be the judge's final decision or an interim decision, such as a ruling to exclude a certain document from being admitted into evidence.

As a party representing yourself, you will perform many of the functions that a lawyer does for a client. If your opponent is represented by a lawyer, you are expected to deal with the lawyer and not directly with your adversary. This means you should make phone calls to the attorney, not your opponent, and when you serve legal papers on your opponent, you should deliver them to the attorney. However, since you aren't a lawyer (who is forbidden from directly contacting someone represented by an attorney), there may be an exceptional situation where, if the opportunity arises, you will want to bypass the lawyer and talk to your opponent directly, perhaps in an effort to settle the case.

You should also be aware, in case you are concerned that your opponent is not getting information from his lawyer, that another rule of professional conduct requires lawyers to communicate certain important information to their clients. For example, if you make an offer of settlement to the attorney, she must communicate it to her client, even if she thinks it's a bad proposal (see Chapter 5, Settlement).

Even when you represent yourself in court, you may want to hire a lawyer as a "coach" to help you find the applicable law and advise you on particular questions as your case progresses. (See Chapter 21, Getting Help from Attorneys: Hiring a Legal Coach, for more on self-help law coaches.)

11. Spectators

Most court proceedings are open to the public, so family members, friends and even total strangers may watch hearings and trials. You may find it helpful to enlist supportive friends to come to court with you and perhaps assist by carrying things and taking notes for you.

Spectators must usually sit in the back of the courtroom behind what is called "the bar"—actually a small fence or gate—that divides the area immediately surrounding the judge and jury from the rest of the room. In some courts, and especially in cases of spousal battering or sexual harassment, judges may grant permission for non-lawyer supporters to sit next to you at counsel table (place at the front of the courtroom where lawyers and pro pers sit while presenting their cases, discussed in Section D, below), to provide moral (though usually not verbal) support. If this is something you feel will help you present your case more effectively, ask the judge for permission.

D. THE COURTROOM AND ITS PHYSICAL LAYOUT

Even though as a pro per you are not expected to perfectly understand court rules and legal principles, you'll want to know where you should sit and stand and where everyone else belongs when you go to court. The more familiar you are with the lay of the land, the more easily you will find your way around—and look and feel confident doing so. Here are those parts of courtroom found in most state and federal courthouses.

1. Spectator Area

The spectator area is usually in the back of the courtroom, often separated from the rest of the courtroom by a bar or low partition. Members of the public sit in this area, as will you if you go to visit a courtroom. After checking in with the clerk, attorneys, parties and witnesses usually stay in this area until the names of their cases are called (announced) by the judge or clerk.

2. Jury Box

The jury box is where jurors sit during the jury selection and throughout trial. Traditionally it seats 12 jurors, although many states now use smaller juries in civil actions. The jury box area remains empty when there is no jury or the jury is out of the courtroom.

3. Jury Room

The jury room is separate from and often behind or adjacent to the courtroom itself. During jury trials, this is where jurors go to evaluate the evidence, deliberate and decide what their verdict will be.

4. Witness Box

This box-like area, also called the witness stand or just the stand, is located to the left or the right of the judge's bench, on the same side of the courtroom as the jury box. It is where witnesses sit when they testify. Before they are asked to testify, witnesses either sit in the spectator area or wait in the corridor outside the courtroom (if the judge has excluded them until they are called to the stand).

It is fairly routine for witnesses to be excluded (kept out of the courtroom until it is their turn to testify) so that their testimony is not influenced by what other witnesses say, but you may have to ask the judge to direct the witness to wait outside. Let your witnesses know ahead of time that they may be excluded so that they won't feel the judge is biased against them if he asks them to leave. You might suggest that they bring a book to read while they wait.

5. Judge's Bench

The judge's bench is the raised wooden desk or podium at the front of the courtroom where the judge sits. No attorneys or parties may go near the bench except upon the judge's request or by asking the court (the judge) for permission to approach the bench. During a jury trial, it's fairly common for the judge or a lawyer or pro per to request a short meeting at the bench (sometimes referred to as "a sidebar conference") to discuss some point out of the jury's hearing.

6. Judge's Chambers

The judge's chambers are his or her private office, often a room adjacent to or behind the courtroom. Judges may ask you to have a conference in chambers during a trial or other proceeding, if they want to go "off the record" and have a quiet place to confer. Judges use such conferences for various reasons—for example, to admonish one or both sides for inappropriate conduct in a jury trial or to urge one or both sides to settle. (See Chapter 5, Settlement, for more on settlement conferences.)

If you are asked to go into chambers and are uncomfortable with whatever is said, you may request that the conference be put on the record. That means the court reporter would come in, or you would all go back into the courtroom so the reporter can record what is said.

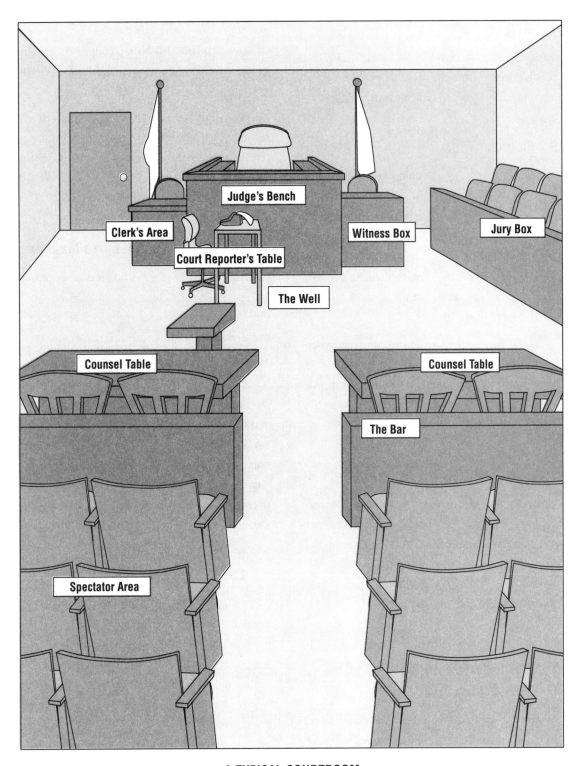

A TYPICAL COURTROOM

7. Clerk's Area

The court clerk usually sits on the side of the judge's bench opposite from the witness box. The clerk is often present during the court's proceedings.

8. Counsel Table

This area, which includes a table or two, chairs and sometimes a podium and microphone, is where attorneys and parties sit during trials and hearings on their cases. In most courtrooms, you make arguments and question witnesses while standing at the podium or microphone, though some judges may allow you to remain at the counsel table or stand closer to the witnesses.

You'll take your place at counsel table when your case is called. If the counsel tables are labeled for plaintiff or defendant, sit at the appropriate table. If they are not, the plaintiff usually sits on the side that is closer to the jury box.

9. The Well

The well is the space between the counsel table and the judge's bench. The court clerk and the court reporter may sit in the well area. Don't go into the well area, unless the courtroom is so small or the architecture is such that you must pass through it to take your seat at the counsel table.

E. COURTROOM RULES, CUSTOMS AND ETIQUETTE

Representing yourself, you may feel a bit insecure, especially before you have had a chance to observe other courtroom sessions. This is normal since you are not trained and experienced in conducting trials, and you may have been treated with hostility or heard stories about other pro pers being treated that way.

Again, just as if you were traveling to a distant land, you will have a more pleasant and productive trip if you follow local customs (in this case courtroom etiquette) and are as polite as possible. This section explains some of those customs.

1. Dress in a Business-like Manner

Generally, in court you should dress as if you were going to a job interview or a professional job—suits for men and suits or dresses for women. Better to overdress than to underdress. Federal courts tend to be more formal than state courts.

In lower courts, such as traffic, municipal or justice courts, however, it's appropriate to dress as you normally dress for your work—particularly if you come to court directly from your job. For example, if you are a contractor, dancer or security guard, and are coming from work, you don't need to change into lawyers' clothes, a suit and tie.

2. Be Courteous to Everyone, Especially Court Personnel

Not only is this a good way to treat everyone, it's particularly important in court, where you are likely to need a bit of helpful advice from time to time. You may also need small favors, such as a five-minute recess or for the clerk to notify you if your case is called and you need to be out of the courtroom for a minute to use the rest room or make a phone call. And you will have questions—even the most experienced attorneys do—such as how to

THE COURTHOUSE AND THE COURTROOM

label exhibits or file legal papers. Court personnel are much more apt to grant your requests and help you out if you are polite. It's as simple as that.

3. Check in When You Enter the Courtroom

When you enter the courtroom, check in with the court clerk. Give your name and case number, and ask if the court's schedule is on time and when the clerk believes your case will be called (heard by the judge). If court is in session when you enter the room, wait until the judge takes a break or pauses long enough after a proceeding is finished that you can discreetly hand the clerk a note with your name and case number, saying you want to check in.

4. Stay Close Until Your Case Is Called

Clerks usually have a good handle on the judge's schedule, but sometimes things go faster than anticipated because other parties aren't ready or a case is settled at the last minute. Or the judge may call cases out of order. Also, some courts schedule hearings in blocks, so that several matters are all set for the same time. In these courts, judges often take the routine or quick matters first and the cases or hearings they feel will take up more time after all the routine items are finished. Sometimes, judges put cases on "first call" or "second call," meaning earlier or later in the time block, and the lawyers or pro pers can request that their case be heard earlier or later depending on their schedules.

For all these reasons, if you need to leave the courtroom, even for a minute, it's best to let the clerk know where you are in case the judge is ready

for your case sooner than expected. Just like the train, sometimes the judge won't wait.

When the judge is ready to hear your case, the clerk or the judge will call out your name and the names of the other parties in your case. You will stand and say that you are present and ready to proceed. When the judge or clerk motions for you or tells you to come forward, you will take your seat at the counsel table.

MASTER CALENDAR SYSTEMS

In some courts, the first judge you are assigned to go see is not the judge who will be presiding over your trial, but what is called the "master calendar judge." The master calendar judge is a bit like a tour organizer who takes bunch of tourists into one central office first and then assigns them to particular tour guides according to what sights they will see, what language they speak or how big the group is. The master calendar judge evaluates a whole slew of cases as to how long they will take and what's likely to be involved in trying them. She sometimes tries to help the parties with settlement negotiations. Then, based on the cases and on availability of particular courtrooms, the master calendar judge assigns those cases that are ready for trial out to other courtrooms.

In assigning the case, the judge might say something like, "Nolo v. Klotchman to Department 2, trailing." This means your case will be heard by the judge in Courtroom 2, but that it will trail (follow) one or more other cases. The Clerk's Office should be able to tell you if your court uses a master calendar system and, if so, how it works.

5. Speak Respectfully to the Judge

As a general rule, you should always stand when addressing the judge. Only if you see that attorneys routinely talk to the judge while seated at the counsel table, as is the practice in some state courts, should you sit while you speak to the judge. Even then, it might be worth showing the courtesy of standing until the judge says you may be seated. If you are unable to stand for medical reasons, tell the judge that at the outset of the proceedings.

Always call the judge "Your Honor" when you speak to him or her. Do not say "Sir" and especially not "Ma'am." In court, by long-running tradition, "Your Honor" is the neutral, respectful term used by all. You are not giving up your democratic dignity by using it.

6. Don't Speak Directly to Opposing Counsel

When your case is being heard, always address the opposing attorney or pro per through the judge, not directly. For example, say, "Your Honor, this morning Ms. Ellis stated here in court that she would not be calling any other witnesses. Now she has stated that she intends to call two additional witnesses. I ask that they not be allowed to testify." Do not turn to Ms. Ellis directly and say, "You said you wouldn't call any other witnesses."

Always address or refer to attorneys, parties and witnesses by last names—for example, Mr. Neustadt or Ms. Doherty. Even if you have talked a lot on the phone and the person has told you to call him by his first name, use last names in court. This is to maintain the formal, respectful courtroom tone.

7. Find Out About Special Procedures

All judges follow the same broad procedural rules discussed in this book. Nevertheless, some judges have their own preferences as to detail, and if you can learn these, you will be well served. One good way to start is by watching your judge in action before your day in court; another is by talking with the clerk or a lawyer who has appeared before your judge. (For more information on researching your judge's background and style, see Chapter 9, Selecting the Decision-Maker.)

8. Don't Speak to the Judge About the Case Without Opposing Counsel Present

Legal rules prevent ex parte (one-sided) contacts with the judge. You wouldn't want the other lawyer to talk to the judge out of your presence; you should follow the same rules. Normally, if a judge or one party suggests a meeting either at the judge's bench (sometimes called a sidebar conference) or in the judge's chambers (office), both sides must be represented. Sometimes it will be up to you to help arrange a mutually convenient time for such a meeting.

9. Never Speak to Jurors About the Case Before the Verdict

If you are conducting a jury trial and happen to pass one of the jurors in your case in the hallway, a nod, smile or "hello" is permissible. But do not enter into any discussion with a juror or comment on your case within earshot of a juror.

10. Be Discreet

Do not discuss your case with witnesses, family members or anyone else in any public place where you can be overheard, such as the elevators, restrooms or cafeteria. The lawyer for your opponent is likely to know many people in the courthouse, and your words may quickly be passed along.

11. Ask for Help If You Are Treated Badly

Once a trial starts, it is normally too late to request a different judge. (See Chapter 9, Selecting the Decision-Maker, for how to challenge a judge before trial.) This does not mean, however, that you are helpless if you are treated in a demeaning or hostile way. For example, if you ask a simple question and are given a stern lecture that only idiots appear in court as pro pers and that you should immediately hire a lawyer, it's pretty clear that you are facing a steep uphill battle. However, you can:

- Ask to speak to the judge privately. If the judge agrees, tell her that you are doing your best to follow the rules, and point out politely that you have the right to represent yourself and be treated respectfully.

- Write a letter to the presiding judge (head or chief judge) of the court. The Clerk's Office can tell you who this is. Describe the specific instances in which you feel you were treated unfairly and ask that another judge be assigned to your case.

- If all else fails, consider filing a written motion with the court requesting a mistrial, disqualifying the judge on the grounds that the judge's bias (prejudice) against pro pers is making it impossible for you to have a full and fair trial.

If the judge's clerks or law clerks treat you unfairly or rudely, follow similar guidelines. First try speaking with them in a polite but firm way. If they do not improve, write a note to the judge (or presiding judge if you don't get anywhere with your judge) about the problems. ■

3

STARTING YOUR CASE

Almost nobody wants to go to court. So people usually attempt to resolve disputes out of court, informally, before filing a lawsuit. For example, if someone owes you money from a contract you both agreed to, you will most likely ask the person for the money before suing. If your request is denied, you may try another phone call, a written request for payment (demand letter) or perhaps a face-to-face negotiation session. Assuming enough money is at stake, your next step might be to show you mean business by hiring a lawyer to call or to write on your behalf. If you still haven't gotten paid, you might suggest a formal mediation or arbitration proceeding. (See Chapter 1, Going It Alone in Court, and Chapter 5, Settlement, for more on these out-of-court processes, called "alternative dispute resolution" or ADR).

Eventually, however, if the person who owes you money continues to refuse to pay, you have a choice to make: you can either bring a lawsuit or write off the money.

Can You Sue? These days, many companies, such as banks, realtors and insurance companies, include mandatory arbitration or mediation clauses in the contracts you sign to do business with them. These provisions mean you must resolve any dispute you have with the company through one of these out-of-court dispute resolution methods; you cannot bring a lawsuit in court.

This chapter describes the process by which lawsuits typically get underway. The most important rules that come into play at this preliminary stage concern how long plaintiffs have to file a lawsuit ("statutes of limitation") and which court has power to hear a case ("jurisdiction"). Next, plaintiffs and defendants set the stage for trial by filing "pleadings" (documents asserting and contesting legal claims). A plaintiff's initial pleading is usually called a "complaint." A complaint asserts one or more legal claims against a defendant and asks a court to do something, award money damages for example. A defendant's initial pleading is often called an "answer." An answer disputes either all or key portions of a complaint. In an answer, a defendant may also ask for legal relief against the plaintiff (money damages, for example) or even against a third party.

Many years ago, pleading rules were extremely technical and rigid, designed to weed out what the law regarded as unmeritorious claims at the earliest possible stage. As a result, many lawsuits never made it past this initial pleading stage. Modern pleading rules are somewhat more relaxed. Complaints and answers determine a case's general boundaries, but usually don't need to be long-winded or contain technical language. (As a result, the "weeding out" function performed by pleading rules in earlier days now falls to other procedures, such as summary judgment motions (see Chapter 6, Section B).) Court systems in some states even use official "check the boxes and fill in the blanks" pleading forms for many common kinds of cases. If such a form is available for your kind of case, simply purchase it from a courthouse clerk. If not, look for "pleading requirements" in your local court's set of procedural rules. Then, to fairly easily find the correct language and format for your case, refer to one of the commercially published attorney "form-books," or "pleading guides," available at any law library.

Read the rules for your local court district. As you might guess, the legal system has not completely escaped its picky past, and judges still occasionally use violations of pleading rules as excuses to get rid of cases before the cases cross the threshold of a courtroom. For instance, except when court-provided "fill in the blanks" forms are available, you are still likely to encounter pleading rules governing such matters as what kind of paper you must use and where to put the staples. You can usually obtain a copy of your local court rules from the courthouse clerk's office. Follow them carefully to make sure that a clerk does not reject your pleading.

RESOURCES ON PROCEDURAL RULES

To locate resources that can help you learn the necessary procedural rules involved in civil lawsuits, see Chapter 22, Legal Research. For a quick summary, try *West's Civil Procedure in a Nutshell*, by Mary Kay Kane (West Publishing Co.). For more detailed information, we recommend the following:

Civil Procedure, by Friedenthal, Kane and Miller (2nd Ed., West Publishing Co.).

Civil Procedure, by James and Hazard (4th Ed., Little, Brown & Co.).

Moore's Federal Practice, by James W. Moore (Matthew Bender).

Federal Procedure Forms, Lawyer's Edition (Lawyer's Coop/Bancroft Whitney).

Fundamentals of Litigation for Paralegals, by T. Mauet and M. Maerowitz (Little Brown & Co.).

A. DO YOU HAVE A GOOD CASE?

Before you decide to file a lawsuit, you should do at least enough research and investigation to make sure that the facts and law support a legally valid claim. For example, the fact that your adversary gave you a menacing look is not a legally valid claim, unless the look was accompanied by some threatening action. Or, if a car lightly touched your fender but did not damage your car or hurt you in any way, you don't have a solid legal claim.

But many of the disputes and injuries that occur in our daily lives do give rise to legally valid claims. A typical problem for which you may want to sue to recover damages (money) is an auto accident in which you suffered broken bones, pain and a damaged car, or a contract breached by a roofer who used materials that caused your new roof to leak.

But even if your claim is valid, it won't be worth your while to bring a lawsuit if your adversary has no money or assets, since you will not be able to collect any money if you win. So before you go to court, be sure to read about collecting judgments. (See Chapter 19, When Your Trial Ends: Judgments and Appeals.)

Also, before filing a complaint think about all the people or businesses who might be legally responsible for the harm you have suffered. This means that you should not focus on only the driver who struck you, the doctor who mistreated you, or the building contractor who added on the room whose roof collapsed. The more legally responsible parties you can legitimately name as defendants in your lawsuit, the better your chances both of achieving a favorable settlement and of collecting a judgment should you prevail at trial. For example:

- In an auto accident case, you plan to sue the driver of a car that struck you. If you do some investigation and find out that faulty brakes may have contributed to the accident, think about adding the brake manufacturer and the auto repair shop that recently worked on the brakes as defendants in your lawsuit. Perhaps after you name them as defendants in your lawsuit, the brake manufacturer and repair shop may be so anxious to avoid bad publicity, legal expenses or the risk of a large adverse judgment that they make quick settlement offers.

- In the case of a doctor who you think mistreated you, your inquiries may indicate that the insurance company that included the doctor in its company's health plan negligently allowed the doctor to practice medicine in areas in which the doctor was not qualified. If so, you might name the insurance company as well as the doctor as defendants in the lawsuit.

- In the case of a building contractor who did a substandard room addition, you may learn that part of the reason for the roof's collapse is that the contractor was itself supplied with substandard roofing materials by a roofing supply company. If so, you might name both the manufacturer and the seller of the roofing materials as defendants in the lawsuit.

Unless you have expertise in the subject matter of the lawsuit, you may not be able to identify all non-obvious individuals or businesses that could be legally responsible for the harm you have suffered. And even when you can identify additional legally responsible parties, you must balance the likelihood of collecting from them against the fact that naming additional defendants increases the scope and cost of case investigation and adds to the overall complexity of your lawsuit. Jurisdictional rules that determine which court has power to hear a case may also make it hard to include all defendants in a single lawsuit. (See Section C below.) In short, you may want to consult a legal coach before filing a lawsuit, to talk about whether the possible financial benefits of adding defendants outweighs the additional time, money and energy you will have to invest in your case.

Don't file a frivolous lawsuit. Investigate before you sue. To reduce the possibility that someone you sue will claim that you filed a groundless lawsuit simply for harassment purposes and in return will sue you for "abuse of process" or "malicious prosecution," make sure that you have what Fed. Rule of Civ. Proc. 11 refers to as "evidentiary support" for the accuracy of the claims in your complaint. This often means that you will have to do some legwork or even hire an expert in the particular field before deciding whether you are legally justified in filing a complaint. Occasionally, you may even encounter rules that require you to demonstrate that a complaint is justified. For example, in many states, if you want to sue a doctor for medical malpractice, you will have to attach to your complaint a physician's certificate attesting to the legitimacy of your claims.

RESOURCES ON EVALUATING YOUR CASE

Shepard's/McGraw Hill publishes a 15-volume series called *Preparing for Settlement and Trial* by the Shepard's Editorial Staff. It's a compilation of articles on current legal topics, such as age discrimination, construction site accidents, securities fraud and products liability. Each article has information to help a lawyer assess the strengths and weaknesses of a case, including checklists that point out what to ask for in discovery and citations to relevant legal authorities.

B. IS YOUR LAWSUIT TIMELY?

You may have a great case, but if you take too long to sue, the defendant can quickly get the case thrown out of court ("dismissed"). That's because "statutes of limitations" protect defendants from being hit with stale legal claims by strictly limiting the time after an alleged harm occurs that a plaintiff has to file a lawsuit. As a plaintiff, you should not spend excessive time negotiating with an adversary or debating whether to file a lawsuit.

1. How Long Do You Have to File?

How long do you have to file a lawsuit? No "one-size-fits-all" answer exists. Every state has its own time limits, and even within a state the period you have to file a lawsuit varies according to the type of claim. For example, rules in one state may allow plaintiffs with personal injury claims (for instance, a broken leg suffered in an auto accident) one year from the date of injury to file suit and plaintiffs who sue for breach of a written contract claims (for example, failure to make good on a promissory note) four years from the date of breach to sue. In another state, personal injury plaintiffs may have two years to sue, and plaintiffs with breach of written contract claims may have five years.

 Forget about statutes of limitations if you file suit within a year. Except for when you sue a government agency (see Sidebar), you almost always have at least one year from the date of harm to file a lawsuit, no matter what type of claim you have or which state you live in. In short, you should have no statute of limitations worries if you sue within this one-year period.

Example: Henry is injured in an auto accident on February 1. On March 1 of the same year, a lawyer whom Henry hires for a couple of hours of advice recommends that he seek compensation for his injuries from the driver of the other car. Henry spends months trying to settle with the other driver's insurance company. Finally, on September 1 of the same year, the insurance company writes to Henry that "We'll pay you $1000.00, nothing more." Henry concludes that the offer is grossly inadequate and decides to sue the other driver. If Henry isn't sure of his state's statute of limitations for personal injury cases, he should be sure to file the suit by February 1 of the next year. If Henry doesn't wait more than a year, his complaint will definitely be timely.

 Special short-time limits for claims against government agencies. Often you cannot sue a government agency unless you first file an administrative claim with the city, county or state of which the agency is a part. Check your state's rules quickly after you suffer harm—you may have as little as 60 days to submit an administrative claim. If (as usually happens) the government denies your claim, the denial letter will tell you how long you have to file a lawsuit in court.

Once you file a complaint on time, a statute of limitations has nothing to do with how long it takes for a case to conclude. However, most states do have separate "diligent prosecution" statutes which require you to move your case to trial within a certain time period or face dismissal.

DEFENDANTS MUST ALERT THE COURT TO A STATUTE OF LIMITATIONS VIOLATION

If you are a defendant who thinks that the plaintiff may have waited too long to sue, you'll also need to check the applicable state or federal limitations period to determine whether the lawsuit is timely. That's because judges rarely throw out late claims on their own. To be sure that a judge dismisses an untimely case, you normally include an "affirmative defense" in your answer, alleging that the plaintiff's complaint is untimely (see Section B3a below). As an alternative to filing an answer, in some courts you can file a "Motion to Dismiss" asking a judge to throw out an untimely complaint.

---

2. When Does the Clock Start Ticking?

Once you have ascertained what statute of limitations applies to your case, your next step is to determine when the clock starts ticking. As mentioned above, in most situations the time starts to run on the "date of harm." However, a huge exception to this general rule exists. The exception protects plaintiffs in situations where they may not be aware for months or even years that they have been harmed. In such situations, statutes of limitations may begin the clock ticking either on the "date of discovery" of the harm, or the date on which the plaintiff "should have discovered" the harm. In short, for some types of legal actions the statute of limitations clock can start ticking at three different times!

- Earliest: The date of harm.

- Later: The date on which the plaintiff reasonably should have discovered the harm. This refers to the date when a judge considers it fair to say that the plaintiff should have known about the harm, even if the plaintiff didn't actually know about it.

- Latest: The date on which the plaintiff actually discovered the harm.

Example: On January 1, a doctor performs a gallbladder operation on Phoebe, but mistakenly removes Phoebe's spleen. The doctor tells Phoebe of the screwup as soon as she wakes up. Phoebe's time period for suing the doctor begins to run on January 1, since the harm occurred on that date and Phoebe actually knew it. If a "two-year" statute of limitations for medical malpractice applies to Phoebe's case, she'd have two years from January 1 to file a lawsuit against the doctor.

Example: Same case, except the doctor tells Phoebe nothing of the surgical screwup. Phoebe is in constant pain following the January 1 surgery. A month later, on February 1, Phoebe talks to another doctor who tells her that she should not be in pain and that she should immediately come in to have it checked out. Phoebe delays going to the doctor until July 1 of the same year, at which time she finds out that her spleen had been removed mistakenly on January 1. In this situation, Phoebe's time period for suing the doctor probably begins to run on or shortly after February 1, because the pain coupled with the second doctor's advice determines when Phoebe should reasonably have discovered the harm.

Example: Same case, except that Phoebe suffers no unusual after-effects following the January 1 surgery. Phoebe is unaware that anything went wrong with the surgery until July 1 of the same year, when an x-ray during a routine medical checkup reveals that her spleen was removed. In this situation, since Phoebe did not discover and could not reasonably have discovered the harm until July 1, most states would measure Phoebe's time to sue from July 1.

CALCULATING THE "DATE OF HARM" WHEN A BORROWER DOESN'T REPAY A LOAN

Promissory notes often require debtors to repay borrowed money by making regular payments (either monthly or annually). Sometimes, but by no means always, promissory notes contain "acceleration clauses" that allow the creditor to sue immediately for the entire amount due on the note if a debtor misses a payment. If a creditor exercises an acceleration clause following a missed payment, the date that payment was due is the "date of harm" for statute of limitations purposes. However, if a note doesn't contain an acceleration clause (or even if it does and the lender chooses not to exercise it), a separate "date of harm" exists for each payment a debtor fails to make.

Example: Assume that a debtor is supposed to make payments on a promissory note on June 1 and December 1. The note does not contain an acceleration clause. The debtor fails to make the June 1 payment. The creditor can sue to try to collect the June 1 payment, but cannot sue for the December 1 payment unless and until the debtor fails to make it. June 1 and December 1 are separate "dates of harm," and the statute of limitations for each harm does not begin until the payment is missed.

Plaintiffs who are minors when they suffer harm also generally have longer than the usual periods within which to file suit. In general, statutes of limitations don't start running (are "tolled") until a minor reaches age 18, no matter how old the minor was when the harm occurred.

Example: Mack Awley, age 12, had been the adorable child star of a hit TV show for seven years when the show went off the air. At that time an accountant told Mack's family that during its entire seven-year run, the show's producer had paid Mack only half of what was due under Mack's written contract. On what date would Mack's time period for suing the producer begin to run? Answer: Most states would measure Mack's time to sue from the date of his 18th birthday. And since states generally have either four- or five-year statutes of limitations for disputes based on breaches of written contracts, Mack might be able to wait until he was 22 years of age to file suit—or 10 years after the "date of discovery" of the underpayments and 17 years after the earliest underpayment! (Of course, Mack's parents or guardians would be wise to file suit on Mack's behalf while Mack is still a minor. A stale case is generally harder to prove, and after years of delay Mack might well be less adorable than he is now.)

SAMPLE STATUTES OF LIMITATIONS PERIODS

The table below sets forth California's statutes of limitations for many common types of lawsuits. Different time periods may apply in your state, so be sure to check your state's rules carefully. However, the California rules are fairly typical and should give you a good idea of what you're likely to find when you read your state's rules. (See Chapter 22 for information about how to look up state laws.)

- Medical malpractice actions: Three years from the date of injury or one year from the date of discovery of the injury, whichever occurs first.

- Breach of an oral contract: Two years.

- Breach of a written contract: Four years.

- Eight years from the victim's 18th birthday or three years after the victim realizes that physical or psychological injury has resulted from childhood sexual abuse, no matter what the victim's age.

- Suits for libel or slander: One year.

- Personal injury claims based on negligence: One year.

- Suits for injuries resulting from domestic violence: Three years from the last act of domestic violence.

 ### RESOURCES ON STATUTE OF LIMITATIONS

Solving Statute of Limitations Problems, by Adolph Levy (Kluwer Law Book Publishers) is an analysis of various statute of limitations issues, written from the plaintiff's perspective.

C.   WHICH COURT HAS POWER TO HEAR A CASE ("JURISDICTION")?

The U.S. and state constitutions, as well as federal and state laws, grant and limit courts' "jurisdiction," which simply means the power to hear and decide a case. To make a legally valid decision, a court must have both "subject matter jurisdiction" (power to hear the kind of case a lawsuit involves) and "personal jurisdiction" (power over the parties involved in the lawsuit).

The reason this is important is that in addition to filing a case on time, a plaintiff has to file it in the proper court. If by mistake you file a case in the wrong court, a defendant may get the case moved (perhaps to a court that's less convenient or favorable to you than if you had chosen the proper court), or even get the case dismissed altogether by filing a "Motion to Dismiss for Lack of Jurisdiction." Dismissal for lack of jurisdiction may be only an inconvenience if you have time to refile the lawsuit in the proper court. But if the statute of limitations runs out before you can do this, your court-picking mistake may mean that the defendant can have your lawsuit thrown out permanently.

For almost every type of case, the rules we talk about below make it pretty simple to figure out in which court you should file your complaint. Be aware, however, that jurisdiction issues can occasionally become extremely complex when they involve such fundamental questions as whether a case should be heard in federal or state court or whether a state may require residents or businesses of a different state to appear in its courts.

"FULL FAITH AND CREDIT"

Under the "Full Faith and Credit" clause of the U.S. Constitution, every state has to honor court cases legally decided in other states. This means that if the court in which you file suit has the legal right to decide a case ("jurisdiction"), you can enforce the judgment anywhere in the country. (You may have to "register" your judgment in another state before you can collect in that state.)

1. Federal Court Jurisdiction

Since the overwhelming majority of cases (such as those involving personal injury claims, divorce, landlord-tenant problems, consumer claims, probate matters and contract disputes) involve state court claims, it is reasonably easy to separate out the few types of cases which must (or can be) filed in a federal trial court (called "Federal District Court"). Each state has at least one federal district court, and populous states contain as many as four federal districts.

One requirement for filing a case in federal district court is that the court have what lawyers call "subject matter jurisdiction." Federal courts have subject matter jurisdiction in two kinds of cases:

"Arising under a federal law" (called "federal question" cases). Federal district courts have subject matter jurisdiction if your case is based on ("arises under") any federal law. Examples include:

- You sue a police officer for violating a federal civil rights statute that authorizes civil damages lawsuits by persons who are unlawfully arrested.

- You own a patent, and sue an individual for manufacturing an item that violates your patent. (Federal law creates patent rights.)

- An owner of a small business, you sue a large company for violating federal antitrust laws.

- Under a federal law aimed at eliminating discrimination by businesses, a civil rights organization sues a restaurant chain for maintaining a policy of discouraging patronage by members of ethnic minority groups.

Diversity of citizenship cases. Federal district courts also have subject matter jurisdiction if you are suing a citizen of a different state (or a foreign national), and you are asking for at least $75,000 in money damages. (The monetary floor may be responsible for the old saying, "Don't make a federal case out of it.") Don't be fooled by the "subject matter jurisdiction" label—if a federal court has jurisdiction based on diversity of citizenship, the subject matter of the case doesn't matter. Examples of federal diversity jurisdiction include:

- As a citizen of New York injured in a traffic accident, you sue the New Jersey citizen who was driving the car that struck you and your complaint asks for damages in excess of $75,000. (You could file the complaint in a federal court in either New York or New Jersey.)

- As a businessperson who is a citizen of Florida, you sue a citizen of Great Britain for breaching a contract and causing you to lose $100,000.

- Bluegrass Corp., a corporation whose headquarters are in Kentucky, sues a company headquartered in Washington for $300,000 for breach of contract based on the Washington company's supplying the wrong kind of grass seed. (You could file the complaint in a federal court in either Kentucky or Washington.)

- A company headquartered in Tennessee sues a Texas Internet news service provider for $125,000 for publishing false information about the company's business operations. (You could file the complaint in a federal court in either Tennessee or Texas.)

CITIZENSHIP

For diversity jurisdiction purposes, individuals can be a citizen of only one state at a time, and are generally citizens of the state in which they maintain a principal residence. A corporation can be a citizen of two states, the state in which it is incorporated and the state in which it maintains its principal place of business. Federal courts have diversity jurisdiction only if complete diversity between plaintiffs and defendants exists.

Example: Cobb, a Georgia citizen, wants to sue Peachy Corp. Peachy Corp is a Delaware corporation with its principal place of business in Atlanta. Diversity jurisdiction does not exist, because Cobb and Peachy are both Georgia citizens.

Example: Cobb, a Georgia citizen, wants to sue Ruth (a Maryland citizen) and Wagner (a Georgia citizen). Diversity jurisdiction does not exist, because Cobb and one of the defendants are citizens of the same state.

 Dual Jurisdiction—when you can file in federal or state court. Most lawsuits that can be filed in federal district court can also be filed in state court. Federal courts have "exclusive" jurisdiction only in a very few kinds of "federal question" cases, such as lawsuits involving copyright violations, patent infringement and federal tax claims. This means that plaintiffs in all "diversity jurisdiction" cases and nearly all "federal question" cases have a choice of suing in federal or state court. Lawyers call the process of deciding which court is best for a plaintiff's case "forum shopping." For example, a plaintiff who has a choice of courts may consider such factors as:

- Which courthouse is closer to the plaintiff's place of work and business? For example, a plaintiff may choose to file in a state court simply because the nearest federal court is 250 miles away.

- Which court has a longer statute of limitations? A plaintiff whose case is untimely under state law would surely choose to file suit in federal district court in a federal question case if federal law provided a longer statute of limitations. (Federal courts use a state's statute of limitations in a "diversity jurisdiction" case.)

- Differences in the judges. For instance, a plaintiff may think that local state court judges have a judicial philosophy that makes them more likely to sympathize with the plaintiff's claim.

- Differences in the jury panel. State and federal courts may have different boundaries for jury selection purposes, and a plaintiff may, for example, file suit in federal court because it selects jurors from a wider geographic area.

Consult a legal coach for advice on forum shopping. Many subtle factors can affect "forum shopping." If you have a choice of courts, it would be wise to consult with a legal coach who has experience in both federal and state courts.

2.   State Court Jurisdiction

State courts almost always have the power to hear cases involving events that took place in the state where the court sits or if defendants reside in or are served with a summons and complaint in that state. This means that unless your case involves one of the few types of cases over which federal courts have exclusive jurisdiction (see Section C1 above), the state court in the state in which you live will probably have jurisdiction to hear your case, whether you're seeking an adoption, guardianship or divorce, suing a landlord or a tenant, have a consumer complaint against a contractor or repair shop, want to go to small claims court, need to probate a will, or are involved in one of the vast variety of other kinds of legal disputes. If you're reading this book and either are or are soon to be involved in a lawsuit, the odds are overwhelming that you'll be in state court.

Example: Dobbs, a Michigan resident, buys a used car from Rick's Used Cars, a Michigan business. A few weeks later, the car breaks down and Dobbs learns that it needs a new engine. Dobbs sues Rick's Used Cars for fraud and breach of contract in Michigan, which has jurisdiction because Rick's is a Michigan business.

Example: Allnut lives in Arizona and is involved in a traffic accident in Arizona with Marlowe, a Texas resident. Allnut could file a lawsuit in Arizona state court, which would have jurisdiction since the accident took place there. (Every state has a "motorist" law that confers jurisdiction on its state courts to hear cases involving all traffic accidents occurring in that state.) Allnut could also file suit in Texas, where Marlowe resides, since state courts almost always have jurisdiction to hear cases filed against defendants who live in the state. (However, Allnut could not file the lawsuit in California or Florida in an effort to combine a vacation with legal business. Neither state is the site where traffic accident-related events occurred or the defendant lives.)

Example: Elaine, a New York citizen, sues Officer Kramer (also a New York citizen) for violating her civil rights by falsely arresting her. Elaine bases the suit on a federal statute, 42 United States Code Sec. 1983, and asks for damages of $10,000. A New York federal court has the power to hear Elaine's case. Since the case is based on ("arises under") a federal statute, the New York federal court has jurisdiction even though Elaine and Officer Kramer are citizens of the same state and Elaine seeks less than $75,000. Alternatively, Elaine could file the lawsuit in New York state court, which would have power to hear the case because the arrest occurred in New York and both Elaine and Officer Kramer live there. The state court has "concurrent jurisdiction" with the federal court and enforces the federal law as it would a state law. Elaine can go "forum shopping" between New York federal and state court.

However, even when you properly decide that the state court in which you plan to file your lawsuit has subject matter jurisdiction, your search for the correct court is not finished. The issues you must next consider include:

• Does the state have a specialized court to hear your type of case? Most states divide up their trial courts' business according to the plaintiff's desired relief and to a case's subject matter; and

• Which county or city court within a state is the proper place for your case? Lawyers call this determining "venue." Let's briefly look at each of these issues.

a.   State courts that specialize according to the plaintiff's desired relief

When states divide up their trial courts' business according to the plaintiff's desired relief, they typically consider the amount of money and the type of remedy a plaintiff seeks. For example, a court may only have the power to award monetary damages up to $5,000, or may have the power to award monetary damages but not to issue a non-monetary ("extraordinary") remedy, such as an injunction (an order that a defendant do something other than pay money, such as to tear down a fence that encroaches on the plaintiff's property).

States use somewhat varied formulas when allocating business to trial courts according to a plaintiff's desired relief. However, the following divisions are typical:

• Small claims courts, hearing cases involving up to $5,000.

• Courts for medium-sized claims, perhaps limited to cases involving up to $25,000.

• Courts for all cases involving higher amounts, or involving requests for injunctions or other non-monetary remedies.

Terminology for different court divisions varies from one state to another. For example, a few states refer to their highest level trial courts as "supreme courts," while other states refer to them as "superior," "district" or "county" courts. Check your state's court rules if you are uncertain about which level of court has the power to hear your case.

Check your state's latest rules on courts' monetary limits. States often amend the dollar divisions between different trial courts. For example, a few states that now limit small claims courts to cases involving up to $5,000 are considering raising the amount to $7,500 or even $10,000

SAMPLE STATE TRIAL COURT STRUCTURES

Set forth below are the general civil trial court structures of seven states, based on the courts' monetary limits. (Source: Bureau of National Affairs, Directory of State and Federal Courts, Judges and Clerks, 1997 edition; data reported through 1994.)

1. **Colorado**

   Small Claims Court—Claims up to $3,500

   County Court—Claims up to $10,000

   District Court—Claims above $10,000

2. **Illinois**

   Small Claims Court—Claims up to $2,500

   Circuit Court—Claims above $2,500

3. **Michigan**

   Municipal Court—Small Claims Court up to $1,750; other cases up to $1,5000

   District Court—Small Claims Court up to $1,750; other cases up to $10,000

   Circuit Court—Claims above $10,000

4. **Texas**

   Justice of the Peace Court—Small Claims Court up to $5,000

   County Court—Claims up to $5,000

   District Court—Claims above $5,000

5. **New York**

   Town and Village Justice Court—Small Claims Court up to $3,000

   City Court—Small Claims Court up to $3,000; other claims up to $15,000

   District Court—Small Claims Court up to $3,000; other claims up to $15,000

   County Court—Claims up to $25,000

   Supreme Court—Claims above $25,000

6. **Pennsylvania**

   Philadelphia Municipal Court—Small Claims Court up to $5,000

   District Justice Court—Claims up to $4,000

   Court of Common Pleas—Claims above $4,000

7. **California**

   Small Claims Court—Claims up to $5,000

   Municipal Court—Claims up to $25,000

   Superior Court—Claims above $25,000

b. State courts that specialize according to a case's subject matter

Just as many restaurants have a limited menu, so do many courts specialize in hearing certain types of cases—regardless of the dollar amount of the case or whether a plaintiff seeks non-monetary relief. Specialization by subject matter allows judges and other court personnel to build expertise and quickly handle a certain type of case. For example, a particular state may have specialized Family Law Courts (hearing divorce, child support and related matters), Probate or Surrogate Courts (hearing guardianship cases, determining the validity of wills and trusts and distributing the property of deceased persons) and, in a few states, even Landlord-Tenant Courts. If a state has set up a specialized court to hear your type of case, that is the court to which it will be assigned regardless of how much money you seek or of whether you seek a non-monetary remedy.

c.   "Venue"

Venue made easy. Venue is almost always proper if you file a lawsuit in the court closest to the place in which the defendant resides or does business. If you are in doubt about venue and don't want to wade through the rules and exceptions, file the lawsuit there.

Assume now that you've considered the amount in dispute and the subject matter of your case and have determined which type or level of state court has the power to hear your case. Next you must think about which county in the state is the correct location for the lawsuit, a task that lawyers generally call "picking the proper venue." Venue rules limit the counties in which a case can be filed in order to spare defendants the needless inconvenience of fighting a case far from where the defendant lives or where relevant events took place. For venue purposes, the correct county can be the county in which:

- the defendant resides or does business;

- a contract was signed;

- a contract was to be carried out;

- an auto accident took place; or

- other events leading up to the lawsuit took place.

Since more than one county can be the correct venue for a lawsuit, often a plaintiff can again court ("forum") shop when deciding in which county to file a lawsuit.

Example: George and Jerry are both citizens of Texas. George lives in North County, near Oklaho-ma, and Jerry lives six hundred miles away in South County, near Mexico. One day George drives south and Jerry drives north, and they collide in the middle of Texas (let's call it Deep in the Heart of Texas County). George wants to sue Jerry. Venue rules probably require George to sue Jerry either in South County (where Jerry resides) or in Deep in the Heart of Texas County (where the collision occurred). George's home base, North County, is not a proper venue for the lawsuit, so Jerry is spared the inconvenience of having to defend himself there.

"FORUM NON CONVENIENS"

The doctrine of "forum non conveniens" allows a defendant to ask a court to exercise discretion to transfer a case to a court that is more convenient to the defendant and has a greater connection to events involved in the lawsuit. For example, diversity jurisdiction rules would allow Dan (a California citizen) to sue Raquelle (a Maine citizen) in California for $100,000 for a traffic accident that occurred in Maine. Almost certainly, the witnesses and all the physical evidence will be in Maine. Raquelle would probably file a motion asking the California court to exercise its forum non conveniens discretion and transfer the case to a federal court in Maine, and the court should grant her request.

---

3.   Personal Jurisdiction

To obtain an enforceable judgment in either a federal or state court, the court must have power over the particular defendant (individual or business) you are suing. Lawyers refer to this as "determining personal jurisdiction." Subject matter jurisdiction rules determine where a plaintiff can file a case; personal jurisdiction rules determine whether a court has power over a particular defendant.

Personal jurisdiction rules are usually the same in state and federal courts. With a few exceptions beyond the scope of this book, federal courts have the same personal jurisdiction as the state courts located in the same state. (For a limited exception giving greater power to federal courts, see Fed. Rule of Civil Proc. 4.)

a. Defendant Resides or Does Business in the State

Determining that a court has personal jurisdiction over a particular defendant is easy when you file the suit in the state in which the defendant resides or does business. The nearly universal rule is that the courts in a state have personal jurisdiction over all people or businesses that are citizens of or do business in that state. For example:

- You sue an Illinois citizen in an Illinois state court for breach of contract. It doesn't matter in which state you're a citizen, or where the events leading up to the lawsuit took place because an Illinois state court has personal jurisdiction over all citizens of Illinois.

- You sue an Illinois citizen in an Illinois federal court for breach of contract. Just like an Illinois state court, an Illinois federal court has personal jurisdiction over all citizens of Illinois. However, to establish that the Illinois federal court also has subject matter jurisdiction, you'd need to be a citizen of some state other than Illinois and ask for damages in excess of $75,000, or the case would have to arise under federal law.

b. Other Ways to Get Personal Jurisdiction

Personal jurisdiction rules can be a bit stickier when you file the suit in a state other than the one in which the defendant is a citizen or does business. To protect a defendant from being sued in a "hostile," possibly far-off location, personal jurisdiction rules require that facts exist that make it fair for a court to exercise power over a non-citizen.

Example: Debbie is a Texas citizen vacationing in Florida. While in Florida, Debbie buys what she is told are two brand new "fully loaded" computer systems at Kevin's Computer Shop. Debbie later learns that the computers are loaded with reused parts and won't perform the tasks that Kevin claimed. Debbie cannot sue Kevin in her home state of Texas. Texas has no personal jurisdiction over Kevin since Kevin is neither a citizen of nor does business in Texas, and Kevin hasn't been served with a summons and complaint in Texas.

Nevertheless, courts can and often do have personal jurisdiction over citizens of and businesses in other states in a variety of circumstances. Here are standard situations in which courts have personal jurisdiction over non-citizens:

- The defendant enters the state in which you filed suit after the case is filed, even if only for a short visit, and you serve the defendant with the court papers (normally a summons and complaint) in the state. (As in the children's game of "You're It," you'd have to find and "tag" the defendant with the papers while the defendant is in the state.)

Example: You sue Herb, an Ohio citizen, for breach of contract in a Minnesota court. After the suit is filed, your process server sees Herb drive into Minnesota for lunch, and serves Herb with the summons and complaint in Minnesota. (Of course, the Minnesota court would also need subject matter jurisdiction. A Minnesota state court has subject matter jurisdiction because Herb was served in Minnesota. A Minnesota federal court would have subject matter jurisdiction if the plaintiff and Herb were citizens of different states and the complaint asked for more than $75,000 in damages, or if the complaint was based on federal law.)

• The defendant caused a traffic accident in the state in which you've filed the lawsuit (and the case grows out of the traffic accident). Remember, all states have "motorist" statutes giving their courts power to decide cases growing out of accidents on their highways, regardless of the parties' citizenship. You could serve the defendant with the lawsuit anywhere, not just in the state where the lawsuit was filed.

• The defendant (individual or business) has engaged in at least a small but significant amount of activity that constitutes "minimum contacts" in the state in which you've filed the lawsuit (and the case involves that activity). "Yuck," you may be thinking—"what the heck are 'minimum contacts'?" You're not alone— many judges and lawyers wonder the same thing. The "minimum contacts" requirement generally means that a defendant (person or business) who is a citizen of a different state must have enough connection to the state where a case has been filed for a judge to conclude that it's fair for the state to exercise power over the defendant. While it's risky to overgeneralize in these situations, a judge would probably conclude that "minimum contacts" exist in the following situations:

- A business with its headquarters in another state maintains a branch office, store or warehouse in the state in which the suit is filed.

- A business with its headquarters in another state sends mail order catalogs into the state in which the suit is filed.

- An individual who is a citizen of another state solicits business by making phone calls to customers or publishing advertisements in the state in which the suit is filed.

- An Internet service provider that is a citizen of another state does business with paid subscribers or takes online orders from customers in the state in which the case is filed.

Example: While on vacation in Vermont, Aura (an Ohio citizen) visits Fred's Vermont Antiques and sees what is labeled as a packet of "ancient Etruscan coins." Fred tells her they are rare and worth much more than the $5,000 he is asking for them. When Aura returns home to Ohio, she calls Fred and buys the coins. She then discovers the coins are actually worth only a few hundred dollars, and wants to sue Fred. Aura will have to file the lawsuit in Vermont. Since Aura made the phone call to Fred rather than the other way around, Fred does not have enough "minimum contacts" with Ohio to support an exercise of Ohio's power over Fred.

A "minimum contacts" claim is stronger when the claim relates to the purpose of the "contacts." Assume that you want to sue a non-resident business, Abel Co., in your state based on Abel's maintaining a bicycle warehouse in your state. If your claim relates to a bicycle that you picked up at the warehouse, a judge is likely to conclude that it's fair to exercise personal jurisdiction over Abel Co. and allow your suit to proceed. But if your claim against Abel Co. grows out of a totally separate problem that has nothing to do with bicycles, the judge may conclude that Abel Co. does not have enough "minimum contacts" and dismiss your case at Abel Co.'s request.

JURISDICTION BASED ON REAL PROPERTY OWNERSHIP ("IN REM" JURISDICTION).

A state has limited jurisdiction (which lawyers call "in rem" jurisdiction) over a non-citizen person or business that owns real property in the state. Jurisdiction in this situation is limited in two ways:

- Jurisdiction extends only to the fair market value of the real property. This means that if you sue a non-citizen who owns an apartment house worth $500,000, the most your judgment can be worth is $500,000.

- In addition, the claim probably has to relate to the property. For example, you could get jurisdiction over the non-citizen owner of an apartment house if you slipped and fell on the property. But you could probably not get jurisdiction over the non-citizen owner if the lawsuit grows out of an entirely separate problem that has nothing to do with the apartment house.

D. HOW A LAWSUIT BEGINS

In the beginning of a lawsuit, the parties must file several documents with the court.

1. Plaintiff's Complaint

The complaint is the document that starts a lawsuit. It sets forth the legal claims and what action the plaintiff (person bringing the lawsuit) wants the court to take.

The names may change, but pleadings are essentially the same. A complaint or initial pleading is called a "petition" in some courts or for some types of cases. When the term "petition" is used, the person suing is called the "petitioner," and the person responding is called the "respondent."

For example, someone hurt in a car accident may sue the other driver. In the complaint, the plaintiff may ask the court to order the other side, usually called the defendant, to pay monetary damages to compensate the plaintiff for bodily injuries and damage to his car from the accident. Translated into everyday language, that complaint may say something like:

"The defendant hit my car. He hit my car because he carelessly ran a red light, which is against the law. I suffered damages in the amount of $100,000 because of his carelessness—$10,000 for the car repairs, $50,000 for medical bills, $20,000 in wages I lost since I couldn't work because of the injuries and $20,000 for the tremendous pain suffered. Therefore, I want the court to order the defendant to pay me $100,000."

To draft (write up) your complaint in the proper format, you should first determine if your court requires you to use a court-approved form. Ask at the Clerk's Office and read the court rules. If you don't have to use a specific court-approved form, follow the example of many lawyers and consult a legal form book in the law library. As the name implies, form books are collections of legal documents written in a fill-in-the-blank style. (See Chapter 22, Legal Research, for more on legal form books.)

! **Sample forms are illustrations, not models.** Throughout this book, you will find examples of legal documents that you are likely to encounter. We include these samples only to give you an idea of what the documents may look like. Because rules differ in different court systems, the actual documents used in your case may vary greatly from the samples. (See Chapter 22, Legal Research, for how you can find forms that meet specific requirements in your court.)

Subject to local variations, complaints commonly include:

① **Identifying information.** Your name, address and phone number goes in the upper left hand corner of the first page. As an option, you may also include a fax number and an e-mail address. This information enables court personnel and the defendant to contact and mail documents to you.

② **A caption.** A caption identifies the court in which you've filed the case, the parties (such as John Doe, "plaintiff" or "petitioner" versus Jane Doe, "defendant" or "respondent"), the case number (issued by a court clerk at the time of filing), and sometimes the type of case. For example, a caption may mention that a complaint is for "Breach of Contract" or "Negligence."

③ **Jurisdictional facts—federal court cases.** To establish a federal district court's power to hear a case (see Section C above), it's up to the plaintiff to include in a complaint information establishing a court's subject matter jurisdiction. (See Federal Rule of Civil Procedure 8-a.) For example, in a federal court "diversity jurisdiction" case, to establish the court's subject matter jurisdiction the complaint must refer to the different states of which the parties are citizens and request damages in excess of $75,000. In a federal question ("arising under federal law") case, the complaint must refer to the federal law on which the case is based. (See Appendix of Forms to Fed. Rules of Civil Proc., Form 2.) Facts showing a federal district court's personal jurisdiction need not be specially mentioned; it's up to the defendant to raise a problem of personal jurisdiction if one exists.

③ **Jurisdictional facts—state court cases.** Stating jurisdictional facts is ordinarily not necessary in state court cases. However, it's usually necessary that the complaint establish venue by identifying the county in which events giving rise to the dispute took place or in which the defendant resides or does business.

SAMPLE COMPLAINT

```
 1 | Nolo Pedestrian
   | [Street Address]            ①
 2 | [City, State, Zip Code]
   | [Phone number]
 3 |
   | Plaintiff in Pro Per
 4 |
 5 |
 6 |
 7 |
 8 |           THE _____ COURT OF _____ COUNTY
 9 |                    STATE OF _____
10 |    ②
11 | Nolo Pedestrian,                        )
   |                                         )
12 |                  Plaintiff,             )
   |                                         )
13 |   v.                                    )   Case No. _____
   |                                         )
14 | Sarah Adams,                            )   COMPLAINT
   |                                         )
15 |                  Defendant.             )
   |                                         )
16 | _____
17 |
18 | ③   1. On approximately January 1, year, at 3 p.m., while plaintiff was crossing Main Street at Elm
19 | Street in the City of _____, defendant Sarah Adams drove her truck through the
20 | crosswalk, negligently failing to stop for plaintiff, and thereby injuring plaintiff.
21 |     2. As a result of defendant's negligent driving, plaintiff's leg was broken, causing substantial pain
22 | and suffering, medical expenses, and lost income.
23 | ④   WHEREFORE, plaintiff prays for judgment against defendant in the sum of $100,000 plus costs and
24 | interest.
25 |
26 |                     ⑤   Nolo Pedestrian _____
   |                         Nolo Pedestrian, Plaintiff in Pro Per
27 |
28 |
```

③ **Factual assertions.** In plain English, you should briefly recite the facts ("allegations") that make up your legal claim. You do not have to set forth all the evidence on which you rely. A short summary of what happened is usually good enough. (Legal form-books, discussed in Chapter 22, have very helpful examples of how to word allegations for common types of legal claims, such as negligence and breach of contract.)

Don't just recite your desired result.
Though your complaint doesn't have to state all the background facts involved in your claim in detail, you do have to do more than make a vague, conclusory statement such as, "The defendant owes me money and I want the court to order him to give it to me." Instead, refer to the key facts giving rise to the debt. For example, if you are suing Denise to recover money she owes you on a written promissory note, refer to the contents of the Note and attach it as an Exhibit to your complaint.

A few states insist on more detailed complaints. Several states (including California and New York) are what lawyers often refer to as "code pleading" or "fact pleading" states. These states require that complaints include facts supporting each "element" of your legal claim (though you don't have to specifically refer to the elements by name or include voluminous details in the complaint). For a discussion of how to identify the elements of a legal claim, see Chapter 7, Section A.

④ **The "prayer for relief."** A complaint has to tell the court what you want by way of legal relief. (The term "prayer" means "request" and is a throwback to olden times when the Church heavily influenced the courts.) Most often you'll ask only for money damages. However, you might also ask the court to order the defendant to do something, such as to tear down a fence that encroaches on your property or to stop circulating a defamatory letter. For example, Knaplund's prayer for relief in the breach of contract example above may ask for "judgment against Defendant Edelstein in the sum of $17,000, plus interest and costs of suit." In some states, the prayer may also ask for a jury trial if you want one. A prayer for relief comes at the end of a complaint.

⑤ **Your signature.** Normally, your last task is to follow the prayer for relief with your signature, identifying you as the person making the legal claims. In many states you can "verify" your complaint by including above the signature line a statement such as "I declare under penalty of perjury that the allegations in the complaint are true." (Look at your state's rules for the exact language.) When you verify a complaint you force the defendant to file a verified and more detailed answer. In some instances, such as petitions for marital dissolution (divorce), a state's law may require that your initial pleading be verified.

SAMPLE FACTUAL LANGUAGE NECESSARY FOR SOME COMMON LEGAL CLAIMS

While modern pleading rules allow for much flexibility, here are examples of acceptable "short summary" factual statements for common types of legal claims:

Negligence:

1. On September 22, (year), Plaintiff Kebo was driving westbound and Defendant Jackson was driving eastbound on Olympic Boulevard.

2. Defendant negligently made a left-hand turn to go north on Main Street, colliding with Plaintiff's car.

3. As a result of Defendant's negligence, Plaintiff suffered loss of income and personal injuries that required hospitalization. Plaintiff will require additional medical treatment and will lose additional income in the future. Plaintiff's car was also damaged beyond repair.

Breach of Contract:

1. On March 12, (year), Plaintiff Knaplund and Defendant Edelstein entered into a contract for certain repairs to Edelstein's house. A copy of the contract is attached to this Complaint as Exhibit A.

2. Plaintiff made all the repairs called for by the contract and has fully performed all obligations required by the contract.

3. Defendant has refused to pay, and continues to refuse to pay, $17,000 that is due and owing under the terms of the contract.

Fraud:

1. On March 31, (year), Plaintiff Even and Defendant Strauss entered into a written contract in which Plaintiff agreed to purchase from Defendant a vacant lot located in Milwaukee County, Wisconsin. The price agreed upon was $125,000. A copy of the contract is attached to this complaint as Exhibit A.

2. Under the terms of the contract, Defendant stated that the lot was suitable for building a home.

3. This representation was false and fraudulent, because Defendant had used the lot for many years for dumping brewery residue, rendering the land clearly unsuitable for human habitation. Defendant knew that the representation was false and made it for the purpose of inducing Plaintiff to enter into the contract.

4. Plaintiff relied on Defendant's representation when purchasing the lot and was damaged as a result.

Promissory Note:

1. On or about February 14, (year), plaintiff Martinez loaned defendant Chung the sum of $10,000. Defendant signed a promissory note (a copy of which is attached as Exhibit "A") agreeing to repay this amount in its entirety to Plaintiff along with interest at the rate of 10% per year on October 14, (year).

2. Defendant did not pay the amount due under the promissory note, and the entire amount plus interest is now due and owing to Plaintiff.

⚠ Be scrupulously accurate when you verify a complaint. Your representation that all statements in your complaint are made under penalty of perjury will ordinarily be taken very seriously by judges. For example, if what you say under oath later in the case—perhaps in an affidavit you submit to the court, during a deposition or when testifying at trial—varies from what you say in a verified complaint, your opponent may offer the contradictory complaint language into evidence to cast doubt on your credibility. This will not happen if your complaint is unverified.

⚠ Check your local court rules before you try to file anything. In many courts, it is customary, and may be required by court rule, to submit papers on "pleading paper," which is just 8.5" by 11" paper with line numbers running down the left side of each page. You can get a supply of this paper at a stationery store. Or, if you use a computer to type your documents, check to see if your word processing program offers it as a built-in option.

Some courts impose other rules on how papers must be presented. A court may, for example, require two holes to be punched at the top of the page, so papers can be inserted directly into the court's file folder. It may require you to attach what's sometimes called a "blue-back"—a stiff piece of blue paper—to the back of your papers.

💡 You can amend your complaint. Pleadings such as the complaint can normally be amended (changed) after they are filed. For example, assume you are Nolo Pedestrian, the plaintiff suing Ms. Adams in her car accident example just above. After you have already filed a complaint against her, you determine that the companies that manufactured the car and the brakes may also be legally liable, and you want to add these companies as defendants.

Typically, if the defendant has not yet responded by filing an answer, you do not need permission from the court to amend. But you do need permission from the judge if the defendant has already answered your complaint. In that case you will have to file another paper with the court, a request for "leave" (permission) to amend your complaint, in which you state the reasons for the changes.

2. Summons

After a complaint is filed with the Clerk's Office (along with the required filing fee), the court issues a paper called a "summons." The purpose of a summons is to let the defendant know she is being sued and to tell her a number of important facts about the case, including the names of the plaintiff and defendant (called the parties), the name, address and phone number of the plaintiff's lawyer (if she has one), the case number (assigned by the Clerk's Office) and the dates by which the next pleading (normally, the defendant's answer) must be filed.

Generally, the plaintiff then arranges for the summons and complaint to be served on (physically delivered to) the defendant. Rules about how a summons and other legal documents must be served (called "service of process") must be strictly followed. If they are not, sometimes the lawsuit cannot go forward. Service of process is governed by Federal Rule of Civil Procedure 4 in federal courts, and you can usually find local service rules in your state's Civil Procedure statutes. (See Chapter 22, Legal Research, for more on finding legal rules and reference books.) Here are some rules about service of process that apply in many court systems:

- Normally, as a party to the lawsuit, you may not personally serve your own complaint and summons (if you are the plaintiff), or your own answer (if you are the defendant). You also cannot serve your own motions (requests for a court order) or subpoenas (court orders compelling someone to come to court). Another person must serve these pleadings for you. In some states, legal documents must be served by a law enforcement officer (sheriff, marshal or constable) or a licensed private process server; in other states, any adult not connected with the lawsuit can serve legal papers.

- A complaint must be served on the defendant within a certain time after it is filed. For example, in federal courts a complaint and summons must be served within 120 days after filing (Federal Rule of Civil Procedure 4(j)) and within 60 days under certain state rules.

- To serve legal documents on a business—for example, when your adversary is a company rather than an individual—you usually don't have to serve them personally. In most cases, it's enough to have the document delivered to the business place and have a copy of the document mailed to the same address.

- Some courts don't require personal delivery at all in certain circumstances; they allow service by regular U.S. mail.

- Courts require proof of service, usually in the form of a signed document that states when, how and on whom the complaint and summons were served. Often, you must file a proof of service whenever you file any type of pleading with the court. (See Federal Rule of Civil Procedure 4(g).) There's usually a deadline for filing. For example, a proof of service must be filed within 90 days of filing the complaint in some court systems.

You can be reimbursed for filing fees. The filing fee that the plaintiff pays when the complaint is filed with the Clerk's Office is considered one of the "fees and costs of suit." That means that if the plaintiff wins the lawsuit, the court may order the defendant to reimburse the plaintiff for the filing fee. U.S. courts typically do not, however, order the losing party to pay the winner's attorney fees.

SAMPLE PROOF OF SERVICE

1	Nolo Pedestrian [Street Address]
2	[City, State, Zip Code] [Phone Number]
3	
	Plaintiff in Pro Per
4	
5	
6	
7	
8	THE _____ COURT OF _____ COUNTY
9	STATE OF _____
10	
11	Nolo Pedestrian,)
	)
12	Plaintiff,) Case No. 12345
	)
13	v.) DECLARATION OF SERVICE BY MAIL
	)
14	Sarah Adams,)
	)
15	Defendant.)
	)
16	_____
17	Ms. Dana Lauren, the undersigned, hereby declares:
18	I am a citizen of the United States. I am over the age of 18 years and not a party to the within
19	action. On February 28, <u>year</u>, at the direction of Nolo Pedestrian, Plaintiff in Pro Per, I served the within
20	COMPLAINT FOR NEGLIGENCE AND SUMMONS on the following interested party by mailing, with
21	postage thereon fully prepaid, a true copy thereof to:
22	Greta Charles, Esq., Attorney for Sarah Adams, Defendant
23	[Street Address]
24	[City, State, Zip Code]
25	I declare under penalty of perjury that the foregoing is true and correct.
26	Executed at [City, State] on February 28, <u>year</u>.
27	
28	*Dana Lauren* Dana Lauren

3. The Defendant's Response

A defendant must answer within a short period of time (often 30 or fewer days) after being properly served with a complaint and summons. For example, under Federal Rule of Civil Procedure 12(a), the defendant has to serve an answer within 20 days after the complaint and summons is served.

If a defendant fails to respond in time, the plaintiff can apply for what's known as a "default judgment." (A default judgment is a court order granting a judgment against the defendant to pay the amount requested in the complaint, based on the defendant's failure to answer or defend against the lawsuit after having been given proper notice.) In some courts, the plaintiff simply files a Request for Default Judgment with the Clerk's Office. In other courts, the plaintiff must appear in court to show the judge that the threshold requirements for a valid claim have been met (this is sometimes called a "prove up" hearing).

Once a default judgment is "entered" (filed and written into the official court records), it has the status of any other judgment. It is as if the plaintiff had conducted and won a full trial. A defendant may, however, move very quickly to have it set aside (undone and taken off the record). A judge will usually set aside a default judgment only if the defendant was not served properly, or if the defendant's failure to answer the complaint or show up in court is excusable. For instance, if the defendant was in the hospital at the time the papers were served, or the defendant's attorney neglected to respond on behalf of the defendant, the judge might set aside a default judgment. (For reference, default judgments in federal courts are governed by Federal Rule of Civil Procedure 55, reasons for setting them aside by Rule 60(b).)

Assuming that as a defendant you are unwilling to let the plaintiff win by default, you generally have to respond to a plaintiff's complaint in writing within 20-30 days of the date you were served. (The summons accompanying the complaint will specify exactly how much time you have.) If you need additional time (for example, you are just about to leave town for two weeks), contact the person (usually an attorney) whose name and phone number is in the upper left-hand corner of the complaint and ask for additional time to respond. Confirm an extension of time to respond with a letter.

⚠️ **Confirming Extensions with the Court.** If your adversary agrees to extend your time to respond, you still may have to file a short notice with the court confirming that the time for response has been extended. Check your local court rules or ask the Court Clerk to see if your state imposes this requirement.

If the opposing party does not agree to extend the time for response, you can go to court with a Motion for Extension of Time to Respond. If you don't have time to do that, file any kind of answer that contests the complaint to prevent the plaintiff from entering a default judgment against you before you return home. You can always amend your answer later when you have more time.

⚠️ **Don't file a frivolous response.** Like plaintiffs, defendants can be subject to monetary penalties if they make false claims or even factual claims not supported by any evidence. (See Fed. Rule of Civil Proc. 11 (b)(4).)

You can respond to the plaintiff's complaint in two general ways:

- Answer "on the merits." This more common method of response typically means filing a pleading known as an "answer" which challenges a complaint's factual accuracy and may also assert affirmative defenses, make claims against the plaintiff and even bring new parties into the lawsuit.

- "Raise technical defects." Typically, this means filing a legal document called a "Motion." Motions focus on procedural issues instead of a complaint's factual accuracy. For example, if you are not a citizen of the state in which you are sued, you may have a basis for filing a motion challenging a court's personal jurisdiction. (You've always heard of "winning on a technicality." This may be your chance!) If the judge dismisses your technical objection and upholds the complaint, you can still file an answer challenging the merits.

Let's look briefly at each type of response.

a. Answer on the Merits

A defendant's answer somewhat resembles a plaintiff's complaint. As does a complaint, your answer will include:

① **Identifying information** in the upper left-hand corner of the first page. (See Section B1 above.)

② **A caption,** which of course will say "answer" instead of "complaint." (See Section B1 above.)

③ **Factual assertions ("allegations")** denying the claims the plaintiff made in the com-plaint. The simplest way to do this is through a "general denial," which states that "defendant denies each and every allegation of the complaint." Assuming that you are eligible to file a general denial, it's fine to do this even if you recognize that some of the plaintiff's allegations are accurate. A general denial simply puts the defendant on record as forcing the plaintiff to "prove it."

In a number of circumstances you are not eligible to make a general denial. Either local court rules (get a copy pronto from the courthouse clerk's office) or the fact that the complaint is "verified" (signed under penalty of perjury) may prevent you from making a general denial. In this situation, you will be required to respond separately to each numbered paragraph of the plaintiff's complaint. In doing so it will probably be necessary to concede the accuracy of certain allegations while denying others. For example, assume that you are sued for negligence, and that paragraph 3 of the complaint states that you negligently made a left-hand turn while driving on Olympic Boulevard and struck the plaintiff's car. Your answer may state that "I admit that I was driving eastbound on Olympic Boulevard on June 3, but I deny each and every other allegation of paragraph 3 of the complaint."

If you do not know whether an allegation in a complaint is true, you may deny "based on information and belief." (See Federal Rule of Civil Procedure 8-b.) For example, if a verified complaint alleges in paragraph 6 that the plaintiff suffered a broken leg, and you have no way of knowing if that is really true, your answer may state that "Defendant has no information or belief regarding the allegation of paragraph 6, and based on such lack of information and belief denies the allegation in paragraph 6."

⚠ **How to avoid the "negative pregnant."** Back in the days when pleading rules were incredibly picky, the "negative pregnant" became one of the legal system's most colorful traps for an unwary defendant. A negative pregnant consisted of a defendant's denial that a sum of money is owed, phrased in such a way that a judge treats it as an admission that some other sum of money is owed. For example, if an answer stated that "Defendant denies owing $50,000," a judge could interpret this as a negative pregnant in which the defendant admits owing $49,999!" Fortunately, the negative pregnant has been largely consigned to the scrap heap of legal history. However, to protect yourself against a judge who decides to make an example of you, play it safe and state that you "deny owing $50,000 or any other sum."

④ **A prayer for relief,** which typically requests that "the plaintiff take nothing" and that the court award court costs to you. If your answer includes claims against the plaintiff (called a counterclaim; see below) or a third party (called a cross-complaint or cross-claim; see below), the prayer for relief will also ask for money damages in a specified amount or "according to proof," just like the prayer for relief in a complaint.

⑤ **Your signature,** which follows the prayer for relief. If the complaint is "verified," you'll probably be required to verify your answer. This means that just above your signature you'll include a statement such as "I declare under penalty of perjury that the allegations in the answer are true." (Check your state's law or a legal formbook for the wording required in your state.)

In addition to denying all or some of a complaint's allegations, your answer may also include "affirmative defenses," "counterclaims," and "cross-complaints." Let's briefly look at each of these.

Affirmative Defenses

Affirmative defenses consist of new factual allegations that under legal rules defeat all or a portion of a plaintiff's claim. As the defendant, you have the obligation to raise any affirmative defenses on which you hope to rely, and at trial you'll have the burden of proving their truth. Common affirmative defenses are listed in Fed. Rule of Civil Proc. 8 (c).

They include:

Statute of Limitations—an allegation that plaintiff failed to file the complaint within the time required by law.

💡 **If the court lacks jurisdiction over you, say it here.** Normally, your answer will not dispute the court's power to hear the case (jurisdiction), since the plaintiff probably filed the lawsuit in the proper court. In the unusual case in which the court's power to hear the case is an issue, you may include that as an affirmative defense or, in the alternative, file a pre-answer motion raising lack of jurisdiction as a technical defect. (See Section 3b below.)

SAMPLE ANSWER

1	Sarah Adams, Defendant
	[Street address]
2	[City, State, Zip Code] ①
	[Phone number]
3	
	Defendant in Pro Per
4	
5	
6	
7	
8	② THE _____ COURT OF _____ COUNTY
9	STATE OF _____
10	
11	Nolo Pedestrian,)
	) Case No. 12345
12	Plaintiff,)
	) DEFENDANT'S ANSWER TO
13	v.) PLAINTIFF'S CIVIL ACTION
	) FOR NEGLIGENCE
14	Sarah Adams,)
	)
15	Defendant.)
	)
16	_____
17	
18	③ Defendant Adams answers the complaint as follows:
19	1. Defendant admits that on Janurary 1, <u>year</u>, she was driving in the vicinity of Elm and Main
20	Streets, but Defendant denies each and every other allegation in paragraph 1.
21	2. Defendant denies each and every allegation in paragraph 2.
22	Defendant asserts the following affirmative defense:
23	Plaintiff is barred from pursuing the cause of action stated in Plaintiff's Complaint under the
24	State of _____'s applicable statute of limitations for negligence actions as it occurred
25	more than two years before the Complaint was filed.
26	④ WHEREFORE Defendant prays that Plaintiff take nothing and that Defendant be awarded all
27	fees and costs of suit.
28	⑤ *Sarah Adams* _____
	Sarah Adams, Defendant in Pro Per

In a negligence case, that:

- the plaintiff's own carelessness (often called "contributory negligence") was the cause of all or some of the plaintiff's injuries; or

- that the plaintiff "assumed the risk" of injury by voluntarily engaging in a dangerous activity, such as rock climbing, playing in a football match or walking next to a building where thousands of pigeons roosted.

In a contract action, that:

- a particular oral contract is invalid because by law (called the "Statute of Frauds") the agreement was required to be in writing—or at least referred to in a document—to be enforceable;

or

- the defendant was a minor at the time the contract was made; or

- the contract was a product of duress, because the plaintiff threatened the defendant with physical harm if the defendant refused to sign the contract.

You and the plaintiff have already settled the dispute. (Lawyers call this "accord and satisfaction.")

⚠ Be sure that your answer states all possible affirmative defenses. If you do not include an affirmative defense in an answer (or get a judge's permission to add an affirmative defense later), you will not be able to offer evidence to support an affirmative defense at trial. A legal coach can help you determine if any affirmative defenses are available to you.

Some states have pre-printed "check box" forms that you can use. You can find them at a law library.

Counterclaims

"Counterclaims" (governed in federal courts by Fed. Rule of Civil Proc. 13) are a way for a defendant to make claims against and seek money damages or other legal relief from a plaintiff. A counterclaim is particularly appropriate in a situation in which you planned to sue the plaintiff before the plaintiff won the race to the courthouse door and sued you first. A counterclaim allows you to use an answer not only to deny a plaintiff's allegations, but also to go on the offensive against the plaintiff. A counterclaim says, in effect, "The plaintiff says I owe money to him? No way—it's the plaintiff who broke the contract and as a result owes me the money I lost." A defendant who wants a judgment against a plaintiff has to include a counterclaim in an answer if the defendant's claim is based on the same series of events as the plaintiff's (lawyers call these "compulsory counterclaims").

Example: You've been sued for negligence. The plaintiff's complaint states that you carelessly made a left-hand turn and collided with the plaintiff's oncoming car. Your answer may set forth a counterclaim in which you allege that it was the plaintiff who carelessly drove into the road from a driveway after you had begun to turn, colliding with you and causing you to suffer personal injuries requiring hospitalization, continuing medical treatments, lost future income and severe damage to your car. If you don't include this counterclaim in your answer, you'll give up the right to seek damages from the plaintiff caused by the accident. (Again, legal formbooks—discussed in Chapter 22, Section B2—set forth sample counterclaims for different kinds of cases.)

Complaint

ATTORNEY OR PARTY WITHOUT ATTORNEY (NAME AND ADDRESS):
TELEPHONE:
FOR COURT USE ONLY

ATTORNEY FOR (NAME):
Insert name of court, judicial district or branch court, if any, and post office and street address:

PLAINTIFF:

DEFENDANT:

☐ DOES 1 TO

COMPLAINT—Personal Injury, Property Damage, Wrongful Death
CASE NUMBER:
☐ MOTOR VEHICLE   ☐ OTHER (specify):
☐ Property Damage   ☐ Wrongful Death
☐ Personal Injury   ☐ Other Damages (specify):

1. This pleading, including attachments and exhibits, consists of the following number of pages:

2. a. Each plaintiff named above is a competent adult
  ☐ Except plaintiff (name):
    ☐ a corporation qualified to do business in California
    ☐ an unincorporated entity (describe):
    ☐ a public entity (describe):
    ☐ a minor   ☐ an adult
      ☐ for whom a guardian or conservator of the estate or a guardian ad litem has been appointed
      ☐ other (specify):
    ☐ other (specify):

  ☐ Except plaintiff (name):
    ☐ a corporation qualified to do business in California
    ☐ an unincorporated entity (describe):
    ☐ a public entity (describe):
    ☐ a minor   ☐ an adult
      ☐ for whom a guardian or conservator of the estate or a guardian ad litem has been appointed
      ☐ other (specify):
    ☐ other (specify):

  b. ☐ Plaintiff (name):
    is doing business under the fictitious name of (specify):

    and has complied with the fictitious business name laws.
  c. ☐ Information about additional plaintiffs who are not competent adults is shown in Complaint—
    Attachment 2c.
    (Continued)

Form Approved by the
Judicial Council of California
Effective January 1, 1982
Rule 982.1(1)
COMPLAINT—Personal Injury, Property Damage,
Wrongful Death
CCP 425.12

Answer

ATTORNEY OR PARTY WITHOUT ATTORNEY (NAME AND ADDRESS):
TELEPHONE:
FOR COURT USE ONLY

ATTORNEY FOR (NAME):
Insert name of court, judicial district or branch court, if any, and post office and street address:

PLAINTIFF:

DEFENDANT:

ANSWER—Personal Injury, Property Damage, Wrongful Death
CASE NUMBER:
☐ COMPLAINT OF (name):
☐ CROSS-COMPLAINT OF (name):

1. This pleading, including attachments and exhibits, consists of the following number of pages:

DEFENDANT OR CROSS-DEFENDANT (name):

2. ☐ Generally **denies** each allegation of the **unverified** complaint or cross-complaint.

3. a. ☐ DENIES each allegation of the following numbered paragraphs:

  b. ☐ ADMITS each allegation of the following numbered paragraphs:

  c. ☐ DENIES, ON INFORMATION AND BELIEF, each allegation of the following numbered paragraphs:

  d. ☐ DENIES, BECAUSE OF LACK OF SUFFICIENT INFORMATION OR BELIEF TO ANSWER, each allegation
    of the following numbered paragraphs:

  e. ☐ ADMITS the following allegations and generally denies all other allegations:

    (Continued)

Form Approved by the
Judicial Council of California
Effective January 1, 1982
Rule 982.1(15)
ANSWER—Personal Injury, Property Damage,
Wrongful Death
CCP 425.12

Summons

NAME AND ADDRESS OF ATTORNEY
TELEPHONE NO.
FOR COURT USE ONLY

ATTORNEY FOR (Name):
Insert name of court, judicial district or branch court, if any, and Post Office and Street Address:

PLAINTIFF

DEFENDANT

SUMMONS (JOINT DEBTOR)
CASE NUMBER

NOTICE! You have been sued. The court may decide against you without your being heard unless you respond within 30 days. Read the information below.

¡AVISO! Usted ha sido demandado. El tribunal puede decidir contra Ud. sin audiencia a menos que Ud. responda dentro de 30 días. Lea la información que sigue.

If you wish to seek the advice of an attorney in this matter, you should do so promptly so that your written response, if any, may be filed on time.

Si Usted desea solicitar el consejo de un abogado en este asunto, debería hacerlo inmediatamente, de esta manera, su respuesta escrita, si hay alguna, puede ser registrada a tiempo.

1. TO THE DEFENDANT (Name):
You are hereby directed to file in this court, within 30 days after this summons is served on you, a written response to the Declaration or Affidavit accompanying this summons, giving any legal reason why you should not be required to pay the unpaid amount of: $ . . . . on the judgment rendered by this court on (Date): . . . . against:
Unless you do so, your default will be entered on application of the plaintiff and the court may enter a judgment against you for the unpaid amount due on the judgment, which could result in the garnishment of wages, taking of money or property, or other relief.

DATED: . . . . Clerk, By _____, Deputy

(SEAL)

2. NOTICE TO THE PERSON SERVED: You are served
  a. ☐ As an individual defendant.
  b. ☐ As (or on behalf of) the person sued under the fictitious name of:
  c. ☐ On behalf of:
    Under: ☐ CCP 416.10 (Corporation)   ☐ CCP 416.60 (Minor)
           ☐ CCP 416.20 (Defunct Corporation) ☐ CCP 416.70 (Incompetent)
           ☐ CCP 416.40 (Association or Partnership) ☐ CCP 416.90 (Individual)
           ☐ Other:
  d. ☐ By personal delivery on (Date):

A written response must be in the form prescribed by the California Rules of Court. It must be filed in this court with the proper filing fee and proof of service of a copy on each plaintiff's attorney and on each plaintiff not represented by an attorney. The time when a summons is deemed served on a party may vary depending on the method of service. For example, see CCP 413.10 through 415.50. The word "complaint" includes cross-complaint, "plaintiff" includes cross-complainant, "defendant" includes cross-defendant, the singular includes the plural.

Form Adopted by Rule 982
Judicial Council of California
Revised Effective January 1, 1979
(See reverse for Proof of Service)
SUMMONS (JOINT DEBTOR)
CCP 989

Proof of Service

PARTY WITHOUT ATTORNEY (My Name and Address):
MY TELEPHONE NO.:
FOR COURT USE ONLY

NAME OF COURT:
STREET ADDRESS:
MAILING ADDRESS:
CITY AND ZIP CODE:
BRANCH NAME:

PLAINTIFF:

DEFENDANT:

PROOF OF SERVICE BY MAIL
(CCP Sections 1013a, 2015.5)
CASE NUMBER

I declare that:

1. At the time of service I was at least 18 years of age and not a party to this legal action.

2. I am a resident of or employed in the county where the mailing occurred.

3. My business or residence address is: _____

4. I served copies of the following paper(s) in the manner shown:
  a. Papers served [list exact titles of paper(s)]:

  b. Manner of service: by placing true copies in a sealed envelope addressed to each person whose name and address is given below and:
    ☐ depositing the envelope in the United States Mail with the postage fully prepaid; or
    ☐ (If deposited at a business:) Placing for collection and mailing following ordinary business practices. I am readily familiar with the business practice for collection and processing of correspondence for mailing with the United States Post Office. The correspondence will be deposited with the United States Post Office on the same date as the date of deposit (below) in the ordinary course of business.
    (1) Date of Deposit: _____
    (2) Place of Deposit (city & state; business address if deposited at a business): _____

5. I declare under penalty of perjury under the laws of the State of California that the foregoing is true and correct. Executed on _____ at _____, California.

Print Name: _____

[Signature of Person Who Served Papers]

Name and Address of Each Person to Whom Documents Were Mailed:

☐ _____ Additional names and addresses on reverse.

PROOF OF SERVICE BY MAIL

Cross-Complaints, or Cross-Claims

More rarely, you may also want to use your answer to bring a new party into the case by including a "cross-complaint" in your answer. (See Fed. Rule of Civil Proc. 13-g.) A cross-complaint in essence blames a new third party for any harm the plaintiff suffered. For example, if you are a defendant in an auto accident case, you may file a cross-complaint against the company that repaired the brakes on your car, claiming that the improper brake repair (and not your carelessness) caused your brakes to fail and your car to collide with the plaintiff's.

b. Raise Technical Defects

Before filing an answer (or sometimes as part of an answer), you might respond to a complaint by filing a Motion to Dismiss, claiming that the case cannot proceed because the plaintiff has violated one or more procedural requirements. (See Fed. Rule of Civil Proc. 12.) Serious procedural violations can result in a judge dismissing a case, and if the statute of limitations expires before the plaintiff can refile it, the procedural error may spell the end of the case. More likely, your valid procedural objections will disrupt the case by forcing the plaintiff to start over with a new complaint or even in a new court. If nothing else, the ensuing fuss and delay may convince the plaintiff that winning the case won't be easy and lead the plaintiff to offer to settle.

The common technical defects you can raise include:

"We'll see your hundred thou and countersue you a million"

- The court lacks power to hear the case (jurisdiction), either over the defendant personally or over the subject matter of the case. For example, perhaps the plaintiff has filed the case in federal court, even though the claim does not arise under federal law and the plaintiff and defendant are citizens of the same state. (See Section C above.)

- Improper service of the summons and complaint. For example, instead of handing you the papers personally, the plaintiff's process server simply discarded them but claimed to have served you.

- The complaint is vague and ambiguous. This response is not usually successful, because modern pleading rules allow each side to postpone providing the details of the case until disclosure and discovery (see Chapter 4, Investigating Your Case). However, if a complaint is so vague that you are not sure of what you supposedly did wrong, you can make a "Motion for a More Definite Statement," which if successful can force the plaintiff to prepare and serve a more factually detailed complaint.

- The complaint fails to state a claim for relief. Essentially, this response asserts that "even if everything the plaintiff alleges is true, there is no valid legal claim." For instance, a complaint would not state a valid claim if it alleged that "I bought a stock recommended by my stockbroker and it went down in value." (By contrast, the claim might have been valid if it alleged that the stockbroker recommended a stock without disclosing that it was a speculative stock to an investor who had previously told the stockbroker that she wanted only conservative investments.)

 RECOMMENDED READING

American Jurisprudence Pleading and Practice Forms Annotated (Lawyers Cooperative Publishing Co.; updated regularly), is a comprehensive, multi-volume guide with numerous forms and examples.

Basics of Legal Document Production, by Cummins (Delmar), contains numerous examples of state and federal pleadings.

Plain Language Pleadings, by Wilson (Prentice Hall), is an attorney assistant's guide to preparation of pleadings. ■

4

INVESTIGATING YOUR CASE

Once the initial legal documents are filed (usually a complaint and an answer; see Chapter 3, Starting Your Case), the parties to a lawsuit typically turn to gathering evidence to prove that their claims (allegations) are true and that their adversary's are not. This phase of a lawsuit is often called "case investigation" or "fact investigation." Think of it this way—although you may personally know exactly what happened, now that you are in the formal legal system you will have to prove it to a judge or jurors who know nothing about you or what happened. And to make your task more difficult, your opponent will probably present a very different version of events. The upshot is that you should approach case investigation with two main questions in mind:

- "What evidence that is legally admissible in court can I find in order to back up my claims?"

- "How can I best present my evidence to a judge or jury in order to convince them that I should prevail at trial?"

Case investigation takes two forms: "informal investigation" and "formal discovery." Informal investigation includes all information-gathering that you can do on your own, working with cooperative people or organizations both before and after a lawsuit is filed. Informal investigation encompasses such activities as:

- conducting interviews;

- collecting documents;

- taking photographs (of damaged property, accident sites or other pertinent objects or locales); and

- finding out about an adversary's insurance coverage.

By contrast, "formal discovery" is a legal process that kicks in after a case has been filed. Formal discovery encompasses a number of investigatory tools, including:

- Interrogatories—written questions directed to the adversary that the adversary must answer in writing and under oath; and

- Depositions—oral in-person questions that the adversary or another person must answer under oath.

One big disadvantage of formal discovery is that it can be expensive. A major advantage is that it doesn't depend on anyone's voluntary cooperation. That is, you can use formal discovery tools to compel an adversary or witness to provide you with information and documents.

A. INFORMAL INVESTIGATION

As mentioned above, informal investigation consists primarily of seeking information and documents from people who will voluntarily cooperate with you. You can informally question or seek documents from anyone, including eyewitnesses, public agencies and police officers. If you are not an attorney, you can also seek information directly from your adversary, even if the adversary is represented by a lawyer. (Lawyers can talk only to an adversary's lawyer.) Obtaining information informally obviously saves the time and expense of formal discovery methods. Like many lawyers, you may be able to gather all the evidence you need to prove your claim (or disprove your adversary's) through informal investigation.

⚠️ **Be aware of "unauthorized investigation" laws.** Some states have "unauthorized investigation" laws that make it a misdemeanor to investigate without a license. If your state has this kind of law, it almost surely does not apply to you if you are self-represented and investigating your own case. However, the law may prevent you from asking a non-licensed friend to question witnesses or perform other investigatory tasks.

As an example to see how informal investigation might work, assume that you are involved in an auto accident in which an uninsured driver ran into your car. Since you do not have uninsured motorist coverage, you file a lawsuit on your own. You may:

- Obtain a copy of the report prepared by the police officer who came to the scene of the accident, by going to the local police station and paying a small fee. This "accident report" may include statements made by the other driver that will help you prove that the other driver was at fault. The report may also give the names and phone numbers of bystanders (including the police officer) whom you can try to question informally.

- Interview eyewitnesses (and if their information is helpful, serve them with subpoenas requiring them to appear in court once you have a trial date). Among the ways of finding eyewitnesses in an auto accident case are getting their names from a police report, talking to bystanders right after an accident posting in the vicinity of an accident notices that ask eyewitnesses to contact you and even putting a notice in the classified section of a local newspaper.

💡 **Gather evidence promptly. Memories fade and scenes change.** If you intend to photograph a scene or interview witnesses, do so as soon as possible after an accident or other event that may end up in court. Any substantial delay may result in your questioning a person whose memory of key events has faded. Similarly, physical changes in a location, road or piece of equipment may take place, perhaps depriving you of useful evidence at trial.

- Prepare audiotapes or written statements at the conclusion of interviews. Be sure that the witness signs a written statement, or states on an audiotape that you are recording the conversation with the witness' consent. An audiotape or written statement should refer to the important facts supporting your version of events and should indicate the date of preparation. While audiotapes or written statements usually are not admissible in evidence at trial, they can nevertheless be extremely valuable during a trial when used to refresh an uncertain witness' recollection (see Chapter 11, Section E4) or cross-examine witnesses who change their stories (see Chapter 12, Section E3 and Chapter 8, Section D3). Also, prompt preparation of an audiotape or written statement setting forth facts favorable to you may discourage a witness from later changing a story to favor the other driver.

Use written statements and audiotapes to improve your negotiating posture. Written or orally recorded statements can help you negotiate a favorable settlement with your adversary or an insurance company (if the adversary has insurance). An adversary or insurance company who realizes that you have witnesses to back up your claims often takes your settlement proposals more seriously.

• Take photos of your injuries, the damage to your car and the scene of the accident. (Use a camera that automatically superimposes dates on photos, or write the date that a photo was taken on the back promptly after you develop the photo.) Either you or a friend can take the photos, but no matter who wields the camera, anyone with personal knowledge of what a photo depicts can lay the groundwork for the photo to go into evidence at trial. (See Chapter 14, Section D for more information on how to get photos into evidence.)

• Obtain from your doctor a copy of a medical report describing your injuries, course of treatment and the likelihood of future physical problems.

• Secure receipts for all medical treatment, psychological counseling, physical rehabilitation and any other "out of pocket" expenses resulting from the accident. Under some circumstances you can recover these fees from the defendant even if your insurance company has paid them. In addition, these expenses document the extent of your injuries and add to the damages you may be entitled to for "pain and suffering."

• If the defendant claims that some other person or business is responsible for the harm you suffered ("the auto repair shop put defective brakes in my car"), ask the defendant for supporting documentation (copies of the brake repair records and any records relating to brake inspections). If the information supports the defendant's claim, you may decide to name the repair shop as an additional defendant in the lawsuit.

• Examine a county's land records to see if the defendant owns real estate in the county, and court records to see if the defendant is involved in any other litigation. This information may help you decide whether the defendant has assets from which you can collect a judgment.

HOW TO DOCUMENT PROPERTY LOSS CLAIMS

You can often use informal investigation to gather the documents you'll need to prove the value of damaged property, such as a car or a stereo. The general rule is that you are entitled to compensation for the "fair market value" of repairing or replacing damaged property. For example, if your car had a fair market value of $3,000 before an accident totaled it, you will be awarded only that amount, even if you have to spend $5,000 to replace it. To informally gather documents you'll need in court to support your claim for the value of a car, you might:

- Purchase a "Kelley Blue Book" or check one out of a library to prove the value of a totaled car. At trial, judges generally take "judicial notice" of a car's Kelley Blue Book value, meaning that the book itself provides evidence of the car's value. You don't need to hire an expert to testify.

- Obtain receipts from car mechanics and similar repairpersons. At trial, to overcome a possible objection that a receipt is inadmissible hearsay (see Chapter 15, Section E), you can testify that you paid (or will pay) the amount stated on the receipt.

- Look in your personal papers for photos that show an item's condition before it was damaged, and for any appraisals done by an insurance company or expert. "Before and after" photos are a great way to document the harm you've suffered.

 Ensuring that evidence is admissible at trial. Gathering information serves little purpose beyond possibly helping foster a settlement if you can't use it if your case goes to trial. Since most documents or objects won't waltz into evidence by themselves, you or another witness will have to "sponsor" them with appropriate testimony showing a judge that they are authentic and in good condition. In other words, you need to produce at trial the favorable witnesses you've talked to informally. The suggestions below will make it easier for you to offer the fruits of your investigative labor into evidence should your case go to trial:

- Keep originals of all documents in a safe place for court; make copies to show to witnesses or to attach to pleadings.

- Do not add writing or punch holes in original documents.

- During an interview, ask witnesses for the names and phone numbers of friends or relatives who will know the witnesses' whereabouts should they move before your case goes to trial.

- If you know your trial date when you interview a favorable witness, serve the witness with a subpoena at the time of the interview. (A subpoena is a court order requiring a person to attend court—you can pick up subpoenas at a courthouse.) This will save you having to locate the witness a second time to serve a subpoena. Alternatively, serve a "subpoena duces tecum" if you want the witness to bring documents or other evidence to court as well. (See Sidebar.)

- Keep any tangible objects you want to offer into evidence (for example, a damaged stereo) in a place where friends and family members cannot meddle with them, preferably under lock and key. This precaution will usually enable you to defeat an adversary's possible claim that an object should not be allowed into evidence at trial because it could have been altered or tampered with.

- Take photographs of the damaged item, especially if it is too large to bring to court or if its condition is likely to change before the date of trial. You can offer photos into trial through your own testimony or that of any other witness who has seen the damaged item and can testify that the photo accurately depicts the item's condition. (See Chapter 14, Section D for more on introducing photos into evidence.)

HOW TO FILL OUT A SUBPOENA DUCES TECUM

A subpoena duces tecum is an official court form available at a courthouse clerk's office. To complete this form, identify the documents you want a witness to bring to court, fill in the name of the person who has custody of them (if you are serving a business or government agency, you may simply refer to the "custodian of records"), and state the relevance of the documents to your case. For example, assume that you want to prove that you had just installed an expensive CD system in your car, which was subsequently totaled. You might serve a subpoena duces tecum on the bookkeeper of the company that performed the installation, asking the bookkeeper to bring to court copies of all records pertaining to the installation of the CD and stating that "I need the installation records to prove my property damage in a car accident case."

When requesting copies of documents, you can often encourage voluntary cooperation by pinpointing the specific information you seek. For example, assume that you sue the Chicken Feed Restaurant after coming down with what you believe was food poisoning. It is important to know if records in your local county health office can help you prove that the Chicken Feed was responsible for your illness. If you ask for "all your records pertaining to the Chicken Feed Restaurant," a health office employee facing hours of hunting for documents, many of which may not be germane to your case, may reply, "Sorry, you'll need a court order." But if your request is easier to deal with (for example, "I'd like a copy of records of any sickness reports made by patrons of the Chicken Feed Restaurant during last July, and a list of the restaurant's Health Code violations for the last two years"), you may get the information promptly without needing a court order.

Some sources may initially be reluctant to disclose information, perhaps fearing that they can be sued for violating a person's privacy. However, don't give up without trying a bit of persuasion. Explain:

- how the information the person has pertains to a case that has already been filed in court; and

- that cooperation is easier for everyone, because if you can't get the information voluntarily, you may have to take the person's deposition or serve a subpoena duces tecum to require the person to turn over documents.

Finding evidence and witnesses may take a bit of ingenuity, perseverance and maybe even a little help from your friends.

- Do your own field investigation. In one case, law students represented a woman who was seeking to collect unemployment benefits after she was fired by a casino. The casino claimed that the woman was not entitled to benefits because she had carelessly allowed a stack of gambling chips to be stolen by leaving them on a counter to which the public had access. To investigate whether the casino's own carelessness could have led to the theft, the law students went to the casino and noticed that a metal grate had recently been installed in front of the counter where the theft occurred. They took a photo of the grate. The photo convinced the hearing officer that the absence of a grate and not the woman's carelessness led to the theft of the chips, and the woman was awarded unemployment benefits.

- If you are trying to contact a witness for whom you have a name but no other identifying information, check with government agencies, such as a motor vehicle department or a utility company. If these agencies are uncooperative (a real possibility), and if a witness is important enough and the amount of money in dispute justifies it, consider hiring a private investigator to locate the witness. Another method of locating a witness for whom you have only a name is to use an Internet "search engine."

- If you are suing an ex-employer for discharging you illegally, consider talking to former employees about their experiences and knowledge of company policies.

- If you are suing a moving company for damaging and losing your personal property, collect insurance records, purchase receipts, photographs and the like to prove ownership and condition of the lost or damaged items.

- If you are suing a government agency, look in your local public library for reports and relevant statistics concerning the agency's operations.

 Large businesses and institutions often insist on subpoenas. Parties to court cases often want records from large organizations, such as hospitals and telephone companies. Such organizations tend to protect themselves from "invasion of privacy" claims by the person whose records you seek by releasing records only after being served with a subpoena. You may find an employee willing to talk to you "off the record," but to secure evidence admissible in court you'll probably need a subpoena.

RESOURCES ON INFORMAL INVESTIGATION TECHNIQUES:

How to Find Almost Anyone, Anywhere, by Tillman (Rutledge Hill Press), is a private investigator's how-to book of techniques for searching for missing persons, with an emphasis on tracing relatives.

B. FORMAL DISCOVERY

The word "discovery" refers to a number of evidence-gathering tools that the legal system makes available to you in order to compel your adversary, witnesses and others with information about your dispute to answer questions and produce documents before your case goes to trial. Laws setting up formal discovery methods were first enacted in the 1930s by legal reformers who believed that requiring parties to lawsuits to exchange information about a case would promote justice by fostering settlement and cutting back on the "surprise" aspect of trials. Reformers also hoped to conserve judicial resources by leaving the discovery process largely in the hands of the litigants themselves, involving judges only if litigants are unable to resolve discovery disputes.

Unfortunately, over the years lawyers have found ways to move into pre-trial discovery the battles that formerly took place in the courtroom, so that the reformers' hopes have been only partly realized. (Though a bit over the top, the 1991 film "Class Action" provides an interesting window into discovery abuse.) For example, some lawyers try to avoid complying with discovery requests by claiming ambiguities in questions that any two-year-old would understand. Other lawyers (often representing big corporations) may drive up the cost of litigation (both to their own clients and to their adversaries) by swamping individuals and small businesses with burdensome discovery requests in order to coerce them into giving up or settling cheap.

As a result, many state and federal courts have streamlined their discovery rules in an effort to combat such abuses. For example, many states have a "disclosure" rule similar to Federal Rule of Civil Procedure 26 (a), enacted in 1993. This procedure requires parties to disclose key information voluntarily, without waiting for their adversaries to request it. The data that parties are supposed to disclose include the identity of expert and nonexpert witnesses, relevant documents and tangible objects and insurance agreements that might cover all or part of a judgment.

In addition to requiring voluntary disclosure, local discovery rules may also limit the number of questions that parties can ask and may set strict time limits for completing discovery. In addition, parties often have a responsibility to "meet and confer" in order to set up a jointly agreed-to discovery plan (see Fed. Rule of Civil Proc. 26-f) and to sort out any disputes before dragging each other into court. When parties disagree over whether information is "discoverable," judges often speed up the process by conducting discovery hearings by phone. Finally, judges are increasingly willing to impose sanctions (ranging from monetary penalties to dismissal of cases) on parties who abuse discovery rules. Judges will expect you to follow discovery rules even if you are self-represented, so seek the advice of a legal coach if you are uncertain of your discovery obligations.

Which is better: informal investigation or discovery? Self-represented litigants, in small cases especially, should almost always attempt to get necessary information by first using informal investigation techniques—particularly to gather information supporting their own legal claims. Formal discovery tends to be so expensive and complex that even attorneys often forgo it unless a substantial amount of money is involved. If your case is a good-sized one, or even if it isn't but you nevertheless plan to use formal discovery methods, follow these general guidelines:

- Take a deposition (a formal discovery method, discussed in Section C, below) to preserve helpful testimony from a witness who may not be available when a case goes to trial (perhaps because the witness is ill or about to move to another state).

- Consider preparing "Requests for Admissions" (another formal discovery device, discussed in Section F, below) to force your adversary to admit quickly that some of your factual claims are accurate.

- Use formal interrogatories and possibly depositions to find out about your adversary's case only if informal methods don't work.

Even if you don't choose to use the machinery of formal discovery, your opponent might. For this reason, you'll want to continue through this chapter to understand how the process works. We briefly examine the four primary formal discovery tools:

- Depositions

- Written Interrogatories

- Requests for Production of Documents

- Requests for Admissions

Pay attention to discovery deadlines. Judges and court rules often set up and enforce strict discovery schedules and time limits. For example, a judge may order that "all depositions are to be completed within 30 days" or that "no discovery is to take place within 30 days of the trial date." Mark such deadlines on a calendar and plan to strictly abide by them. If an unexpected delay arises or an adversary's misconduct prevents you from meeting a deadline, you may have to request extra time from a judge by filing a Motion for Extension of Time to Complete Discovery in court. A simpler alternative is to ask your adversary to "stipulate" (agree) to an extension of time. However, this will probably not work if your adversary has intentionally caused the delay or if your local court follows a "fast track" pretrial system that aims to reduce court backlogs by setting short time limits and giving only judges the power to extend them.

C. DEPOSITIONS

Depositions normally consist of face-to-face questioning in an office setting. (Federal Rules of Civil Procedure 27-32 outline deposition procedures in federal court cases; most states have similar procedures.) You can depose anyone you have reason to think has information relevant to your case. This includes your adversary, an expert witness hired by your adversary or a potential witness for you or your adversary. In style, depositions resemble courtroom testimony. A court reporter places a witness (colorfully called a "deponent") under oath and records the testimony (and may videotape or audiotape it as well). The court reporter later produces a written deposition transcript. The deponent is supposed to look over the transcript, change answers if necessary and sign the transcript. (But if a deponent does significantly change an answer, you can try to undermine the deponent's credibility at trial by offering evidence of the change to the judge or jury. See Chapter 12, Section E3.) What happens to a transcript after a deponent signs it varies from state to state. In many, transcripts are filed in court once they are signed. In other states, signed transcripts are kept by the party taking the deposition and filed in court only if the party wants and is legally entitled to read from the transcript at trial.

Although you always hope to uncover evidence helpful to your case, a deposition's main purpose is to help you assess the strength of your opponent's case by learning in advance how much an adverse witness will harm you if the case goes to trial. For this reason, it is crucial that you realize that you gain nothing by trying to avoid harmful testimony at a deposition. If a witness has bad things to say, better to find out about them as early as possible and not be surprised by them in the middle of trial. During a deposition you also have a chance to observe a deponent's demeanor, allowing you to estimate whether a judge or jury is likely to believe the deponent.

1. Advantages and Disadvantages of Taking Depositions

The four main formal discovery tools often work best in combination. For instance, you may send out a set of written interrogatories to uncover witnesses your adversary knows about, then take depositions of those witnesses, and finally send your adversary a request to admit that a fact testified to by a witness in a deposition is true. However, because formal discovery can be expensive and time consuming, you should be aware of the general advantages and disadvantages of each discovery tool. Depositions generally have these advantages:

- You can offer a deposition transcript into evidence at trial if the deponent is unavailable to give live testimony. This rule explains why you might consider deposing a helpful witness who may not be available to testify at the time of trial. (By contrast, the hearsay rule would probably bar you from offering an informally made written statement or audiotape into evidence. See Chapter 15, Basic Rules of Evidence, Section E.)

- If an adversary's witness whose deposition you have taken testifies significantly differently at trial than at the deposition, you can read the inconsistent deposition testimony into the trial record to impeach (attack) the deponent's credibility. By contrast, impeachment is not nearly as effective if a judge or jury hears only your testimony that a witness informally told you something different.

Example: You have sued your former employer for violating state law by firing you for missing work because you served on a jury in a lengthy trial. Before trial you take the deposition of your former supervisor, Paul Chepick. At the deposition, Chepick testified that your work performance had been satisfactory before you went on the jury. At trial, Chepick testifies that you were fired not because of your jury service, but because of a number of work-related problems. Because Chepick's deposition testimony contradicts his trial testimony, you could read the deposition testimony into the record at trial to call his believability into question. (For another example of how to use deposition testimony to attack a witness' credibility at trial, see Chapter 12, Section E3.)

- As compared to conducting discovery by asking written questions (interrogatories), depositions allow for more flexibility in questioning because you hear a deponent's answer before you ask the next question. For example, assume that a deponent unexpectedly refers to an important business meeting that you had no idea had taken place. In a deposition, you can immediately follow up the remark with questions about what took place during this meeting. (By contrast, you have to prepare all of your written interrogatory questions ahead of time, before you know any of the answers. Yes, sending out a second set of interrogatories is a possible option when a first set turns up unexpected information, but one that is unwieldy and often requires a judge's permission.)

- You can take anyone's deposition. You can depose your adversary, an employee who works for your adversary or an ordinary or expert witness hired by your opponent—even your opponent's attorney! For an expert you'll probably have to pay an hourly fee, which can be quite high (see Chapter 18, Expert Witnesses), but an ordinary witness is usually reimbursed only for travel expenses to attend the deposition. (By contrast, you can send written questions (interrogatories) only to your opponent, not to an ordinary or expert witness.)

- You elicit the testimony of an individual deponent. While your adversary's lawyer will probably attend the deposition and can consult with the deponent during recesses (breaks in the testimony), it is the deponent who has to answer the questions. (By contrast, attorneys often play a major role in preparing the answers to written interrogatories and usually advise clients how to answer them in a way that provides you with as little information as possible.)

- You can use a deposition to learn and ask about documents (or other tangible items) by simply using a Notice of Deposition (for your opponent) or a subpoena duces tecum (for a non-party witness) to list items you want the deponent to bring to the deposition.

Unfortunately, deposing an adversary or a witness who supports your adversary also has considerable disadvantages. Weigh these considerations very carefully before you decide to take a deposition:

- Depositions are the most expensive of discovery tools. Even if you are representing yourself (and therefore not paying an attorney to take or attend a deposition), you must pay a court reporter to transcribe the testimony and prepare a written transcript. While costs vary somewhat by locality, it's not unusual for a court reporter to charge up to $5.00 per page of transcript. A day of deposition testimony fills up about 150 pages, meaning that a day-long deposition may cost you around $750. You probably won't have to purchase a transcript if you simply attend a deposition taken by your adversary. (If you want and have the legal right to use at trial a transcript that you haven't purchased, you might have to send the adversary a subpoena to make sure the adversary brings the transcript to trial.) If you lose the case, however, a judge might order you to pay your adversary's deposition expenses. (By the same token, if you win, ask the judge to order your adversary to pay your deposition costs.)

- If you haven't investigated a case thoroughly enough to know which witnesses are most likely to have important information, you may end up paying dearly to depose a witness whose main answers are "I don't know." (By contrast, written interrogatories give you access to "corporate knowledge." When you send interrogatories to an adversary that is a business or other entity, any employee with knowledge has to contribute to the answers.)

Example: You have sued a record company for releasing a song that you believe violates your copyright. You take the deposition of Jan Winter, a record company executive who you think was in charge of releasing the song and therefore knows all about the decision to publish it. However, at the deposition Jan testifies repeatedly that she had nothing to do with the song since she worked in a different division of the company until after it was released. You've spent lots of money and learned nothing. (By contrast, if you had first sent interrogatories to the record company asking for the names of people in charge of releasing the song, you might have been able to target the most knowledgeable deponent.)

Ask your adversary to designate a deponent. When your opponent is an organization and you are not sure who to depose, consider asking the adversary to identify and bring to the deposition the most knowledgeable employee. For example, in the record company case, your Notice of Deposition might have directed the company to "produce for deposition the employee who is most knowledgeable about the process by which the song was developed and published." See Fed. Rule of Civil Proc. 30(b)(6). If the adversary tries to give you a hard time by producing someone who knows nothing about the song, you could go to court and ask a judge to order the adversary to pay your wasted deposition expenses.

- Effective deposition questioning is a difficult skill, even for many attorneys. You have to pose questions carefully in order to be confident that you know how adverse witnesses will testify at trial. If questions are vague or you forget to cover a topic, you won't be prepared for your opponent's evidence at trial or to show that a witness has changed a story and therefore should not be believed.

- Your adversary's lawyer can be present at a deposition. The attorney may throw you off track by objecting to your questions. Too, an adversary's attorney can help witnesses "refresh their recollections" during recesses. Finally, seeing you in action will allow the attorney to estimate your own credibility, and by listening to your questions learn more about your case than you learn about the adversary's.

- If you depose an adverse witness who becomes unavailable for trial, you enable the adversary to offer the deposition transcript into evidence at trial.

2. How to Take a Deposition

Once you've decided to take a deposition, check your local court rules. Pay particular attention to the time window for taking depositions and know how to notify a person whose deposition you want to take. Under all rules, you'll need to select a date and location for the deposition, arrange and pay for a court reporter's presence (many are listed in phone books) and give the deponent and opposing counsel (or your self-represented adversary) at least 10 days' written notice. Even better, as a courtesy, talk to all the necessary people ahead of time and arrange a mutually convenient date and location.

Written notice procedures tend to differ depending on whether the deponent is the adverse party or some other person. In most states, you set up a deposition of your adversary by using a document generally called a "Notice of Deposition." In some states, if you want the adversary to bring documents to the deposition (so that you can examine them and ask questions), you can simply list those documents in the notice. However, in states that follow Fed. Rule of Civil Proc. 30 (b)(5), you'll have to request documents by sending out a separate form called a "Request for Production of Documents." (See Section E, below, for more on Requests for Production of Documents.)

If you want to depose a "non-party witness" (someone other than your adversary), you'll probably have to serve the witness with an official court form called a "Subpoena re Deposition." If you want the non-party witness to bring documents to the deposition, use instead a form carrying the fancy title "Subpoena Duces Tecum re Deposition." (These forms should be available from a court clerk.) List the documents you want the witness to bring along, and state briefly how they pertain to the case. Lawyer formbooks, discussed further in Chapter 22, Legal Research, will contain sample language that you can adapt to your situation.

Lawyers usually take depositions in their offices, but any office will do. If you have a convenient office or can borrow one, use it. You'll probably feel more comfortable on familiar turf! Otherwise, you may arrange to use either your adversary's or the court reporter's office.

Videotaped depositions. Rules in many courts allow for videotaping of depositions, usually in addition to having a court reporter present. While this procedure is optional and adds to a deposition's cost, a videotape can be particularly desirable if you want to preserve favorable testimony from a witness who may not be available at trial. That's because showing a videotape of an unavailable witness' deposition testimony to a judge or juror is likely to be more impressive than reading a transcript of the testimony.

SAMPLE NOTICE OF DEPOSITION, PAGE 1

1	Nolo Pedestrian
	[Street Address]
2	[City, State, Zip Code]
3	[Phone Number]
	Plaintiff in Pro Per
4	
5	
6	
7	
8	THE _____ COURT OF _____ COUNTY
9	STATE OF _____
10	

11	Nolo Pedestrian	)	
12		)	Case No. 12345
	Plaintiff,	)	
13	v.	)	NOTICE OF DEPOSITION
14	Sarah Adams,	)	
15	Defendant.	)	

17 TO EACH PARTY AND TO EACH ATTORNEY OF RECORD IN THIS ACTION:

18 YOU ARE HEREBY NOTIFIED THAT THE DEPOSITION OF _____

19 will be taken at _____, _____, commencing at _____ and

20 continuing from day to day thereafter.

21 YOU ARE FURTHER NOTIFIED THAT: *(check and fill in appropriate boxes)*

22 [ ] <u>Non-Party deponent:</u> The deponent is not a party to this action. So far as known to the

23 deposing party, the deponent's address and telephone number are as follows:

24 _____

25 _____

26 Said deponent has been served with a Deposition Subpoena.

27

28

SAMPLE NOTICE OF DEPOSITION, PAGE 2

1   A COPY OF THE DEPOSITION SUBPOENA IS ATTACHED HERETO AND SERVED HEREWITH.

2

3   [ ] <u>Deponent is a corporation or other entity:</u> The deponent is not a natural person. The

4 matters on which the deponent will be examined are as follows: *(describe in detail so that*

5 *corporation will produce "most qualified" person to testify)* _____

6 _____

7

8   [ ] <u>Items to be produced by deponent-party:</u> The deponent, who is a party to this action,

9 is required to produced the following documents, records or other materials at said deposition:

10 *(describe materials or categories of materials in detail)* _____

11 _____

12

13   [ ] <u>Recording proceedings:</u> The deposing party intends to cause the proceedings to be

14 recorded both stenographically and by *(audio/video)* _____ tape.

15

16   [ ] <u>Expert witness video</u>: The deponent is an expert witness or a treating or consulting

17 physician. The deposing party intends to make a video tape recording of the proceedings and

18 reserves the right to use said video tape recording at trial in lieu of live tertimony from the

19 deponent.

20

21

22   *Nolo Pedestrian*

23   Nolo Pedestrian, Plaintiff in Pro Per

24

25

26

27

28

How to prepare to take an effective deposition. Follow these tips to learn as much information as you can at a deposition:

- Prepare a list of questions before you take a witness' deposition. You need not slavishly follow the list, but having one to refer to should prevent you from forgetting important topics.

- Bring (or subpoena) copies of any written statements about the case that the deponent has previously given. For example, bring the police report if the witness gave a statement to a police officer who included it in the report, or the witness' own affidavit if one was attached to a pleading filed in court. Ask the deponent to amplify on and fill any holes in a statement's contents, then check to see if the deponent in any way contradicts a prior statement. If so, you might ask the witness to repeat the contradictory statement. That way, if you impeach (attack the credibility of) the witness at trial, the witness cannot easily wriggle out by saying, "I made a careless mistake during my deposition."

- Bring copies of any other documents you want to question the witness about, regardless of whether the witness wrote the document or has any connection to it. For example, you may want to know whether the witness ever saw a document, the date on which the witness saw it or whether the witness is aware of the information in the document.

- Review and bring along all paperwork relating to the case organized chronologically, including the complaint, answer and any motions or court rulings. These documents can help if an issue arises concerning the relevance of your questions.

Okay, shift gears and assume that everyone is present at the deposition. What do you do when it's time to start? Before getting into the facts of a case, it's a good idea to begin with what lawyers call a "deposition preamble." This consists of a series of questions lawyers often ask to try to prevent deponents from weaseling out of their deposition testimony at trial. Routine preamble questions include:

- "Are you under the influence of any medication?"

- "Have you had a chance to review any previous statements you've given to your lawyer or anyone else in connection with this case before coming here?"

- "Have you had a chance to meet and discuss the case with your lawyer before coming here today?"

- "If you don't understand a question, will you tell me that so that I can rephrase it?"

- "Do you realize that you are under oath, just as if we were in a court of law?"

- "Is there any reason you can't give your best testimony today?"

Such questions tend to undermine explanations that deponents may come up with if they change their testimony at trial. For example, a hostile witness who doesn't raise a fuss during the preamble and who then at trial greatly exaggerates or contradicts testimony given at the deposition will have a tough time explaining his statements that "I couldn't concentrate at the time of my deposition because I was really feeling ill," or "I hadn't had a chance to review the facts of the case with my attorney at the time of the deposition." Once past the preamble, you can ask questions seeking case-related information. In doing this it is important to realize that the scope of discovery is very broad, far wider than at trial. For example, you can ask a witness about rumors he has heard or opinions he has formed, even though these questions would probably be out of bounds at trial, so long as the answers might "reasonably lead to the discovery of admissible evidence." While each case is factually unique, these general guides may help you think of questions to ask:

- Ask questions that take a deponent through a story chronologically rather than topic-by-topic. Following a chronological format helps you understand the deponent's story and as a result question thoroughly. For example, ask questions such as:

  - "After the June meeting, what's the next thing that happened?"

  - "Before you heard what you referred to as a squeal of brakes, did anything else happen?"

- Ask "wrap-up" questions before leaving one topic to move to another. Wrap-up questions give deponents an opportunity to search their own memories for details that you haven't brought up. For example, before moving on from questioning a deponent about a meeting that occurred on June 1, conclude by asking, "Is there anything else you can recall that took place during the June 1 meeting?" The answer may be an unexpected windfall. But even if, as is usually the case, the deponent responds, "I don't recall anything else," the answer can be very valuable. If at trial the deponent suddenly remembers additional information that helps the other side, the answer allows you to cast doubt on the witness' believability by reading the contradictory deposition testimony to the judge or jury.

- Use a combination of open and narrow questions. Open questions may elicit information you would not have thought to ask about and may encourage witnesses to describe events in their own words: "Please tell me everything that you can recall about the June 1 meeting." Narrow questions allow you to probe for precise information: "Did Johnson say anything about upgrading computers during the June 1 meeting?"

- Refer directly to the allegations of your complaint or answer when questioning your adversary. For example:

  - "Your answer alleges that my own negligence caused the accident. Please tell me what I did that you think was negligent."

  - "Your complaint alleges that I was driving carelessly. Do you know of any witnesses to my alleged careless driving?"

  - "Your complaint asks for economic losses you suffered due to my alleged breach of contract. Please specify the losses to which the complaint refers."

- Show documents and tangible objects to a deponent and ask about their contents. To do this you may use either materials that you brought with you or that you asked the deponent to bring along. (Be sure to take the time to carefully read documents and study objects that a deponent brings before asking questions.) For example: "Your statement to the police officer indicates that you had left your eye doctor moments before you saw the accident. Please tell me why you went to see the eye doctor."

Marking exhibits. When you plan to refer to a document during deposition questioning, have a copy available and ask the court reporter to mark the copy as an exhibit. For example, if you've questioned a deponent about a letter that the deponent wrote to Aunt Sally, ask the court reporter to "mark this copy of the letter to Aunt Sally as Exhibit A." The exhibit will accompany the deposition and you can refer to the document as well as the deposition testimony if you have a reason to use the deposition at trial. (See Chapter 14, Exhibits.)

• Use documents to refresh a deponent's recollection. For example: A construction worker says that he cannot recall what grade of wood was used on the exterior of your house. You may respond, "Please look over the construction agreement that's been marked as Exhibit A and see if that refreshes your recollection."

• Ask if the deponent knows of any other person or document that might have information pertaining to your case. For example:

– "You testified that the subject of computer upgrades was discussed during the June 1 meeting. Are you aware of any document, memo or report that supports your testimony?" "Have you talked to anyone who has told you that she or he recalls this subject being discussed at that meeting?"

– "Following the accident, did you talk to anyone who said that they saw any part of it?" (If the answer is yes): "Please give me the names, addresses, phone numbers and any other information you have that would help me to contact the persons you talked to."

• Don't be afraid to ask for details of unfavorable evidence; remember that a deposition is your chance to find out how bad the case against you will be if you go to trial. A deposition is not the place to argue your side. As best you can, try to pretend you're representing someone else and trying to find out how the witness can hurt this "other person."

For example, if a deponent testifies to seeing you having drinks in a bar shortly before you drove off in your car, you might continue with:

Open questions to encourage the deponent to describe events in the deponent's own words:

– "You testified that you saw me drinking in a bar on the night of the accident. Please tell me everything you can remember about my activities that night."

– "Can you recall anything about my physical condition that night?"

– "You said that I seemed a bit tipsy. Please explain what you mean."

– "Anything else you can recall?"

Narrow questions asking for details:

– "Over what period of time did you see me in the bar?"

– "You testified that you saw me holding a drink. Did you see how many drinks I had?"

– "Could you tell in any way what I was drinking?"

• Ask questions concerning a deponent's general background. The information may suggest topics you wouldn't have thought of and may allow you to estimate the deponent's general credibility. For instance, you may ask about a deponent's:

– family background (including marital status)

– education

– employment history

– organizations to which the deponent belongs

– the deponent's relationship to your adversary, the adversary's lawyer or witnesses

– the deponent's financial interest in the case (this topic is particularly appropriate for an expert witness, because the size of the expert's fee may suggest a motive for the expert to bend an opinion in your adversary's favor)

– convictions of crime, if any.

HOW A DEPOSITION BACKGROUND QUESTION PAID OFF BIG TIME

In the mid-1980s, a group of families sued two Woburn, Mass., businesses for poisoning groundwater and causing leukemia deaths and other physical injuries. During a deposition of a doctor who had important information that helped the plaintiff, a defense lawyer asked about the doctor's marital status. The doctor mentioned an ex-wife, who, after being tracked down by the defense, provided negative information about the doctor's personal background. The plaintiff's lawyer, fearing that the jury might learn of the background, decided not to have the doctor testify at trial. (*A Civil Action*, by Harr, Vintage Books, p. 190.)

• Probe a deponent's credibility by questioning the basis of a deponent's ability to observe and recollect. For example, you may ask whether a deponent has any special reason to be able to recall what happened months or years earlier. And you might ask whether the deponent has any physical limitations. Finally, you might also ask about any external conditions (weather, darkness, background noise) that may have interfered with the deponent's ability to see or hear what happened. Questions you may ask along these lines include:

– "Is there any reason why you remember what took place during the June 1 meeting?"

– "Please describe your activities on the day that the accident took place, up until the time you heard the screech of brakes."

– "Do you ordinarily wear glasses?" (If the answer is yes): "Were you wearing them at the time of the accident?"

• Deponents can often be hard to pin down, especially when you try to elicit information they'd prefer not to provide. One good approach is to watch out for "weasel words" and qualifiers and insist on definite responses. For example, a deponent testifies, "I might have left my glasses at home." Since "might have" are clearly weasel words, you will want to follow up by asking, "Please answer yes or no. Did you leave your glasses at home?"

• Look in a law library for lawyer "practice guides" that suggest areas of deposition questioning for specific types of cases. For example, a practice guide might suggest topics that you should probe in a breach of contract or an auto accident case. One well-known and quite comprehensive source is *Bender's Forms of Discovery*, a 10-volume treatise updated regularly.

After you've finished questioning, your opponent's lawyer can also question the deponent. Often, opposing counsel will ask either no or a very few questions. This makes sense since the deponent is probably on your opponent's side, meaning the opponent can use informal questioning to get additional information out of your sight and hearing.

3. Defending Your or a Witness' Deposition

As a party to a lawsuit, you have a right to be present at every deposition your adversary takes. Lawyers call this "defending a deposition." (Lawyers occasionally save their clients money by skipping doing this and ordering a transcript instead.) If you are a self-represented litigant, you automatically defend a deposition when yours is taken. Below are suggestions that can help you or a deponent who supports your side of the case (and is willing to meet with you beforehand) to testify as completely, accurately and credibly as possible. This is important because solid depositions strengthen your bargaining position. Moreover, following this approach should prevent you or a deponent who supports your side of the case from getting into a messy situation in which you later have to explain to a judge or jury why you or a deponent have changed your deposition story or can suddenly remember details at trial that were not mentioned months earlier at a deposition.

Your adversary can ask about any pre-deposition discussions you have with a witness. Your adversary's lawyer can ask a witness what you said to the witness before the deposition started. Or as lawyers put it, your pre-deposition discussions aren't "privileged." Therefore, don't say anything that would embarrass you or hurt your credibility if the witness were to repeat it during the deposition.

The following tips can help you or your witness testify fully and accurately at a deposition.

- Just as you would do if you were getting ready to take a deposition, prepare in advance by going over the pleadings and any case-related written statements made by you or your witness, such as demand letters sent to your adversary, affidavits attached to a pleading or motion (for example, as part of a summary judgment motion; see Chapter 6, Pre-Trial Motions and Hearings), or even letters written to a newspaper about the incident giving rise to the lawsuit. Similarly, review all pertinent documents that constitute the "paper trail" leading to litigation. For example, in a breach of contract case this would include any memos that you or a witness might have written preceding the signing of a contract and the contract itself.

- Don't volunteer information. Listen carefully to questions, and answer only what you are asked. You or a witness may be tempted to defend your position with long, rambling answers, but such answers almost inevitably provide an opponent with useful information. (If you really want a witness to elaborate on an answer, wait until the end when you will have a chance to ask questions.)

- If you don't understand a question, or a question is confusing because it has several parts, ask the questioner to rephrase it.

- Ask for a recess if you become mentally fatigued, need a bathroom break, or just need time to think. During this time, you can continue to refresh your recollection with statements or other documents.

- Object if you think that a question is improper. However, you should then go on to answer it unless a question is totally irrelevant or asks about legally privileged information—for example, conversations you've had with your legal coach. (See Section C4 below, "Deposition Objections.")

- Tell the truth.

4. Deposition Objections

Just as during a trial, lawyers and self-represented parties can object to each other's questions during depositions. (See Fed. Rule of Civil Proc. 30 (d)(1). Also see Chapter 16, Making and Responding to Objections, for a discussion of common objections and objection procedures.) But because judges are not present at depositions, no immediate ruling on your objection's validity is possible. Typically, a judge rules on a deposition objection only if the side taking the deposition wants to read the objected-to testimony into the record at trial (and has a legal basis for doing so). If the trial judge determines that the objection was proper, the judge will probably not permit the objected-to testimony to be read at trial.

Again, because judges are not present at depositions, a deponent normally answers an objected-to question just as if no objection had been made. For example, an attorney defending a deposition may object that a question calls for hearsay, and then tell the deponent to "go ahead and answer the question." The big exception to the "go ahead and answer" practice occurs when the basis of an objection is that a "question is improper because it calls for privileged information." (The Sidebar below, "Privileged Information," explains why.)

An attorney may try to take advantage of you. If you defend a deposition as a self-represented litigant, an attorney might try to take advantage of you (and the absence of a judge) by bullying you or one of your witnesses with rapid-fire repetitive questions in an effort to confuse you into providing conflicting answers and/or asking questions so far afield that they are outside even the broad scope of discovery. You can object to an attorney's questions just as you could at trial, which has the effect of preserving the objection until such time as a judge reads the transcript (see discussion above). But if you're asking the questions, don't stop just because an attorney repeatedly objects to your questions—the attorney may just be trying to rattle you. To get the information you want, simply persevere with your questions no matter how obstreperous the attorney is. However, in an extreme situation in which an attorney is repeatedly insulting or intemperate, it may be appropriate to terminate a deposition and promptly file a motion in court and use the transcript as a basis of a request for a judge to impose sanctions (penalties) on the attorney.

PRIVILEGED INFORMATION

As you've seen, deponents are normally expected to provide information that may be legally objectionable, leaving it to a judge to rule on admissibility later if an effort is made to introduce the information into the trial record. The big exception occurs when a question seeks "privileged information." In all states, and subject to various exceptions, legal privileges exist for confidential communications between attorneys and client, spouses, physicians and patients, and ministers and congregants. Depending on a state's law, privileges may also exist in some other situations, such as between psychotherapists and clients. A privilege also exists for an attorney's "work product," meaning an attorney's strategic papers and files. (For a good general discussion of privileges, see Lilly, *Introduction to the Law of Evidence,* (West Group; 3d ed. 1996.) Because when a privilege exists the protection of privacy outweighs the need for the truth, neither you nor any other witness has to reveal privileged matter, whether at a deposition or a trial. For example, you do not have to reveal the case-related private conversations you've had with your legal coach, or a personal conversation you had with your spouse following a car accident or the making of a contract. Nor can you ask your adversary for a copy of the adversary lawyer's "trial strategy memo," because that represents the lawyer's privileged "work product."

Example: You ask your adversary, "Please tell me what you and your attorney talked about before we started the deposition." The question calls for privileged information and the deponent does not have to answer it.

Example: Amanda Nolo, a self-represented litigant, discusses her case with a friendly witness before the adversary takes the witness' deposition. The adversary's lawyer asks, "What did you and Nolo talk about before the deposition?" The question is proper. Since Amanda Nolo is not a lawyer, no privilege exists for conversations between her and the witness.

Deponents who are unaware of the protection for privileged material may unwittingly disclose it during a deposition, in which case the privilege is waived. That is why a lawyer who represents a deponent usually instructs the deponent not to answer a question that seeks legally privileged information. If you are self-represented, you don't have the right to instruct a deponent to refuse to answer a question that calls for privileged information. However, you can interrupt a deposition to advise a friendly deponent that a question calls for privileged matter, and leave it to the deponent to decide whether or not to answer it.

RESOURCES ON DEPOSITION

American Jurisprudence Pleading and Practice Forms (Lawyers Cooperative Publishing Co; updated regularly), is a multi-volume treatise; Vol. 8-A has numerous examples of deposition forms.

Basics of Legal Document Production, by Cummins (Delmar), reviews fundamentals of various discovery tools and contains many examples and sample forms.

The Effective Deposition, by Malone and Hoffman (National Institute for Trial Advocacy Practical Guide Series), is a comprehensive guide to deposition rules and techniques, based on the Federal Rules of Civil Procedure.

All is not necessarily lost if you neglect to object to an improper question or answer during a deposition. You might be allowed to make the objection for the first time at trial should your opponent seek to read improper deposition testimony into the record. This happens when the deposition testimony that your opponent wants to read into the record is improper, and the opponent couldn't have cleared up the impropriety with more questions had you objected during the deposition. However, the safest course is to become familiar with grounds for objection and to make objections for the record whenever you are uncertain. You especially need to object if your objection concerns the form of a question or answer (say, a question is leading or is vague). You cannot make a "form" objection at trial if you failed to make it during the deposition. (See Fed. Rule of Civil Proc. 32 (d)(3)(B).)

D. WRITTEN INTERROGATORIES

Written interrogatories are questions that you or your adversary must answer in writing, under oath. (See Federal Rule of Civil Procedure 33; most states follow similar procedures.) Court rules usually give the answering party—called a respondent—30 days to answer. However, because answering interrogatories often means searching records and gathering documents, judges usually grant a party's Motion for Additional Time to Answer. Realizing this, parties usually informally stipulate (agree) to a request by their opponents for a reasonable amount of additional time to answer.

1. Advantages and Disadvantages of Sending Interrogatories

Compared to depositions, written interrogatories have these advantages:

- Your only interrogatory expense is the time it takes you to prepare them, and you don't have to pay a court reporter or arrange for videotaping or a date and location. You prepare the questions at your convenience and serve them on your adversary by mail.

 Save time and money by sending out interrogatories before taking depositions. Interrogatory answers can pinpoint the witnesses who are likely to have important information, reveal documents that you can use when questioning witnesses, and supply background information that you would otherwise have to ask about during a deposition. As a result, your deposition questioning can target key witnesses and can be shorter and more efficient.

- The scope of your questions can be very broad. Whether you take a deposition or send out interrogatories, you can seek information "reasonably calculated to lead to the discovery of admissible evidence."

- When you send interrogatories to an organization, you are entitled to "corporate knowledge," or the collective memory of all employees and representatives, not merely the single witness whose deposition you are taking. A typical preface to interrogatory questions instructs the recipient to "furnish all information known by or in possession of yourself, your agents, and your attorneys, or appearing in your records."

Example: You have sued a hospital for negligently allowing Doctor Rex to perform a medical procedure for which you claim that Doctor Rex was not qualified. You ask, "Please describe the process you followed to investigate Doctor Rex's qualifications to perform the above-mentioned medical procedure." An individual deponent might be able to testify only about a small part of the investigation.

The interrogatory, by contrast, should reveal the combined investigation activities of various individuals.

However, just like depositions, interrogatories have a number of downsides that often limit their utility. (Remember, we advised you earlier to rely on informal investigation to the extent it is possible!) These include:

- Court rules are likely to limit the number of interrogatories you can ask. Federal Rule of Civil Procedure 33 (a) allows 25 questions (including a reasonable number of subparts), unless a judge gives you permission to ask more. Few states allow more than 50.

- Interrogatories are inflexible. Court rules often limit you to a single set of interrogatories. Even if this isn't true (or a judge makes an exception in your case and allows a second set), you have to prepare and send out a whole set of interrogatories before you receive any responses. This means that you often don't have the information (the answer to question # 1) which might allow you to make more pointed inquiries (questions # 2 and 3), as you normally would at a deposition.

- You may pose interrogatories only to the opposing party. You cannot send interrogatories to witnesses or other third persons.

- Interrogatory answers are frequently prepared with strong input from lawyers. Lawyers tend to provide narrow answers that cover up rather than reveal helpful information, and to try to avoid answers entirely by claiming that questions are ambiguous, vague, unduly burdensome, seek legal conclusions or violate the attorney-client privilege. (These types of re-sponses are especially likely if you represent yourself and your opponent has a lawyer.) While you can file a motion asking a judge to compel your adversary to answer your question, this process can be time-consuming and frustrating.

Example 1: In a personal injury case, your interrogatory asks, "Please identify the witnesses you have talked to or taken statements from, and attach those statements (or summaries) to your answers." The probable response: "Objection—the question asks for the attorney's work-product and is protected from disclosure under Federal Rule of Civil Procedure 26(b)(3)." Solution: Ask only for the names and addresses of witnesses, not for the attorney's decisions about which witnesses are worth talking to or taking statements from. (Sample proper interrogatory: "State the full name and address of each person known to you who witnessed or claims to have witnessed the collision between the plaintiff's and the defendant's cars on May 4, (year).") If you want to know what the witnesses saw or heard, you'll have to interview them informally or take their depositions.

Example 2: You are the plaintiff in a breach of contract case, and your interrogatory asks, "Please identify all documents in your possession that pertain to the case." The probable response: "Objection—the question is vague and overbroad." Solution: Narrow your requests. For example, a more acceptable interrogatory would be, "Please identify any documents in your possession pertaining to conversations between Sam Spade and Plaintiff relating to the contract described in Plaintiff's complaint."

- Lawyers rarely provide, and judges rarely insist that they provide, lengthy answers to broadly worded interrogatories. The legal culture generally allows for summary responses to open-style interrogatories, perhaps out of a sense that information should not be too available "on the cheap." If you want to elicit a full story, you'll probably have to take a deposition.

Example: You ask, "Please describe the process leading to the hospital's hiring of Doctor Rex." Instead of a lengthy, fully detailed answer, you're likely to get something closer to, "Thorough review of past employment and numerous committee discussions and analysis."

2. Drafting Interrogatories

Without experience, you'll probably find it hard to draft clear, unambiguous interrogatories. One way around this problem is to consult a legal treatise such as *Bender's Forms of Discovery*, which has predrafted questions for specific kinds of cases. (Unfortunately, *Bender's* won't be of much help if it doesn't have specimen interrogatories for a case with facts similar to yours.) Another possibility is to have your proposed interrogatories reviewed by your legal coach, if you have one. The coach can probably quickly provide suggestions for tightening up your questions.

**RESOURCES ON
INTERROGATORIES**

Bender's Forms of Discovery (Matthew-Bender; regularly updated), is a 10-volume treatise with sample interrogatories for numerous kinds of cases, including products liability, employment discrimination, slip and fall and building construction.

American Jurisprudence Pleading and Practice Forms Annotated and *Basics of Legal Document Production* (both cited in Resource Box at the end of Section C above).

SEVEN TIPS ON DRAFTING GOOD INTERROGATORIES

The following suggestions should help you draft more effective interrogatories.

① If court rules in your jurisdiction provide for voluntary "disclosure" of pertinent documents and witnesses, do not begin to prepare interrogatories until your adversary has completed disclosure and you've had a discovery-planning meeting with the adversary's lawyer. That way you'll have additional background information that can help you pinpoint specific topics on which to focus interrogatories.

② Because you can submit only a limited number of interrogatories, use sub-questions to reduce the number of interrogatories you use to cover a single topic. Remember, however, that sub-parts must be reasonable in number. Lawyers rarely succeed when they try to evade limits on the number of interrogatories by adding 20-30 sub-parts to a question.

Example 1: "Please state whether you wear prescription corrective lenses. If the answer is 'yes,' please also state the vision problem for which you have a prescription and the prescription."

Example 2: "During the past five years, have you suffered any other personal injuries? If your answer is 'yes', please state for each injury:

a. the date of the injury;

b. where you were at the time of the injury;

c. how the injury took place;

d. the nature and extent of the injury;

e. the name and address of each medical facility or office in which you received treatment for the injury;

f. whether and from whom you sought compensation for that injury."

③ If you are going to ask a series of interrogatories about a single event or document, define the event or topic in a "Definitions" section that comes before the questions. This way you don't have to describe the defined event or topic every time you refer to it in an interrogatory.

Example 1: "Definitions. The following term used in these interrogatories has the following meaning: The term 'September 22 contract' refers to the contract signed by plaintiff and defendant on September 22 and attached as Exhibit 'A' to these interrogatories."

Example 2: "Definitions. A request for any 'document' refers to all writings of any kind, including but not limited to correspondence, memoranda, notes, pamphlets, books, computer printouts, fax documents, graphs, photographs, videotapes and electronically stored records, whether stored on tapes, cassettes, computers or other similar devices." (Whew! You wouldn't want to say this more than once!)

④ When you ask for information, also ask if your opponent has any document or record reflecting that information, and if so to include a copy of the document with the answers. This saves you having to seek the document in a separate "Request for Production of Documents."

Example: "Do you contend that you shipped the widgets to plaintiff on March 12? If so, please state whether you have in your possession or control any document or record indicating that such a shipment was made and attach a copy of any such document or record to your answers to these interrogatories."

⑤ Ask your adversary to set forth the facts on which its legal claims are based.

Example: You are the defendant in a personal injury action; the plaintiff's complaint asks for "damages of no less than $100,000." You might submit an interrogatory such as "Please identify separately each element of harm (economic, physical, psychological or otherwise) for which you seek damages, the dollar amount you seek for each element of harm and the facts constituting each element of harm."

⑥ When serving interrogatories on an entity such as a corporation, ask for "the identity of each person who participated in preparing the answers to these interrogatories, and of each document that was consulted in the course of preparing answers to these interrogatories." The answers can help you to decide which if any individuals to depose and what documents to request.

⑦ Make use of "form" interrogatories drafted by attorneys. Legal formbooks and attorney "practice guides" are available at any good-sized law library. Such guides typically contain specimen interrogatories for use in specific types of cases. For example, a formbook may have a set of "Plaintiff's Interrogatories in a Breach of Shopping Center Lease Case." Consult formbooks for your type of case before preparing a set of interrogatories. (See Chapter 22, Legal Research, for tips on how to use legal formbooks.)

E. REQUESTS FOR PRODUCTION OF DOCUMENTS; SUBPOENAS

We have so far discussed several ways of obtaining or inspecting and copying documents (or other objects), including:

- Making informal requests to cooperative witnesses or businesses;

- Asking for voluntary disclosure;

- Using a "Notice of Deposition" or a "Subpoena Duces Tecum re Deposition" to order a deponent to bring documents to a deposition;

- Asking a party to attach documents to answers to interrogatories.

Several additional if less common methods to gain access to written materials exist, including:

- Sending your opponent a "Request for Production of Documents." (See Federal Rule of Civil Procedure 34; most states have similar rules.)

- Serving a non-party with a subpoena ordering the recipient to allow you to inspect and copy designated materials. (See Federal Rule of Civil Procedure 45; many but not all states provide for this option.)

A request for a document must be precise enough that the recipient can reasonably determine what you want. For example, a request to "produce every document that has anything to do with this case" is likely to be objected to as vague. The requirement that your request be specific often means that you have to delay sending out a Request for Production of Documents until you know enough about the case to identify the documents you're after. (On the other hand, a recipient can't avoid furnishing a document because "your request failed to mention the weight of the paper on which the report was printed.")

 It's proper to request documents you can't identify. You do not necessarily have to know a document's exact title, or even that it actually exists, to send a Request for Production of Documents to your opponent or issue a Subpoena for Production of Documents to a third party. For example, you might serve a subpoena on a hospital, asking the hospital to send you copies of (or to allow you to inspect and copy) "all records, reports, notations, charts, x-rays, results of medical tests or any other document (as defined above) pertaining to General Hospital's treatment and care of Penny Sillen on February 13-15, (year)." The obvious advantage of wording a subpoena this broadly is that it may well produce documents whose existence you are unaware of.

A recipient has to allow you to inspect or copy a document so long as it's in the recipient's "possession or control." The "or control" language is important. It means that a scummy recipient can't play "hot potato" with a document, giving it to an attorney or friend and then responding, "I'd love to give it to you but I can't; it's not in my possession."

Example: You might phrase Requests for Production of Documents in an auto accident personal injury case as follows:

"Plaintiff Les Ismore requests that Defendant produce the following documents for inspection and copying at Ismore's business office at 950 Campion Way, Leamington, OH, between the hours of 2:00 P. M. and 4:00 P. M. on March 31, (year):

1. The document of title ('pink slip') to defendant's Ford Explorer. (This can help you prove that the defendant owned the car and is therefore legally responsible for your injuries.)

SAMPLE REQUEST FOR PRODUCTION OF DOCUMENTS

```
1   Nolo Pedestrian
    [Street Address]
2   [City, State, Zip Code]
3   [Phone Number]
4   Plaintiff in Pro Per
5
6
7
8           THE _____ COURT OF _____ COUNTY
9                    STATE OF _____
10
11  Nolo Pedestrian                          )
                                             )   Case No. 12345
12                    Plaintiff,             )
                                             )   NOTICE OF DEPOSITION
13  v.                                       )   REQUEST TO DEFENDANT ADAMS FOR
                                             )   PRODUCTION OF DOCUMENTS
14  Sarah Adams,                             )
                                             )
15                    Defendant.             )
    _____        )
16
17         Plaintiff Nolo Pedestrian requests, pursuant to Federal Rule of Civil Procedure 34 which our state has
18  adopted, that Defendant Sarah Adams produce the following documents by delivering them to the office of
19  Nolo Pedestrian located at [Address] within 30 days from the date of service of this Request:
20         1.   Registration and proof of ownership of the truck driven by Defendant Adams which struck Nolo
21  Pedestrian on January 1, year.
22         2.   Receipts and records showing all maintenance and repairs to the truck referred to in Request 1
23  above, during the one-year period before January 1, year.
24         3.   Copies of Defendant Adams' business records reflecting Adams' appointments on January 1, year,
25  the day of the accident in question in this lawsuit.
26
27                                          Nolo Pedestrian
                                            _____
28                                          Nolo Pedestrian, Plaintiff in Pro Per
```

2. The defendant's automobile insurance policy that provides insurance coverage for defendant's Ford Explorer. (This can help you decide if you are likely to be able to collect a judgment in your favor.)

3. Any other insurance policy (including 'umbrella insurance') that insures the defendant against liability growing out of an automobile accident. (Same purpose as No. 2.)

4. Receipts for and records of any repairs or servicing done on defendant's Ford Explorer during the one-year period immediately preceding the date of the accident that is the subject matter of this lawsuit. (This can help you decide if the defendant failed to make necessary repairs, or whether a repair shop or parts manufacturer might also be liable for your injuries.)

5. Defendant's appointment book for the date of the accident. (This may help you prove that the defendant could have been distracted at the time of the accident, as might be the case if the defendant was late for a critically important meeting or had just received disturbing medical news.)"

RESOURCES ON REQUESTS FOR PRODUCTION

American Jurisprudence Pleading and Practice Forms Annotated and *Basics of Legal Document Production* (both cited in Resource Box at the end of Section C, above).

REQUESTS TO EXAMINE OBJECTS OR INSPECT LAND OR BUILDINGS

Discovery rules generally also allow you to request production of "things" and to request entry on an opponent's land to make an inspection. For example, if you claim that you were injured by a piece of poorly designed automotive equipment, you may request that "Defendant produce the Sherr 9000 tire inflator for inspection and testing at the offices of Burridge Testing Labs at 30 Clifton Avenue, Coventry, MD, on June 3, (year)." Or, if you claim that a ditch dug by your next-door neighbor is improper because it causes flooding on your property, you may "request that Defendant permit Plaintiff and Plaintiff's engineering expert to enter Defendant's property located at 229 Elm Drive on March 27, (year) at 2:00 P.M. for the purpose of inspecting and photographing the property."

You or your adversary may respond to a Request for Production of Documents in a variety of ways, depending on such factors as convenience, the way records are kept and the number of records. Standard alternative ways of responding include:

- Mail copies of the documents to the requesting party, with the sender bearing the copying costs.

- Bring the originals to the requesting party and let that party undergo the cost of copying.

- When the records are voluminous, make them available at the place where they are usually stored and allow the requesting party to inspect and copy them. (The recipient of a Request to Produce can't ship documents to the North Pole and tell the other side to go there to inspect them!)

- Object. Common objections are that a request is "unduly burdensome" (too much trouble, given the amount of money in dispute), or "too vague and overbroad."

- Reply that "there are no documents in the possession or control of Defendant that correspond to Plaintiff's Request Number 2."

F. REQUESTS FOR ADMISSIONS

Requests for Admissions are written statements or assertions that you prepare and serve on an adversary in an effort to secure the adversary's admission that facts are true or that documents are genuine. (See Federal Rule of Civil Procedure 36; most states have similar rules.) Requests for Admissions are not designed to "discover" information from an adversary, but to make life easier at trial. That's because once you or an adversary admits that a fact is true or that a document is genuine, the admission can be offered as evidence at trial and cannot be disputed.

Example: In an auto accident case, you serve the following Requests for Admission on the defendant:

- "Admit that the following fact is true: 'On February 29, defendant Sarah Adams consumed two martinis between the hours of 9 A.M. and 10 A.M.'"

- "Admit that the following document is genuine: A letter dated March 1 and signed by Sarah Adams."

If these requests are admitted (either by answering them affirmatively or by failing to deny them within the time set by law, often 30 days), you can offer the requests into evidence to prove that Sarah Adams consumed two martinis and wrote the March

1 letter. Moreover, the defendant cannot try to contradict this evidence.

As a self-represented litigant, you must be especially alert if you are served with Requests for Admissions. First, you must respond in writing within 30 days, or everything in the request is "deemed admitted." Second, you cannot automatically deny every Request for Admission, figuring that, "I can't lose by denying." To the contrary, if your case goes to trial, and your opponent proves a fact to be true or a document to be genuine after you denied a Request for Admission, the trial judge can force you to pay whatever it cost your opponent to make the proof—including attorney's fees! (See Federal Rule of Civil Procedure 37-c.)

If you don't have a document or are uncertain as to how to answer a Request for Admissions, often the safest course is to respond by saying that "I neither admit nor deny the requested fact because I do not have sufficient information to do so." This will usually protect you against having to pay your adversary's expenses for proving that the fact is true, unless a judge concludes that you answered in bad faith or could have readily found out whether a fact was true or a document genuine.

Requests for Admissions are usually served near the end of the formal discovery period. That's because if you serve requests on an opponent before the opponent has had a reasonable opportunity to investigate the case, your opponent will almost certainly deny them or answer by citing "lack of sufficient information." And a judge is unlikely to penalize the opponent for failure to admit at this early stage, even if you prove at trial that a fact is true or a document is genuine. Similarly, it is not usually until case investigation is nearly done that you can identify the facts and documents that you want to include in a set of Requests for Admissions.

SAMPLE REQUEST FOR ADMISSIONS

1	Nolo Pedestrian
	[Street Address]
2	[City, State, Zip Code]
3	[Phone Number]
	Plaintiff in Pro Per
4	
5	
6	
7	
8	THE _____ COURT OF _____ COUNTY
9	STATE OF _____

10		)
	_____	) Case No. _____
11	Plaintiff,	)
		) REQUEST FOR ADMISSIONS
12	vs.	)
		)
13	_____	)
	Defendant.	)
14	_____	)

15 REQUESTS FOR ADMISSION, SET NUMBER _____, ARE HEREBY PROPOUNDED TO:

16 (name of each party from whom admissions requested) _____

17 BY:(name of propounding party) _____

18

19 YOU ARE HEREBY REQUESTED TO ADMIT the truthfulness of each of the facts set forth below; and the

20 genuineness of each document, a copy of which is attached to this Request.

21 EACH OF THE FOLLOWING FACTS IS TRUE:

22 1. _____

23 2. _____

24 EACH OF THE FOLLOWING DESCRIBED DOCUMENTS, COPIES OF WHICH ARE ATTACHED TO THIS

25 REQUEST, IS GENUINE:

26 3. _____

27 4. _____

28 DATED _____   SIGNATURE _____

5

SETTLEMENT

Salmon swimming upstream to spawn in an obstacle-filled river have a far better chance of accomplishing their goal than a case has of making it all the way to trial. Informal estimates are that around 90% of cases filed in court wind up being settled rather than resolved by the verdict of a judge or jury. This conventional wisdom is reinforced by a recent study led by Jonathan Hyman for the New Jersey Administrative Office of the Courts. Not only did just 10% of all the cases in the New Jersey sample go to trial, but 12% of these cases settled after a trial had started. Thus, the Hyman study also confirmed another basic truth about litigation: it's never too late to settle.

Settlement is a popular option for a number of reasons:

- As a plaintiff, you can take advantage of the time value of money. The dollar you get by settling now may be more valuable than the two dollars you may get years down the road.

- As a defendant, you may gain psychologically by putting a lawsuit behind you and exchanging a fixed loss now for the uncertainty of an open-ended and possibly much more expensive future judgment.

- If you are self-represented, no matter whether you are a plaintiff or a defendant, the biggest benefits of settlement can be extricating yourself from a complex and often alien and hostile legal system, and saving the hundreds of hours you may otherwise have to spend doing legal research, talking to witnesses, gathering documents, engaging in numerous other case-related activities and ultimately going to court.

- Settlement affords both plaintiffs and defendants the certainty of a known result. By comparison, the outcome of a trial is always in doubt. (Lawyers are fond of referring to trial as a "crapshoot.") Even the most solid case can occasionally succumb to such factors as lost exhibits, disappearing or forgetful witnesses, a hostile judge or a rogue jury.

- Settling often allows both sides to tailor the outcome to meet their specific needs. For example, if a business dispute goes to trial, a judge may be limited to awarding the plaintiff money damages that the defendant cannot pay. By settling, the parties might structure future dealings in such a way that the plaintiff is paid off over time or is guaranteed future contracts that more than make up for the money the plaintiff lost.

"Why don't you fellows just go outside and settle this in the parking lot?"

Example: Daniel and Julia see an orange on the sidewalk. When both lunge for it, a nasty argument ensues. In court, a judge would probably have to award the entire orange to Daniel or Julia according to a legal rule—perhaps to the one who saw it first. However, in settlement discussions the parties might realize that Daniel wants the orange to use its peel in a recipe, while Julia wants it only for the the pulp to make orange juice. In short, the orange can be divided so that both parties get what they want. In this way, a settlement can produce a mutually satisfactory "win-win" outcome that the legal system could not.

For these and many other reasons, settlement is often in your best interests—even though it almost always means that you have to back off from an earlier hard-line position. Or, as Sir Winston Churchill put it, better to "jaw, jaw, jaw" rather than wage "war, war, war."

Since every case that settles is one fewer that the formal legal system has to find time and room for, legislators and judges think that settlement is also in the best interests of the legal system. The upshot is that after a complaint and answer are filed and before a case goes to trial, you will inevitably encounter judges, backed by court rules and procedures, encouraging you to consider settlement. Accordingly, this chapter provides a guide to the post-filing settlement procedures you are likely to encounter and offers suggestions for dealing with them effectively.

TRY SETTLING BEFORE LITIGATING

Waiting to try to resolve a dispute until after court papers have been filed ordinarily makes little sense. Disputants should—and most probably do—attempt to settle their arguments before going to court. In fact, the filing and serving of a complaint is often an admission that these early settlement efforts have failed. Paradoxically, a complaint itself can often serve as a settlement device in the sense that it represents one side telling the other, "I mean business and you'd better be willing to compromise if you want to avoid a long and nasty fight."

One way to achieve a fair and effective settlement before going to (or being dragged into) court is to employ techniques known collectively as "alternative dispute resolution." Prominent among these techniques are negotiation (trying to resolve a dispute by talking to another person face-to-face) and mediation (trying to resolve a dispute with the help of a neutral third-party mediator). While you have undoubtedly engaged in negotiations and even informal mediations your entire life, these activities are more likely to result in fair and satisfactory outcomes if you learn and employ the best information on effective use of these techniques. Among the good resources you can consult to increase your knowledge and skill in negotiation and mediation are:

RESOURCES ON SETTLEMENT

Settle It Out of Court: How to Resolve Business and Personal Disputes Using Mediation, Arbitration and Negotiation, by Thomas Crowley (Wiley and Sons), contains information on the wise and effective selection of arbitrators and mediators as well as how to craft workable settlement strategies.

Getting to Yes: Negotiating Agreement Without Giving In, by Fisher & Ury (Houghton Mifflin), is still considered a "Bible" on how to promote settlement by focusing on underlying needs and objective positions rather than personalities.

How to Mediate Your Dispute, by Peter Lovenheim (Nolo Press), an excellent guide to the mediation process, including how to prepare for a mediation and what happens during mediation.

How to Win Your Personal Injury Claim, by Joseph Matthews (Nolo Press), a focused resource on how to successfully negotiate with insurance companies in personal injury and property damage cases.

The Pocket Lawyer: Solve Your Own Legal Disputes, by Sullivan and Judge Warren McGuire (Venture 2000), a useful review of the major alternative dispute resolution techniques, written for non-lawyers.

A. COURT-ORDERED ("JUDICIAL") MEDIATION

Mediation is a descendant of dispute-resolution methods used by village or tribal elders in ancient times. In mediation, you discuss a dispute with your opponent and a neutral, usually professionally-trained, third person called a mediator. The mediator's role is to facilitate discussion, help disputants focus on concrete issues, offer settlement proposals and, if the process gets that far, help the disputants craft a written settlement agreement. A mediator has no power to impose a solution. Because mediations so often produce settlements, courts in many localities require parties in some kinds of cases to go through mediation before their cases can proceed towards trial.

Every state sponsors low-cost, voluntary, community-based mediation programs in specific fields, usually including neighbor disputes, consumer problems, landlord-tenant problems and child custody and visitation disputes. In addition, many mediators who specialize in divorce and business disputes practice privately. The upshot is that mediation is so widely available that one way or the other, you may well have voluntarily participated in a mediation before going (or being taken) to court. Whether or not this is true, if you find yourself in Small Claims Court, in a child custody dispute, or if your case involves a "small" amount of money (often, $50,000 or less), a judge is likely to suggest strongly or even order you and your opponent to try mediation. Of course, if mediation does not produce a settlement, your case continues on through the court system.

The American Arbitration Association (AAA), to which many mediators belong, states that "in most cases mediation results in a settlement." Other mediation groups generally concur. Therefore, because it is quite likely that you will resolve your dispute with a mediated settlement and not a court judgment, you'll obviously want to guard against a disadvantageous result by preparing carefully for mediation. The following tips should help you achieve a satisfactory mediated settlement:

- You will be attempting to resolve the case with your opponent personally, even if your opponent is represented by a lawyer. (Lawyers sometimes attend mediations, but only to counsel clients and facilitate the discussion.) However, recognize that a representative of a business or other large organization is likely to have prior mediation experience, and will be savvy about and at ease with the process, and may be a lawyer to boot. To gain something of an equal footing, you should understand exactly how mediation works by reading a book such as Peter Lovenheim's *How to Mediate Your Dispute* (Nolo Press). (See Sidebar, "Try settling before litigating," above.)

- Think in advance about possible mediated outcomes that you would find satisfactory. While a mediator may suggest ideas you haven't considered, getting a head start on your thinking can help you evaluate new proposals. While you want to keep an open mind, it is particularly important that you think in advance about an acceptable "bottom line" compromise position so that you don't find yourself conceding too much.

- Bring documents and other exhibits supporting your legal claim. Even though no judge or jury is present to declare a winner or loser, tangible objects lend force to your points and provide you with psychological support.

- Remember that the idea behind mediation is not to produce winners and losers, but to find solutions (often creative ones beyond the power of a judge to order) that meet both parties' real needs (but not always their fondest wants or expectations) so far as is possible.

Though specifics many vary somewhat from state to state, the following guidelines are typical of how you are likely to encounter mediation as part of the formal legal system. A judge often has the power to order mediation of any civil lawsuit involving less than $50,000, and of all child custody and visitation disputes. The parties often have a chance to agree on a mediator of their choosing, but in some instances the judge simply appoints one from a panel of available mediators. When a judge orders the parties to mediate, the mediator's fees are paid by the court. Mediations are more informal than trials. Mediations take place in office settings, not in courtrooms, and operate without regard to evidence rules, meaning that disputants are free to say whatever they want and to back it up with whatever information they consider important.

Example: Hilary has invested $20,000 to become a partner in a bagel/flower shop business started by Skye. Hilary asks for her money back after becoming convinced that Skye seriously understated the level of competition in their locality. When Skye refuses, Hilary sues Skye for fraud and breach of contract; Skye denies Hilary's allegations. At an early stage of the litigation a judge orders the parties to try mediation. During mediation, Hilary refers to "reliable rumors I've heard about a national bagel chain's plan to open a couple of nearby outlets in the next few months." In a trial, a judge would probably rule that Hilary's reference to rumors (no matter how "reliable") is inadmissible on the grounds of vagueness and hearsay (see Chapter 15, Basic Rules of Evidence). However, Hilary is entirely free to talk about rumors in mediation, and her statements have as much force as Skye and the mediator are willing to give them.

If mediation doesn't produce a settlement—and remember that neither a mediator nor a judge can force you to accept a mediated solution—your case proceeds towards trial. Nothing you or anybody else says during mediation is admissible as evidence at trial. For example, your opponent can't testify that during the mediation you admitted that "I might have been driving a few miles over the speed limit."

To help you understand how mediation works, consider how the mediation in Hilary's and Skye's dispute might unfold. (*How to Mediate Your Dispute,* by Peter Lovenheim (Nolo Press), describes six stages of a typical mediation; p. 1.28. The discussion below tracks those stages.) Depending on the complexity of a dispute and the attitudes of the parties, these stages may be completed in an hour or two or may continue over several days. But no matter how long it lasts, the mediation is likely to proceed as follows:

- **Stage 1:** The mediator reviews the goals and rules of mediation and encourages the disputants to work cooperatively towards a settlement. For instance, a mediator might remind Hilary and Skye that "I encourage each of you to be honest with the other and to honestly try to come to an agreement. I won't take sides, and I'll keep everything you say confidential."

- **Stage 2:** Each disputant has an uninterrupted chance to describe her view of what the argument is all about and to offer possible solutions. For example, Hilary and Skye in turn could describe their understanding of the events, documents and conversations leading up to the agreement. They could then each discuss their perceptions of the level of compe-

tition the new business will face. Finally, both could set forth their desired basis upon which to resolve the dispute. Initially, for instance, Hilary might demand "my money back right now," while Skye might say that "I want to keep Hilary's money in the business for at least one year, but I am willing to sign a note promising to pay her back in a year with interest."

- **Stage 3:** The mediator tries to get the parties to identify and agree on the issues that must be dealt with in order to resolve the dispute. In this case, the mediator might identify "level of expected competition" and "duration of the partnership agreement" as issues that Hilary and Skye absolutely must discuss.

- **Stage 4:** The mediator meets privately (caucuses) with each disputant to discuss the strengths and weaknesses of each person's position and tries to refine settlement ideas. In a private caucus with Hilary, for example, the mediator might want to discuss her ability to prove Skye's alleged misrepresentations and what information she might consider relevant to a decision to keep the partnership going.

- **Stage 5:** The mediator and the disputants again meet to continue working towards a solution. Sometimes the parties might find it best to agree to adjourn the mediation for a week or two so that they can seek out or develop additional information. When the mediation continues, all three will meet together to see if settlement is a realistic possibility.

- **Stage 6:** Mediation ends with a resolution that is summarized in writing, or with a joint decision to return to the court system because agreement cannot be reached and further efforts would be futile. In this case, one possible settlement would consist of Skye agreeing to increase Hilary's interest in the partnership by 5% or 10% to compensate her for the unanticipated risk presented by additional competition. Another possibility would be for the two parties to agree to change their merchandise mix to avoid head-to-head competition. If settlement is agreed to, the mediator would help the parties reduce the agreement to writing, report back to the court and file papers dismissing the case.

B. COURT-ORDERED ("JUDICIAL") ARBITRATION

Many states give judges a second way to resolve "smaller" cases (generally those involving $50,000 or less) without going to trial. This consists of court-ordered or "judicial" arbitration, a kind of informal trial. In states that authorize both court-ordered mediation and court-ordered arbitration, you'll need to check your local court rules to find out whether you can have any input into which procedure a judge orders you to follow. If you and your opponent agree, it might even be possible for a judge to order that both procedures occur. That is, if court-ordered mediation fails to produce an agreement, you might ask the judge to order the case to arbitration.

Like mediation, arbitration is designed to be a less expensive alternative to resolving a dispute in court. However, arbitration is more like a trial than is mediation. That's because you and your adversary present oral testimony, documents and other tangible exhibits to a neutral third party (in this case an "arbitrator") who is empowered to make a decision (usually called an "award"). Arbitrators are professionally trained in arbitration procedures, and are usually lawyers or retired judges. Most courts maintain panels of arbitrators, and a judge will appoint one for your case. The arbitrator's fee (often around $100 per case or hearing day) is paid by the court. (In some localities parties whose cases involve too much money to be covered by court-ordered arbitration can request voluntary arbitration, in which case they pay the arbitrator's fees themselves.)

Arbitrations typically take place in the arbitrator's conference room, and the arbitrator need not strictly abide by rules of evidence. Moreover, an arbitrator can try to fashion an outcome that is "fair," even if the outcome is different from what might happen in court. Following the presentation of evidence, the arbitrator issues a written award.

The arbitrator can make an award regardless of whether the parties agree with it, unlike in mediation. However, the award resulting from court-ordered arbitration is ordinarily non-binding. That is, if you are not happy with the outcome of court-ordered arbitration you can reject an arbitrator's award and insist that your case be returned to the court system. When your case goes back to the court system, you are eligible for a trial (which lawyers often call a "trial de novo"), just as if the arbitration never took place. (However, in many states you can be saddled with court costs if you reject an arbitration award and don't achieve a better outcome at trial than you did in the arbitration.) If neither you nor your opponent asks for a trial de novo, the arbitrator's award becomes the court's judgment and is generally enforceable to the same extent as a court judgment.

Example: Assume that a judge orders Hilary and Skye's bagel/flower shop dispute to arbitration. After hearing evidence, the arbitrator decides that Hilary is entitled to dissolve the partnership and be returned the $20,000 she invested in the business. However, Skye rejects the award and goes to trial in an effort to uphold the partnership agreement and keep Hilary's money in the business. Unless a judge or jury holds that the partnership agreement is valid, Skye will probably have to reimburse the county for the arbitrator's fee and pay Hilary's costs of trial (though probably not her attorneys' fees).

⚠️ **Mandatory arbitration.** The court-ordered arbitration system we describe here is just one type of arbitration. Another form is non-judicial mandatory arbitration, in which the arbitrator has the power to issue a binding award. Without realizing it, you may have entered into a contract which provides for "binding arbitration" in the event of a dispute and just about eliminates your ability to go to court. For example, if you have an account with a stock brokerage, are a member of a health care plan, or live in a condominium, it is likely you have signed a document that provides that any dispute will be resolved exclusively through arbitration rather than through the court system. Courts generally uphold provisions for mandatory and exclusive arbitration, and do not overturn arbitrators' awards so long as procedures were fairly followed.

Since arbitration procedures closely resemble trials and arbitrators are almost always lawyers or retired judges, you should prepare for an arbitration in much the same way you would for trial. For instance, you should figure out what you have to prove (see Chapters 7 and 8, What You Need to Prove at Trial), gather the documents you'll need and present any witnesses who can back up your contentions after working with them carefully to be sure that their testimony covers the key points. Nevertheless, you should find it easier to represent yourself in an arbitration because evidence rules are relaxed and the proceedings are likely to be less formal than a trial.

C. OFFERS OF JUDGMENT ("STATUTORY OFFERS")

An "offer of judgment" is a written offer made by a defendant to a plaintiff proposing to settle a case on the terms set forth in the offer. (See Fed. Rule of Civil Proc. 68; most states have similar provisions.) If you receive an offer of settlement that is even marginally reasonable, consider it seriously before saying "no." The reason is that you may lose money if you refuse the offer of judgment and the outcome of trial is less favorable to you than the offer. In that event, the judge may order you to pay any court costs the defendant incurs after you turn down the offer, such as witness fees and court reporter fees—but usually not the defendant's attorneys' fees.

An offer of judgment can unfairly pressure you into a quick decision if you receive it early in the case, before you've had a chance to evaluate the strength of your case and your adversary's . If you receive an offer of judgment before you've had a chance to engage in informal investigation or formal discovery (see Chapter 4, Investigating Your Case), consider these responses:

SAMPLE OFFER OF JUDGMENT

Offer of Judgment

To: Plaintiff Nelly Nolo, in pro per.

Defendant Really Big Corporation offers to allow judgment to be entered against it and in favor of plaintiff Nelly Nolo in the sum of ten thousand dollars ($10,000) plus costs of suit incurred by plaintiff to the date of this offer.

This settlement offer is made pursuant to Rule 68 of the Federal Rules of Civil Procedure and Rule 408 of the Federal Rules of Evidence, and is not to be taken as an admission of any liability or wrongdoing on the part of defendant Really Big Corporation.

This offer shall remain open for ten days after service of the offer on plaintiff Nolo.

Date: _____

_____
Attorney for Defendant

- Ask your adversary to extend your time to reply. An offer may give you as little as ten days to reply, and a request for a month or even longer is reasonable if the offer is made before you've had a chance to investigate.

- If the adversary refuses to extend your time to respond and later asks the judge to order you to pay costs under a law such as Federal Rule 68, explain to the judge that such an order would be unfair because the offer was made at a time when you could not reasonably have been prepared to accept it. (Your argument will be stronger if you can show the judge that you asked for an extension of time to respond to a statutory offer and your adversary refused the request.)

D. PRE-TRIAL SETTLEMENT CONFERENCES

Part of what happens between the time of filing initial pleadings and trial is that a judge will conduct one or more "pre-trial conferences." (See, for example, Federal Rule of Civil Procedure 16.) During a pre-trial conference (which doesn't usually take place until after you've had a chance to gather documents and evidence), a judge will meet with you and your adversary's lawyer for any of a variety of purposes. For example, a judge may use a pre-trial conference to schedule hearings on motions or try to shorten the trial by getting you and your adversary to stipulate (agree) to particular facts. However, probably the most important reason that judges schedule pre-trial conferences is to facilitate settlements. Rules such as Fed. Rule of Civil Proc.

16 (a) authorize judges to order the attendance (either in person or by telephone) of parties who have the power and authority to settle the case.

The style that judges use to conduct pre-trial settlement conferences varies widely. Some judges act much like mediators, trying to facilitate discussion and help the parties arrive at their own settlements. Others take a more active role, sizing up "what a case is worth" and trying to cajole or occasionally even browbeat the parties into a settlement (sometimes by caucusing with each side individually, as mediators often do). Some judges require parties to prepare confidential (not shown to the adversary) "settlement memoranda" justifying their settlement demands or offers. Finally, judges sometimes even ask lawyers to cut their fees to facilitate a settlement.

If you are a self-represented litigant, you'd obviously like to know in advance what to expect from your judge during a settlement conference. Unfortunately, since these conferences usually take place in judges' private offices (often called "chambers"), you won't have a chance to watch your judge in action in another case. However, you can consult with your legal coach, who may have experience with the judge or know someone who does. Another option that may prove helpful is to ask a judge's clerk or secretary about a judge's preferred method of conducting a settlement conference.

When thinking about what sort of settlement you would accept, it is important to be realistic about what is likely to happen if your case goes to trial. If you are a plaintiff, ask yourself questions such as:

- "What are my chances of winning?"

- "How much money am I likely to receive?"

- "How much time and energy will it take to prepare for trial and how will that expenditure of time and energy affect my business or other activities?"

- "How long will the trial take and to what extent will it disrupt my life?"

- "Will I have a hard time collecting the judgment if I win?"

If you are a defendant, ask yourself questions such as:

- "What are my chances of winning?"

- "How much time and energy will it take to prepare for trial and how will that expenditure of time and energy affect my business or other activities?"

- "How long will the trial take and to what extent will it disrupt my life?"

- "What's the possibility that a judge or jury will order me to pay much more than I could settle for now?"

- "Can the publicity of a lawsuit hurt my reputation or business?"

 If you have limited experience with the court system, get help before going into a settlement conference. As a self-representing party, you may not have enough experience with the legal system to feel that you can answer the above questions with any degree of accuracy. You might ask a legal coach to help you craft a reasonable settlement offer and evaluate the other side's offer.

At a pretrial conference it is easy to feel like an "outsider," especially if your adversary is represented by a lawyer. You might even feel as if the judge and your adversary's attorney are ganging up to force you to accept a bad settlement. On the other hand, a judge's experience can help guide you to a settlement outcome that is at least as good as you are likely to achieve at trial. While it's important not to be buffaloed into saying "yes" to a bad settlement, you'll also want to avoid being so angry at your adversary or so emotionally invested in your case that you pass up a chance for a reasonable compromise. Again, a pre-settlement conference discussion with your legal coach can guide you towards a realistic settlement outcome.

PRESSURE TO SETTLE: THE CONSQUENCES OF SAYING "NO" TO A JUDGE

If you are self-represented, you may be concerned that refusing a settlement that a judge is urging you to accept will turn the judge against you at trial. Start by understanding that in many localities the judge who presides over a settlement conference is not the same judge who will preside at trial. In any event, most judges' court rulings will not be affected by your refusal to settle. However, if a judge's behavior or statements during a settlement conference indicate that the judge may have already arrived at an unfair conclusion about your case, the laws of most states allow you to file a "Motion to Disqualify" asking that another judge be assigned to preside over your trial. (Attorneys' "practice guides," available in a law library, will probably have a sample Motion to Disqualify.)

E. POST-SETTLEMENT DOCUMENTS

Settlements are typically accompanied by a number of documents. (This is the legal system, after all!) The terms of the settlement may be set forth in a written settlement contract that may be called a "Release" or a "Stipulation for Dismissal." If your adversary's lawyer prepares the contract, you'll obviously want to read it over carefully and perhaps ask for modifications before signing. A settlement contract is enforceable in court, the same as any other kind of contract. And if you later claim that the adversary is not living up to the settlement, only the written contract, not the oral discussions leading up to it, will establish your rights and obligations.

The language of a release (sometimes also called a "General Release" or a "Release of All Claims") is often quite broad, typically terminating all of a plaintiff's claims (existing and unknown) against all existing and potential defendants. Your state may have a law providing that releases do not extend to claims that you don't know about; if so, you'll probably have to waive (give up) that protection in the release agreement.

For example, if you receive $10,000 to settle your personal injury claim, you will probably be asked to sign a release not only on your behalf, but also on behalf of your "heirs, agents and assigns." In addition, the release will probably state that the settlement covers every possible type of injury, including "personal injuries, property damage, physical disabilities, medical expenses, lost income, loss of consortium and all other claims that have been or could have been brought, whether now known or which might become known in the future." It may seem unfair for you to be asked to settle possible claims that you aren't even aware of, but courts routinely uphold this type of broad release language and rely on it to justify barring future lawsuits growing out the events referred to in the release. As a result, before signing a release you should be certain of the full extent of your property losses and personal injuries.

Example 1: You slip and fall outside a department store, and sue the department store for improperly maintaining the sidewalk in front of the store. You agree to drop the suit in exchange for a payment of $5,000, to compensate you for medical expenses of $1,500, lost wages and "pain and suffering." You sign a broadly worded "Release of All Claims" under which you agree to dismiss the lawsuit and irrevocably release the department store from any future claim growing out of your fall. A month later, your doctor tells you that your injuries are not responding as well to treatment as the doctor expected, so you'll need around six months of additional therapy costing an additional $2,000. You cannot refile the case or seek additional money from the department store. The release terminated all your claims, both known and unknown.

Example 2: Same case. The department store offers to settle your case by paying you $5,000 if you'll dismiss the case and sign a General Release of All Claims. Trying to decide whether to accept the offer, you check with your doctor, who tells you, "At this point I can't be certain how much more treatment you need. Normally you'd be looking at a few months of therapy costing around $1,500. But you've been a little slow to respond to treatment, so you could be looking at expenses of twice that or even more." In this situation, you should probably ask for additional time to accept or reject the settlement offer, until you have a firmer sense of the extent of your medical bills. If you accept the offer and sign the release, you'll have no recourse if your medical expenses turn out to be greater than you thought.

SECRET SETTLEMENTS

It is common for a release to require that you keep confidential the amount of money you receive in settlement. For example, a release may state, "This settlement is confidential, and neither party shall disclose the terms of the settlement to anyone, whether orally or in writing. Failure to maintain confidentiality voids the settlement." Such language is especially popular with businesses that fear that public disclosure of settlement terms will encourage litigation. If you want to settle, you'll probably have to agree to confidentiality.

A "Stipulation for Dismissal," when filed with the court, means the case will be terminated, usually "with prejudice." The term "with prejudice" indicates that the case cannot later be reopened or refiled as a separate action.

 RESOURCES ON RELEASES

For additional examples of release forms, see:

101 Law Forms for Personal Use, by Robin Leonard and Marcia Stewart (Nolo Press).

How to Win Your Personal Injury Claim, by Joseph Matthews (Nolo Press). ■

6

PRE-TRIAL HEARINGS AND MOTIONS

You will likely have to appear in court at least once, and maybe several times, before your trial occurs. The most common reasons are to attend pre-trial conferences and hearings on motions. These proceedings, and the legal documents filed in conjunction with them, are the focus of this chapter.

A. PRE-TRIAL CONFERENCES

At some point before your case goes to trial, the court may require one or more pre-trial conferences. (For reference, in federal courts, pre-trial conferences are governed by Federal Rule of Civil Procedure 16.) The main purpose of a pre-trial conference (sometimes called a status conference) is to identify the issues remaining to be resolved and focus the evidence that will be presented at trial. But judges can also use them to set discovery deadlines, and a trial date and ensure that your case is moving along. Some courts will resolve these issues by telephone so the parties do not have to go to court. Check with the Clerk's Office in your court.

Often, you and your adversary must prepare and bring to this conference a document called a "pre-trial memorandum." This specifies the uncontested and contested legal and factual issues, the exhibits that will be introduced and witnesses who will testify at trial, and the jury instructions (rules the judge will read to the jurors before they go off to reach a verdict).

Your court may have special forms; ask at the Clerk's Office. If it doesn't, you can find forms for pre-trial memoranda in the law library, in form books on civil litigation. (See Chapter 22, Legal Research.) Sometimes a pre-trial memorandum must be prepared jointly—that is, you must meet with your adversary (by phone, by mail or in person) to coordinate and provide the information requested by the court. This process (sometimes called a "meet and confer") encourages parties to settle the case before it goes to trial or at least agree on certain issues so as to narrow the scope of the dispute.

B. PRE-TRIAL MOTIONS

A motion is a request, usually in writing, for a judge to make an order (decision or ruling) with regard to a legal issue that arises in the course of a lawsuit. The issue may simply be a scheduling matter, such as in a motion to request a continuance (extension of time). For example, you may want to request that the trial itself be postponed from May 1 to June 1. Or, the issues may be complex and cut to the very heart of the case, such as a motion for summary judgment (a request for the judge to make a final judgment without going to trial because affidavits establish that the facts are not in dispute).

Making and responding to motions (called motion practice) can be confusing, but do not let it daunt you. If you believe there are issues you can or should resolve before trial, you may benefit from filing a motion. If your adversary files a motion, review and analyze the facts and legal issues in the motion and any documents attached to it. Go over them with your legal coach, if you have one. Then, carefully provide enough factual and legal analysis (described below) to formulate reasoned responses, and present your position to the court in a written response and orally at the court hearing, if one occurs.

1. Motions: An Overview

Since this book's main focus is trial, the information on motions is meant as background. This chapter highlights some of the important rules and procedures involved in pre-trial motion practice, but it is not a comprehensive guide. Courts have rules you should consult governing how and when motions can be filed.

a. When Motions Are Made

Depending on what you're asking the court to do, a motion can be made before, during or after trial. Some motions are made orally and others in writing, depending on the rules of court and the type of decision you are requesting that the judge make. For example, during trial, parties make oral motions to strike (delete improper testimony from the record). This chapter focuses mainly on motions that arise before trial, most of which must be made in writing. Check the rules in your court to be sure.

b. Who Can Make a Motion

Only a named party to the case, such as you or your adversary, may file a motion. Witnesses, for example, may not make motions.

c. The Basic Motion Process

The party bringing a motion usually must write several documents (discussed below, in Section 3). Then, the opposing party has a chance to oppose the motion. Unopposed motions are often granted by the judge without a hearing. If the motion is opposed, frequently the judge will decide, based on the parties' papers alone without scheduling a hearing in court, whether to grant or deny the motion. If a hearing is scheduled, it will be before a judge (no jury) and will likely be relatively short—often much

---

MOTIONS MADE DURING AND AFTER TRIAL

The following motions can be made during and after trial:

- **Motion in Limine**. A request for a court order excluding irrelevant or prejudicial evidence, typically made at the outset of a jury trial. (See Chapter 16, Making and Responding to Objections.)

- **Motion to Strike**. A request that the judge delete improper testimony from the trial record. It's usually made after the judge has ruled that particular testimony is not admissible. (See Chapter 16.)

- **Motion for a Directed Verdict**. Typically made in a jury trial after the plaintiff has presented evidence, this motion is a request that the judge rule against the plaintiff without letting the matter go to the jury. The usual reason is that the plaintiff has not established the legal claims as a matter of law. (See Chapter 19, When Your Trial Ends: Judgments and Appeals.)

- **Motion for Judgment Notwithstanding the Verdict ("JNOV")**. Also in jury trials, this is a request by one party for the judge to rule against the other party, after the jury has already decided in the other party's favor. This motion effectively asks the judge to overrule the jury (See Chapter 19, When Your Trial Ends: Judgments and Appeals.)

---

less than 30 minutes. A hearing gives the parties a chance to answer questions from the judge and argue the motion.

Some judges do not even preside over trials, only motions (called "law and motion" courts or divisions in courthouse lingo). Because these courts are busy, the judge has probably considered similar motions countless times before and likely has many other motions on calendar the same day as yours; you may have only a few minutes to state your reasons for wanting or objecting to the motion. The judge's ruling on a motion may be made at or after the hearing. If it's made later, you will be notified about the judge's decision by mail.

d. Frivolous Motions

A party must have a valid legal basis for filing a motion.

Some people use motions for reasons other than what they state in their papers—for example, to delay proceedings or to increase their adversary's costs, perhaps in an effort to force their adversary to drop the case or settle cheaply and quickly. Do not do this. Make sure any motion you bring is truthful and that what you request is legitimate.

Judges have begun to crack down on frivolous (without a valid legal basis) motions. A party who can show that the other side has filed a frivolous motion may request sanctions (punishment—usually a fine) against both that party and her attorney. If one side files a series of frivolous motions, the judge may even rule that the other side wins the case.

If your adversary has acted outrageously, in a way that prejudices your case, you can make a motion for sanctions. For example, you may ask for sanctions if your adversary has asked for repeated continuances seemingly for the purposes of delay or harassment. Or, ask for sanctions if your adversary refused to stipulate and forced you to go to court for a continuance even though you gave an excellent reason (such as your being in the hospital) why the earlier date was not suitable.

Like other motions, a motion for sanctions should state what you want and why, and should include supporting documentation describing what

happened, such as a declaration or affidavit, discussed in Section 3, below. For example, if your adversary repeatedly forces you to come to court on frivolous motions, you may ask the court to order him to pay your expenses in preparing for and attending those hearings.

 Don't ask for sanctions unless your adversary's conduct is outrageous. Sanctions are serious business, and most judges do not impose sanctions unless a party's conduct is fairly outrageous. It makes sense to ask for sanctions only in extreme cases, and to be sure of the facts before you make accusations.

2. Is a Motion Necessary?

Before making a written motion or responding to one made by your adversary, try to informally reach an agreement. For example, if you need to postpone a deadline, you might ask your adversary to agree to a "continuance." If the other side agrees, you can prepare a document called a "Stipulation to Continue [insert name of what's been continued]." Ask the court clerk and check the rules in your court for any special procedures for preparing and filing one. Typically, both you and your adversary must sign the stipulation and file it with the court. If both sides agree, the court will probably grant the continuance without requiring either you or your adversary to appear in court. The clerk will then schedule the matter for a later date, as agreed, and notify the parties of the new date and time.

A sample of a stipulation for a continuance of the hearing date on a motion for summary judgment is shown below.

SAMPLE STIPULATION TO CONTINUE

1	SARAH ADAMS
	[Street address]
2	[City, State, Zip Code]
	[Phone number]
3	
	Defendant in Pro Per
4	

8 THE _____ COURT OF _____ COUNTY

9 STATE OF _____

11	Nolo Pedestrian,	)	CASE NO. 12345
		)	
12		)	
	Plaintiff,	)	
13		)	STIPULATION TO CONTINUE HEARING ON
	v.	)	PLAINTIFF'S SUMMARY JUDGMENT MOTION
14		)	
	Sarah Adams,	)	
15		)	Date: April 15, 19XX
	Defendant.	)	Time: 10:00 a.m.
16		)	Place: [Court Address]
		)	[City, State, Zip Code]
17		)	Courtroom 10
	_____	)	

20 Defendant Sarah Adams and Plaintiff Nolo Pedestrian agree to the following:

21 The parties jointly request that Plaintiff's Motion for Summary Judgment, set for hearing before this

22 Court on April 15, 19XX, be continued to a date and time convenient to the Court, on or after June 15,

23 19XX.

25 *Sarah Adams* _____   *March 8, 19XX* _____
   Sarah Adams, Defendant in Pro Per   Date

27 *Nolo Pedestrian* _____   *March 1, 19xx* _____
   Nolo Pedestrian, Plaintiff in Pro Per   Date

3. What Goes into a Motion

Your motion must tell the court exactly what you want and why you want it. Unfortunately, legal proceedings are rarely that simple; you must put your request and reasoning in the form the court requires and expects. (For reference, Federal Rule of Civil Procedure 7(b) governs the form of motions in federal courts.) This section discusses documents you typically must prepare in order to make a motion.

a. Notice of Motion

A legal document called a "Notice of Motion" gives notice to (informs) your adversary that you are bringing the motion, so that she has time to prepare for the court hearing and possibly respond in writing. Your Notice of Motion should tell the other party:

1. When the motion will be heard. This means the court hearing date, time and place.

2. The grounds (reasons) for your motion.

3. What supporting documents you will be referring to in your request to the judge, such as "points and authorities" (written legal arguments which support the reasons for your motion with citations to relevant laws) or declarations or affidavits (sworn factual statements).

b. The Motion

The motion is your request to the judge for a specific court order. It states what you want and why you are entitled to that particular order. To justify your request, sometimes it's enough to include a short reference to the rule of law that entitles you to the order, especially for routine matters. (See sample motion for continuance in Section 7, below.) Other times, however, especially in more complex motions, you may need to list (cite to) other relevant legal authorities, such as court cases, and explain how those authorities support your position. This type of explanation and citation is called a Memorandum of Points and Authorities. (Consult a legal form book or your self-help law coach for more on how to prepare this type of document. See Chapter 22, Legal Research.)

c. Supporting Documentation

As supporting documentation, you may need to include statements of facts in the form of a declaration or affidavit (see sample, below, in Section 7). You may also include copies of other relevant documents as exhibits (attachments).

4. Scheduling a Court Hearing on a Pre-Trial Motion

Some motions are made, responded to and ruled on by the judge in writing—all without a court hearing. In some courts, motions can be argued on telephone conference calls. But many times, a party bringing a motion must obtain a court hearing date for the judge to consider and rule on a motion. The court clerk can tell you how to obtain a hearing date in your court. In many places, you schedule a date by phoning the court. The clerk will assign you a hearing time and enter your case on the court docket (calendar) for that day.

When you phone the clerk, be prepared to give your case name and number, the type of motion and an approximate time you want to schedule the hearing (if you have a choice). For example, you might say: "Yes, this is Sarah Adams, the defendant in Pedestrian v. Adams, Case No. 12345. I would like a court date, if possible in about six weeks, for a summary judgment motion."

Sometimes, courts have a particular time or day of the week devoted solely to hearing motions ("law and motion" day) or special law and motion judges (different from the judge who will conduct your trial). When you call, ask the clerk when motions are heard.

Double-check the judge's calendar. Court schedules sometimes change at the last minute. For example, judges sometimes try to clear their calendars (hear routine or uncontested matters first, then move on to disputed and or complex proceedings) or otherwise change their calendars around. It is good practice to check with the judge's clerk the day before just to verify the time of your hearing and how early you should be there. This may have an extra advantage, too, of showing the clerk that you respect the courtroom routine and appreciate the clerk's help.

5.   Serving and Filing Your Documents

To give your adversary adequate notice, you must often have the papers served at least ten to 15 days before the motion is due to be heard in court. Federal Rule of Civil Procedure 6 (d) requires notice of at least five days for most types of motions; local rules often extend that time period.

Most courts allow you to serve (deliver) your Notice of Motion, Motion, Reply and related documents by mail. (Federal Rule of Civil Procedure 5, Sections (a), (b) and (c), and your state's equivalents govern how service must be made.) The papers you serve should include a copy of your proof of service, a signed document stating when, how and on whom the Notice was served. Keep a second copy of the proof of service for your records and file

the original with the court, as required by your court's rules.

 Ask the court for time to respond to a motion. If your adversary schedules a motion and gives you less than one week's notice of the hearing date and time, you may want to let the judge know. The judge may reschedule the hearing or reprimand your adversary—especially if you have not had time to respond or prepare. To protect yourself, always note the date you receive documents from your adversary or the court.

Typically, you are not allowed to serve your own documents; check the rules in your court. Often you must have an adult who is not a party to the lawsuit mail or deliver your documents. The person who actually serves your motion for you is the one who should sign the proof of service.

In addition, you must typically file originals with the court. (See Federal Rule of Civil Procedure 5 (d) and (e) or the rules in your state which govern filing papers with the court.) You can file legal papers in person at the courthouse Clerk's Office (where you filed your complaint or answer), or you may be able to file documents by mail. Check your local rules and talk to a clerk (or your legal coach), for other rules, such as the number of copies you must file. You may want to take an extra copy to the court to "conform" (stamp the document as filed on the date received) and give back to you for your files. If you file your documents in person, you can wait for your conformed copy. If you mail the documents, you may need to send an extra copy clearly marked "Please Conform and Return to [your name and address]" with a self-addressed, stamped envelope.

6. Court Hearings on Motions

Before a judge grants or denies a written motion, the judge may hold a brief court hearing. There are no jurors and normally no witnesses, although sometimes a judge will want to hear testimony in connection with a complex motion. But, typically, any factual information from you, your adversary or a witness is presented in the form of a declaration or affidavit—a statement of facts personally observed, which is dated and signed under penalty of perjury.

Some judges issue a tentative ruling, based on the papers you and your adversary have filed, a day or two before the hearing. It states which way the judge is inclined to rule (for or against the motion) and sometimes the reasons for the judge's decision. Ask the court clerk if your judge makes tentative rulings and when you can call to find out a particular ruling. It may help to know in advance what the judge thinks so that you can use the hearing to respond to the judge's particular concerns.

On the day of your hearing, the clerk will call out the name of your case when it's your turn. You and your adversary will go to counsel table to argue the motion. Whoever brought the motion (called the movant or moving party) will usually argue first. After the movant, the respondent (party responding to the motion) argues. Both sides make points based on the law and the facts, showing why the judge should or should not grant the request. Since the judge already has documents setting out the parties' positions, it is usually unwise to repeat exactly what is in the papers. The whole hearing typically lasts no more than ten to 15 minutes.

Watch a motion hearing before arguing one. A good way to get a feel for how argue a motion is to go sit in on a motion in the court where you will argue before your hearing. Note where people sit and stand, where the microphones are, how much time the judge seems to spend with people and what types of questions she is asking. Also, use any time you have before your hearing begins to review your own notes and observe carefully what the judge seems to expect from others arguing before you.

Though a hearing is not a trial, you should observe the same formalities when arguing a motion. Stand when you make your presentation, and address the judge as "Your Honor." Don't talk directly to or argue with your adversary (or her lawyer). (See Chapter 2, The Courthouse and the Courtroom.)

At the end of the hearing, the judge will often make a final decision, either orally or in writing. Other times, the judge may decide to take the matter "under submission." That means the judge will think about it and let you know the ruling later, in writing.

If the judge makes an oral ruling, take detailed notes to be sure you know its exact terms. Also make sure you know who is in charge of writing up the order and notifying all interested parties (people who are affected by the ruling). Sometimes the clerk prepares the order for the judge to sign; other times the judge asks one party (most often the winning party) to draft the order for the judge to sign, and give notice of the court's order. If you are asked to draft an order, refer to your notes and check with the clerk as to exactly what form the notice should take. One good approach is to ask the clerk for a sample and a list of everyone who must be notified.

WHO MUST BE NOTIFIED

In many cases, the notice list (names and addresses of the interested parties who should be notified about court decisions in the case) is relatively short: your adversary and the court. However, a notice list can be quite long. For example, even in the most routine bankruptcy matters, notice of motions must often be given to all creditors (people owed money).

Because notice can be defective (invalid) if necessary people are not included, find out who must be "noticed" (notified) of specific decisions that arise in your case. Do this by checking your state and local rules about notice (or federal and local rules if you are in federal court). Also, if the judge asks you to draft an order, ask the judge directly who must be given notice.

Don't rely on these sample motions. The sample motions in this chapter are only illustrations. To draft (write) a motion in your case and be certain you are using the format and language required by your court, refer to your local court rules and a legal form book. Form books, often used by lawyers to prepare motions, also contain helpful explanations about the relevant legal references and factual information (called "Points and Authorities") you may need to include to support the position you are taking in your motion. (Chapter 22, Legal Research, discusses form books.)

7. Common Pre-Trial Motions

This section focuses on common pre-trial motions: those relating to continuances, discovery issues, summary judgment and dismissing a complaint. It contains sample motion papers and dialogues from court hearings to give you an idea of what may come up when you bring or respond to a motion.

a. Motion to Dismiss

If a defendant thinks the plaintiff's claims are not legally valid, the defendant can ask the judge to dismiss the complaint before trial. Essentially, the defendant is saying, "Even if everything the plaintiff says in the complaint is true, the plaintiff isn't entitled to anything from me." The defendant makes this request by filing a motion to dismiss a complaint for failure to state a claim (in some courts this is called a demurrer, pronounced "de murr er").

For example, say the plaintiff's complaint asserts a legal claim of assault, alleging that you gave the plaintiff a menacing look. A look, though perhaps frightening and even rude, does not by itself amount to an act for which the plaintiff can bring a valid lawsuit. Only if you had also taken some threatening action, such as swinging your fist, would the plaintiff have a legally valid claim of assault.

If the motion is denied, and the complaint is held to be valid, the defendant will have a short time (often another 30 days) to answer the complaint. If the motion is granted and the complaint dismissed, the judge may allow the plaintiff a chance to amend (fix), refile and reserve the complaint and summons on the defendant.

b. Motion for a Continuance

The purpose of a motion for a continuance is to delay the date of a hearing, settlement conference, deposition or even the trial itself. For example, if you will be hospitalized for surgery when a motion is supposed to be heard, or if a witness will be out of the country on the date set for trial, ask for a continuance.

Some courts routinely grant one continuance, especially if the other side does not object; others want to see a good reason for the delay before they grant a continuance. This may be especially true in courts that have adopted "fast track" or expedited procedures—streamlined systems to move cases along at a faster pace than in traditional systems. You may be granted a continuance if a scheduled surgery causes you to be hospitalized but denied a continuance if you are simply going on vacation.

If you are the moving party, and you cannot reach an agreement with your adversary about a postponement, you will need to tell the judge, in your papers, why the current date is bad. Next, point out that you and the other side have discussed the problem. The judge will likely appreciate your efforts to handle the matter in a friendly way.

If you oppose a continuance, emphasize in your reply papers why a delay would prejudice (hurt) you. For example, you may point out that an important witness will not be available if trial is delayed. Or you may argue that the other side appears to be requesting repeated continuances in an effort to stall or force you to settle.

For example, assume you are Sarah Adams, a building contractor whose truck struck a pedestrian (named Nolo) as he crossed Elm and Main Streets. Mr. Nolo has sued you; you are the defendant and you are representing yourself. You had barely sent your answer (reply to the plaintiff's complaint) when the plaintiff's attorney sent you a Notice of Motion for Summary Judgment (request for the judge to resolve the case without going to trial because the facts are not in dispute).

You believe the plaintiff's attorney is bringing the motion because he thinks you will be easily intimidated as a pro per, and won't know how to respond. You think he's hoping to get a quick court judgment or advantageous settlement if he moves fast, before you get a chance to prepare. All you know for sure is that you were not driving carelessly, and that you dispute the plaintiff's claim that you were negligent. In addition, you believe that investigation may reveal that the plaintiff's injuries did not come from your truck, but from some pre-existing injury. To oppose the motion, you will need to show that there is a factual dispute that should go to trial. But you need additional time to gather evidence about what really happened. So far, you have not had a chance to conduct any discovery or other investigation.

You should first contact the other side and ask them to agree to continue the hearing to a later date. You do, and they refuse. (Keep records of your request and their refusal.) You are left with two choices:

1. Oppose the summary judgment at its scheduled date and time, with little evidence to back up your legal position.

2. File a motion for a continuance of the summary judgment motion hearing, so you have time to find at least enough evidence to show that there is a genuine dispute of facts.

You decide to bring the continuance motion. After calling (or writing, if your rules require it) the clerk to get a hearing date for your continuance motion (see Section 4, above), you draft a Notice of Motion, Motion and Declaration, which might look something like the ones shown below. A sample reply, which your adversary might file to oppose you motion, is also shown below.

SAMPLE NOTICE OF MOTION AND MOTION REQUESTING CONTINUANCE

1	SARAH ADAMS
	[Street Address]
2	[City, State, Zip Code]
	[Phone Number]
3	
	Defendant in Pro Per
4	

THE _____ COURT OF _____ COUNTY

STATE OF _____

Nolo Pedestrian,   ) CASE NO. 12345
)
                                    Plaintiff,   ) NOTICE OF DEFENDANT'S MOTION AND
) MOTION REQUESTING CONTINUANCE OF
           v.   ) PLANTIFF'S SUMMARY JUDGMENT MOTION;
) DECLARATION OF SARAH ADAMS
Sarah Adams,   )
) Date: March 17, 19XX
                                    Defendant.   ) Time: 10:00 a.m.
) Place: [Court Address]
)   [City, State, Zip Code]
)   Courtroom 10
_____   )

TO PLAINTIFF AND HIS ATTORNEY(S) OF RECORD:

You are notified that on March 17 at 10 a.m. in Courtroom 10, Defendant Adams will bring a

motion to continue the Plaintiff's Summary Judgment Motion. The Plaintiff's Summary Judgment

Motion was originally scheduled for April 15, 19XX. The Defendant will move the court to continue that

date for at least 60 days so that Defendant has adequate time to conduct discovery and respond to

the Plaintiff's Motion.

This Motion is based on the Notice of Motion, the Motion itself and the attached Declaration of

Defendant Adams. Any responses to this Motion must be served not later than March 12, 19XX.

Date: March 6, 19XX

                                    _____*Sarah Adams*_____
                                    Sarah Adams, Defendant in Pro Per

SAMPLE MOTION

1

2

3   <u>MOTION REQUESTING CONTINUANCE OF</u>

4   <u>PLAINTIFF'S SUMMARY JUDGMENT MOTION</u>

5

6   Defendant Adams moves this Court for an order continuing the hearing on Plaintiff's Summary

7   Judgment Motion, presently scheduled for April 15, 19XX, to a date not less than 60 days after April

8   15, 19XX. In support of this motion, Defendant asserts:

9   　　1.   Defendant was served on February 28, 19XX, with the Plaintiff's Summons and Complaint.

10   　　2.   Defendant was served on March 5, 19XX, with the Plaintiff's Notice of Hearing on Summary

11   Judgment Motion scheduled for April 15, 19XX.

12   　　3.   Because Defendant has not had adequate time to conduct discovery, Defendant cannot

13   adequately respond at this time to the Plaintiff's Motion.

14   　　4.   Under Federal Rule of Civil Procedure 6(b), this Court has discretion to extend the time period in

15   which Defendant must respond to the Motion and continue the date at which Plaintiff's Motion will be

16   heard.

17   　　WHEREFORE, Defendant requests that this Court continue the hearing date of Plaintiff's Motion to a

18   date not earlier than 60 days after April 15, 19XX, and extend the amount of time within which

19   Defendant must respond to that Motion accordingly.

20

21   Date: March 6, 19XX   *Sarah Adams*
     　　　　　　　　　　　　　　　　　　　　　　　　Sarah Adams, Defendant in Pro Per

22

23

24

25

26

27

28

SAMPLE DECLARATION OF SERVICE BY MAIL

1	SARAH ADAMS
	[Street Address]
2	[City, State, Zip Code]
	[Phone Number]
3	
	Defendant in Pro Per
4	
5	
6	
7	
8	THE _____ COURT OF _____ COUNTY
9	STATE OF _____
10	

11	Nolo Pedestrian,	) CASE NO. 12345
		)
12	Plaintiff,	) DECLARATION OF SERVICE BY MAIL
		)
13	v.	)
		)
14	Sarah Adams,	)
		)
15	Defendant.	)
		)
16		

17   Ms. Dana Lauren, the undersigned, declares:

18   I am a citizen of the United States. I am over the age of 18 years and not a party to this action. On of

19   March 6, 19XX, at the direction of Sarah Adams, Defendant in Pro Per, I served the within NOTICE OF

20   DEFENDANT'S MOTION AND MOTION REQUESTING CONTINUANCE OF PLAINTIFF'S SUMMARY

21   JUDGMENT MOTION; DECLARATION OF SARAH ADAMS on the following interested party by mailing,

22   with postage thereon fully prepaid, a true copy thereof to:

23   Loretta Charles, Esq.
       Attorney for Nolo Pedestrian
       [Street Address]
24   [City, State, Zip Code]

25   I declare under penalty of perjury that the foregoing is true and correct.

26   Executed at [City, State] on the 6th day of March 19XX.

27   *Dana Lauren*
                                     Dana Lauren
28

SAMPLE REPLY OPPOSING MOTION

1 | LORETTA CHARLES, Esq.
[Street Address]
2 | [City, State, Zip Code]
[Telephone]
3 |
Attorney for Nolo Pedestrian, Plaintiff
4 |
5 |
6 |
7 |
8 | THE _____ COURT OF _____ COUNTY
9 | STATE OF _____
10 |
11 |) CASE NO. 12345
Nolo Pedestrian,   )
12 |)
Plaintiff.   ) NOTICE OF OPPOSITION TO DEFENDANT'S
13 |) MOTION REQUESTING CONTINUANCE OF
v.   ) PLANTIFF'S SUMMARY JUDGMENT MOTION
14 |)
Sarah Adams,   )
15 |) Date: March 17, 19XX
Defendant.   ) Time: 10:00 a.m.
16 |) Place: [Court Address]
) [City, State, Zip Code]
17 | _____) Courtroom 10 _____
18 |
19 | TO DEFENDANT ADAMS, IN PRO PRO:
20 | Plaintiff objects to Defendant's Motion to Continue Plaintiff's Summary Judgment Motion originally
21 | scheduled for April 15, 19XX. Defendant has had ample time to investigate. The facts are clear and
22 | not in dispute, and the Court's and parties' time would be greatly economized by going forward with
23 | the Motion on the date and time scheduled. This Notice of Opposition to Defendant's Motion is based
24 | on the Notice itself and the attached Declaration of Plaintiff Pedestrian.
25 |
26 | Date: March 9, 19XX   *Loretta Charles*
_____
27 | Loretta Charles, Esq.
Attorney for Plaintiff Nolo Pedestrian
28 |

SAMPLE DECLARATION OF PLAINTIFF

DECLARATION OF NOLO PEDESTRIAN

I, Nolo Pedestrian, declare under penalty of perjury that:

1. I am the Plaintiff, Nolo Pedestrian, in the case of Pedestrian v. Adams (Case No. 12345) currently pending in the _____ Court of _____ County in the State of _____.

2. On or about February 28, 19XX, I caused Defendant Sarah Adams to be served with a Complaint and Summons.

3. On or about March 5, 19XX, I caused Defendant Sarah Adams to be served with a Notice of Motion and Motion for Summary Judgment.

4. The defendant has had approximately 10 days from the date she received the Complaint, and nearly two years since the accident occurred, to investigate this case.

5. The facts are clear and undisputed in this simple negligence action. They are set out in the Summary Judgment Motion and Declarations supporting that motion, which was filed with this Court on or about March 5, 19XX.

The above is true and correct to the best of my personal knowledge.

Date: March 8, 19XX   Signed: _Nolo Pedestrian_
                         Nolo Pedestrian, Plaintiff

SAMPLE DECLARATION OF DEFENDANT

DECLARATION OF SARAH ADAMS

I, Sarah Adams, declare under penalty of perjury:

1. I am the Defendant Sarah Adams, and I am acting as my own attorney in the case of Pedestrian v. Adams (Case No. 12345) currently pending in the _____ Court of _____ County in the State of _____.

2. On February 28, 19XX, I received the Plaintiff's Summons and Complaint.

3. On March 5, 19XX, I received notice of the Plaintiff's Summary Judgment Motion originally scheduled for April 15, 19XX.

4. As of March 5, 19XX, when I received the notice, I had not yet had time to take any discovery to obtain information I need to adequately defend myself in the pending case.

5. I intend to send at least one set of interrogatories to the Plaintiff. I also plan to depose Cynthia White, a witness at the scene of the accident.

6. On March 5, I phoned Plaintiff's lawyer and explained to her that I need additional time in order to conduct and complete this discovery so that I can adequately respond to the Plaintiff's Summary Judgment Motion. But she refused to agree to a continuance.

7. After the Plaintiff refused my request to continue the Summary Judgment Motion. I prepared this Motion for Continuance and had it set for the earliest available court date, March 17, 19XX.

I declare under penalty of perjury that the foregoing is true and correct.

Date: March 6, 19XX   Signed: _Sarah Adams_
                         Sarah Adams, Defendant in Pro Per

The date for the hearing on the continuance motion arrives. You arrive in court, a few minutes early, dressed in a businesslike manner, and check in with the clerk, giving your name and the case name and number. You then wait until your case is called. Finally you hear the clerk or judge say "Nolo Pedestrian v. Sarah Adams. Are the parties present?" If you and your adversary have both checked in, the clerk may tell the judge that you are here. You both stand to signify your presence. When the judge calls or motions for you to approach, you take your places at counsel table.

In this instance, you are the moving party (the one making the motion), so you will likely be called on first. Typically the judge will ask what you have to say. Here's what might follow:

1   You:

Good morning, Your Honor. I am Sarah Adams, the defendant in this matter. I am a building contractor here in [city], and I am representing myself. The reason I am requesting a continuance is simple. The plaintiff scheduled a summary judgment motion two weeks after my answer was filed. I have not had time to thoroughly investigate the case. I plan to serve interrogatories on the plaintiff. I will also probably take one or more depositions. I feel strongly that once I have investigated more thoroughly, I will be able to demonstrate that I was not careless.

2   Judge:

This is not trial, and I don't want to hear arguments or testimony.

3   You:

Your Honor, I was merely trying to say that I think I will be able to show very soon that there

are significant factual disputes, but I need more time. This summary judgment motion is premature. And, having to go forward with one now would unfairly prejudice my right to a fair hearing in this case.

As you see by the judge's comment, the judge may interrupt to ask questions or steer you toward the proper issues. Here the judge may continue with questions about the discovery you plan to take, the facts as you know them right now or whether you have tried to get the opposing party to stipulate to a continuance. The judge may also turn to your adversary.

4   Judge:

What are your objections to such a continuance?

5   Your adversary (Responding Party):

Your Honor, as stated in our papers, we feel the defendant has had ample time to conduct discovery. We have not been served with any interrogatories or received notice about any depositions. We don't believe the defendant really intends to conduct any discovery. The defendant just wants to try to keep this matter pending as long as possible to force a settlement. My client is injured....

6   Judge:

Do you have any response?

7   You:

Well, yes, Your Honor. That is simply not true. I have no hidden agenda of forcing a settlement. I just want to be treated fairly and to have sufficient time to prepare. My adversary is represented by counsel, but I am not a lawyer and I am not as familiar with all of the legal proceedings. I have been working on interrogatory questions and will get them out as soon as I possibly can. Just 60 more days, which can't possibly hurt them, would be most helpful for me to get the facts straight and know how to respond to the summary judgment motion.

8 **Judge:**

Motion granted. Defendant will have an additional 60 days to respond to plaintiff's summary judgment motion.

If the judge rules your way, don't allow your elation to get in the way of your need to clarify some key information. You need to record the exact date and time the case is continued to and find out whether, as the victorious party, you will be responsible for preparing the court order (the document, signed by the judge, that officially changes the date of the hearing).

c. Discovery Motions

If problems arise during discovery, you or your adversary may need to go to the judge with a motion asking the court to order the other side to comply with discovery requests. If you send interrogatories, for example, and your adversary refuses to answer one or more of them, you can file a motion asking that the judge compel an answer. If a person who is ordered to answer still refuses to do so, the judge can sanction (fine) or hold him in contempt of court. Contempt of court usually means imposing a fine or even a short jail sentence if he continues to refuse to comply with a court order.

The flip side of a motion to compel a response to discovery is called a motion for a protective order —an order allowing you not to answer certain questions. (In federal courts, these orders are al-

lowed under Federal Rules of Civil Procedure 26(c) and 30 (d).) A party can seek a protective order if the other side's discovery request causes undue annoyance, embarrassment, oppression or expense.

 Try to get your adversary to agree before you file a motion. Before filing a motion to compel a response to discovery or for a protective order (to avoid having to respond to discovery), try to get your adversary to give you some or all of the information voluntarily. For example, if your adversary doesn't respond adequately to your interrogatories, don't rush into court. Instead, try to work out the problem— perhaps by rephrasing the questions. You might even write a formal letter setting forth why you believe you have a right to the information (if they are objecting) or why you feel you should not have to reveal the information (if you are objecting to your adversary's discovery requests).

A persuasive letter indicates that you mean business and are not willing to drop the issue, and it may resolve the dispute. And if your negotiations ultimately fail and you eventually bring a motion, the letter (which you can attach as an exhibit) shows the judge that you attempted to resolve the matter without costing the court time and money, but that the other side simply refused to cooperate.

You may want to consult your legal coach before answering questions to see if they are improper. But it is generally improper to ask questions that:

• Force someone to reveal a confidential, privileged communication, such as a statement made to a lawyer during a lawyer-client consultation, to a doctor during a medical examination or to a spouse.

- Require an enormous amount of time, money or other resources to comply with. For example, if you are a small business owner and you are asked to produce every piece of paper you signed having to do with your employees for the last three years, you may ask that the request be confined to a shorter, more relevant time period or otherwise narrowed.

- Are asked to harass rather than to discover some admissible evidence—for example, a question about sexual history or a possible past criminal record.

- Are in no way relevant to the case. Although the standard for relevance in discovery is much looser than in the trial itself, neither you nor your adversary can seek information about matters that are totally unrelated to the case.

(Federal Rule of Civil Procedure 37 and your state's equivalents govern discovery disputes.)

If the court finds you have shown good cause for a protective order, the judge can help you out in a variety of ways, from blocking your adversary's entire discovery request to limiting the people who must attend a deposition, sealing (keeping confidential, out of the public record) the discovery or otherwise regulating the request.

Resolve discovery disputes with a phone call if you can. Since discovery problems are frequent, and going to court to resolve them is expensive and wasteful, many courts have established a phone conference procedure so that a judge can quickly resolve such disputes. Check with the court clerk or your judge's clerk to see if such a procedure is available.

Obviously, if you are initiating a motion to compel, it is because you need the information and believe your request is reasonable. Your papers must tell the judge why this is true. Usually this means saying how it will be helpful to lead you to relevant evidence in your case, and that it will not hurt or unfairly prejudice your adversary to reveal it.

If you are opposing your adversary's motion, you need to give the judge a good reason why you should not have to turn over the information requested. The grounds listed above are some of the reasons you may assert.

For example, say a request asks you to describe each and every conversation you've had with your business partner, Edwin, during the last ten years. Especially if you and Edwin do business on a daily basis, putting together the description requested would be a full-time job for many months, if not impossible. In this case, you will at least want to have the request narrowed down.

To illustrate this motion, turn again to the case about the auto accident at Elm and Main, Nolo Pedestrian v. Sarah Adams. This time, assume that you are the plaintiff. You were crossing the street when the defendant's truck hit you. You are trying to prove that the defendant, a building contractor, had gotten a phone call reporting a missed job site inspection just before the accident occurred. You will try to show at trial that the call caused her to be distracted and drive carelessly. As part of your discovery, you have requested these documents:

- records pertaining to all other traffic accidents in which Defendant has been involved, to see if she has had other similar accidents

- business books and records from her business, to determine how common missed inspections are, and how much money is at stake because of a missed inspection

- her phone bill for that month, to verify the exact time the inspection phone call was received.

You served the defendant with a request for production of documents asking for driving and business records. She refused to produce these documents because she is represented by a lawyer who is trying to bully you. You get the feeling they think that if they refuse your discovery requests, you won't know what to do and may just give up without fighting. But you have confidence in yourself (and you have this book), so you fight back. You bring a motion to compel the production of the requested documents.

Before you can go to court, of course, you have to get a hearing date, and draft, file and serve your motion to compel. (See Sections 4 and 5, above.) When your hearing date arrives, after you check in and wait for your case, your hearing may proceed as follows.

1 **Judge:**

Mr. Pedestrian, I have read your papers, and you have undoubtedly seen my tentative ruling. I am inclined to grant your request as to the business records and phone bill, and order Ms. Adams to produce them immediately. But I am going to deny the driving record request. Do you wish to add to your written arguments?

2 **You (Plaintiff Pedestrian):**

Yes, Your Honor. I would ask that the court also order the respondent to produce the driving records. It is essential to my case to see how many other people have suffered from her negligence in the past.

3 **Judge (turning to the respondent/defendant):**

Do you have any response?

4 **Ms. Miller, Defendant's attorney (Respondent):**

Yes. As Your Honor knows, such evidence, even if it existed, would be inadmissible evidence of prior acts—not to mention irrelevant to what happened on the day of the accident in question. We should not be required to produce that driving record now or ever, and strongly urge that your tentative ruling be made final as to that issue.

[For more on why such evidence would not be admissible in court, See Chapter 15, Basic Rules of Evidence.]

5 **Judge:**

So ordered. Ms. Adams does not have to produce her driving records. Now, as to the business records and phone bill. Respondent, do you have any good reason why the movant should not be allowed to inspect these?

6 **Ms. Miller:**

Again Your Honor, these records are irrelevant to the case. My client's business had nothing to do with the accident. Plaintiff ran in front of my client's truck, she tried to swerve, but....

7 **Judge:**

This is not the trial. I am not going to hear evidence today. Your client has her version, and the plaintiff has his. Unless you can tell me why he should not be allowed to fully investigate his theory, which includes reviewing your business records, I will order you to produce them.

8 **Ms. Miller:**

Your Honor, even if you were to believe my client's business records are relevant, which we contend they are not, the plaintiff's request is too broad. He has asked for all my client's business records from the past five years. If he is really just concerned about the cost of missed inspections, then at least we would ask that you limit the request to those inspections we missed during the month of the accident only. Otherwise, their request will put my client out of business. She'll have to spend all her time going through back records, and will lose many new projects because of it.

9 | **Judge (turning to you):**

Any response?

10 | **You:**

Nothing I haven't written in my papers, Your Honor. The defendant's business records are essential for me to prove how much the fact that she missed an inspection that day distracted her and caused her to be careless. We must look at one year's worth of figures, at the very least, to make an accurate….

11 | **Judge:**

O.K. I will allow the request but limit it to the six months before the accident and to only those documents directly related to missed site inspections. Movant, will you draft the order and give notice?

12 | **You:**

Yes, Your Honor, I will prepare the order.

To follow up on exactly how the order should read, you might say something like this:

13 | *Your Honor, could you please review your exact order and possibly have your clerk give me a sample? I have never prepared an order and I want to be sure it is correct.*

14 | **Judge:**

The clerk can assist you as to the format and, again, my order was that your request for the driving records is denied. The request for the phone bill was granted and the request for the business records was granted in part. Defendant is ordered to produce all business records pertaining to missed inspections in the past six months and the phone bill in questions. Next matter on calendar, Jack v. Jill.

d. Summary Judgment Motion

Trials often occur for one of two reasons: either people don't agree about what happened (the facts) in a given situation, or they don't agree on the correct legal consequences of certain facts they all admit happened. If you and your adversary agree on the important facts, but do not agree on what law should be applied, you don't need to go to trial. The judge can take your agreed-on version of the facts, determine how the law should apply to the situation and issue a ruling—all without a trial.

To ask a judge to rule on a case in this way, either side makes what's called a motion for summary judgment. This can save you and your adversary a tremendous amount of money, since it cuts down or eliminates costs such as subpoenaing and preparing witnesses, preparing arguments and taking time off work for trial.

Try to settle the case before bringing a summary judgment motion. Before going to court on a summary judgment motion, you will likely want to enter into some settlement negotiations with your adversary, to try to resolve the case without the costs to either of you of paying for the court hearing.

When you bring a summary judgment motion, you are asking the judge (there is no jury) to base her ruling on the undisputed facts, which you and your adversary have presented in documents. These may include documents called affidavits or declarations (sworn statements of parties or witnesses), contracts or other evidence. If you don't want the judge to decide the case based on your adversary's summary judgment motion, you need to show, in your reply and at the court hearing if one is scheduled, that some facts are disputed. And you must say why a trial is needed—for example, that it is crucial you have the opportunity to cross-examine your adversary's witnesses. Stress the legal policy favoring a party's right to go to trial.

⚠️ **Don't be scared by a summary judgment motion.** Summary judgment motions are sometimes used by lawyers to try to intimidate pro pers, claiming that no facts are in dispute when plenty really are. Don't fall for this. Assess the facts on both sides, and if you continue to believe you have a genuine dispute, fight the motion by filing an Objection to Summary Judgment Motion. Include in your Objection a written statement of the factual questions you believe exist, supported by affidavits or declarations.

If a summary judgment motion is denied, then you will proceed with the trial. But if the motion is granted, the judge will make a final decision for or against you by applying the law to the agreed-upon facts. In making that decision, the judge will not have any live witnesses, just the written evidence you and your adversary have submitted and the legal arguments you each have made in your papers. You will not have a chance put witnesses on the stand to testify or cross-examine the other side's witnesses, as you would in trial. But the judge's summary judgment will be binding just like the judgment or verdict rendered in a completed trial.

Summary judgments are final. You cannot have a trial after the summary judgment if you don't like the court's decision. For this reason, it's wise to prepare thoroughly if you are bringing or defending against a summary judgment motion. (For reference, see Federal Rule of Civil Procedure 56 and your state equivalents.)

Just as with the other motions, remember to properly schedule and notice your court hearing, and file and serve the necessary documents. (See Section 3, 4 and 5, above.)

Here's how a summary judgment hearing might proceed. Assume that the defendant contractor, Sarah Adams, from the car accident example above, is responding to the plaintiff's summary judgment motion. The plaintiff is represented by a lawyer but Adams is not. Arguments at the hearing may proceed as follows:

1 Judge:

I have Plaintiff's summary judgment motion and Defendant's opposition to that motion here. Unless you, Ms. Adams, can tell me why I should not, I intend to grant plaintiff's motion, and decide this case as a matter of law based on the facts presented to me. It seems to me that the facts are not disputed, and that it is in the interests of efficiency and all parties involved for me to decide the legal questions now, without proceeding to trial.

2 Adams:

Your Honor, it is true there is some evidence we both agree to. We both agree that my truck hit the plaintiff at Elm and Main. But there are several other very important facts about which we don't agree.

First, the plaintiff was injured only slightly by my truck. According to Dr. Even's affidavit, which I've included in my opposition papers, the plaintiff's serious injury, the one he really wants money for, was a pre-existing injury. The plaintiff's declaration states that injury was caused by my truck hitting him. We clearly have a fact dispute and Your Honor [or the jury, if you will have one] must listen to all the evidence and decide who is right.

Second, the plaintiff contends that I was distracted and not paying attention to the road at the time of the accident. But, as I submitted in my sworn declaration, this is not true. I was driving especially carefully at the time, because I had expensive kitchen cabinets in my truck. My statement shows that I was only going 15 m.p.h. Then, without warning, the plaintiff dashed out from between two parked cars. These are crucial questions of fact, and they need to be decided in trial.

3   **Plaintiff's attorney, Ms. Charles:**

By way of response, Your Honor, you have all the facts necessary to make a fair, full and final determination of law in this case. The plaintiff's declaration states he was crossing the street at Elm and Main. No one disagrees. It further states that as he entered the street, the defendant's truck hit him. No one disagrees. The facts are clear. The only thing left to do is determine whether or not the defendant was negligent—an issue of law, Your Honor. Both sides have put forth detailed evidence in the declarations attached to our motions, the ar-

guments have been set forth, and it would be a clear waste of time and money for the court and everyone involved to start dragging witnesses into court for each and every point in the case.

4   **Adams:**

Your Honor, I should not be deprived of the right to cross-examine the plaintiff and his witnesses. My affidavit indicates that he ran out in front of my truck, and that I was watching the road carefully. The plaintiff wants you to decide the matter on the papers so his story will not be exposed to cross-examination. But my right to a fair trial will be denied if you grant this motion, Your Honor. I renew my request that you deny the motion and that a trial date be selected.

5   **Judge:**

In light of Ms. Adams' arguments this morning, and given that it appears there are significant issues of fact and credibility, I have decided to deny the plaintiff's motion, and the matter of Pedestrian v. Adams will proceed to trial. The clerk will notify you when a trial date has been selected.

RESOURCES ON PRE-TRIAL MOTIONS

American Jurisprudence, Pleading and Practice Forms Annotated" (Lawyers Cooperative Publishing, updated regularly), a comprehensive multi-volume treatise with discussion and examples of many different kinds of pretrial motions.

Pre-trial, by Thomas Mauet (Little, Brown 1995) Chap. VII describes the motions process and has sample forms. ■

7

WHAT YOU NEED TO PROVE AT TRIAL:
THE PLAINTIFF'S PERSPECTIVE

Once your case gets to trial, you must prove that the claim (or claims, if you have more than one) you made in your complaint are accurate. To do this you'll have to prove specific facts. This chapter explains how to figure out exactly what facts you have to prove to win your claim, and how to organize a Legal Claim Outline which identifies the elements you have to prove, the facts with which you will prove them and the evidence you will offer at trial to prove these facts.

A. THE ELEMENTS OF A LEGAL CLAIM

It is essential that you understand that any legal claim you make almost certainly consists of separate elements. It's a little like a beam of light passed through a glass prism; what at first looks like a unitary beam of light in fact consists of separately colored bands. In the same manner, what looks like a unitary legal claim based on negligence, breach of contract, breach of warranty or almost any other type of claim in fact consists of separate legal elements. To win a claim, you must prove each and every one of its elements at trial.

To demonstrate how claims are made up of separate elements, let's examine three common legal claims.

1. Claim for Negligence

Negligence occurs when one person's carelessness causes harm to another. How does the law define how careful we must be? Lawyers often describe it this way: we must all exercise "ordinary and reasonable care." If we don't, we are negligent, and if our negligence causes harm we are legally responsible to pay for it. Here are some common examples of negligence:

- a traffic accident is caused by careless driving

- a store employee neglects to mop up a wet spot on the floor, causing a customer to fall

- a road is poorly designed, resulting in a car sailing over an embankment

- a bank fails to provide adequate safety for an Automated Teller Machine, resulting in robbery of a customer.

Here's where the concept of legal elements comes in. Start by understanding that you cannot win at trial just by showing that a defendant behaved carelessly. You have to prove each of the legally required elements of a claim for negligence, which (in most states) are:

1. **Duty:** The defendant owed you a legal duty of care.

2. **Breach of Duty (Carelessness):** The defendant acted unreasonably.

3. **Causation:** The defendant's carelessness directly caused you harm.

4. **Damages:** You suffered economic losses, property damage, personal injuries or psychological distress.

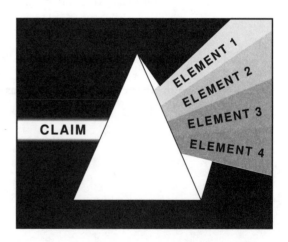

UNDERSTANDING CAUSATION

In some books describing negligence, as well as in some standard (form) complaints for negligence, you may see a reference to an element called "proximate cause" or "legal cause." These terms are just another way of saying that a defendant is liable for negligence only if the negligence directly causes the harm.

For example, assume that a defendant carelessly hits you with a car and breaks your right leg. Recovering from surgery to your right leg and walking with the aid of a cane, you slip on ice and break your left leg. You sue the defendant for both injuries. The defendant will probably be liable (legally responsible) for damages attributable to the injury to your right leg because she directly caused the injury. But probably, the defendant would not be liable for your broken left leg; a judge would not regard the defendant's negligence as a direct (proximate) cause of that injury.

Difficult issues can arise over whether a defendant's negligence is the direct cause of your injuries. If you are in doubt about whether you can prove causation, contact a legal coach with experience in personal injury cases as long before trial as possible.

2. Breach of Contract Claim

A breach of contract occurs when a person violates the terms of a legally valid contract. Here are some typical breach of contract situations:

- A seller refuses to honor an oral agreement to sell a consumer a car at the agreed-upon price.

- A manufacturer ships defective products to a retailer.

- A borrower fails to repay a loan.

- A company refuses to pay agreed-upon compensation to an independent contractor.

Like a negligence claim, a claim for breach of contract consists of individual elements, and to win at trial you must prove all of them. The elements you have to prove are:

1. **Formation:** You and the defendant had a legally binding contract.

2. **Performance:** You did everything you were required to do under the contract.

3. **Breach:** The defendant failed to perform as required by the contract.

4. **Damages:** The defendant's breach produced actual economic losses.

 Oral contracts are often valid. Many people think that a court will enforce contracts only if they are in writing. However, oral agreements are often enforceable, though you may have more difficulty proving their terms. A law known as the "Statute of Frauds" (so named by the English in 1677, which gives you some idea of the pace of change in legal terminology) will tell you whether yours is one of the relatively few types of contracts that must be in writing to be enforced. To find your state's Statute of Frauds, look in an index to your state's civil laws or ask a law librarian for help.

3. Legal Malpractice Claims

Legal malpractice occurs when an attorney fails to use at least ordinary legal skills when representing a client. Generally, the elements necessary to establish a legal malpractice claim are:

1. **Duty:** The defendant attorney owed you a duty to use at least ordinary legal skills.

2. **Carelessness:** The defendant attorney failed to use at least ordinary legal skills in carrying out a task.

3. **Causation:** The defendant attorney's careless-ness directly caused harm to you.

4. **Damages:** The harm you suffered resulted in actual economic loss to you.

There is a higher standard of care for professionals. If you compare the ele-ments of an ordinary negligence claim with the elements of a legal malpractice claim, you will see that they are largely identical. The difference is that a professional (for example, an attorney, doctor or architect) cannot avoid liability by showing that she simply acted reasonably. An attorney, for ex-ample, must act with the care and knowledge of a competent attorney. For further information on professional malpractice, consult a torts (civil wrongs) treatise in your law library. (Chapter 22, Legal Research, discusses how to use treatises.)

B. HOW TO FIND THE ELEMENTS OF YOUR CLAIM

You may have to do a bit of legal research to track down the elements of your claim. The complaint that you used to initiate your lawsuit may not identify your claim's elements, because many court systems do not insist that complaints do so. If your claim is based on your adversary's violation of a statute, the text of the statute may not identify the separate elements that you have to prove. In fact, the elements of a claim may be buried in appellate court opinions which you may have dif-ficulty finding.

Here are some places to look for the elements of your claim:

• Your state's book of standard jury instruc-tions. Jury instructions identify the elements

of claims, which you must prove whether your case will be tried with or without a jury.

• Books called legal outlines, written as quick refreshers for law students on subjects such as torts and contracts, typically list the elements of common claims. They are generally avail-able in law bookstores near law schools.

If you need more help, consult your self-help legal coach or a law librarian. (See Chapter 22, Legal Research, for additional suggestions on doing your own legal research.)

Once you identify the elements of your claim, list them in the Legal Elements sec-tion of your trial notebook. (See Chapter 17, Orga-nizing a Trial Notebook.)

C. PROVING EACH ELEMENT

As the plaintiff, you must prove each element of a claim or lose the case. To illustrate this critical point, let's focus briefly on a typical attorney malpractice claim. Assume that you wish to file a lawsuit against your former attorney, Jean Blue. About two years earlier, you went to see Blue after you were injured on your neighbor's property. Blue agreed to handle your case but neglected to pursue it. When she finally filed a lawsuit on your behalf against your neighbor, the legal time lim-it in which the suit could have been filed (the statute of limitations) had expired, and your suit was thrown out of court.

In assessing whether you can win a malpractice suit against Blue, start with two obvious points: Blue had a duty to represent you competently, and her failure to file suit before the statute of limita-tions expired is carelessness that constitutes a

LEGAL CLAIMS

Most small lawsuits involve breach of contract or negligence claims, which are discussed above. But there are hundreds of other legal claims. A few of the more common ones are defined below.

⚠️ **This list is for general background information only.** Each state has its own rules on the specific elements required to prove these legal claims, and you must know those elements before trying to bring or defend against a lawsuit. Chapter 19, Legal Research, explains how to find your state's list of the elements of a legal claim.

Assault. The plaintiff has a reasonable fear or concern that the defendant is about to commit an immediate battery. (Assault can also be a criminal offense.)

Example: Someone threatens you with a knife.

Battery. The defendant deliberately and offensively (that is, in a way the plaintiff would not permit) touches the plaintiff. (Battery can also be a criminal offense.)

Example: Someone hits you.

Breach of fiduciary duty. A fiduciary (someone who occupies a position of trust) fails to live up to that duty of trust, and as a result the person to whom the fiduciary owes the duty of trust suffers loss.

Example: A trustee (someone who is in charge of the property in a trust) spends trust money for her own use instead of using it for the trust's beneficiary.

Conversion. The defendant intentionally converts to his own use some property of the plaintiff.

Example: You lend your stereo to a friend, who later sells it without your permission and keeps the money.

Defamation (libel and slander). The defendant makes to third persons (or causes to be made to third persons) a statement about the plaintiff, and the statement harms the plaintiff's reputation.

Example: A newspaper prints statements that falsely claim a teacher had been convicted of a crime.

False imprisonment. The defendant intentionally and unlawfully restrains the plaintiff's freedom of movement.

Example: A salesperson refuses to let a shopper leave a store when there's no legitimate reason to think the shopper was trying to steal anything.

Fraud (intentional misrepresentation). The defendant knowingly makes a statement that misrepresents a fact, with the intention of inducing the plaintiff to rely on that statement, and the plaintiff justifiably relies on that statement and suffers loss.

Example: A salesperson tells a prospective buyer that a water purification system will make water safe, when the salesperson knows that it won't. The buyer, relying on the statement, buys the system and as a result loses the money spent on it.

Private nuisance. The defendant prevents or disrupts the plaintiff's use and enjoyment of his property.

Example: Your neighbor lets his dogs bark at all hours of the day and night, making it impossible for you to use your back yard.

Public nuisance. The defendant causes a health or safety hazard to the residents of a particular area.

Example: A chemical plant lets toxic fumes drift onto neighboring property, posing a health threat to the residents.

Trespass. The defendant goes onto someone else's property without permission.

Example: Your neighbor parks her car in your front yard.

breach of that duty. So the first two elements (listed in Section A, above) are satisfied.

But as you can see from the list of elements, you must also show that as a result of the breach you suffered actual economic loss. Logically, to do this you must be able to convince the judge or jury that you would have won the suit against your neighbor had Blue filed it on time. Put another way, if the judge or jury decides that you would have lost the case against your neighbor, Blue's breach of duty didn't actually harm you, and you would lose the malpractice case.

D. YOUR BURDEN OF PROOF

As the plaintiff, you carry the "burden of proof." This means that in order to win at trial, you must convince a judge or jury that *each element* of your legal claim is true or you lose.

But how convincing does your proof have to be? In most civil cases, your burden of proof is "a preponderance of the evidence." In other words, even if a judge or jury thinks that the probability that you have proved the truth of an element is only slightly better than 50%, you have successfully carried your burden of proof as to that element.

A higher burden of proof is, however, occasionally required. In a few types of civil cases, such as those involving claims for fraud and breach of an oral agreement to make a will, you may have to prove the truth of each element by clear and convincing evidence. While no precise mathematical difference separates "clear and convincing evidence" from "a preponderance of the evidence," your evidence generally has to be stronger to win a claim requiring this higher burden of proof.

When preparing for trial, be sure you know what burden of proof you have to meet. The best sources of this information are jury instructions for your type of claim, a legal treatise that discusses the elements of your type of claim or your self-help law coach. (See Chapter 22, Legal Research.)

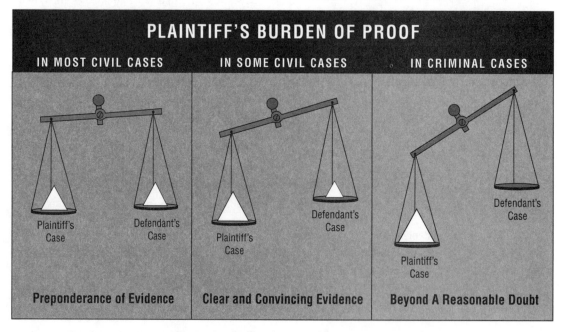

PLAINTIFF'S BURDEN OF PROOF

| IN MOST CIVIL CASES | IN SOME CIVIL CASES | IN CRIMINAL CASES |

Plaintiff's Case — Defendant's Case

Defendant's Case — Plaintiff's Case

Defendant's Case — Plaintiff's Case

Preponderance of Evidence   **Clear and Convincing Evidence**   **Beyond A Reasonable Doubt**

Explain the burden of proof to a jury. To illustrate the civil burden of proof during closing argument, many plaintiff's attorneys like to hold their arms out to either side in imitation of a scales of justice. They then tilt very slightly to one side to indicate that if the plaintiff's evidence has moved the judge or jury even slightly in the plaintiff's direction, the plaintiff has met the burden of proof.

You may not want to be so theatrical at trial. But you will want to let the jury know that you don't need to prove any element of your legal claim beyond a reasonable doubt, as a prosecutor must do in criminal cases; convincing the jury by 50.01% is good enough. (See Chapter 13, Closing Argument.)

E. HOW TO IDENTIFY FACTS PROVING THE ELEMENTS OF YOUR CLAIM

You might reasonably think that once you've identified the elements of your claim, you can tell exactly what facts you have to prove to win at trial.

Unfortunately, it's not so simple. As you can see from reading the lists of elements (Section A above), legal elements are abstract concepts. The abstract language of legal elements is no accident; elements have to be stated in broad terms if they are to apply to a wide variety of possible conduct.

For example, let's look more closely at the second element of a negligence claim: that the "defendant breached the duty of care." This language doesn't refer to any specific, provable conduct. For example, in an auto accident case it doesn't tell you whether you should prove that a defendant driver breached the duty of care by speeding, driving under the influence of alcohol or driving carelessly in some other manner.

Similarly, in a claim for breach of contract, one element you have to prove is that you and the defendant had a "legally binding contract." This language doesn't tell you what exactly makes a contract legally binding.

The abstract language of legal elements would not be a problem if you or a witness could go into court and simply testify that, "While driving on June 3, the defendant breached the duty of care," or that "The contract was legally binding." But testimony must refer to what witnesses actually saw and heard—what was said in conversations, what people did, how events unfolded. You and your witnesses must testify about happenings *in your specific case* that satisfy the legal elements. After hearing about the competing versions of what actually took place, it is up to a judge or jury to decide whether a duty of care was breached, whether a contract was legally binding or whether any other legal element has been satisfied.

There is no magic way to identify the facts that will satisfy each element in your case. For the most part, it works just fine to rely on your everyday experience and common sense. For example, assume that you are suing a door-to-door seller of a water purifying system for fraud. You claim that the salesperson induced (tricked) you to purchase the system by making false claims about it. After doing some research, you find that one of the elements of a fraud claim is that the defendant made a false statement "with knowledge of its falsity." You know that neighbors who previously bought the same system from the same seller had complained to the seller that the system did not improve their drinking water. Your common sense should tell you that this is a fact you can prove to satisfy the "knowledge of falsity" element. You can then line up your neighbors to testify and provide evidence of this fact.

Common sense won't always suffice, however. For example, in a breach of contract case, you may find that in order to prove the element, "legally binding contract," you must prove "consideration." But "consideration" is another abstract term, and you may not know its meaning in a legal context. In such situations, an easy method of making sure you know what you have to prove is to consult a law dictionary. (By the way, "consideration" refers to the profit or other benefit that each party to the contract was to receive.)

LAW DICTIONARIES

Two excellent law dictionaries, which should be readily available in any public or law library, are:

Law Dictionary, by Stephen Gifis (Barron's Educational Series).

Dictionary of American Legal Usage, by David Mellinkoff (West Publishing Co.).

A reference book that may help you identify facts that satisfy legal elements is *American Jurisprudence Proof of Facts* (Lawyers' Cooperative Publishing Co.). This is a multi-volume treatise that discusses how to prove hundreds of legal claims. While the facts you will have to prove in your case will undoubtedly be different from the facts discussed in the treatise, the treatise may assist your understanding of what you have to prove.

To illustrate how to identify facts that satisfy abstract elements, this section provides examples for three kinds of lawsuits: negligence, breach of contract and attorney malpractice, the three legal claims described in Section A above. Even if your claim is one of these, the facts you will have to prove in your case will of course be different. But the process you will go through to identify facts will be very similar.

Identifying facts is crucial. We cannot overstate the importance of making sure that you know before trial what facts you will try to prove to satisfy each element of your claim. Otherwise, you may lose at trial not because your witnesses were not credible or because your claim was an improper one, but because you neglected to prove facts to satisfy each element of your claim.

A good way to organize your thoughts as you go through this process is to make an outline of each element, the facts you will need to prove it, and the evidence you will use to prove the facts. (Samples are shown below.) It will let you know, at a glance, if you have identified facts to prove each element, and it will also be a good reference for you during your trial. Depending on the type of claim you have made, your outline may have as many as four, five or six elements. Devote a separate page to each grouping of element, fact and evidence to organize your case as clearly as possible. (If the same item of evidence is relevant to more than one fact, simply include it on more than one page. Section F, below, discusses evidence.)

A fact by any other name is still a fact. In the course of your legal research, you may run across the terms "material facts" or "ultimate facts." This is simply more legal jargon, which refers to facts that satisfy legal elements. All the facts set forth below are material facts or ultimate facts.

1.   Claim for Negligence

Your story: About 3 p.m. on March 31, you were standing on the corner of Elm and Main Streets, waiting to cross the street. When the light in your direction turned green, you stepped off the curb into the crosswalk. You had gotten about one-third of the way across the street when you suddenly saw a truck driven by the defendant, Sarah Adams, bearing down on you. You tried to get out of the way, but the truck struck you. You suffered a broken leg, which took four months to heal, and were left with a permanent limp. An eyewitness will testify that you were in the crosswalk when the truck made a left turn and struck you.

Adams is a building contractor. During her deposition, she admitted that her truck struck you and that just moments before the accident she had gotten a call on her car phone telling her about a missed inspection on a big job she was working on, and that she turned left to visit that job site. Adams denies that she drove carelessly.

You file a complaint against Adams for negligence and find the list of elements you must prove. (See Section A, above.) Now you're ready to write down a specific fact that satisfies each element. Do not worry about your exact words—this process is only for your benefit. Neither the judge nor the defendant will ever see your list.

Element 1:
The defendant owed me a legal duty of care.
Fact:
At the time of the accident, Adams was driving a truck in the immediate vicinity of where I was a pedestrian crossing the street.

You may not need to prove the duty of care. As a general rule, a defendant has a duty of care towards anyone who is likely to be harmed by the defendant's careless conduct. Because Adams admits striking you, you would probably not need evidence to prove this fact.

Element 2:
The defendant acted unreasonably.
Fact:
Adams made a left turn when she was thinking about a job problem and not paying attention to pedestrians in the road.
Element 3:
The defendant's carelessness directly harmed me.
Fact:
Being hit by Adams' truck broke my leg and left me with a limp.

Watch out for the "preexisting injury" defense. In many personal injury cases, a defendant will try to deny causing your injuries by offering evidence that an injury you say resulted from the defendant's conduct actually existed before that conduct took place.

Element 4:
I suffered economic losses, personal injuries and psychological distress.
Fact:
My broken leg had to be operated on. I lost two weeks of work, was on crutches for four

months, was in constant pain during that
period and had medical expenses of $50,000.
Also, I was left with an embarrassing
permanent limp, soreness and stiffness.

2. Claim for Breach of Contract

Your story: On February 14, you hired the defendant, Von Jarrett, a contractor, to build an addition of 600 square feet onto your house. The price was $75,000. The written contract called for a down payment of $5,000, and then for periodic payments, tied to defined completion stages, until the job was finished. The contract called for the addition to be completed by June 14.

Jarrett stopped working around the beginning of April and demanded an additional $20,000 over and above the $75,000 to finish the job. Because you had properly made all due interim payments and because by refusing to continue working Jarrett breached the contract, you refused to pay the additional money and hired another contractor to complete the work. After you hired the new contractor, you learned that Jarrett had used substandard materials, which had to be replaced. Your total cost for the addition (including replacing the substandard materials) ended up being $110,000. You also had to pay $3,000 extra to stay in a hotel two months longer than you anticipated.

Element 1:
We had a legally binding contract.
Fact:
On Feb. 14, Jarrett made a written promise to
build a 600-square-foot addition onto my
house, and I promised in writing to pay a total
of $75,000 by the time the job was complete.

Exchange of promises is sufficient. In a contract case, one party's promise is adequate "consideration" for another party's promise. Stripped of legal jargon, this means that if each party receives a benefit from the other's promise (which is almost always true in a business transaction), a contract is formed unless the judge regards the transaction as a gift from one party to the other.

Element 2:
I did everything I was required to do under the
contract.
Facts:
I paid Jarrett a down payment of $5,000 and
when the first and only stage of the work was
completed by Jarrett an additional $15,000.
In addition, I provided Jarrett with complete
access to my property to do the work. That's
all the contract required me to do.
Element 3:
Jarrett failed to fulfill his side of the contract.
Facts:
Jarrett stopped working on the addition in
early April, when the addition was only partially
complete. Jarrett also refused to complete
the addition unless I promised to increase the
total contract by $20,000 even though I had
made all payments due under the contract.
Also, Jarrett did not use the quality of
materials called for by the contract.
Element 4:
Jarrett's breach produced actual economic
losses.

Facts:

Because of Jarrett's refusal to complete the job for the contract price and his substandard work, I had to hire another contractor to complete the addition according to plan, for a total cost of $110,000. My damages include the $35,000 that I had to pay in excess of the $75,000 contract price for the addition, as well as $3,000 in additional living expenses because I couldn't live in the house for two extra months while the addition was completed.

3. Claim for Legal Malpractice

Your story: A number of years ago your stepmother hired an attorney to draft a will leaving her entire estate to you. After she signed the will, your stepmother gave birth to a son. Sometime later, she wanted to make sure that the son would get no part of her property. Your stepmother called the same attorney, who assured her that no change in the will was necessary—all of the stepmother's property would still go to you under the will. After your stepmother's death you discovered that under your state's law, which was in effect when your stepmother called the attorney, the son was automatically entitled to half ($60,000) of your stepmother's estate despite the terms of the will. Your state's law, known as a "pretermitted heir statute," states that a child born after a will is made takes half of the estate no matter what the will says, unless the child is specifically disinherited.

Element 1:

The lawyer owed me a duty of professional care.

Fact:

Defendant is a licensed attorney who was hired by my stepmother to prepare a will leaving all her property to me.

 State laws vary as to a lawyer's duty to a will beneficiary. Your claim against the lawyer can succeed only if the lawyer's duty of professional care extends to you, the beneficiary under the will. In some states, a lawyer has no duty towards will beneficiaries, but only to a client (here, your stepmother). If your case arises in one of these states, the claim would not succeed even though the lawyer was careless.

Element 2:

The lawyer failed to use at least ordinary legal skills.

Fact:

After the lawyer drafted a will for my stepmother which made no reference to a child, my stepmother told the lawyer that she had given birth to a son and asked if she had to change her will to make sure all her estate went to me. The lawyer mistakenly told her that she did not have to change her will to disinherit the son.

Element 3:

The lawyer's carelessness was the direct cause of harm to me.

Fact:

Because of the lawyer's advice, my stepmother failed to change her will to disinherit her son.

Element 4:

I suffered actual economic losses.

Fact:

I lost $60,000 that I would have received had the will been changed to disinherit the son.

! **Disinheritance laws in your state may be different.** If you are involved in a dispute involving children omitted from a will, check your state's "probate" or "wills" laws very carefully. In most states, a child omitted from a will is entitled to a share of a parent's estate only if the child was born after the will was signed. But in a few states, a child omitted from a will may receive a share of a parent's estate even if the child was already alive when the will was signed.

F. LOOKING AHEAD TO TRIAL: ORGANIZING YOUR EVIDENCE

Once you have an outline of the facts satisfying each element of your claim, you can add greatly to its usefulness by taking the next step: listing under each fact the most important evidence you will introduce to prove it.

💡 **If your opponent agrees, you don't have to prove everything.** A stipulation is an agreement between you and your adversary. You can stipulate to many things, including the truth of a fact. To arrange for a stipulation, before trial simply ask your adversary to agree to certain facts. For example, you might say, "Are you willing to stipulate that you are a licensed attorney and that my stepmother hired you to prepare her will?" If necessary, support your request for a stipulation with reasons, saying something like, "The stipulation will save us both time, because I won't have to present evidence. And you don't really dispute this fact anyway." Once you and your adversary reach an agreement, write out its terms, sign it and ask your adversary to sign it as well. That way you will prevent your adversary from suddenly denying the existence of a stipulation at trial and leaving you unprepared to offer evidence. (For a sample stipulation, see Chapter 14, Exhibits.)

For example, look back at Element 1 in the legal malpractice case. The fact that satisfies the element of duty is that the defendant was a licensed attorney who was hired by your stepmother to prepare a will leaving all her estate to you. Under this fact, list the evidence you will offer to prove it. For example, the will may be bound in a cover that has the defendant's name and address on it, and you may have a canceled check showing payment by the stepmother to the defendant for the will. You could also produce evidence by demanding that the defendant bring to court the file showing that your stepmother had been a client. Finally, the defendant may stipulate (agree) that he is an attorney and that your stepmother hired him to prepare her will. If the attorney stipulates to this fact, you needn't prove it at trial. In that event, your outline of facts and evidence for Element 1 will look like the one shown below.

Claim: Legal Malpractice

Element 1:

The lawyer owed me a duty of professional care.

Fact satisfying Element 1:

Defendant is a licensed attorney who was hired by my stepmother to prepare a will leaving all her estate to me.

Evidence to prove fact:

a. Defendant has agreed to stipulate that he is a licensed attorney who prepared my stepmother's will.

b. The will names me as sole beneficiary.

You can use this same procedure for each element that you have to prove. For a somewhat more complex example, look back at Element 2 in the same legal malpractice case. To satisfy this element you have to introduce evidence that after the lawyer drafted the will, your stepmother told the lawyer that she had given birth to a son and asked if she had to change her will to make sure all of her estate went to you, and that the lawyer told her that she did not have to change her will to disinherit the son.

As you can see, one thing you have to prove is that the will that the attorney drafted made no reference to a son. The will itself is evidence of this fact, and you should include a reminder in your Legal Element Outline to introduce the will into evidence. (See Chapter 14, Exhibits.)

Offering evidence of what your stepmother told the attorney, and what she was told in return, may be more difficult. Your stepmother, your most obvious source of evidence, is deceased.

Of course, the defendant may admit the conversation—but you would hardly be going to trial if the defendant admitted this fact. Perhaps you or another relative or friend heard your stepmother talking to the defendant, or at least heard her say that she was going to find out from the attorney if she needed to change her will. In addition, you may have to call another estate planning attorney as an "expert witness" to testify that the defendant's failure to advise your stepmother to change her will was legal malpractice. An expert's testimony may be necessary because the average judge or jury is unlikely to know what "competent legal skills" are in this context. (See Chapter 18, Expert Witnesses.)

Let's briefly look at Elements 3 and 4. To prove that the lawyer's advice was the direct cause of your stepmother's failure to change her will, you may offer evidence (from you, a relative or a friend) that your stepmother said that she was not going to change her will because her lawyer said that she didn't have to. And to prove that you lost $60,000, you may offer evidence of the will itself (which demonstrates that your stepmother wanted you to inherit her entire estate), testimony from the son that he received $60,000 of your stepmother's estate, or receipts and records from your stepmother's estate proving that $60,000 of the estate was paid to the son.

Claim: Legal Malpractice

Element 2:
The lawyer failed to use at least ordinary legal skills.

Facts satisfying Element 2:
After the lawyer drafted a will for my stepmother which made no reference to a child, my stepmother told the lawyer that she had given birth to a son and asked if she had to change her will to make sure all her estate went to me. The lawyer mistakenly told her that she did not need to change her will.

Evidence to prove fact:
a. My stepmother's good friend James went with her to the attorney's office and heard the lawyer tell my stepmother she didn't need to change her will to leave me everything.
b. Expert witness will testify that the lawyer's mistaken advice was legal malpractice.

After you complete the outline of the facts and evidence necessary to prove each element of your claim, put it in your trial notebook. The outline will be a big help in guiding your presentation of evidence at trial. (See Chapter 17, Organizing a Trial Notebook.)

G. LEARNING ABOUT YOUR ADVERSARY'S CASE

Even though you're a plaintiff, you should read Chapter 8, which discusses trial preparation from the defendant's perspective. Understanding how the defendant is likely to attack your case at trial gives you a chance to prepare a response.

RESOURCES ON SPECIFIC LEGAL CLAIMS

American Bar Association Guide to Consumer Law: Everything You Need to Know About Buying, Selling, Contracts and Guarantees (Times Books), covers consumer disputes, including basic contract law; residential leases; warranties; automobile sales, leases and repairs; consumer credit; buying and selling a home; and insurance.

American Bar Association Guide to Family Law: The Complete and Easy Guide to the Laws of Marriage, Parenthood, Separation, and Divorce (Times Books), covers claims involving cohabitation and premarital agreements, divorce, alimony, child support and custody and domestic violence.

Every Tenant's Legal Guide, by Janet Portman and Marcia Stewart (Nolo Press), covers eviction defense, housing discrimination, housing repairs and maintenance and comes with a diskette with blank forms.

How to Win Your Personal Injury Claim, by Joseph Matthews (Nolo Press), covers auto accident disputes.

Every Employee's Guide to the Law, by Lewin Joel III (Pantheon), covers employee rights, workers' and unemployment compensation.

The Employer's Legal Handbook, by Fred Steingold (Nolo Press), covers claims regarding hiring, paying and discharging workers.

Neighbor Law: Fences, Trees, Boundaries, & Noise, by Cora Jordan (Nolo Press), covers boundary and personal disputes.

Patent, Copyright, & Trademark: A Desk Reference for Intellectual Property Law, by Stephen Elias (Nolo Press), covers trade secrets, copyrights, patents, and trademarks.

The Rights of People Who Are HIV Positive, by William Rubenstein, Ruth Eisenberg and Lawrence O. Gostin (Southern Illinois University Press), covers the rights of people with HIV and AIDS (ACLU guide).

Money Troubles: Legal Strategies to Cope with Your Debts, by Robin Leonard (Nolo Press), covers sales fraud, credit cards, car loans, collection agencies and credit discrimination. ■

8

WHAT YOU NEED TO PROVE AT TRIAL:
THE DEFENDANT'S PERSPECTIVE

As a defendant, you prepare your case in much the same way as a plaintiff does: figuring out exactly what you want to prove at trial and deciding what evidence you'll present to prove it. Begin by following these three steps:

1. List each legal claim (for example, breach of contract, fraud or both) that the plaintiff made in the complaint.

2. List the elements of each claim—that is, what the plaintiff must prove to win on the claim. (See Chapter 7, What You Need to Prove at Trial: The Plaintiff's Perspective.)

3. Identify the facts with which the plaintiff is likely to try to satisfy each element.

   Once you have finished Step 3, you then do one or both of the following:

   a. Identify evidence you can offer to disprove the facts you listed in Step 3.

   b. Identify your own facts that contradict the facts that you listed in Step 3, and identify evidence you can offer to prove your own facts.

You'll end up with an outline that looks like the one shown below.

Depending on the type of claim the plaintiff has made, your outline may have as many as four, five or six elements.

Legal Claim:

Element 1:

Plaintiff's fact for Element 1:

Evidence disproving this fact:

a.

b.

c. (etc.)

My contradictory fact:

Evidence proving my fact:

a.

b.

c. (etc.)

Element 2:

Plaintiff's fact for Element 2:

Evidence disproving this fact:

a.

b.

c. (etc.)

My contradictory fact:

Evidence proving my fact:

a.

b.

c. (etc.)

Now let's go through these steps and see how following them can help you to win at trial.

A. IDENTIFYING THE ELEMENTS OF THE PLAINTIFF'S LEGAL CLAIM

Legal claims consist of discrete elements, and a plaintiff must prove every element to win on that claim. Chapter 7, What You Need to Prove at Trial: The Plaintiff's Perspective, explains how to identify the elements of common claims, such as negligence or breach of contract. It is imperative that you read this material, because you need to build your defense around those same elements. Using the instructions in that chapter, list the elements of each claim the plaintiff made in the complaint.

Don't rely on the plaintiff's complaint. The plaintiff's complaint will state whether you have been sued for negligence, breach of contract, fraud or some other legal claim. However, the complaint probably will not list the elements of the legal claim, because court rules in most states do not require it.

B. IDENTIFYING THE PLAINTIFF'S FACTS

As Chapter 7 also explains, all legal elements are abstractions. Knowing what legal elements the plaintiff must prove doesn't tell you the specific facts the plaintiff will try to prove at trial. For example, knowing that one element of a plaintiff's negligence claim is that you acted carelessly doesn't tell you specifically what the plaintiff will try to

prove you did that was careless. The plaintiff must try to prove specific facts at trial for each of a claim's elements, and you must try to anticipate what those facts are.

Fortunately, figuring out the facts a plaintiff will try to prove to satisfy each legal element usually does not require technical legal knowledge on your part. Using common sense, you can usually identify the plaintiff's facts by matching what you know about the plaintiff's case to the elements the plaintiff has to prove.

For example, from Chapter 7, you know that there are four elements of a negligence claim:

1. **Duty of care:** You owed the plaintiff a legal duty of care.

2. **Breach of duty:** You acted unreasonably.

3. **Causation:** Your carelessness caused the plaintiff harm.

4. **Damages:** The plaintiff suffered economic or other loss.

Now assume that you are a defendant in a negligence case based on an automobile accident. You know from your settlement discussions with the plaintiff's lawyer that the plaintiff's position is that you were exceeding the speed limit, and that the plaintiff suffered a broken arm, incurred medical bills of $10,000 and lost a week's wages at work. Common sense tells you that the fact that the plaintiff will try to prove to satisfy the element of "breach of duty of care" is that you were speeding, and that to prove "damages" the plaintiff will try to prove that his arm was broken, he had medical expenses of $10,000 and he lost a week's wages. You can begin organizing this information in outline form, like the one shown below.

Legal Claim: Negligence

Element 1:

Duty of Care

Fact Plaintiff will try to prove:

The plaintiff was in an area where he was likely

to be harmed if I drove carelessly.

Element 2:

Breach of Duty

Fact Plaintiff will try to prove:

I was speeding when the accident occurred.

Element 3:

Causation

Fact Plaintiff will try to prove:

My speeding caused the plaintiff to suffer a

broken arm.

Element 4:

Damages

Fact Plaintiff will try to prove:

As a result of his broken arm, plaintiff had

medical bills of $10,000 and lost a week's

wages.

Usually, you can find out all you need to know about the plaintiff's case through informal discussions and standard pre-trial contacts. Some of these opportunities include:

- **Your personal dealings with the plaintiff and the plaintiff's associates.** You almost certainly will have had a variety of contacts with the plaintiff, employees or other business associates of the plaintiff and with the plaintiff's lawyer leading up to the filing of the lawsuit. Most lawsuits are preceded by oral discussions and written demands that provide information about the plaintiff's legal position.

- **Negotiation and settlement discussions.** Even after the lawsuit is filed, you and the plaintiff (or the plaintiff's lawyer) will probably discuss possible settlement of your dispute, either informally or in a pre-trial conference conducted by a judge. (See Chapter 6, Pre-Trial Hearings and Motions.) During these discussions, you should be able to find out most of what you need to know about the plaintiff's case. In trying to convince you to agree to a certain settlement figure, the plaintiff will probably refer to the facts he is prepared to prove at trial and much of the evidence he will rely on to prove them.

Settlement offers and statements can't be admitted at trial. The law's policy is to encourage litigants to settle disputes before trial. To encourage litigants to speak openly during settlement discussions (whether conducted by a judge or between the parties informally), no court system allows dollar offers to settle or statements made during settlement discussions to be admitted as evidence. (See for example Federal Rule of Evidence 408.) So while you will learn information about the plaintiff's case during settlement discussions, you cannot offer evidence that the plaintiff offered to settle the case or of any statements made by the plaintiff during those discussions.

- **Direct inquiry.** Don't overlook that favorite information-seeking device of generations of parents and teachers: ask! Most people are socialized to respond to direct questions, and they are likely to follow that habit during pre-trial discussions. For example, you know that in a negligence case the plaintiff has to prove that you behaved carelessly. If you are unsure about what the plaintiff claims you did that was negligent, you may ask, "In what way do you claim that I was careless?"

- **Formal discovery.** As a non-lawyer, you may be reluctant to initiate formal discovery, such as depositions, interrogatories and requests for admissions. But if informal methods of finding out about what facts the plaintiff will try to prove have not worked, discovery may be worth a try. For instance, in a negligence case you can send an interrogatory to the plaintiff asking, "Please state each and every fact you rely on that demonstrates that I was careless." Similarly, to find out about the plaintiff's claimed damages, during a deposition you can ask the plaintiff, "Please tell me all the personal injuries you claim you suffered as a result of the accident." In both instances, the plaintiff must respond to your questions under oath.

Formal discovery, although it's more expensive than informal methods of learning about facts, does have a big advantage: the way you use it at trial. For example, an admission made in response to your request for admission is binding on the plaintiff if you present it at trial. That means, for example, that if the plaintiff admits in response to your request for admission that "the car was blue," the plaintiff can't argue the point at trial.

Similarly, if the plaintiff (or a witness for the plaintiff) gives a different answer while testifying at trial than she gave at her earlier deposition, you can impeach (attack the credibility of) the witness by bringing up the inconsistent deposition answer. For instance, assume that at trial the plain-

tiff testifies that "the light turned green when I was about 50 feet away from the intersection." During her pre-trial deposition, however, she testified that "the light turned green when I was about 10 feet from the intersection." You can impeach the plaintiff's testimony at trial by introducing the conflicting deposition testimony to show that her story has changed. If you can successfully impeach the plaintiff or the plaintiff's witnesses on one or two important points, the judge or jury may doubt the credibility of her entire case. (Impeachment techniques are discussed in Section D, below, and in Chapter 12, Cross-Examination.)

C. DEFEATING ANY ONE ELEMENT OF A CLAIM

To win at trial, the plaintiff must prove facts for each and every element of a claim. In most civil cases the plaintiff's burden is to convince a judge or jury that facts are true by a "preponderance of the evidence," which is the same thing as saying that the plaintiff must establish that the chances are at least slightly better than 50% that the plaintiff's facts are true.

But as the defendant, you have one big advantage over the plaintiff. To win on a claim, you need only prevent the plaintiff from proving the truth of at least one fact for that claim. Because the plaintiff and not you has the burden of proof, you do not have to prove that the plaintiff's evidence is untrue. You only have to raise enough doubt in the judge's or jury's mind about any one element to prevent the plaintiff from winning.

For example, assume that you are sued for negligence. At trial, the plaintiff succeeds in proving three of the four elements of negligence by a preponderance of the evidence. That is, the plaintiff persuades a judge or jury that (1) you acted carelessly; (2) your careless actions were the direct cause of the plaintiff's loss; and (3) your careless actions produced actual damages. However, the plaintiff is unable to convince the judge or jury by a preponderance of the evidence as to the remaining element, that you had a duty towards the plaintiff to act carefully. You win! The plaintiff met the burden of proof for three of the four elements of negligence, but not for the fourth.

This kind of scenario is very plausible. For example, in one recent case a number of investors sued an accounting firm for conducting an audit negligently. Relying on the audit, the investors had invested money in a company, and lost money when the company turned out to be in far worse financial condition than the audit suggested. The court decided that the accounting firm was negligent and that its negligence directly caused economic damages to the investors. However, the court also decided that the accounting firm had no duty towards the investors because the firm had no idea who the investors might be. The result: the accounting firm won the case.

D. DISPROVING THE PLAINTIFF'S FACTS BY IMPEACHING WITNESSES

Once you have a good idea of the facts the plaintiff will offer to satisfy each element of a claim, you should next identify any evidence you can offer to disprove them. Remember, if you can prevent the plaintiff from proving any one element, you win. One way to disprove the plaintiff's facts is

to come up with evidence that casts doubt on the credibility of your adversary's evidence. If the judge or jury simply doesn't believe the plaintiff's key testimony on some fact, chances are the judge or jury will conclude that the plaintiff has not met the burden of proving that fact. Damaging a witness's credibility is called "impeaching" the witness.

If you are going to impeach an adverse witness during trial, normally you have to identify evidence casting doubt on credibility before trial. To help you look for such evidence when you are talking informally to potential witnesses or perhaps even taking a deposition, here is an overview of the common ways to attack a witness's credibility. Most of them should be familiar to you from everyday life.

1. Bias

If you have evidence suggesting that a witness has a financial or emotional interest in the outcome of a case, you can offer it at trial to show that the witnesses is biased. For example, assume that the lawsuit against you is based on negligence, and the fact the plaintiff is trying to prove is that you were driving too fast. (This fact satisfies one of the elements of negligence, "breach of duty of care.") To support this claim, the plaintiff plans to call a witness to testify that you were driving 50 m.p.h. in a residential area. If you can get the witness to admit that she has made disparaging remarks against the social group to which you belong or that she is a close friend or relative of the plaintiff, or stands to gain financially if the plaintiff wins, the judge or jury may conclude that the witness has a bias that casts doubt on the believability of her testimony. Similarly, you can argue that a doctor called as an expert witness by the plaintiff to testify to the severity of the plaintiff's injuries is biased if you can show that the doctor has received a large payment to examine and testify for the plaintiff.

2. Impaired Ability to Observe

Evidence indicating that a witness did not have a good opportunity to see what the witness claims to have seen can be very helpful to your case. For example, in the same negligence case, if you can show that the witness saw you driving for only a split second, had terrible eyesight, saw you from a long distance or had consumed three martinis a half hour before seeing the accident, you can attack the witness's believability based on her impaired ability to observe.

3. Prior Inconsistent Statements

Evidence that before trial a witness made statements that conflict with the witness's trial testimony can make for a devastating attack on credibility. For instance, if at trial a witness testifies that you were driving 50 m.p.h., and you then introduce a sworn deposition or even an oral statement by the same witness saying you were going 40 m.p.h., or saying that he couldn't tell how fast you were going, you can cast serious doubt on his credibility.

If you can offer evidence to impeach the plaintiff's version of events, include it in your Legal Claim Outline. For example, if you have evidence that a witness for the plaintiff, Johnson, made two oral statements that are inconsistent with his expected testimony, you would update Element 2 in your Legal Claim Outline as follows:

Legal Claim: Negligence

Element 2:

Carelessness (Breach of Duty)

Fact Plaintiff will try to prove:

I was going about 50 m.p.h. when the accident occurred.

Evidence disproving this fact:

a. Johnson told a police officer after the accident that he didn't get a very good look at my car before the accident.

b. Johnson told me on the telephone that he didn't think that I was going more than 40 m.p.h.

E. PROVING YOUR VERSION OF EVENTS

As a defendant, you are not limited to trying to disprove what the plaintiff claims are facts. You may also testify and call witnesses in support of your own version of events. And remember that to prevail, you needn't convince the judge or juror that your version is correct; you simply need to offer enough evidence to lead the judge or juror to doubt that the plaintiff has carried his burden of proof as to any single element. This second approach is the legal equivalent of the sports saying, "The best defense is a good offense."

To prepare to offer your own version of events, again simply use common sense and the information you gather before trial. Look at the list of elements and identify for any or all elements a contradictory fact for which you can offer credible evidence. For example, assume that you have been sued for breach of contract. The plaintiff, Andrea, claims that after a series of negotiations you orally agreed on September 22 to buy her stamp collection for $15,000. After checking the elements necessary to prove a breach of contract claim, you see that one of the elements that Andrea must try to prove is that a binding contract was formed. In this case, the fact that she will try to prove for that element is that on September 22 she agreed to sell and you agreed to buy her stamp collection.

But you deny agreeing to buy the stamp collection. Your version of the September 22 conversation is that you agreed to buy Andrea's stamp collection for $15,000, but only if she also threw in her coin collection. Andrea said that she would think about your proposal and get back to you. That's the last you heard from her until you were sued. So at trial you will try to prove a contradictory fact for the element of "binding agreement." To show that there was no binding agreement, you will try to prove that you offered to buy Andrea's stamp

and coin collection for $15,000 and that Andrea never accepted your offer. In your Legal Claim Outline, you will list this information as shown below.

Legal Claim: Breach of Contract

Element 1:

There was a legally binding contract.

Fact Plaintiff will try to prove:

On September 22, I agreed to buy her stamp collection for $15,000.

Evidence disproving this fact:

My contradictory fact:

On September 22, I offered to buy her stamp and coin collections for $15,000, but she never agreed to my proposal.

Evidence for my contradictory fact:

a. My testimony that this is what happened on September 22.

b. Testimony of dealer Jim Pelowski, who says that on September 24 plaintiff offered to sell her stamp collection to him for $15,000. This shows that she didn't reach an agreement with me.

F. PUTTING THE DEFENSE STRATEGIES TOGETHER

Let's put the two defense approaches you've just read about together in a single example to help you understand how you can use both to defend yourself at trial. We'll use the negligence claim introduced in Chapter 5; put yourself in the position of the defendant, Sarah Adams.

Here's the scenario: The plaintiff contends that at about 3 p.m. on March 31 he was standing on the corner of Elm and Main Streets, waiting to cross the street. When the light in his direction turned green, he stepped off the curb into the crosswalk. He had gotten about one-third of the way across the street when he saw your truck bearing down on him. He tried to get out of the way, but failed and your truck struck him. As a result he had to undergo an operation for a broken leg that took four months to heal, had medical expenses of $20,000 and was left with a permanent limp. The plaintiff will offer evidence that you are a building contractor, and that just before the accident you received a call on your car phone from your office informing you of a missed inspection on one of your big remodeling jobs. He will argue that the call distracted you, and that you carelessly neglected to see him in the crosswalk. He will produce a witness who claims to have seen you looking out the driver's side window of your truck instead of straight ahead.

You agree with the plaintiff that at about 3 p.m. you were driving a pickup truck approaching the intersection of Main and Elm, and that you had just gotten the call from your office about the missed inspection. But you will offer evidence that missed inspections are fairly common, and that the phone call in no way distracted you. Also, you were driving with expensive kitchen cabinets in the back of your truck, so you were driving especially carefully. After waiting for traffic coming the other way to clear, you made a left turn onto Elm. As you did so your eyes were on the road. You plan to offer evidence that the plaintiff's witness, who will say that she saw you looking out your driver's side window, is the plaintiff's fiancee, and so is biased. In addition, you will impeach her with her state-

ment to a police officer at the scene of the accident that she was not paying close attention to your truck before it struck the plaintiff.

Your version of what happened next is that as you straightened out and started driving at a normal rate of speed on Elm, the plaintiff suddenly ran out from between two parked cars directly into the path of your truck. You braked, but could not avoid hitting the plaintiff. Nevertheless you were not going much more than 5-10 m.p.h. when you struck the plaintiff, and do not believe that you broke his leg. Indeed, an orthopedic doctor who examined the plaintiff's X-rays and other medical records at your request is prepared to testify for you that the plaintiff's leg problem was an old injury that was not caused by your hitting him.

Based on the information above, at trial you can attack the credibility of at least one of the plaintiff's facts. That is, you can impeach the plaintiff's witness based on her possible bias and the inconsistent statement she made to a police officer. You can also try to prove two contradictory facts of your own based on your evidence: that you were driving carefully and that you did not cause the plaintiff to break his leg. Based on this information, your Legal Claim Outline will look like the one below.

Once you have completed it, place your Legal Claim Outline in your Trial Notebook. Devote a separate page of your notebook to each element you plan to contest. This way you will not get confused in the heat of trial as to what evidence pertains to which fact. If the same evidence pertains to more than one element, simply include it on more than one page.

Legal Claim: Negligence

Element 1:

I had a legal duty of care towards Plaintiff.

Fact Plaintiff will try to prove:

At the time of the accident, I was driving a truck in the immediate vicinity of where the plaintiff was a pedestrian crossing the street.

Evidence disproving this fact:

None. [You might as well stipulate (agree) to the truth of this fact. You will not contest this fact. As a matter of law, you had a duty to the plaintiff to drive safely. Whether the plaintiff was in the crosswalk, running out from between two cars or standing on his head and barking for a fish, the plaintiff was in the vicinity of your truck.]

Element 2:

I breached the duty by acting carelessly.

Fact Plaintiff will try to prove:

I drove carelessly by making a left turn while not paying attention to pedestrians in the road.

Evidence disproving this fact:

The plaintiff's witness is not credible—as his fiancee, she is biased. Also, she has made inconsistent statements about her ability to observe. She now says that she saw me looking out the driver's side window, but right after the accident she told a police officer that she wasn't paying close attention to my truck before the accident.

My contradictory fact:

I was driving carefully with my eyes on the road.

Evidence proving my fact:

Nothing was distracting me; phone calls about missed inspections are routine. Also, I was driving especially carefully because I had expensive kitchen cabinets in the back of my truck that I was going to deliver to another job.

Element 3:

My careless driving directly caused harm to the plaintiff.

Fact Plaintiff will try to prove:

Being hit by my truck directly caused the plaintiff's leg to be broken.

Evidence disproving this fact:

I have no information to impeach the plaintiff.

My contradictory fact:

I did not break the plaintiff's leg; any leg problem that he had was due to an old injury not caused by my truck.

Evidence proving my fact:

Dr. Even will testify based on examining the plaintiff's medical records that the plaintiff's leg problem was caused by an old injury.

Element 4:

Plaintiff suffered economic losses and personal injuries.

Fact Plaintiff will try to prove:

Plaintiff's broken leg had to be operated on. He was on crutches for four months, was in pain during that period, and he has a permanent limp. His medical expenses were $20,000.

Evidence disproving this fact:

None. All these things may be true, but I wasn't the cause of them and I wasn't careless. ∎

9

SELECTING THE DECISION-MAKER

Trial by jury is one of the traditions of the Anglo-American legal system. But many cases, especially civil cases, are decided by a judge sitting without a jury. Some kinds of cases never have a jury; only a judge is allowed to decide them. Usually, however, the parties themselves decide whether a case is tried to a jury. In most court systems, judges decide cases unless one of the litigants makes a timely pre-trial request for a jury trial and posts jury fees.

This chapter discusses your role in choosing who will decide your case. You'll learn how to find out if you are entitled to a jury trial. And you'll see that even if you are, as a pro per litigant you are almost always better off choosing a judge trial. However, yours may be the unusual case that should be tried to a jury, or your adversary may put in a jury trial request. Therefore, this chapter also takes you through the entire jury selection process.

A.   ARE YOU ELIGIBLE FOR A JURY TRIAL?

Whatever your personal preference between judge and jury, a jury trial may not be available for your case. For example, you are not entitled to a jury trial if you are seeking not money but an order that your adversary do something (injunctive relief), such as tear down a building that encroaches on your property. Also, in most states you cannot have a jury trial in cases involving child support and child custody. In most other cases, such as those involving personal injury, breach of contract, professional malpractice, libel or slander, you are entitled to a jury trial.

> **AND YOU THOUGHT WE WON OUR INDEPENDENCE**
>
> The reason that jury trials are not available in all kinds of cases is that many of our legal procedures trace their roots to England, where in centuries past there were two kinds of courts, law courts and equity courts. Each handled different matters. Jury trials were available in courts of law but not in courts of equity. Today, even though these ancient distinctions between courts have largely disappeared, your right to a jury trial often depends on whether English courts would have dealt with your case in the law or equity courts. Ironically, England, which started the whole mess in the first place, has nearly eliminated jury trials in civil cases altogether.

Check out your options. If you are considering requesting a jury trial, first check with the court clerk to make sure that you are entitled to one. If the clerk cannot tell you, seek the advice of an experienced trial lawyer.

B.   ARE YOU BETTER OFF WITH A JUDGE TRIAL OR A JURY TRIAL?

As a pro per, you are generally better off trying your case to a judge than to a jury. By not going before a jury, you eliminate a number of procedural hassles. For example, you do not have to worry about:

- how long before trial you have to make a jury request

- depositing jury fees with the court

- preparing jury instructions. (Chapter 13, Closing Argument, discusses jury instructions.)

In addition, a judge trial is likely to be more informal and easier for you to conduct than a jury trial. For example, in the absence of a jury your judge may not insist on strict adherence to courtroom procedural rules and rules of evidence. And, of great importance, you can reasonably expect a judge to ignore inflammatory, irrelevant or other inadmissible evidence from your adversary that slips by you because of your unfamiliarity with evidence rules. Jurors, however, may well be influenced by the evidence even if the judge tells them to disregard it. (See Chapters 15, Basic Rules of Evidence, and 16, Making and Responding to Objections.)

Despite the additional complexities a jury trial brings, you may prefer one because you think that a jury will be more sympathetic to your case than a judge. But whether a judge or a jury trial is more likely to produce a favorable result is a complicated question, one that many experienced lawyers readily acknowledge rarely has an easy answer. Lawyer "folk wisdom" often points to choosing a jury if a case has emotional appeal, and choosing a judge if a case is complex and based on technical legal questions. However, even lawyers are wary of such broad stereotypes. Your knowledge of the attitudes and values of the people in your community is probably more relevant than general folk wisdom.

For example, assume that you have sued two police officers for using excessive force when mistakenly arresting you. If the trial will take place in a conservative law-and-order community where likely jurors regularly back "the boys (or girls) in blue," but several local judges have a reputation for being highly independent of local politics, you may want to choose a judge trial. By contrast, if many of the people in the community have themselves been victimized by overzealous police officers, and local judges have close ties with police officer associations, you may be better off with a jury trial.

As a rough guide to juror attitudes, talk to acquaintances who seem representative of the people who are likely to become jurors. How do they react to your case? Even allowing for feelings of personal friendship, do they seem sympathetic to your position? Or do they have a negative reaction, perhaps because your case seems to depend on legal technicalities? Such discussions can help you decide whether to opt for a jury trial.

C. YOUR OPPONENT'S RIGHT TO CHOOSE A JURY

Be aware that you may end up with a jury trial even if you prefer a judge trial. This is because your adversary has an independent right to request a jury trial. If your adversary requests a jury trial, you will have one whether or not you want one.

D. DISQUALIFYING A JUDGE

Judges wield much power, even in jury trials. A judge, not a jury, decides what evidence may be admitted and (subject to broad guidelines) how other important procedural rules will be applied. A judge even has the power to overturn a jury verdict and either enter a different verdict or order a new trial. (See Chapter 19, When Your Trial Ends: Judgments and Appeals.)

If you are unhappy with the background or the attitudes of the judge who has been assigned to preside over your case, consider disqualifying the judge, whether or not you plan to have a jury trial.

1. Automatic Disqualification

Under federal law and the laws of many states, you have the right to disqualify your assigned judge even when a jury will decide your case. For example, in California and in federal court, you have the right to file an affidavit (your sworn statement) to disqualify a judge on the ground that the judge is biased. (Cal. Code of Civil Procedure § 170.6; 28 United States Code § 144.) You needn't prove that the judge is prejudiced. Once you file the affidavit, another judge is automatically assigned to preside over the trial. However, this free disqualification is almost always a one-shot opportunity. You must accept the next judge who is assigned unless you can prove that the new judge is actually biased against you or has an obvious conflict of interest.

Watch your deadlines. Your right to disqualify a judge is likely to be subject to strict time deadlines. You may have as little as ten days after a judge has been assigned to preside over your trial to disqualify the judge. Check your local rules carefully for deadlines for disqualifying a judge.

2. Who Will Be Your Judge?

Some court systems use "all-purpose judges," meaning that the judge assigned to your case the moment it is filed will preside over all court pro-ceedings, from pre-trial motions to trial. If your case is assigned to an all-purpose judge, you may have plenty of time to check out and consider disqualifying her.

But in other court systems, you may not learn who will preside over your case until the day it is set for trial. If you find yourself in this kind of court system (and you can easily find out by asking the court clerk when you file a complaint or answer), you will have to check into the backgrounds of the various judges to whom your case may be assigned. Armed with that knowledge, you can disqualify a judge within the time allowed if you decide to do so.

Beware of pro tem judges. Because judges pro tem don't have independent status (they serve at the pleasure of the court) they can be less likely to make a controversial ruling than a regular judge for fear of not being rehired. Even more important, since many pro tems do not conduct trials as frequently as judges and do not attend judges' training and continuing education sessions, they may not be as familiar with the law that affects your case. Nolo Press (the publisher of this book) regularly receives complaints about inadequate pro tem judges.

3. Investigating a Judge

Your right to disqualify a judge is of little use unless you know enough about the judge's background and attitudes to make an informed judgment about how fair your judge is likely to be. Here are some of the ways to investigate a judge:

· **Check with lawyers, especially your self-help law coach if you have one, about the judge's reputation.** Ask what kinds of cases the judge handled before going on the bench, about whether the judge is generally plaintiff-oriented or defendant-oriented, how the judge might react to your type of case, and what the judge's attitude towards a pro per litigant is likely to be.

· **If you live in an area that has a newspaper directed towards lawyers, find out if it publishes biographies of judges.** Many legal newspapers publish judicial profiles that describe judges' law practice backgrounds, their attitudes towards litigation and the community organizations to which they belong. Often, judicial profiles also contain capsule "reviews" by attorneys who have appeared in a judge's court. (In California, these biographies are compiled in a regularly updated book called "Judicial Profiles," which is available to the public in law libraries.)

· **If you have time, sit in the courtroom while the judge who is assigned to your case presides over a different trial.** Observe the judge's attitude, listen to the rulings the judge makes and watch how the judge works with parties, lawyers and witnesses. Though you cannot make definitive judgments based on a short observation, you may gain some insight as to whether the judge will be fair-minded in your case.

E. MAKING A TIMELY JURY TRIAL REQUEST

Even if your case is eligible for trial by jury, in most court systems it will be tried by a judge alone unless you or your adversary makes a jury trial request. Jury requests must usually be made in writing well in advance of trial and even before a trial date is set. For example, if your case is in federal court, your "demand" for a jury trial must be served on your adversary not later than ten days after service of the last pleading, often the defendant's answer. (Federal Rule of Civil Procedure 38.) And in California, a party wanting a jury trial must make a written Notice of Motion for a jury trial within five days after an "at issue memorandum" has been filed. (Rule 377 of the California Pre-trial and Trial Rules.) (An "at issue memorandum" is simply a document indicating that all parties have been served and estimating the likely amount of time required for trial. Your court system may well require the filing of a similar document, though it may not go by the same name.) If you miss the request deadline, you waive (give up) the right to a jury trial.

If you want a jury trial, carefully check your court's rules for the deadline for making the request. Rules about deadlines for jury trial requests are often found in a book of civil procedure rules or local court rules. If you have difficulty finding the rule for your court system, ask a court clerk or a law librarian or check with your legal coach.

⚠ **Pay jury fees on time.** People selected as jurors receive a small amount of money for each day they serve, and in civil cases the parties themselves pay this money. In most court systems, whoever requests a jury usually has to pay a deposit of one day's jury fees (often $50-150) before trial. You can lose your right to a jury trial if you fail to post jury fees on time.

💡 **You can recover jury fees from your adversary if you win.** Jury fees are a "cost of trial," which ordinarily the loser of a trial must pay to the winner. If the jury decides the case in your favor, be sure to ask the judge to order your adversary to reimburse you for any jury fees you paid.

F. HOW THE JURY SELECTION PROCESS WORKS

The exact procedures for selecting a jury vary from one court system to another, but they are in general the same in all courts. On the day your case goes to trial, when your case is called, a group of prospective jurors is selected at random from a large pool of prospective jurors. If the jury will consist of the traditional 12 jurors, about 30 prospective jurors will be called. But because in many court systems civil juries consist of only six or eight jurors, the jury pool is likely to be correspondingly smaller.

The pool of prospective jurors is bought into the courtroom, and a smaller group of 12 (or fewer) jurors is chosen at random and seated in the jury box. After they are seated jurors are often referred to by number, with "Juror No. 1" typically occupying the seat in the upper left hand corner of the jury box. This group is the initial jury panel. The other prospective jurors remain in the courtroom, ready to replace any prospective jurors who are excused (dismissed) from serving on the jury.

Once the prospective jurors are seated in the jury box, the judge (or the judge and the parties) ask them questions. The goal of this questioning process, which goes by the old French term, "voir dire," is to select a fair and impartial jury. (By the way, don't worry about the exact pronunciation of voir dire. Like recipes for Caesar salad dressing, everyone's is different. For what it's worth, we pronounce it "VWAR-DEER.")

Initially, jurors are usually questioned by the judge about their general personal backgrounds, such as their marital status, occupations and previous jury service. Then either the judge or you and your adversary will question them further, searching for biases that might prevent them from being fair and impartial. These questions typically relate directly to the evidence that will be offered in the upcoming trial. For example, say you're suing an attorney for legal malpractice for giving erroneous advice about a will, as a result of which you didn't get an inheritance. It makes sense for you (or the judge) to question the prospective jurors both as to their experiences with or biases for or against attorneys. In addition, you may ask them if they have ever received property through a will or failed to receive property when they expected to.

Similarly, if you are involved in a negligence case and there is a claim that you or your adversary had been drinking before an accident, you (or the judge) will probably question the prospective jurors about their attitudes towards and experiences

SELECTING THE DECISION-MAKER **9 / 7**

with alcohol. For instance, they will probably be asked whether or not they drink, what they think about people who drink and whether they think it possible for a person to drink alcohol without becoming drunk.

WHO QUESTIONS THE PROSPECTIVE JURORS?

Traditionally, lawyers did almost all of the voir dire questioning. However, over the years many judges have come to believe that allowing lawyers to question prospective jurors takes up too much time and is used by lawyers to try to persuade jurors of the merits of their case rather than to simply select a group of impartial jurors. For example, a defense lawyer in a negligence case may ask, "Ms. Johnson, just because Ms. Nolo happened to get hurt when she came uninvited to my client's house, you don't think that she should automatically recover any damages, do you?" By asking dozens of questions such as these, some lawyers have managed to make jury selection take longer than the trial itself! As a result, today many judges conduct most or all voir dire questioning.

If your case will be tried to a jury, find out ahead of time how the judge who will preside over your trial handles voir dire. You will probably have to ask the judge's court clerk, because local court rules may leave the procedure up to the judge. Here are the likely alternatives:

- Your judge may ask only a few background questions and leave most of the questioning to you and your adversary.

- The judge may conduct most of the voir dire but allow you and your adversary a limited amount of time to ask questions afterwards.

- The judge may conduct all of the voir dire, but invite you and your adversary to submit written questions that the judge may choose to ask.

Many voir dire questions are asked of the jury panel as a whole. For example, you may ask, "Have any of you personally hired an attorney in connection with a will?" Other questions are put to individual prospective jurors. For instance, assume that a prospective juror named Mike Asimow raised his hand in response to your question about having hired an attorney in connection with a will. You may then ask a question such as, "Mr. Asimow [or "Juror No. 3"], please tell me about your experience with the attorney."

After the panel of jurors has been questioned, you and your adversary are allowed to excuse prospective jurors in a process called "challenging jurors." (See Section G. 2, below, for more on this process.) Prospective jurors are challenged and excused one at a time, with the plaintiff usually getting to exercise the first challenge. For example, a plaintiff may say, "I wish to excuse Juror No. 5." (In some courts, the parties send notes to the judge indicating which prospective jurors they want to excuse. The judge then does the actual excusing, so that the remaining jurors cannot blame a friend's dismissal from the panel on either party.)

If the judge allows the challenge, the challenged juror will be sent back to the jury room, and a new prospective juror will be selected at random from the original jury pool. The new Juror No. 5 is then questioned, and then the defendant has a turn to challenge a juror. The defendant can then challenge any one of the original prospective jurors or the new No. 5. Or the defendant can temporarily pass, meaning that the right to challenge goes back to the plaintiff.

Keep track of jurors. If you will have a jury trial, devote a section of your trial notebook to jury selection. You can include in that section a box chart which, for a 12-person jury, looks like this:

Juror 1	Juror 2	Juror 3	Juror 4	Juror 5	Juror 6

Juror 7	Juror 8	Juror 9	Juror 10	Juror 11	Juror 12

As each potential juror takes a seat, write the juror's name in the numbered space corresponding to her seat in the jury box. If that juror is removed, cross out the name and write in the new one. In the remaining space, take notes on the jurors' answers during voir dire questioning so that you can ask follow-up questions (if you are able to) and exercise challenges.

The question-and-challenge process continues until both sides accept the same group of jurors, or until both sides have challenged as many prospective jurors as they are allowed by local court rules. At that point the court clerk officially swears in the jury and trial—mercifully—begins.

G. YOUR RIGHT TO CHALLENGE JURORS

Since part of the jury selection process entails challenging and excusing prospective jurors, you need to understand the two kinds of juror challenges and the important distinctions between them.

1. Challenges for Cause

A challenge "for cause" asks a judge to excuse a person as a prospective juror on the ground that a legal impediment to that person's service as a juror exists. Normally, the impediment is something in a person's background or answers to questions indicating that the person is not fair and impartial. You and your adversary are allowed an unlimited number of challenges for cause, because you are both entitled to jurors who are fair.

Sometimes, the basis of a challenge for cause is so obvious that a judge herself will excuse a juror as soon as it becomes apparent. For example, assume that in response to a judge's initial background questioning, a prospective juror states that she is personally acquainted with you or your opponent. That juror will probably be excused by the judge at once on the ground that it is almost impossible for a person who knows one of the parties to judge a case fairly on the evidence presented in court. Likewise, a judge will immediately excuse a prospective juror who has a job that will inevitably bias the juror's attitudes towards you or your adversary. For example, assume that you are suing a lawyer for legal malpractice. The judge will probably excuse for cause any prospective jurors who are lawyers or who work for insurance companies that write legal malpractice insurance. Finally, the judge will probably excuse for cause any prospective jurors who appear to be ill or infirm or unable to serve for the length of time your trial is likely to last.

Usually, however, judges do not excuse jurors on their own. It is up to you to ask the judge to excuse a juror for cause on the ground that the juror's personal background or voir dire answers demonstrate bias against you. The judge will grant your request if she agrees that a prospective juror is biased.

To persuade a judge to grant your challenge for cause, you may have to convince the judge that a prospective juror is biased. Your adversary can also get into the act and may well try to persuade the judge that the juror has not demonstrated bias. After all, the same answers that prompt you to think that a prospective juror may be biased against you will probably lead your adversary to want that person to serve on the jury.

Let's illustrate briefly how an argument over a challenge for cause might proceed. Assume that you are the plaintiff in a negligence lawsuit. You know that there will be evidence that you drank a beer one hour before the accident, and that the defendant will argue that because you had been drinking the accident was your fault. During voir dire, Juror No. 3, Ms. Morrow, said that she does not drink, that she does not serve liquor of any type in her house and that in her opinion, people would be far better off if they never drank alcohol. At the same time, she said that she could be fair to you, and would not decide the case against you simply because you had taken a drink. However, you do not trust Juror No. 3 to decide the case fairly; based on what she said and how she said it, you think she is likely to be biased against you because you had a drink. Here is how you might try to persuade the judge to excuse Juror No. 3 for cause:

1 **Judge:**

Ms. Nolo, it is your turn to challenge.

2 **You:**

Your Honor, I challenge Juror No. 3 for cause.

3 **Judge:**

What is the basis of your challenge?

4 **You:**

Your Honor, she said that she is a lifelong teetotaler. She never drinks, she does not associate with people who drink, and she thinks that nobody should drink. She is entitled to that belief, but I don't think that someone who has those beliefs can give me a fair trial. There will be some evidence that I had a beer, and from what she said, it's clear that she'd be biased against me because of that.

5   **Judge:**

Mr. Scott [opposing counsel], *any response?*

6   **Mr. Scott:**

Yes, Your Honor. We oppose the request and ask that you deny the challenge for cause. Ms. Morrow described her beliefs, which many people share, but she said that she will be fair, that she will listen to the evidence for both sides, and that she will base her decision strictly on the evidence and not on her personal beliefs. I see no basis for a challenge for cause.

7   **Judge:**

Well, based on what I heard, she said she could be fair and has in no way prejudged the case. If we kicked everybody off the jury who doesn't drink or thinks drinking is a social problem, we'd have trouble putting juries together. I don't think there's enough here to sustain a challenge for cause. I'm going to deny the request.

Losing a request to dismiss a juror for cause is not uncommon. As long as a prospective juror claims to have an open mind and promises to base a decision strictly on the evidence, many judges feel that a challenge for cause should not be granted. But having lost the argument, you may still be able to remove Juror No. 3 by exercising a peremptory challenge, discussed in Section 2, below.

2. Peremptory Challenges

A peremptory challenge is one that you can exercise for any reason whatsoever. Unlike a challenge for cause, you don't have to explain or justify your challenge to the judge. For example, perhaps you want to excuse Juror No. 8 because she has an occupation that suggests to you that she will not give you a fair shot, because she smiled at your adversary but not at you or because she dresses in a way that you do not like. Or maybe your intuition tells you, "This is not a person who I want making a very important decision that affects my future."

The point is that you have a right to excuse any prospective juror with a peremptory challenge by simply telling the judge that you wish to "thank and excuse Juror No. 8."

If all this sounds too good to be true, be aware of a major restriction on peremptory challenges: you get only a few. This makes sense—if the number of peremptory challenges were unlimited, you or your adversary could excuse all the jurors in the pool. The exact number of allowed peremptory challenges varies from one court system to another. For example, in federal civil trials, each party gets only three peremptory challenges. (28 United States Code § 1870.) In California, each party gets six peremptory challenges, while Arizona allows four peremptories each. (Cal. Code of Civil Procedure § 231; Ariz. Rule of Civil Procedure 47(e).)

Before trial, read your state statutes and court rules very carefully and talk to the court clerk so that you know how many peremptory challenges you will be allowed. You do not want to use up your last peremptory challenge on a whim, only to have the next prospective juror be someone you really do not like. Remember, your adversary has the same number of peremptory challenges as you, and may excuse jurors who you really want to have on the jury.

 Make a challenge for cause rather than a peremptory challenge whenever possible. If you think that a prospective juror's background or responses to voir dire questioning demonstrate bias against you, always try to convince a judge to excuse a juror for cause before you exercise a peremptory challenge (assuming that you have a peremptory left). Since excusing a juror for cause does not cost you one of your precious, limited number of peremptory challenges, you are much better off convincing a judge to grant your challenge for cause than exercising a peremptory challenge.

But if you have no peremptory challenges left, do not challenge a juror for cause unless you are confident your challenge will be granted. It's almost always a bad idea to have a juror on the panel who you have unsuccessfully challenged for cause. If the juror you tried to dismiss for cause did not think ill of you before you argued that she was biased, think of how she is likely to feel towards you after you have pointed out in public why she is likely to be unfair! (For example, return to the example of your challenge to Ms. Morrow in Section 1, above.)

H. WHAT JURORS SHOULD YOU CHALLENGE?

Just reading about the jury voir dire process may convince you that you are generally better off with a judge than a jury trial. Deciding who is likely to be fair-minded and who may be biased can be a difficult task. However, the fact that you are not an attorney does not put you at a big disadvantage. For example, in a recent nationally reported case, a judge granted a defense attorney's request to excuse a juror in the middle of a trial, on the ground that the juror appeared to be biased against the attorney's client. After he was excused, the juror told reporters he was in fact very sympathetic towards the lawyer's client! Most trial attorneys admit that selecting jurors is based as much on intuition and common sense as on anything else, and that your most crucial tasks are to listen and observe carefully. If you pay close attention to what prospective jurors say and how they say it, there is no reason why you cannot do as good a job of selecting jurors as an attorney.

Perhaps no area of the law has been as dominated by lawyer folk wisdom as selection of jurors. Traditionally, lawyers have drawn upon broad stereotypes when deciding whether to exercise peremptory challenges. For example, people who belonged to certain groups were said to be more emotional, and therefore good plaintiffs' jurors. People with other backgrounds were thought to be careful with money and therefore good defense jurors. Today, in our multicultural and complex society, broad stereotypes tend to be of little value. You are probably better off learning as much as you can out about each prospective juror's personal background and evaluating how someone with that background is likely to react to your evidence.

For example, if you are 25 years old and were injured in a traffic accident when going from one party to another at 2 a.m., you may not want a 74-year-old person who never goes out at night to sit on your jury. If you claim that you were illegally fired from your position as an executive earning over $100,000 a year, you may not want a person who works for the minimum wage sitting on your jury. And if you are a tenant seeking the right to remain in your apartment by fighting what you claim is an unlawful eviction notice, you may not want a landlord on your jury. Admittedly, such decisions also rest on stereotypes: that a 74-year-old shut-in might resent a young "party animal," that a person who works for minimum wages might be unable to identify with a corporate executive and that one landlord will sympathize with another. But at least these assumptions rest on specific factors rather than broad categories.

I. WHAT TO ASK PROSPECTIVE JURORS

Whether or not you are allowed to question jurors yourself (remember, some judges only let you submit questions for the judge to ask), think carefully about what information will help you decide whether a person can be fair and impartial in your case.

Word your questions in a way that encourages prospective jurors to talk about their experiences and attitudes, rather than give yes or no answers. For example, compare these questions:

a. Will you be biased against me just because I had one beer to drink an hour before the accident?

b. How do you feel about someone who drinks one beer and then drives a car an hour later?

You don't have to play the voir dire game. As an alternative to the approach of questioning and challenging prospective jurors, at least one authority, California Superior Court Judge Rod Duncan, suggests that a pro per litigant may be better off simply standing up and saying something like, "These look like good and honest people to me. I'm not a lawyer and neither are they, and I trust them to apply the law fairly. No questions." Or, you might make the same type of statement and ask only, "Will any of you hold it against me because I'm not a lawyer and I may make a few mistakes trying to represent myself?"

An advantage of this approach is that you show from the outset that you are not going to try to pretend you are a lawyer. Particularly if your adversary is represented by counsel, the jurors may empathize with your "little guy vs. big guy" approach. On the other hand, to fully carry out this alternative approach you have to be willing to forgo all challenges. You should, however, be able to rely on your judge to excuse on his or her own any prospective juror who demonstrates an obvious bias against you.

A prospective juror can answer the first question yes or no. But even a juror who says no may harbor attitudes that would prevent the juror from being fair and impartial towards you. The second question, by contrast, encourages the juror to talk. The answer may give you a better gauge for deciding whether to exercise a challenge. Remember that a prospective juror's "body language" and how you and a juror relate to each other as people is probably at least as important as any specific response the juror gives.

 List the topics you plan to cover during voir dire. In the jury selection section of your trial notebook, write down the topics you plan to ask about during voir dire. You won't need to ask general background questions; the judge will ask those. Instead, focus on the facts of your case.

Unless your judge allows you only to submit written questions, do not write out specific questions. If you do, you may keep your face buried in your notes rather than maintaining eye contact with the juror you are questioning and talking as one person to another.

Here's an example of how to prepare for and conduct voir dire questioning. Say you're the plaintiff in a breach of contract case, suing a building contractor for doing shoddy work and then stopping work on a 600-square-foot room addition to your home. Before trial, you made a note in your trial notebook to ask prospective jurors about their previous contacts with building contractors, whether they had any problems and if so how the contractor handled them and whether they were especially sympathetic towards contractors.

1   **You:**

Ms. Sossin, I believe you said that you had some work done by a building contractor, is that right?

2   **Juror:**

Yes, we did.

3   **You:**

When was that?

4   Juror:

Let's see, I guess a little over four years ago.

5   You:

What did the work involve?

6   Juror:

It was just after my husband and I moved into our house. We loved it, but the den was very small. I have a large collection of Beatles albums, posters and other memorabilia, and I wanted a larger den to display them in. So we knocked out the back wall and extended the den by about 10 feet. Altogether, we added about 150 square feet to the room.

7   You:

Did you hire a contractor to do the work?

8   Juror:

Yes.

9   You:

How did you go about finding a contractor?

10   Juror:

Well, we called on a couple of ads, and asked friends for some recommendations. I think we got about three or four estimates, and went with one that was not the cheapest, but that seemed like he'd do a good job.

11   You:

How did the job turn out?

12   Juror:

Very well. No major problems, maybe a couple of the usual little ones.

13   You:

What do you mean by "little ones?"

14   Juror:

I remember one problem was the ceiling. I know I asked for a smooth ceiling, but he sprayed that cheaper stuff that looks like cottage cheese up there. When I said that wasn't what we wanted, he said there must have been a misunderstanding, that the price he had quoted was for the ceiling he had sprayed. It turned out that's what the contract said; we knew we had asked for a smooth ceiling and didn't notice that the contract said something different. We worked it out; we paid a little more and got our smooth ceiling.

15   You:

Were you happy with how the contractor worked that problem out?

16   Juror:

Yes, I'd say so. The remodel cost a little more than we thought it would, but he said that he charged us less for a smooth ceiling than he would have if it had been in the contract in the first place.

17   You:

Any other problems that you remember?

18   Juror:

No.

19 You:

As you know, in this case I'm suing a building contractor for doing substandard work and refusing to finish my job. Is there anything about the experience you had with your contractor that might make you lean towards one side or the other in this case?

20 Juror:

Not at all.

21 You:

As you sit there now, what is your attitude about building contractors, based on your own personal experience and any other things you've heard about?

22 Juror:

I'd say that the person we dealt with was very professional, but I've heard that not all contractors are that way. I guess they're like people in any other line of work—some good ones, some not so good.

23 You:

Do you think you can give both sides a fair trial in this case?

24 Juror:

Oh, yes.

25 You:

You wouldn't pay more attention to what the defendant says just because you were satisfied with the contractor you worked with?

26 Juror:

Not at all.

27 You:

Would you have any special sympathy for the defendant just because he's a building contractor?

28 Juror:

No.

29 You:

All right, thank you Ms. Sossin; I appreciate your candor. Now, Mr. McCalla, I believe that you also raised your hand….

Transcript Analysis: These questions do a good job of getting the prospective juror to discuss her experiences with a building contractor. Although you ask directly whether she has any special sympathy towards contractors (No. 27), you mostly ask her to talk about those experiences. No matter how she answers No. 27, you may decide to exercise a peremptory challenge if you think that her other answers and manner of speaking suggest that she is likely to feel favoritism towards your adversary.

Your entry for this juror in the jury selection box chart of your trial notebook might look like the following:

Juror 3
• Hilary Sossin
• Mid-20s
• Graphic artist
• Married - no kids
• Never served on jury
• Had work done by contractor
Satisfied, only "little problems"
Doesn't seem particularly pro or
anti building contractors

Ask voir dire questions in a conversational manner. Studies suggest that many prospective jurors resent attorneys' voir dire questioning, feeling that they have somehow been placed on trial. They may be even more resentful of questions coming from a pro per, especially if you try to come off sounding like Perry Mason. So when you ask voir dire questions always be polite, avoid lawyer imitations and err on the side of brevity. Try to ask questions "person-to-person," apologize if you ask a question that even you cannot understand, and even try to smile when appropriate.

Keep this respectful attitude even if you plan to exercise a peremptory challenge against a juror. Jurors often empathize with each other, and you don't want a juror on the panel who is angry at you for excusing a fellow juror in an unkind way.

J. ALTERNATE JURORS

If the judge thinks that your trial will last more than a few days, the judge may seat (impanel) a regular jury panel of 12 (or fewer) jurors as well as one or two alternates. The alternate jurors sit next to the regular jurors and listen to all of the testimony, but do not take part in the deliberations or the decision unless one of the regular jurors drops out. That way, the trial doesn't have to start all over again if a juror becomes ill or for some other reason must cease acting as a juror.

If no alternates have been selected, and a juror drops out before the conclusion of your trial, or more jurors drop out than there are alternates to replace them, one possibility is to start the trial all over again. That may involve relocating witnesses, missing additional days of work and incurring additional expenses. Another possibility is to ask your adversary to stipulate (agree) to proceeding with the remaining jurors. If you both agree, a judge will almost always allow you to proceed with fewer than the regular number of jurors. Obviously, you are more likely to prefer this latter possibility if you think the trial has gone well. If the trial has not gone well, the former possibility gives you a chance to present a stronger case to a new jury. And don't overlook the possibility that your threat to insist on a whole new trial may strengthen your bargaining position if you and your adversary decide to reopen settlement discussions.

RESOURCES ON JURY SELECTION

Jury Selection in Civil and Criminal Trials, by Ann Fagan Ginger (Lawpress Corp.). A two-volume treatise on analyzing and selecting jurors, with particular emphasis on civil rights and law reform types of cases.

Jury Selection, by Judge Walter Jordan (Shepard's/ McGraw-Hill). A single-volume treatise that describes common legal grounds for exercising challenges for cause and provides sample voir dire questions for both plaintiffs and defendants in a variety of kinds of civil cases. An appendix lists how many peremptory challenges are allowed in each state.

Fundamentals of Trial Techniques, by Thomas Mauet (Little, Brown & Co.). Chapter 2 contains a short overview of jury selection procedures and sample questions.

Jury Selection, by V. Hale Starr and Mark McCormick (Little, Brown & Co.). This book provides sample voir dire questions for a variety of cases and reviews some of the psychological literature on non-verbal communication. It also has a lengthy review of a simulated voir dire exercise, complete with pictures and backgrounds of prospective jurors. ∎

10

OPENING STATEMENT

Opening statement is your first opportunity to outline the evidence you plan to offer the judge or jury. Like a good map, your opening statement should guide the judge or jury through the testimony they are about to hear and documents they will see.

Giving an overview—the big picture of your case—is important. Oral testimony is normally presented during trial by a number of different witnesses in a question-and-answer format, and it can be difficult for the judge or jury to follow. They can easily get lost in the details and miss your overall story. Also, if a particular part of your witnesses' testimony is crucial to your case, you can flag it in your opening statement, so the judge or jury will pay special attention to it during the trial.

It's important to keep in mind, though, that your opening statement should provide only a preview of your case. It is not the time to argue how the evidence proves you should win—that comes much later, at closing argument. (See Chapter 13, Closing Argument.)

A. SHOULD YOU MAKE AN OPENING STATEMENT?

Opening statements are optional, and lawyers sometimes choose not to make them. (In legal jargon, this is called "waiving" opening statement.) Sometimes, in relatively uncomplicated cases, they figure the judge will pick up all the necessary information soon enough. Or, the judge may already have a good idea what the case is about from the pre-trial conference. (See Chapter 6, Pre-Trial Hearings and Motions.) In fact, it is for this rea-

son—to avoid repetition—that many lawyers waive their opening statements when trying a case to a judge alone.

You may not even be given the chance to make an opening statement. Your judge may consider an

---

HOW A TRIAL PROCEEDS

1. *Jury Selection**

2. Opening Statements

   • Plaintiff's Opening Statement

   • Defendant's Opening Statement**

3. Plaintiff's Case

   • Plaintiff's Direct Examination of Plaintiff's Witnesses

   • Defendant's Cross-Examination of Plaintiff's Witnesses

4. Defendant's Case

   • Defendant's Direct Examination of Defendant's Witnesses

   • Plaintiff's Cross-Examination of Defendant's Witnesses

5. Closing Arguments

   • Plaintiff's Closing Argument

   • Defendant's Closing Argument

6. *Jury Instructions*

7. *Jury Deliberation*

8. Verdict/Judgment

*   Italicized stages occur only in jury trials.

** Defendant may choose to postpone making an opening statement until just before she presents her case (see Section B, below).

opening statement a waste of time, especially if there is no jury, and may not let you make an opening statement. If this happens, you may have to just proceed with the case. But you can try to assure the judge, diplomatically, that your statement will be brief. Also, you can tell the judge that you believe an opening statement will clarify an important point.

If you are the plaintiff, you should rarely if ever voluntarily forgo your opening statement. You want to make the most of this opportunity to tell the judge or jury about your case. After all, the burden of proof is on you, so it is an excellent idea to get the first words in.

If you are the defendant, you likely will want to give an opening statement on the theory that the best defense is a good offense. But you may decide not to make an opening statement or to make a very brief one, if your defense rests primarily on undermining the plaintiff's evidence.

For example, if your strongest theory is that the plaintiff has insufficient evidence to prove one of the elements of her claims, you may not need to outline your own evidence. Your opening statement may be quite effective if it merely states that, as the defendant, you are not obligated to prove anything, that the burden of proof requires the plaintiff to prove every element of her claims by a preponderance of the evidence and that the evidence will clearly be insufficient for the plaintiff to meet that burden. (See Chapter 7, What You Need to Prove at Trial: The Plaintiff's Perspective, and Chapter 8, What You Need to Prove at Trial: The Defendant's Perspective.)

 Don't dwell on the burden of proof in opening statement. You may not argue during opening statement. (See Section D, below.) Since the judge may regard comments about the burden of proof and the insufficiency of the evidence as argument, keep them brief.

B. WHEN TO MAKE YOUR OPENING STATEMENT

As the term suggests, opening statements are made at the very start of a case. In a jury trial, opening statements are made after the jury has been selected and sworn in. In a judge trial, the time for opening statements occurs right after the court clerk or judge calls (announces) the case for trial.

The judge will probably ask you, if you're the plaintiff, whether you want to make an opening statement. But because some plaintiffs trying a case before a judge alone choose not to make an opening statement, the judge may assume you wish to skip your statement and start the trial by asking you to call your first witness. If this occurs, ask the judge for permission to make your opening statement.

Defendants have a choice about when to make an opening statement. The defendant who wants to make one can either:

- Make an opening statement immediately after the plaintiff's opening statement; or

- Wait until after the plaintiff has presented all her evidence and the defendant has cross-examined all the plaintiff's witnesses, before the defendant calls her own witnesses. This is called "reserving" opening statement.

If you are the defendant, there are at least a couple of advantages to making your opening statement right after the plaintiff's. Perhaps the most important is that you immediately show the judge or jury that there are two sides to the story. If you don't deliver your opening then, you take a risk that the plaintiff's story will become fixed in the jurors' or judge's mind before you get to present your evidence.

However, there also can be advantages to reserving your opening statement until after the plaintiff has testified, presented all her witnesses and you have had a chance to cross-examine those witnesses. You not only may avoid revealing evidence the plaintiff doesn't know about, but you also have a chance to tailor your statement to the plaintiff's evidence. Finally, your opening will be fresh in the minds of jurors or the judge when you present your evidence. This allows your statement to serve as a more effective road map through your evidence.

Pick whichever order seems best in your case, but don't be overly concerned about your decision. There is no one right way.

"Mornin' folks."

C. HOW TO PUT TOGETHER YOUR OPENING STATEMENT

In some cases, opening statements include explanations of legal principles, trial procedures and other information, but the main objective is to preview or outline the evidence. When representing yourself, your best bet is almost always to make a brief opening statement, probably no more than five minutes, and stick to the essentials discussed below. It is even more important to avoid giving a long opening statement in a judge trial than in a jury trial. Judges, unlike jurors, are used to following along with testimony and figuring out what is essential to a case.

1. Introduce Yourself and Your Main Witnesses

If the judge who presides over your trial is new to you, introduce yourself. As a short and sweet introduction, you may say:

Good morning, Your Honor. I am David Martinez. I am a homeowner and I am representing myself today in this case for breach of contract against the defendant, Ira Isaacs, the building contractor who repaired my roof.

During a jury trial you may omit this if you already introduced yourself during jury selection. If, however, the judge conducted all the jury questioning and you never got to mention your name, go ahead and introduce yourself to the jury now.

You can also introduce the various witnesses—perhaps previewing a bit of what they will testify about during trial. As the defendant in a negligence case, for instance, you can say:

Good afternoon, Your Honor. I am the defendant in this case, Sarah Adams. I am a building contractor here in town, and I am representing myself in this case brought by the plaintiff, Mr. Pedestrian. Both Mr. Pedestrian and myself will testify, as will three other main witnesses. Ms. Cynthia White will be testifying about how Mr. Pedestrian crossed in the middle of the street, darting out between several parked cars, and about how difficult it was to see him. And Kevin Reback, a college student and part-time salesperson will testify that I was driving at a safe, normal speed. And, Dr. Even will testify about Mr. Pedestrian's pre-existing injury to the leg he claims was hurt by the accident.

2. Explain the Purpose of Your Opening Statement

After you introduce yourself, briefly tell the judge or jury what's coming in your opening statement. For example, in a jury trial you might say:

Ladies and gentlemen, I will briefly tell you about the testimony you will hear and the documents I am going to introduce into evidence in this case. Since you will hear detailed accounts from witnesses later, for now I will just summarize the main points.

If your case is before a judge alone, you might say,

Your Honor, as you know I am representing myself today. I will do my best to present all of my evidence as clearly as I can and follow the court's rules to the best of my ability. So, very briefly, I will go over the witnesses you will hear from and documents I plan on introducing into evidence to give you an idea of what this case is about in a nutshell.

Don't be surprised if the judge cuts you off at this point, especially if this same judge handled your pre-trial conference. If you feel strongly that your opening statement will be helpful, ask the court to allow you just one minute to make a certain point. Otherwise, proceed, as the judge will likely direct you, to call your first witness.

3. Summarize Your Evidence

If you are the plaintiff, during trial you must prove facts supporting each element of your legal claims. (See Chapter 7, What You Need to Prove at Trial: The Plaintiff's Perspective.) Accordingly, in your opening statement, you will want to mention at least some of the evidence that you will offer to provide that proof.

Let's look at an example based on a legal malpractice case. You are suing your deceased stepmother's attorney for legal malpractice because the attorney failed to advise your stepmother, in response to her request, that she needed to change her will to disinherit a child born after the will was signed. Even though the will says you are to receive everything, because of the attorney's neglect you are now being forced to share your stepmother's estate with the child. You may say:

The evidence will show that my stepmother called the defendant and asked whether it was necessary to change her will after having a new child who she did not want to take any of her property. The defendant admits he is a licensed attorney in this state. You will hear from my stepmother's best friend that she heard my stepmother say she wanted all her property to go to me and not to her son. My stepmother did not want him to have her money because she knew he had problems, and she believed he would waste the mon-

ey. She also knew I had two children to support. You will also see proof in letters she wrote me through the years saying that she wanted me to have all her property. But because the defendant negligently advised her, the son she wanted to disinherit will get half her property, and some $60,000 that my family and I need desperately will now go to him—just what my stepmother wanted to prevent.

Although it's unlikely, a case can be dismissed if the plaintiff's opening statement is deficient. A defendant can ask the judge to dismiss the lawsuit (this is called declaring a nonsuit) if the plaintiff's opening statement shows that the plaintiff does not have evidence to prove each of the required elements of her legal claims. So, if you are the plaintiff, when summarizing the evidence, be sure to at least touch on some facts which help prove each element of your legal claims. (See Chapter 7, What You Need to Prove at Trial: The Plaintiff's Perspective.)

If you are the defendant, however, it's best not to ask the judge to dismiss the lawsuit for this reason. Judges usually allow plaintiffs some, and often a great deal of, leeway. And by saying what evidence the plaintiff has failed to prove so early in the case, you may end up helping the plaintiff fix the defects and present sufficient evidence on all the right points during the trial.

4. Tell the Judge or Jury What You Want

Ask explicitly, at the outset, for the ultimate result you want. This sometimes gets lost in the many details presented during trial. Make it easy for the judge or jury to know what you want from them. For example:

Your Honor, after hearing all the evidence, I hope you will rule that the defendant breached our contract to repair my roof, and order that he pay me the $20,000 I had to pay to get it repaired properly.

D. WHAT NOT TO SAY DURING OPENING STATEMENT

There are two important pitfalls to avoid when you make your opening statement: Do not discuss evidence that may not become part of the court record, and do not argue.

1. Don't Refer to Evidence That May Not Be Presented

If you are not sure what a witness will say, don't tell the judge or jury what you think the witness will testify to. There are two good reasons for this. First, if your speculation turns out to be wrong, your opponent (or even the judge) may point out your misrepresentation during closing arguments. This can make you look bad. Second, if you distort key testimony or misrepresent a crucial fact, and it becomes clear that your opening prejudiced your opponent's case, your adversary can ask the judge for a mistrial.

If the judge declares a mistrial, he or she will stop the trial and set a new one. A mistrial is granted when something jeopardizes a party's right to a fair trial. For example, assume you hope the defendant will testify that she had three martinis before she got in her truck and that she was not watching the road when she hit you, but you are not sure exactly what she will say. If you tell the jury that the defendant consumed the three drinks before the accident, and it turns out that no evidence is admitted to support your assertions, you may have seriously damaged the defendant's chances of getting a fair trial. And you'll raise the chances of the judge declaring a mistrial.

 Use "The evidence will show" in your statement. It can be helpful to introduce some of your comments with the phrase, "The evidence will show…." This forces you to stick to evidence you can and will prove during trial and not shift into argument. Even if you omit the phrase when you actually speak in court, writing it in a draft statement before trial may serve as a reminder to summarize only evidence you know will be presented.

Similarly, do not refer to documents or other exhibits that you are not certain will be admitted into evidence. For example, do not refer to a business record you hope to introduce unless you are certain you can lay a foundation showing it is trustworthy. (See Chapter 14, Exhibits.)

How do you know what evidence you can refer to so that you can make a legally bulletproof opening statement? There are a number of ways to be sure you are on safe ground. It's safe to mention evidence if:

- You can testify about that evidence from your own personal knowledge.

- It involves a fact that was referred to in a letter, business or government record, or other admissible exhibit that you will present in evidence. (See Chapter 14, Exhibits.)

- Your opponent or a witnesses corroborated the information in pre-trial discovery. For example, your adversary made the statement in interrogatories or requests for admission, or a witness or your opponent said so in deposition.

- One of your witnesses, whom you have interviewed many times, has stated this information very clearly each time you interviewed her. While there is always some risk that even one of your own witnesses may change a story on the stand, if you have interviewed the person thoroughly before trial, and you trust her, you can probably feel comfortable that the evidence will not suddenly change at trial.

2. Do Not Argue

You are not allowed to argue during your opening statement. In addition to the usual meaning of "argument"—raising your voice or demeaning your adversary—in this context, argument also means going beyond just stating what you will prove and how you will prove it. Demonstrating why the facts and law compel the judge or jury to arrive at a particular result is considered argument. You can think of it this way: your opening statement should be a preview, not an analysis.

Unfortunately, the line between merely presenting evidence and arguing about or analyzing that evidence is not always clear. To help you stay on proper footing, let's look at some of the verbal techniques that are generally considered argument, so that you can avoid them in your opening statement.

a. Don't Discuss Credibility

The credibility (believability) of each witness is important—often critical—to the resolution of a case. The judge or jury will likely accept evidence from someone they believe but discredit what they have difficulty believing. You will strive to bring out both positive and negative credibility issues in your direct and cross-examinations, as well as in your closing argument. But during opening statement, you are not allowed to say why the judge or jury should believe you or your witnesses or why they should discount the testimony of your opponent's witnesses.

Let's look again at an example using the attorney malpractice case about the will dispute (Section C.3, above). Your stepmother's best friend, Lori Van Lowe, a clinical psychologist by profession, will testify on your behalf. She is not to receive anything under the will and doesn't stand to gain anything from the case. The only reason she is testifying is that, as a close friend and confidante of your stepmother, she likely knew better than anyone else what your stepmother wanted.

This background may show that Ms. Van Lowe is a credible witness. And in your closing argument, you will be allowed to tell the judge or jury exactly how the information demonstrates her credibility. (See Chapter 13, Closing Argument.) During your opening statement, however, you must confine yourself to simply stating the evidence, or else you may slide over the line into impermissible argument. For example, it is acceptable to say:

Ladies and gentlemen, a woman named Lori Van Lowe will be one of the chief witnesses in this trial. She was a close friend and confidante of my stepmother, so she knew better than anyone else what my stepmother wanted. Ms. Van Lowe, a clinical psychologist by profession, will not receive anything under my stepmother's will—no matter who wins this case.

By contrast, it is *impermissible* argument to say:

Ms. Van Lowe is believable. She has nothing to gain from saying I was to take under the will. She knows about human nature because she's a psychologist. And, she is far more believable than the lawyer, whose professional reputation is at stake.

b.   Don't Draw Inferences from Evidence

Another no-no during opening statement (though an essential part of your closing argument), is drawing inferences from evidence. By drawing an inference, we mean linking the evidence to the facts you are trying to prove or disprove.

For example, let's look at an item of evidence in a breach of contract case. Assume you are the plaintiff who hired a builder to put a new roof on your home. After the roof was completed, a storm hit, and the neighbor's tree fell onto your home. The roof caved in immediately. An inspection showed the builder used ultra-thin plywood instead of the stronger product you contracted for.

In your opening, you can properly say:

As the contract which will be put into evidence in this case shows, on January 4, I hired the builder Corrie Kaufman to put a new roof on my house. After the roof was completed, a storm hit and the neighbor's tree fell on our home. The roof caved in immediately.

*We then hired Danica Bradley, a building inspector who will be testifying about the report she made, which showed that the builder used **G**" plywood instead of the **H**" plywood we contracted for.*

But you cannot ask the jury to make an inference about the facts. For instance you may *not* say:

After the roof was completed, a storm hit, and the neighbor's tree fell on our home. The roof caved in immediately. It's obvious that the builder used inferior quality wood because he was trying to earn extra profits at my expense.

In the first (proper) example, you have evidence from the inspector that the builder actually used **G**" plywood, a breach of the contract term that required using a thicker grade of wood. But in the second (improper) example, you are asking the jury to make an inference that the roofer used thin plywood to make extra profits. Without specific evidence to support this assertion, you must wait until closing argument to ask the judge or jury to draw this inference.

Let's take a look at another example. Assume you are the plaintiff in a car accident case. You sued the defendant, Sarah Adams, for negligence because her truck hit you at Elm and Main Streets. To help prove that the defendant was speeding, you will offer evidence that just before the accident she got a call on her car phone telling her about a problem on one of her jobs, and she changed course to drive to the job site.

It would be proper to say:

Ladies and Gentlemen, you will hear evidence that just before the accident, Ms. Adams got a call on her car phone telling her about a problem on one of her job sites, and she changed direction to go at once to that job site.

It would be improper to add to the above remarks:

Ms. Adams must have been very upset by the phone call, and in a hurry to get to the job site. That's why she was speeding.

In the proper example, you refer only to the evidence that will be testified to. In the second example, you improperly tell the jury what inference to draw from the evidence. The second example is, however, perfectly proper for your closing argument.

c.   Don't Personally Attack Your Adversary

It is clearly inappropriate to attack your opponent personally. Don't, for instance, add to your comments above by saying:

And besides, it's clear that this slimy builder [pointing and making a face at the defendant] was trying to make a quick buck. He screwed me because he knew I didn't have the time to stand there and watch every minute of work he did.

The judge may sharply reprimand you for such attacks, and if you are trying your case to a jury, you will not impress and may greatly offend them. In rare instances, a judge may feel you so violated the rules and prejudiced your opponent as to merit a mistrial. So stick to the evidence and be respectful, even if your adversary *is* slimy.

If your adversary personally attacks you, take the high road. Don't fall into the trap and argue back. The judge or jury may find your opponent's comments just as distasteful as you do, causing them to lean in your favor. If the comments get too offensive, either object (that the comments are not within the proper scope of opening statement) or ask to speak to the judge at the bench. Then tell the judge that you feel your opponent's comments are inappropriate and prejudicial. Request that the judge admonish (reprimand and warn) your opponent to stop making them.

E.   TIPS FOR REHEARSING AND PRESENTING YOUR OPENING STATEMENT

Most of these suggestions apply any time you speak in court, and they are especially helpful for a strong opening statement.

1.   Use an Outline, but Don't Read a Speech

After deciding what you want to say, write out your opening statement. Then, practice saying it, both alone in front of a mirror and with a trusted friend, to hear how it flows and to get comfortable with it. Also, you may ask your legal coach to briefly review it and make suggestions for improvement or warn of any impermissible material you have inadvertently included.

In court, however, do not read the full opening statement. Reading word-for-word makes you sound stilted and boring, and it keeps you from making important eye contact with the judge or jurors. Instead, outline your key points on a sheet of paper. Keep the outline in your trial notebook, which you will take to court with you. (See Chapter 17, Organizing a Trial Notebook.) Take a quick look at your outline before you go up to speak, and then refer to it as needed during your opening statement. You can look down briefly and verify that you are on track as you pause between sentences or thoughts. Remember, the outline is just a guide. You can still do a fine job if your actual statement varies from it.

A completed sample outline is included in Section F, below. The general format for your outline may look like the one shown below.

Opening Statement Outline

1. Introduce Yourself and Your Main Witnesses
Me: I'm not an attorney, but I'll try my best
Witness #1:
Witness #2:
2. Roadmap (what you plan to cover in your statement and what they can expect in trial)
Summary now; details about testimony and exhibits later, during trial.
First you will hear evidence then you will decide case. Judge will instruct you on law.
3. Summarize Evidence
  (element-by-element for your claims)
  a. Element 1:
  (evidence supporting element 1)
  b. Element 2:
  (evidence supporting element 2)
  c. Element 3:
  (evidence supporting element 3)
  d. Element 4:
  (evidence supporting element 4)
4. Bottom Line:
Rule in my favor; Order

Remember, this is your case. You know the facts. You don't have to memorize details, just say what happened. And if you go to court with a good outline, you can use it as a checklist of points. That way you can relax and be assured you won't forget important items.

2. Speak Slowly and Strongly

Speak a bit more slowly than you do in normal conversation. This allows you to think clearly as you talk and helps the judge or jury follow your points. Also, speaking slowly makes it less obvious when you pause to find something in your notes or to think about how to phrase a particular point. (Use this same technique later in the trial, when you are asking questions of witnesses or making arguments to the judge or jury.)

Practice speaking slowly. Many people speed up without even realizing it because they are nervous in court. You may find it rather difficult to slow down if you are used to speaking rapidly.

Also, you must speak up. The judge or court reporter will likely tell you if you can't be heard, but jurors may not feel comfortable doing this. You don't want jurors deciding against you because they didn't hear something you said.

3. Stand at the Lectern

Standing is proper whenever you speak in court. It is a sign of respect. Standing gives you an air of authority and control. It also helps you project your voice. In most courtrooms, there will be a lectern for you to use, but if one isn't available stand behind counsel table.

F. SAMPLE OPENING STATEMENT

Let's look at a completed opening statement in a case where you are a pedestrian suing a building contractor named Sarah Adams for negligence. Adams' truck hit you as you walked across Elm Street, at the corner of Elm and Main streets. In your jury trial, your opening statement may proceed as follows:

1 *Good morning. My name is Nolo Pedestrian. I am representing myself in this action against the defendant, Ms. Adams. I am not an attorney, and I don't know all the technical rules of trial, but I will do my best.*

2 *The evidence you will hear today will show that at about 3:00 on the afternoon of March 31, I was crossing the street at Elm and Main. I was in the crosswalk when the defendant's truck hit me.*

3 *You will hear me and others testify under oath about the details of the accident. So for now, let me just give you an overview, to help you follow along.*

4 *First, I will testify. I will tell you when I saw her truck coming at me. Then I'll explain how I tried to get out of the way. I'll tell you how she hit me and broke my leg. I'll explain how it took four full months for my leg to heal, and I'll show you the doctor bills that back it up.*

5 *Then you will hear from a witness, Cynthia White, a stranger to me at the time, who saw the whole accident. She will confirm just how the defendant hit me.*

6 *Then evidence will be presented showing that just moments before she struck me, the defendant got a call on her car phone telling her about a missed job inspection.*

7 *You will hear all this testimony. And I'll show you some photos and doctor bills.*

8 *Then, after the judge gives some important instructions on how you should weigh the evidence, it will be up to you to deliberate earnestly and make the right decision. I hope that decision will be to hold the defendant responsible for the pain and loss of income she caused, and to award me the $100,000 I need and deserve to recover from this injury. Thank you."*

Transcript Analysis: In No. 1, you set the tone as a respectful person representing yourself and trying your best. And in No. 2, you properly use "the evidence will show" technique to give a nice preview of the facts of the case, being sure to stay on the right side of the line between reviewing evidence and impermissibly arguing your case. Next, in No. 3 you signal that you are just giving the judge and jury a road map and not every detail.

In No. 4, you preview your own testimony and the exhibits you will introduce. You are properly careful not to present too much detail in your opening statement lest you bore the judge or jury and risk their not listening carefully during trial. You appropriately avoid saying why they should believe you over the defendant.

No. 5 illustrates the dangers of stating what you expect another witness will say. If Cynthia White doesn't testify as you promised, your opponent may point the contradiction out to the judge or jury, making you look foolish. And if the misrepresentation is severe, your adversary can ask for a mistrial.

What you have promised here is that Ms. White will "confirm just how the defendant hit" you. So long as you are reasonably certain she will confirm this (you have interviewed her many times and know that she saw things the same way you did), you are probably fairly safe with this statement, especially since you did not put specific words in her mouth.

In No. 6, you refer to evidence from the defendant. You normally should not discuss the defendant's testimony or evidence you think the defendant will present. There is too much risk of getting it wrong. But in this example you are on fairly safe ground mentioning the defendant's phone call, especially if you have other evidence of the call, such as her phone bill (if she called out), a note on an inspection form that she had the conversation, her own admission that she got the call, or a witness who saw her holding the phone to her ear. That way, if she denies being on the car phone before the accident, you can introduce your other evidence.

You properly do not ask the jury to draw the inference that the reason the defendant hit you was because the call distracted her and she wasn't paying attention to the road. That would be impermissible argument, well beyond the scope of previewing the facts. You will have a chance to tie the evidence to the facts you need to prove and convince the judge or jury they stack up in your favor during your closing argument. (See Chapter 13, Closing Argument.)

Last, in No. 8, you properly ask for a ruling in your favor. That alone is not considered argument. It can be helpful to let the jury or judge know from the outset what you want, and may bring you one step closer to winning.

G. SAMPLE OUTLINE FOR YOUR TRIAL NOTEBOOK

Though it may be helpful for you to write out your full opening statement in order to practice it, you will want to summarize it in an outline form to actually use as you speak. That way, you will not read word for word but you also won't forget important points. An outline for the sample opening statement above is as follows. Yours may look different, but so long as you hit the main points it should be helpful for you.

Introduction

I'm not an attorney, but I'll try my best.

The Evidence Will Show… (basic facts, e.g.,
Adams driving on public streets, Elm and
Main—hit me in crosswalk.)

(This covers element 1, Duty to drive with care)

Roadmap

- This opening statement is a "roadmap"
- I will summarize testimony and exhibits now,
  give details later, and tell you a little bit
  about the order in which things will proceed.

Summary of Evidence

I will testify, White will testify and Adams'
records show:

- She was distracted when driving, she was
  looking down and talking on the car phone
  rather than paying attention to the road.
  Adams' business records show this
  (This covers element 2, Breach of Duty,
  Adams driving carelessly)
- White will testify: she saw Adams' truck hit
  me.
  (This covers element 3, Causation, her
  carelessness caused my injury)

I will testify:

- I paid money in doctor bills, lost money
  from being out of work for four months;
  and have suffered tremendous pain.
  (This covers element 4, Damages)

Bottom Line

- After you hear all the evidence, the judge will
  instruct you and you will decide.
- Rule in my favor; Order that the defendant
  pay $100,000 for my pain, doctor bills and
  lost wages.

RESOURCES ON OPENING STATEMENTS

For more detail on preparing effective opening statements, you may look for a continuing education or lawyer practice guide in your state on "Opening Statement." You can also consult:

Trial Advocacy in a Nutshell, by Paul Bergman (3rd Ed., West Publishing Co.), an easy-to-read, helpful and inexpensive paperback about effective and persuasive trial techniques. Chapter 5 covers opening statements.

The Trial Process: Law, Tactics and Ethics, by J. Alexander Tanford (The Michie Co.), a textbook on trial practice which includes excerpts from many other leading books and dialogues of trial scenarios.

Fundamentals of Trial Techniques, by Thomas Mauet (Little, Brown & Co.).

Trying Cases to Win: Voir Dire and Opening Argument, by Herbert Stern (Wiley & Sons), includes sample opening statements.

A Winning Case: How to Use Persuasive Communication Techniques for Successful Trial Work, by Noelle Nelson (Prentice Hall), a clinical psychologist's guide to oral persuasion. ■

11

DIRECT EXAMINATION

irect examination is your primary chance to explain your version of events to the judge or jury and to undercut your adversary's version. It consists of your own testimony and the testimony of your witnesses in response to your questions.

Despite the dramatic images presented in movies and television, you are unlikely to either uncover significant helpful information when you cross-examine your adversary's witnesses or to change a judge's or jury's mind with a stirring closing argument. Direct examination is your best chance to tell your side of the story to the judge or jury, and well-organized and credible direct examinations are the key to success at trial. This chapter will help you plan and carry out persuasive direct examinations.

Know exactly what you need to prove or disprove. Direct examination testimony should be built around the legal claim or claims set out in the plaintiff's complaint. If you are the plaintiff, you must prove facts that satisfy each element of a claim. If you are the defendant, it is your job to disprove one or more of your adversary's facts. If you are uncertain of a claim's elements and the facts you are trying to prove or disprove, reread Chapters 7 and 8.

A. DIRECT EXAMINATION AS STORYTELLING

This chapter will help you with many of the technical aspects of direct examination, including the kinds of questions you are allowed to ask and how to comply with the requirement that a witness's testimony be based on personal knowledge.

But leaving aside the mechanics for a moment, it's important that you understand that presenting an effective direct examination is very similar to telling an absorbing story in an ordinary social situation. You'll want to focus a judge's or juror's attention on the events that are the most important to your claim or defense by spending time on the details of those events. You'll move more quickly through less important events. And you'll want to make sure each of your witnesses tells a clear, easy-to-follow story that dramatically builds to the main events by drawing out evidence in chronological order. Have your witnesses testify as much as possible in their own words, so a story sounds like it is coming from them and not from you. And, if you have photographs or any other records to back up your witnesses' stories, introduce them into evidence as testimony unfolds to convince your key listeners (judge or jury) that the stories are accurate. (Chapter 14, Exhibits, explains how.)

B. OVERVIEW OF DIRECT EXAMINATION PROCEDURES

Direct examination begins after opening statements. The plaintiff begins by conducting direct examination of her first witness, who may be the plaintiff herself. The defendant then has a chance to cross-examine that witness. The plaintiff then puts on her next witness, and again the defendant has the opportunity to cross-examine. Only after the plaintiff finishes presenting witnesses ("rests her case") does the defendant conduct direct examination of his witnesses. After each one of the defendant's witnesses testifies, the plaintiff similarly has an opportunity to cross-examine.

💡 **Direct examination controls the scope of cross-examination.** When it's your turn or that of your adversary's to cross-examine, questions must relate to the topics covered during direct examination. For example, if you call a witness only to testify to your whereabouts at 8 a.m., your adversary cannot cross-examine that witness about a series of events having nothing to do with where you were at 8 a.m.

After the direct and cross-examination of each witness, the judge normally excuses the witness from further testimony. This means that neither you nor your adversary can ask any more questions of the witness unless you get the judge's permission to question the witness further. This questioning is called "redirect examination." If you want to ask your witness more questions following your adversary's cross-examination, say something like, "Your Honor, before you excuse the witness I'd like to ask a few more questions on redirect examination." Redirect is limited to the scope of cross-examination, meaning that you may only ask questions pertaining to the subjects that your adversary went into on cross-examination. You cannot rehash all of a witness's direct examination testimony on redirect; the purpose of redirect is to offer evidence in response to testimony your adversary brought out during cross-examination.

After your redirect, a judge may also allow your adversary to conduct brief "recross," limited to the scope of your redirect. After that, the witness will definitely be excused, and your next witness will be called. Then the cycle of direct, cross and perhaps redirect and recross repeats itself until you have called all of your witnesses.

As you can see, at each successive stage of testimony, the scope of questions is limited to what was covered during the preceding stage. This means that each phase of testimony is narrower than the one that came before. This funnel effect can be a problem if you conclude a witness's direct examination without asking about an important subject, since the scope rule would seem to forbid you from going back and opening up a new subject after your adversary cross-examines. Happily, a possible solution exists as long as a witness has not been excused. You can ask the judge for permission to "reopen" the witness's direct examination when it is your turn to conduct redirect. Say something like, "Your Honor, I know that this is redirect, but I ask permission to reopen the direct examination to ask just a few questions." Your request to reopen tells the judge, "Oops, I forgot something. As long as the witness is still right here, it's only fair to give me a chance to ask about it now." Usually, the judge will (especially in non-jury trials) grant your request, so you aren't unfairly punished for forgetting to ask some questions.

C. PREPARING FOR DIRECT EXAMINATION

Just like a play in a theater, an effective direct examination is usually the result of careful planning. Here are the important steps you should take before trial to present your strongest possible case.

DIRECT EXAMINATION

1. Subpoena Your Witnesses

A subpoena (sometimes spelled "subpena") is a court order to a witness to come to court. A properly subpoenaed witness who fails to show up at the time and date specified is subject to arrest.

Once you are assigned a trial date, ask the court clerk to issue a subpoena for each of your witnesses. Subpoenas are free, and are usually issued in blank. You can easily fill in the name of the case, the witness's name, the time and date the witness must appear and other necessary information. In some court systems you can personally serve a subpoena on a witness, but in many others you must get the marshal, licensed process server or an adult friend to serve your subpoenas.

You should subpoena all of your witnesses, even friendly ones who are anxious to testify for you. This is not a sign of distrust. Unless you have subpoenaed a witness, your judge may deny your request for a continuance (postponement) of the trial if an emergency or illness prevents the witness from coming to court on the day of trial. The witness can also show the subpoena to his supervisor at work to be excused to attend the trial.

All court systems impose limits on who you can subpoena, when the subpoena must be served and how much you must pay witnesses for their attendance at trial. (See for example Federal Rule of Civil Procedure 45.) While these rules vary somewhat from one court to another, here is an overview of typical requirements.

- **Territorial limits.** Most courts' subpoenas are legally valid only if served on a witness who lives or works within certain territorial limits, often around 100-150 miles from the courthouse. A subpoena served on a person who is outside these limits is ineffective, and the person does not have to obey it.

- **Witness fees.** In most court systems, you must tender (offer) to the witness, in advance, the court attendance and mileage fees set by your local statute—typically about $30-$60 per day.

You can recover witness fees if you win. After trial, the judge has the power to award "costs of suit," including witness fees, to the winning party. So if you win the trial, ask the judge to order your adversary to pay your witness fees.

- **Time limits.** Your subpoena must be served on a witness long enough before trial to give the witness reasonable notice of when she is to come to court. For a witness whom you have already informed of the trial date and who has no conflicting demands, serving a subpoena the day before trial may be reasonable. For other witnesses, reasonableness may require service of a subpoena weeks in advance of trial.

Find out about "on call" procedures. Ask the court clerk if the court rules in your state have an "on call" procedure. With an on call procedure, a subpoenaed witness does not have to report to the courtroom until you need the witness's testimony. The witness agrees to come to court when you telephone and ask her, but need not waste hours sitting idly in the courthouse corridor.

- **Subpoena duces tecum.** If you want a witness to bring receipts, records, notices or other documents and articles to court, ask the clerk to issue a "subpoena duces tecum." A subpoena duces tecum has space for describing the documents you want a witness to bring to court. Fill it out, identifying exactly what documents the witness is to bring. Then have the subpoena duces tecum served on the witness. (For information on how to fill out a subpoena duces tecum, see Chapter 4, Investigating Your Case.)

2. Outline Your Direct Examination

You must know what you're going to ask before you're standing in the courtroom and the judge tells you to call your first witness. To organize your questioning, it's helpful to make an outline for each direct examination you plan to conduct. A sample is shown below.

In the direct examination section of your trial notebook, include an outline of your testimony and one for each witness whose direct examination you plan to conduct. (See Chapter 17, Organizing a Trial Notebook.)

Some attorneys like to include in their outlines both all the evidence they plan to elicit during a witness's direct examination, and also the questions they plan to ask. While writing out a few important questions and answers makes sense, don't write down too much detail. Direct examinations rarely proceed exactly according to plan, and a pre-determined list of dozens of questions may end up confusing you more than it helps.

An outline is usually adequate if it refers to the main points in a witness's story and includes a few questions you want to be sure to ask. If you plan to offer any exhibits such as business records or photographs into evidence during a witness's testimony, your outline should refer to those exhibits and the "foundational" evidence you have to introduce to make the exhibits admissible. (See Chapter 14, Exhibits.)

Direct Examination Outline

Witness: _____

Background Information: _____
_____
_____

Important Evidence: _____
_____

Important Questions: _____
_____
_____

Exhibits to Introduce into Evidence: ____
_____
_____

Make sure your outline is user-friendly.
You'll want to use your direct examination outline for each witness when you ask questions. So as you make it, think of the little details that can affect your questioning. For example, if you have sight problems, write extra big or copy your typed outline on a photocopy machine that enlarges. You may also find it useful to use a fluorescent marker to highlight the most important testimony.

3. Rehearse Each Witness's Testimony

Even though you may have talked to a witness often, always have a final meeting with the witness to rehearse your questions and the witness's answers. You want the witness to know what evidence you are after and the kinds of questions you will ask. You don't need to script every word of your direct examination, but the rehearsal will help your witnesses testify completely and confidently. You may wish to follow the lead of many attorneys and actually run through a practice direct examination. And if you know or strongly suspect the types of questions your adversary is likely to ask on cross-examination, it is a good idea to ask them yourself during rehearsal to give your witness practice in coping with them.

Before rehearsing testimony, consider returning with the witness to the scene of important events, assuming that its appearance has not changed radically. The visit may lead the witness to remember details that add credibility to the witness's testimony.

Some witnesses think that it is improper to rehearse testimony before trial. But it's both proper and routine, and your witness should know that. Also, remind your witness that the purpose of the rehearsal is not to influence the witness's testimony; all you want is the truth. That way, if your adversary asks on cross-examination whether you coached your witness to make up a story, your witness can answer honestly, "No. Ms. Nolo and I talked about what she was going to ask me, but she just told me to tell the truth."

If you are going to ask a witness to identify a document or a photograph or to draw a diagram as part of direct examination, make sure you rehearse this. You don't want a somewhat nervous witness suddenly becoming unable to identify an important exhibit in the middle of trial! (See Chapter 14, Exhibits, for information on how to admit exhibits into evidence.)

For example, say your case involves an auto accident in an intersection. During the rehearsal, you and the witness can draw the intersection, including fixed landmarks such as traffic signals and crosswalks. At trial, you may begin the witness's testimony about the diagram by asking the witness what has already been drawn and then asking the witness to make further markings—for example, paths of cars—as the direct testimony unfolds. (See Chapter 14, Exhibits, for an example of how to do this.)

"Eileen Willis, come on down!"

Practice your questioning. An unexpected answer or objection may throw you off stride and cause you to ask leading or other improper questions. The best way to prevent this is to practice your questioning, both during rehearsal with each witness, perhaps with a friend, and in your own mind.

Mentally formulate different questions for eliciting the same evidence in response to different answers a witness may give and then think about which of the possible questions will be proper and which improper. If necessary, write out specific questions that you have difficulty phrasing properly and include them in your outline to give you the comfort of a written backup. This pre-trial practice will prepare you for the unexpected developments that almost always occur during trial.

When you rehearse with your witnesses, you can also offer a few suggestions that may enhance the credibility of their testimony:

- Remind a witness to make occasional eye contact with the judge or jury while testifying. People often come across as more credible when they look listeners right in the eye. Tell the witness something like, "I'll ask you, 'Please tell the jury what happened after the chicken crossed the road.' Then you should look at the jury when you answer."

- Ask a witness to dress in conservative business attire. A witness need not wear a suit or expensive clothes, but should dress in a manner that indicates respect for the court.

Familiarize yourself with your judge's direct examination procedures. Before trial, visit the courtroom where your trial will take place. Ask the clerk whether your judge has any general rules about direct examination. For example, one judge may insist that you stand at a podium when asking questions; another may allow you to sit at counsel table. Most judges, however, will not let you stand next to the witness or wander about the courtroom when asking questions. Also, if you plan on showing an exhibit to a witness, find out whether your judge will allow you to personally hand the exhibit to the witness or whether you should give it to the bailiff to hand to the witness.

Violating such rules will not make or break your trial. But knowing how a judge expects you to question witnesses lets your judge know that you have prepared thoroughly and seriously, frees you to concentrate on your witness's testimony and allows your witnesses to relax and present convincing testimony.

D. PRESENTING YOUR OWN TESTIMONY ON DIRECT EXAMINATION

As you undoubtedly know from watching movies and TV, direct examination usually unfolds in a question-and-answer format: an attorney asks questions, and a witness answers them. But what happens when you are a pro per litigant serving both as attorney and witness?

A humorous answer was provided by the movie *Bananas.* In one of the well-loved courtroom scenes,

Woody Allen is representing himself in a trial. When it comes time for him to testify, he asks a question from counsel table, runs up to the witness stand to answer it, runs back to counsel table to ask another question, and so forth.

Luckily, the procedure in real courtrooms is not nearly so strenuous. Normally, when it is your turn to testify, tell the judge something like, "Your Honor, I'm now going to testify in my own behalf." Then walk to the witness box, remain standing and swear or affirm to tell the truth. Then sit in the witness chair and give your evidence as you would tell a story. Because most judges are used to the question-and-answer procedure, however, you may find that the judge occasionally stops your narrative and asks questions.

 You can look at notes to refresh your recollection. If you think you have forgotten to say something while testifying, ask the judge for permission to review your notes. Say something like, "Your Honor, I think I've forgotten something here. May I have permission to return to the counsel table for a moment to review my notes?" Just like any other witness, you may review any document to refresh your recollection. (See Section E, below.) Once your memory is refreshed, return to the witness box and carry on with your testimony.

For example, assume that you are a tenant, and the landlord is suing you for not paying your rent. You are testifying on your own behalf, trying to prove that you legally refused to pay because the landlord failed to maintain your apartment in a habitable condition. (Many states have a law requiring landlords to keep rental units livable.) Your testimony about the leaky ceiling problem in your apartment might look like this:

1 **You:**

The worst time I remember was on March 12. I came home from work and saw about five separate leaks in the living room. There were more in the bedroom and the kitchen. A couple of leaks I couldn't even put a bucket under, because the water was just dripping down the walls.

2 **Judge:**

Excuse me, Mr. Nolo. The water dripping down the walls, are you referring to leaks in the living room?

3 **You:**

Yes, Your Honor.

4 **Judge:**

So three of the leaks were away from the walls and you put buckets under those, but the other two you couldn't?

5 **You:**

That's right.

6 **Judge:**

All right, please continue.

7 **You:**

Well, I got right on the phone and called the landlord and told him about the leaks. He said that he'd get around to it when he had a chance, but that a lot of his tenants were complaining so I'd just have to wait my turn. Well, two weeks went by ....

Transcript Analysis: Here, you present your testimony largely in story form. As is common, however, the judge interrupts to ask questions. When she does, you stop your narrative to answer the questions, and then continue telling your story.

Testify first or last. Whether you are the plaintiff or the defendant, you may call your witnesses and testify personally in whatever order you choose. However, you are generally better off testifying either first or last.

The usual advantage of testifying first is that you give an overview of your whole case and have a chance to capture a judge's or jury's immediate attention. By testifying last you lose this chance to frame your case but gain the opportunity to address problems that arose during the testimony of your other witnesses and make a strong final impression. If you or your adversary request it, the judge is likely to order all witnesses to remain out of the courtroom until after they testify. But as a party to the case you can be present throughout the trial. Thus, you may be the only witness for your side who is personally aware of problems that arise during other witnesses' direct examinations.

E. HOW TO QUESTION WITNESSES

When it's your turn to question a witness, you may not know where to start. This section gives you a structure that will let you plan an effective direct examination.

Do not make speeches. A frequent complaint of judges is that pro per litigants often violate the orderly process of trial by making argumentative speeches during direct examination instead of presenting evidence through testimony and questions. The time to make a speech summing up your case is closing argument, not direct examination.

For example, assume that your landlord is trying to evict you from your apartment for making excessive noise in violation of a lease provision requiring tenants not to disturb the neighbors. You call Bernie Rhodes as a witness to testify that there was no excessive noise on the two nights that, according to a landlord's witness, your stereo was blaring. Examine this sample testimony:

1 **You:**

Now Mr. Rhodes, tell us about June 3 and 4.

2 **Your Witness:**

Mr. Nolo, those were the nights that you and I were working on the Keck proposal. It was due on June 5, and we were working pretty much all night in your apartment on both those nights.

3 **You:**

Did we play the stereo in the apartment on those nights?

4 **Your Witness:**

I remember that we played it a little one of the nights when we stopped to have a pizza, but I know it wasn't real loud.

5   **You:**

Do you remember if anyone knocked at the door asking us to turn down the volume?

6   **Your Witness:**

No, I'm sure that didn't happen.

7   **You:**

Your Honor, this proves what I've been saying all along. Mr. Rhodes was inside the apartment with me on both nights and as he told you there was no loud music. We were working on a very important proposal that had to be finished, and there's no way we'd mess ourselves up by blasting a stereo.

Transcript Analysis: Your outburst in No. 7 is an improper speech. When conducting direct examination of a witness, you are limited to asking questions. It is improper for you to argue about the credibility and significance of evidence, until closing argument.

---

1.   Begin With Background Questions

Direct examination begins when you call a witness (yourself or someone else) to the stand, and the witness takes an oath to tell the truth. At that point the judge will turn to you and say something like, "You may proceed."

After taking a deep breath, you may want to start right in on the witness's story. But before you do, ask a few questions about the witness's personal background. Witnesses who are not used to giving testimony or being in court often gain confidence (and therefore look more credible) when they can begin their testimony by talking about their own

background. At the same time, the personal background testimony tends to humanize witnesses in the eyes of a judge or a jury.

For example, here is how you might begin the direct examination of your witness, Ilene Johnson:

1   **You:**

Ms. Johnson, are you employed?

2   **Your Witness:**

Yes. I'm the assistant manager of the Brentwood branch of First Savings and Loan.

3   **You:**

How long have you been employed at the bank?

4   **Your Witness:**

Just about eight years now. I started out as a teller and then went through a management training program. I became an assistant manager a little over three years ago.

5   **You:**

Could you briefly tell us what you do as an assistant manager?

6   **Your Witness:**

I'm basically responsible for hiring and training the teller staff.

7   **You:**

All right. Now, turning your attention to the afternoon of March 12….

If a witness is not employed, consider other possible background topics. For example, if a witness is in college, ask the name of the college and the witness's course of study. Or if a witness is a parent, ask the names and ages of the witness's children. Obviously, you want to emphasize information that makes the witness appear to be someone the judge or jury can rely on. So if your witness is serving a life sentence for murder, or if the witness's only interests are TV talk shows and soap operas, you may want to skip personal background questioning altogether!

No matter what theme you choose to pursue, your background questioning should not generally be much longer than the sample above, since technically the information is not relevant to the meatier testimony the witness will give. But if you are brief, judges normally allow background questions so that the witness can relax and the judge or jury can learn a little bit about the person.

> **BACKGROUND QUESTIONING OF EXPERT WITNESSES**
>
> Background questioning of witnesses must usually be brief because the information you elicit has nothing to do with whether a witness's testimony is accurate. Not so with an expert witness, who by definition is a person whose special skills or knowledge enables her to interpret evidence that is beyond the understanding of the average judge or juror. Before an expert witness testifies, you have to demonstrate to the judge that the witness has special knowledge, skill or experience. This ordinarily requires extensive background questioning about the witness's qualifications. (See Chapter 18, Expert Witnesses.)

 Don't nominate your witness for the Nobel Prize. Most judges will not allow you to ask about honors and achievements a witness may have received or good deeds a witness may have performed. For example, a witness may be the Employee of the Month, the Citizen of the Year, a volunteer in the pediatrics ward of a hospital or the Little League President. Judges typically think of this kind of information as going beyond personal background and into a witness's moral character, and evidence of moral character is rarely admitted in civil trials.

2. Ask Legally Permissible Questions

After you conclude background questioning, you are ready to ask questions to elicit a witness's story. All questions fall into one of four broad categories:

- narrative questions
- open questions
- closed questions
- leading questions.

Rigidly classifying a question in one category or another is unimportant. What is essential is that you become familiar enough with these different types of questions to know which types you are usually allowed to ask at different stages of a trial and which you are not. During direct and redirect examination you are primarily limited to asking open and closed questions.

In addition, familiarity with the different types of questions allows you to adjust your questioning technique according to whether you want a witness to tell a story in his or her own words (use open questions), or to testify to specific information (use closed questions).

a. Narrative Questions

Narrative questions are broad and open-ended. They ask a witness to describe an entire series of events. Here are some examples:

- "Please tell us everything that happened on February 14."

- "Describe the events leading up to the signing of the contract."

Because narrative questions allow witnesses to describe events in their own words, they have the advantage of avoiding any suggestion that you are telling a witness what to say. However, many judges believe that if questions are too open-ended, witnesses (especially non-expert witnesses) will refer to legally improper evidence and waste time with irrelevant digressions. Your judge may not allow you to ask narrative questions or may severely restrict your use of them.

b. Open Questions

Like narrative questions, open questions invite witnesses to testify in their own words. But typically an open question limits a witness to a description of a specific event or condition. Open questions are one of your principal direct examination tools, because most witnesses make their best impressions on a judge or jury when they are allowed to be themselves and tell a story in their own words.

Here are some open questions:

- "Can you describe the condition of the car after the accident?"

- "What happened when you entered the room?"

- "After you received the letter, then what happened?"

- "Please tell us what was said in this conversation."

- "How did he react when he found out that they would not extend the lease?"

- "Please describe the condition of my daughter when we picked her up from my ex-spouse."

Because open questions allow witnesses to respond in their own words but do not invite a long story (narrative) of an entire series of events, most judges allow them. In their view, open questions pose less of a risk that a witness will refer to improper evidence or digress into irrelevancies.

c. Closed Questions

Closed questions ask witnesses for specific pieces of information. They do not invite a witness to expand on an answer. Here are some examples:

- "What color was the car?"

- "On what day of the week did the meeting take place?"

- "After you told her that the tool sets were back-ordered, how did she reply?"

- "What time was it when my ex-spouse brought my son home?"

- "How long was it until I was returned to regular job duties?"

- "What's the last thing the manager said before closing the door?"

Just like open questions, closed questions are one of your principal direct examination tools. Sometimes you do not want witnesses to describe events in their own words. Instead, you want to focus the judge's or jury's attention on a specific piece of information. You may want to do so either because a witness has neglected to mention the information in response to an open question, or because you want to emphasize particular testimony that a witness has already given.

d. Leading Questions

Leading questions suggest the answer you want a witness to give; they are basically statements in question form. Examples:

- "The car was red, wasn't it?"

- "Isn't it true that he never said anything about needing the manager's approval?"

Because they indicate your desired answers, leading questions violate the guiding principle of direct examination: that your job is to ask the questions, and your witnesses' job is to provide the information. If you ask leading questions of friendly witnesses, the witnesses are very likely to agree to whatever you say. So if your adversary objects, the judge will probably not allow you to ask leading questions during direct examination. (See Chapter 16, Making and Responding to Objections.)

Despite the general policy forbidding leading questions during direct examination, they are permitted in a variety of special circumstances. The

two most common arise when you elicit evidence of a witness's personal background or evidence that is "preliminary." Preliminary evidence is undisputed evidence that you want to run through quickly, in order to get to important testimony. Examples:

- During personal background questioning you may ask, "You've been employed by the school district for over 15 years now?"

- Your adversary agrees that a meeting took place on August 31 but disputes what was said during the meeting. Before you ask your witness what was said during the meeting you may ask, "A meeting took place on August 31, correct?"

- Your ex-spouse admits that he has done carpentry work for a Mr. Edwards and a few others, but claims that he does not earn enough to pay court-ordered child support. Before going into how much Edwards paid your ex-spouse, you may ask Edwards, "My ex-husband did carpentry work for you during June and July of this year, is that correct?"

- Your adversary admits that Dr. Phibes, an expert on the valuation of coin collections, examined your coin collection but disagrees with Phibes' opinion as to its value. You may properly ask Dr. Phibes, "Now, you examined my coin collection, right?"

- You call an auto mechanic to testify to the extent of the necessary repairs to your car following an accident. Your adversary admits that the mechanic repaired your car on June 22-23, but disagrees that all of the problems were caused by the accident. You may properly ask the mechanic, "You are the Exoff mechanic who repaired my car on June 22 and 23, right?"

You can also ask a leading question when you want to help a witness find her place in the story if your direct examination has been disrupted by a somewhat lengthy court recess. For example, say that your witness testified that the traffic light in your direction was green when you entered the intersection. Following that answer, the court recesses for lunch. When you resume after lunch, you may begin by asking the witness, "Before lunch, you testified that the traffic light in my direction was green when I entered the intersection, correct?" Though the question is leading, you are not putting words in the witness's mouth. You are simply repeating evidence the witness has already given to get the witness (and the judge and jury) back on track following a break in the testimony.

You may also ask leading questions during your direct examination of a "hostile" witness. (See Section F, below.)

3. Establish a Witness's Personal Knowledge

When you're planning the testimony you want to elicit on direct examination, it's crucial to understand that you must show that a witness is testifying from personal knowledge. (This rule doesn't apply to expert witnesses; see Chapter 18, Expert Witnesses.) This means that you must show that a witness personally observed, heard, smelled, touched or tasted whatever the witness is testifying about. Second-hand information may be good enough for TV talk shows and supermarket tabloids, but it won't work in court—a judge or jury can't take it into account in arriving at a verdict.

Make sure you understand other evidence rules. In addition to the requirement that a witness have personal knowledge, a variety of other evidence rules affect the admissibility of evidence, such as the "relevance rule." The most important of these rules are discussed in Chapter 15, Basic Rules of Evidence. Please be sure to read and understand that material before planning your testimony.

Usually, you do not have to make any special effort to show that a witness has personal knowledge; the testimony itself demonstrates it. For example, assume that you have brought suit against the owner of a dog that bit you on October 3. You call Jordan Miller as a witness to testify to the dog's attack on you. After the personal background questions, your direct examination of Miller continues as follows:

1 You:

Mr. Miller, where were you about four o'clock on the afternoon of October 3?

2 Witness:

I was outside my house, watering my front lawn.

3 You:

Did you see me that afternoon?

4 Witness:

Yes, I saw you walking your dog about two houses down from mine.

5 You:

Did anything happen to me as I was walking my dog?

6 **Witness:**

Yes. You were attacked by a German shepherd.

Transcript Analysis: With no need of complicated techniques, you have established that Miller has personal knowledge because he testified that he personally saw what happened to you.

Now let's see how the personal knowledge requirement works when you want a witness to testify to another person's statement. Jordan Miller is still testifying, and you want to ask him about what the dog owner said after his dog bit you. This portion of Miller's direct examination goes like this:

7 **You:**

Mr. Miller, what happened next?

8 **Witness:**

The German shepherd ran back across the street. Then a man came running over and said that he was very sorry for what his dog had done.

9 **You:**

How do you know this is what he said?

10 **Witness:**

I was standing only a few feet away from him; I could hear very clearly.

11 **You:**

Did he say anything else?

12 **Witness:**

Yes, he said that the dog got out of his yard through a hole in the fence that he hadn't had time to fix.

13 **You:**

Do you see the man who made those statements?

14 **Witness:**

Yes, he's sitting over there [indicating the defendant].

Transcript Analysis: Again, without any special effort you have shown that Miller has personal knowledge of what the defendant said after the attack.

HOW TO IDENTIFY PEOPLE IN THE COURTROOM

Pointing to a person in the courtroom while testifying is often the only way a witness can identify who made a statement or engaged in some other type of conduct. For example, in the dog bite case testimony above, a witness points out your adversary as the person who made a certain statement. But be careful how you ask a witness to identify a person in the courtroom. It is improper to ask a leading question such as, "Is the defendant sitting over there the person who made the statement?" Instead, as in the example, ask a non-leading question: "Do you see the man who made those statements?"

Pointing isn't always the only way to identify someone. If a witness personally knows the person whose conduct you want the witness to talk about, you can simply ask, "Who made the statement?" and expect the witness to say something like, "It was Doris Defendant who said that."

If a witness points to a person in the courtroom, the court reporter cannot record the silent gesture. To make sure the record reflects the identification, say something like, "May the record show that the witness pointed to Doris Defendant."

Now let's look at an example where a witness lacks personal knowledge. Assume that Miller's direct examination continues like this:

15 **You:**

Mr. Miller, do you know whether this dog has ever bitten other people?

16 **Witness:**

Yes, the dog bit three others before she bit you.

Transcript Analysis: In this example, you have not shown that Miller has personal knowledge of the dog's previous attacks. For all the judge can tell, Miller may know about three prior attacks only because other people have told him about them. Miller would then be testifying to second-hand information. So if your adversary objects, or perhaps even if he doesn't, the judge is likely to exclude the evidence in No. 16, meaning that the judge or jury could not consider that evidence in arriving at the verdict. (See Chapter 16, Making and Responding to Objections.)

If you forget to show that a witness has personal knowledge, normally you can readily fix the problem. Here is how you could do so in the Miller example:

17 **Judge:**

Ms. Nolo, that last answer [No. 16] is improper because you have not demonstrated that the witness has personal knowledge of previous attacks by the dog. I'm striking that answer from the record.

18 **You:**

Sorry, Your Honor. Mr. Miller, let me ask you this. Did you ever personally see the dog bite other people?

19 **Witness:**

Yes. I've seen that same dog attack and bite three other people.

Here, with just one additional question you have shown that Miller has personal knowledge of the prior attacks, and the testimony in No. 19 will be admissible (assuming, of course, that it does not run afoul of other evidentiary rules; see Chapter 15).

Special Personal Knowledge Rules for Conversations: Many judges apply a special personal knowledge rule for conversations. Before asking about what people said to each other (either in person or on the telephone), they want the witness to testify to three things:

* when the conversation took place

* where the conversation took place

* who was present during the conversation.

For example, assume that you are the owner of an apartment building and that you have brought suit to evict a tenant, Denise Beilenson, for keeping dogs in her apartment in violation of her lease. You have called Shelly Resnik as a witness to testify that she was present when Beilenson admitted to you that she was keeping three golden retrievers in her apartment and that she had no intention of getting rid of them. Your direct examination of Resnik might go as follows:

1 **You:**

Ms. Resnik, do you remember a conversation between me and Ms. Beilenson about dogs?

2 **Witness:**

Yes, I do.

3 **You:**

When did this conversation take place?

4 **Witness:**

If I remember right it was on the 13th of April.

5 **You:**

And where did the conversation take place?

6 **Witness:**

Down by the apartment's swimming pool.

7 **You:**

Was anyone else present during this conversation?

8 **Witness:**

No, just the two of you were talking. I was sitting a few feet away but I didn't notice anyone else around.

9 **You:**

Now, please tell us what was said during this conversation.

Transcript Analysis: Having shown that the witness knows when the conversation took place (No. 4), where it took place (No. 6) and who was present (No. 8), you have satisfied the personal knowledge rule for conversations and in No. 9 properly proceed to elicit what was said. True, question No. 1 indicates to the witness that you want to hear testimony about a dog conversation, which to a stickler may seem leading and therefore improper. But few judges would deem it either

leading or an improper question. The usual rule is that you can call a witness's attention to the subject matter of his or her testimony as long as you do not indicate your desired answer.

 Don't worry if a witness doesn't remember exact details. The fact that a witness can't remember an exact date, time or other background fact about a conversation (or other event) rarely defeats personal knowledge so as to prevent admissibility of testimony concerning the conversation. If your witness cannot be specific, elicit her or his best estimate. Even testimony that "The conversation took place in early April," or that "It took place sometime in April," will usually be good enough to show personal knowledge.

4. Refresh a Witness's Recollection If Necessary

You should almost always rehearse a witness's testimony before trial. (See Section C, above.) Nevertheless, even the best prepared witness may suffer a lapse of memory while testifying. For example, in response to a question you know a witness can answer, the witness might respond, "I don't remember." If this happens, do not panic. It's perfectly proper to attempt to "refresh the witness's recollection" with a document that refers to the information the witness has forgotten.

You can use any helpful document as a refresher, such as the forgetful witness's deposition or an informal written statement. The document needn't have been personally prepared by the forgetful witness; you may refresh one witness's recollection with the statement of a different witness, a receipt, a police report or any other document.

Assuming that you have handy a document that you think will refresh the flagging memory of your forgetful witness, here's a little ritual you should follow:

Step 1: Ask the witness whether looking at the document might help refresh his recollection.

Step 2: If the witness responds that looking at the document might help, mark it as an "exhibit," show it to your adversary and then ask the judge for permission to approach the witness. (See Chapter 14, Exhibits.) When permission is granted, walk to the witness box and show him the specific portion of the document that contains the information you hope will refresh his recollection.

Step 3: Take the document away from the witness and return to the place where you are asking questions.

Step 4: Ask the witness if his memory is refreshed.

Step 5: If the answer is yes, go on and ask the question necessary to produce the testimony.

 Your adversary may introduce the "refreshing" document into evidence. In federal court and most state courts, you cannot offer the document you use to refresh a witness's recollection into evidence, unless of course it's admissible for some other reason. (See Federal Rule of Evidence 612.) However, your adversary is allowed to offer the document into evidence if the adversary chooses to do so. Therefore, be careful about the document you use to refresh recollection. If it contains information that your adversary wants to get before the judge or jury, the document may prove more helpful to your adversary than to you.

Here is an example of how the process works. You are examining Mr. Houston. He has unexpectedly forgotten information a building contractor told him about the type of wood the contractor was to use on the front of his house. Luckily, you have a document referring to the forgotten information, and proceed as follows:

1 **You:**

Mr. Houston, did the contractor say anything about the kind of wood he would use for the front of the house?

2 **Witness:**

Hmmm— I'm pretty sure he did, but I just can't remember.

3 **You:**

Do you think it might refresh your recollection if you looked at the estimate the contractor prepared? [Step 1]

4 **Witness:**

It might.

5 **You:**

Your Honor, I'm holding a written estimate marked Exhibit A. Counsel for the plaintiff has seen it. May I approach the witness for the purpose of refreshing his recollection? [Step 2]

See Chapter 14 for a discussion of marking and using Exhibits.

6 **The Judge:**

Go ahead.

7 **You:**

Okay, Mr. Houston, please look Exhibit A over, especially this section right here [pointing].

After waiting a few moments, you pick up the document and take it back with you to where you are asking questions. [Step 3]

8 **You:**

Now do you remember what kind of wood the contractor said he would use on the front of the house? [Step 4]

9 **Witness:**

Yes, I do.

10 **You:**

And what did he say? [Step 5]

11 **Witness:**

He said he would use cedar siding.

 Remove the document before eliciting your desired testimony. When refreshing recollection, remember to remove whatever document you have shown the witness before asking if the witness's memory has been refreshed (see No. 7). The reason is that under the evidence rule barring "hearsay," the witness cannot testify to what the document says. (See Chapter 15, Basic Rules of Evidence.) But if the witness testifies to his or her present recollection as refreshed by the document, no hearsay is involved.

OFFERING DOCUMENTS AND OTHER OBJECTS DURING DIRECT EXAMINATION

Tangible objects such as receipts, letters, business records, photographs and computer printouts are often extremely important at trial. They convince a judge or jury of the accuracy of your testimony and that of your witnesses. They also add interest to your presentation of evidence (remember the old saying that "a picture is worth a thousand words") and provide hard evidence to support fallible human memory.

At trial, any tangible object that you want to introduce into evidence is called an "exhibit." While presenting exhibits is not usually difficult, you generally have to follow a number of preliminary steps (called "laying a foundation") before your exhibits can be received in evidence. Different types of exhibits require different steps. For example, the foundation necessary to introduce a photograph into evidence is very different from that required to introduce a business record into evidence. For this reason, we've given exhibits a chapter of their own. (Chapter 14, Exhibits.) Because you will typically offer exhibits into evidence during direct examination, make sure that you understand the material in Chapter 14 before you plan direct examination testimony.

F. HOSTILE WITNESSES

Subject to subpoena limitations, you can call and question any person who has information helpful to your case, even your adversary or someone else who is antagonistic to you. If you decide to call such a person as a witness, ask the judge for permission to treat the person as a "hostile witness." If a judge rules that a witness is hostile, you have the right to conduct direct examination of the witness with leading questions. (See for example Federal Rule of Evidence 611, Texas Civil Rule of Evidence 611 and similar rules in almost all other states.)

For example, assume that you are involved in a child custody dispute with Jan, your ex-spouse. You are pretty sure that a co-worker of Jan's has seen Jan drunk on at least two occasions in the presence of your young children. You want to call the co-worker as a witness to help prove that Jan should not be awarded custody of the children. On the other hand, you know that Jan and the co-worker are dating. The co-worker is unwilling to meet with you informally, and you cannot afford to take the co-worker's deposition. Moreover, according to Jan the co-worker supports Jan's request for custody.

In this situation, if you do subpoena the co-worker as a witness, at the trial ask the judge for permission to approach the bench before beginning the co-worker's direct examination. Tell the judge that the co-worker has been uncooperative, and ask for permission to treat the witness as a hostile witness. The judge may grant immediate

APPROACHING THE BENCH

permission or delay a ruling until after the co-worker begins testifying and the judge has a chance to evaluate if the witness is antagonistic to you. When and if the judge rules that the witness is hostile, you may ask leading questions.

The advantage of leading questions is that you can limit the witness's testimony to the specific topics that support your claims. They do not give an antagonistic witness an opportunity to launch into areas supporting your adversary that you don't want to cover. For example, here are some of the questions you might ask the co-worker in the child custody case:

- "You have been dating Jan for about three months, correct?"

- "You and Jan took my children to a football game last October 9, right?"

- "And Jan got drunk at the game, right?"

- "Jan had so much to drink that you had to help Jan to the car?"

- "And my children were with you the entire time?"

While of course you have no guarantee that a hostile witness like the co-worker will answer honestly, leading questions at least allow you to control the subject matter of the testimony.

⚠️ **Other evidence rules are important too.** A variety of other rules also affect whether direct examination questions are proper. For example, you should avoid questions that are "compound" or "vague," or call for "hearsay" or "character evidence." These additional rules are described in Chapter 15, Basic Rules of Evidence.

G. THE JUDGE'S ROLE

It is important to recognize that judges have a good deal of discretion over what questions they will allow you to ask. For example, federal judges may exercise "reasonable control over the mode and order of interrogating witnesses and presenting evidence." (Federal Rule of Evidence 611 (a).) No two judges interpret the term "reasonable" in exactly the same way. The same question that Judge A considers a proper "open" question, Judge B may consider an improper 'narrative" question. Similarly, a judge will often allow much more deviation from strict rules of evidence in non-jury trials than in jury trials because the judge feels capable of ignoring any improper evidence you bring out by your questioning.

Pay attention to any instructions a judge gives you about how to question a witness. If you are uncertain about whether you can ask a certain kind of question, do not be afraid to ask your judge for permission to approach the bench and ask the judge how to elicit the information you want.

For example, let's examine how to ask a judge for help if your adversary makes an objection that confuses you. You have just concluded preliminary questioning and now want to ask your witness to testify to a conversation in which your adversary agreed to buy your car.

1 **You:**

Can you please tell the jury what was said during this conversation?

2 **Opponent:**

Objection, Your Honor. That calls for a narrative response.

3 Judge:

I'll sustain the objection.

4 You:

Your Honor, I'm a bit confused. May we approach the bench?

5 Judge:

Briefly. Both counsel please approach the bench.

6 You (at the bench):

Your Honor, I didn't think this question called for a narrative answer. I just want the witness to testify to what was said during this one conversation. I'm not quite sure what to do.

7 Judge:

Ms. Nolo, I sustained the objection because I think your question is too broad. Ask a narrower question; don't try to get the whole conversation with one question. Please resume your places and proceed.

8 You (back at the podium):

Let me ask you this. Tell us how the conversation got started.

9 Witness:

The first thing I remember is that you told the defendant that you were willing to reduce the price of the car by $500.

10 You:

And how did he reply?

Transcript Analysis: Here, the judge exercises discretion by sustaining a narrative objection to a question that many other judges would consider proper (No. 3). Rather than guess at the problem and getting yourself more confused, you ask for permission to approach the bench and then ask for help (No. 6). The judge makes a suggestion (No. 7) and you then begin to go step-by-step through the conversation (Nos. 8-10).

THE ROLE OF OBJECTIONS IN ENFORCING EVIDENCE RULES

A party to a lawsuit who believes that the other party has violated a rule of evidence or procedure during trial can object. For example, if your adversary asks an improper leading question during direct examination, violates the personal knowledge rule or commits some other evidentiary sin, or an adverse witness improperly rambles on in response to a proper question, you may say "Objection" and succinctly state the reason for your objection. If the judge deems the objection valid ("sustains" the objection), the information cannot be considered by the judge or jury in arriving at its verdict. A judge can also rule that evidence is inadmissible on her own, without waiting for a party to object. (See Chapter 16, Making and Responding to Objections.)

H. A SAMPLE DIRECT EXAMINATION

Let's look at a sample direct examination transcript, followed by an analysis of the questioning techniques. This transcript has been shortened for illustrative purposes. A real direct examination is likely to be considerably longer.

This example is based on a negligence case (first described in Chapter 7, What You Need To Prove at Trial: The Plaintiff's Perspective) in which a building contractor named Sarah Adams allegedly made a careless left turn and as a result struck you while you were in a crosswalk. Adams admits striking you with her truck, but claims this occurred only because you suddenly ran out from between two parked cars a short distance north of the intersection.

After testifying yourself to what happened, you call Cynthia White as your next witness. Ms. White was at the intersection and saw the accident. In your direct examination of her you want to emphasize that you were in the crosswalk and that Adams made the left turn carelessly because she was not paying attention to the road. You subpoenaed Ms. White even though she was very willing to come to court and describe what she saw. Then, under your local court's on call procedure, you phoned her when the court broke for lunch and asked her to come to court at 1:30. Ms. White is escorted to the witness stand by the bailiff, placed under oath by the clerk and seated. You go to the podium and begin asking questions. The direct examination goes as follows:

1   **You:**

Ms. White, please state your full name for the record.

2   **Witness:**

Cynthia White.

3   **You:**

Ms. White, are you employed?

4   **Witness:**

Not at the moment. I'm going to college.

5   **You:**

Which college do you attend?

6   **Witness:**

Vernal College in Atlantic Highlands. I'm working on a Masters in psychology.

7   **You:**

So you've already completed your undergraduate work?

8   **Witness:**

Yes, about seven years ago. Then I went to work to earn some money so I could go back to school.

9   **You:**

Ms. White, were you at the intersection of Main and Elm at about 3 p.m. on the afternoon of March 31 of last year?

10   **Witness:**

Yes, I was.

11   **You:**

And did you see an automobile accident?

12   **Witness:**

Yes.

13   **You:**

Where were you when the accident occurred?

14   **Witness:**

I was in my car, stopped for a red light. I was heading south on Elm, and I was stopped just north of Main waiting for the light to change.

15   **You:**

Were any cars stopped in front of you?

16 Witness:

No, I was the first car in line. Actually, traffic was pretty light, and I don't know if anyone was behind me.

17 You:

Did you notice me at that intersection?

18 Witness:

Yes I did. I saw you step off the curb and begin to walk across Elm. The light was green for you.

19 You:

Is there any particular reason that you noticed me?

20 Witness:

I heard some young children shouting on the corner where you had been standing, so I looked over in your direction. That's when I saw you step off the curb.

21 You:

Did I walk into any particular area of the street?

22 Witness:

Yes, you were in the crosswalk.

23 You:

What happened after you saw me step off the curb into the crosswalk?

24 Witness:

I turned to look out my front window to see if the light had changed to green yet. That's

when I saw her [pointing to the defendant Adams] heading east on Main and begin to make a left turn to go north on Elm.

25 You:

Let the record reflect the witness is pointing to the defendant, Sarah Adams. Then what happened?

26 Witness:

She speeded up as she made the left turn. Then I suddenly realized that you were in the crosswalk, and I looked to see if you were in any danger. Just about then is when her truck ran into you.

27 You:

How long were you watching the truck before you saw it hit me?

28 Witness:

That's hard to say exactly. I'd say about five seconds.

29 You:

And can you estimate the truck's speed during the time it was making the left-hand turn?

30 Witness:

At least 30-35 m.p.h., much too fast.

31 You:

How long have you been driving?

32 Witness:

Over 15 years.

33   **You:**

Before her truck hit me, could you see where the defendant was looking while she made the left turn?

34   **Witness:**

Yes, I could see her. At least part of the time, she was looking back over her right shoulder out the back window of her pickup truck.

35   **You:**

Is there any reason you can remember that?

36   **Witness:**

Yes, seeing her look behind her like that is what made me think that you might be in danger, and that's why I turned back to see if you were still in the crosswalk.

37   **You:**

After the truck hit me, what happened?

38   **Witness:**

Well, I pulled over to the curb and ran into a store to call an ambulance. Then I went out and stayed with you until the ambulance came.

39   **You:**

And what was the defendant doing?

40   **Witness:**

She pulled over to the opposite curb, and just sat in the cab of her truck until the police came about ten minutes later.

41   **You:**

Thank you. No further questions at this time, Your Honor.

Transcript Analysis: You begin Cynthia White's testimony with a few personal background questions (Nos. 1-8). Since Ms. White is not employed, you quite properly ask a few questions about her college studies. These questions probably help her relax, and they tell the judge or jury a little bit about her.

Then you properly show that Ms. White is testifying from personal knowledge (Nos. 9-12). Note that No. 9 is a leading question because all the information is in the question, leaving the witness only to answer "yes." But a judge will probably allow you to ask this leading question, since it is preliminary: Adams does not dispute the fact that White was at Main and Elm and that an accident took place at that location.

Ms. White's testimony is in the form of a story. You begin by setting the scene before the accident (Nos. 13-17), and end by showing what happened immediately afterwards (Nos. 37-40). Within the story is certain crucial evidence that you want to emphasize. For example, you want the judge or jury to know that Ms. White had a particular reason to see you step into the crosswalk (No. 20) and to see the defendant looking back over her shoulder (No. 36). You also show that she observed the defendant's truck long enough to estimate its speed (Nos. 28-30). While there is no minimum amount of time a witness must observe a truck to have sufficient personal knowledge to be able to estimate its speed, a judge will probably think that under ordinary circumstances five seconds is more than adequate. Also, you suggest that because Ms. White is an experienced driver, her estimate of speed is likely to be reliable (No. 32).

In eliciting Ms. White's story, you use a variety of types of questions. For example, Nos. 19 and 23 are open questions. They allow Ms. White to testify in her own words, but since they do not invite her to narrate an entire series of events they are permissible.

By contrast, Nos. 27, 29 and 31 are closed questions; you ask for specific pieces of information. This is perfectly sensible; you need to have the witness testify to the speed of the truck (No. 30), and you have to show that she saw the truck long enough to be able to give an estimate (No. 28). Yet, neither question is leading; you do not suggest how long Ms. White saw the truck, or what its speed was.

Finally, look at Nos. 39 and 40. On the surface, you are just completing the story of what happened. But the fact that the defendant did not get out of her cab to check on your condition after the accident seems cold-hearted. That information may make a judge or jury feel sympathetic towards you and hostile towards the defendant. While you cannot offer evidence on the ground that "it paints me in a sympathetic light," or because "it shows that my adversary is really a jerk," often you can get in this kind of emotional evidence in the course of telling the story.

Look at the witness you're questioning.
Whether you stand at a podium or sit at the counsel table when asking questions, lay your outline in front of you. As each witness testifies, check off information to make sure you do not overlook important evidence. However, look at the witness who is testifying as much as possible and not at your outline. A judge or jury may lose interest in a witness's testimony if your face is buried in an outline and you are not paying attention to the testimony.

RESOURCES ON DIRECT EXAMINATION

For additional discussion and examples of direct examination, see:

Trial Advocacy in a Nutshell, by Paul Bergman (West Publishing Co.), Chapter 7 is a guide to direct examination.

Trying Cases to Win: Direct Examination, by Herbert Stern (Wiley & Sons), has numerous direct examination examples. ∎

12

CROSS-EXAMINATION

Cross-examination is your opportunity to question any witness who testifies against you, including your adversary. Among non-lawyers, cross-examination is surely the most misunderstood phase of trial. For starters, forget about all those TV and movie dramas where a snarling cross-examiner shouts angry questions at a beleaguered witness from a distance of two inches. In fact, nothing will bring the wrath of a judge down upon a pro per litigant (or a lawyer) quicker than overly argumentative cross-examination questions. Normally, you must cross-examine from a podium or counsel table, and the manner of questioning must show respect to the judge and the system of justice at all times. The fact that you believe a witness to be a damnable liar does not change this one bit.

A second popular misconception concerns how much helpful evidence you can realistically hope to elicit during cross-examination. Again, TV and movies create a false image, this time that lawyers routinely win cases during cross-examination by tricking witnesses into blurting out vital information. But in the real world, an adverse witness is unlikely to change major portions of his story just because you question his credibility. So while you'll want to do the best job you can on cross-examination, you'll probably win or lose on the strength and credibility of your testimony and that of your witnesses on direct examination. (See Chapter 11, Direct Examination.)

A. AN OVERVIEW OF CROSS-EXAMINATION

Your adversary will probably conclude a witness's direct examination by saying, "No further questions at this time." The judge will then turn to you and say something like, "Ms. Nolo, you may cross-examine."

If you are at all uncertain about what you will ask on cross-examination, ask the judge for a few minutes to think about your questions. Lawyers are often granted this courtesy, and you should be entitled to no less. Use the time to look over the cross-examination outline in your trial notebook (see section H below). In general, you are best off asking no more than a few questions. Otherwise you may end up rehashing the entire direct examination, pointlessly giving your adversary's witness a chance to repeat damaging information.

Once you begin to cross-examine, behave exactly as you did (or will do, if you are the defendant) during direct examination. As on direct, all you are permitted to do during cross-examination is ask questions. You may not make speeches commenting on an adverse witness's testimony, argue with a witness or approach the witness without the judge's permission.

 It's okay to read prepared questions during cross-examination. On cross-examination it is usually effective to read prepared questions to an adverse witness. Unlike with direct examination of a friendly witness, a judge or jury won't dismiss the testimony you elicit as scripted.

After you finish cross-examination, your adversary may ask the court to ask additional questions on redirect examination. This gives the adversary a chance to bring out additional testimony in response to testimony you elicited during cross-examination, but is not to be used to rehash a witness's entire direct testimony. Following redirect you will be allowed to ask questions on recross-examination, after which the judge will probably excuse the witness.

1. The Two Goals of Cross-Examination

You can pursue two goals during cross-examination. One line of questioning is affirmative: you seek to produce evidence from a witness called by your adversary that supports your version of events. This will be possible more often than you may think. Few witnesses are all good for one side and all bad for the other.

 Repeat helpful evidence from direct examination. Do not be surprised if your adversary asks her witness to testify to some information during direct that is helpful to you. It is an oft-used tactic. Your adversary may hope that by "hiding" information that helps you in a long direct examination, the judge or jury will overlook it. But to counter this tactic, you have the right to elicit the same helpful evidence during your cross-examination, even if it involves asking a witness to repeat exactly the same testimony already given on direct. Doing so emphasizes it for the judge or jury.

The second goal is to impeach adverse witnesses; that is, to cast doubt on their credibility. Using the impeachment techniques discussed later in the chapter (Section E below), you try to give a judge or jury a reason to distrust the accuracy of the adverse witness's testimony.

It's fine to pursue both goals. You do not have to choose between goals one and two. During cross-examination of a single witness, you may try both to elicit information supporting your version of events and to impeach harmful evidence. When you do pursue both goals, as a general rule seek the affirmative information first. An adverse witness may be far less cooperative after you have tried to impeach her!

2. The Permissible Scope of Cross-Examination

The questions you ask during cross-examination must pertain to (be "within the scope" of) the topics that were explored on direct examination. Impeachment of a witness is allowed because you are attempting to weaken the credibility of direct examination testimony. But if you try to ask about a topic not addressed in your adversary's direct examination that supports your version of events, your adversary may object that your questions are beyond the scope of direct. In response, you may point out to the judge that she has discretion under evidence rules (such as Federal Rule of Evidence 611) to interpret the scope of direct rule broadly. (And many judges do so.)

Even if the judge sustains (agrees with) your adversary's objection, all is not lost. You can recall the same witness to the stand yourself after your adversary finishes presenting all of his evidence (rests his case), and ask the same questions that you were not allowed to ask on cross-examination. When you do recall the witness, ask the judge to rule that the witness is a "hostile witness." A judge's ruling that a witness is hostile to you gives you the right to ask leading questions even though technically you are conducting the witness's direct examination. (Hostile witnesses are discussed further in Chapter 11, Direct Examination.) In fact, pointing out to the judge that it will be a waste of court (and witness) time for the same witness to return to court at a later time is often an effective argument for asking a judge to overrule (deny) your adversary's beyond the scope objection.

B. SHOULD YOU CROSS-EXAMINE?

You have a right to cross-examine every witness who testifies against you, but you are by no means required to do so. Perhaps it makes sense to some people to climb a mountain just "because it is there," but cross-examining a witness just because she is sitting in the witness box is foolish.

If you don't reasonably expect to elicit information that helps prove your version of events, and you don't think that you can impeach the witness on an important point, don't cross-examine. When the judge invites you to cross-examine, just say, "No questions." That way the witness cannot take advantage of your cross-examination to retell his story. And if you do not cross-examine, your adversary cannot conduct redirect examination, eliminating yet another chance for the witness to repeat his version of events.

Because adverse witnesses' stories are likely to sound better to a judge or jury the second or third time around, one of the worst things you can do on cross-examination is to conduct an aimless "fishing trip." You "fish" when you ask a question in the hope that a witness will give a response that impeaches him, but without factual support for that hope. For example, assume that an adverse witness testifies that you ran a red light. You ask on cross-examination, "What were you doing when you saw me run the light?" You have no idea what the witness was doing, but hope that the witness will respond that he was memorizing the Gettysburg Address or was otherwise so preoccupied that he couldn't possibly know what color the light was. Unfortunately, in this situation a witness will almost invariably give an answer that solidifies his direct examination testimony. For example, he might answer, "Your question reminds me that I was studying the traffic at that intersection in meticulous detail as part of a government research safety project." If your only alternative is to fish, you are far better off saying, "No questions."

While setting out any general rules about cross-examination is risky, here are some types of witnesses that should cause you to think twice or thrice before cross-examining:

- Expert witnesses, who are likely to know much more about the subject of their testimony than you do and thus are especially likely to retell their story during cross-examination. (See Chapter 18, Expert Witnesses, for more on this issue.)

- Witnesses who you think have even more damaging information than your adversary elicited during direct examination. Don't give them a second chance to hurt you.

- Witnesses with whom a judge or jury is likely to sympathize, such as children or elderly or infirm witnesses.

 Offering impeachment evidence during direct examination. As any devotee of Perry Mason reruns knows, because of its dramatic effect, impeachment often takes place during cross-examination. However, cross-examination is not the only time you can offer impeaching evidence. Though it may be less dramatic, usually you can also introduce impeachment evidence when it is your turn to conduct direct examination.

For example, instead of asking a plaintiff's witness during cross-examination whether he had consumed three martinis a half hour before he supposedly saw you driving too fast, you can impeach the witness by later calling your own witness to testify that the plaintiff's witness was seen drinking martinis. The advantage of this choice is that the plaintiff's witness cannot undercut the force of the impeachment by immediately offering an explanation such as, "Yes, I did have three martinis, but I take medication that renders them as harmless as lemonade." The disadvantage is that you may lose the impeachment evidence altogether if you cannot produce your impeachment witness at trial.

C. HOW TO ASK QUESTIONS ON CROSS-EXAMINATION

It's crucial not to allow an adverse witness to retell her entire story on cross-examination. Fine advice, you may say. But just like, "Buy low, sell high," the key is in figuring out how to do it.

1. Ask Leading Questions

During cross-examination, the key to eliciting evidence without giving a witness a chance to retell a story is to ask leading questions. (Leading questions are explained in Chapter 11, Direct Examination.) Because they call on witnesses to respond only by saying yes or no, leading questions do not give a witness a chance to rehash direct examination testimony.

Questions are leading when they suggest the desired answer. Leading questions are improper on direct examination, when you're questioning your own witnesses, on the theory that a friendly witness will give the suggested answer even if it's not completely accurate. But leading questions are proper on cross-examination, because there is little risk that an adverse witness will falsely agree with you. Here are some typical leading questions:

- "You never told me the date the inspector would come by to inspect the plumbing, did you?"

- "The first time that you saw the light it was already red, correct?"

- "Isn't it true that you couldn't actually tell which person said 'Stop'?"

Since each of these questions is nothing more than an assertion of the answer you want the witness to give asked in the form of a question, you can see why leading questions—especially short, unambiguous ones—typically limit the scope of a witness's answer. In each example, the only answer the witness is called on to give is yes or no.

Stay in control during cross-examination. Increase the power of leading questions on cross-examination by asking them in a firm (not nasty) voice that suggests that you expect nothing more than yes or no in response. And to further inhibit an adverse witness from straying from your script, keep your questions short.

For example, if you want an adverse witness to agree that "The wolf huffed and puffed until he blew the house down," break it up into two questions: "The wolf huffed and puffed, correct?" and "He continued to huff and puff until he blew the house down, isn't that right?"

2. Interrupt Non-Responsive Witnesses

Despite your best efforts, an adverse witness may attempt to give a narrative response to a leading question. For example, assume that the following dialogue takes place during your cross-examination:

You:

And then Jill came tumbling after, right?

Witness:

You could say that, but you've got to remember that Jill and her brother Jack had only one pail between them. I know for sure that Jack was carrying the pail....

Here, even though your question calls for a yes or no answer, the witness launches into a retelling of his story. Fortunately, you have the power to stop the witness from pontificating. Quickly hold up your hand and say, "Excuse me." When the witness pauses, ask your next question. If the witness continues to talk, ask the judge to intervene by saying something like, "Your Honor, I object; the witness is not answering my question." Assuming that the judge agrees with (sustains) your objection, ask the judge to delete the answer from the record ("strike the answer") and to tell the jury (if there is one) to disregard the testimony the witness gave before you could stop him from talking. If the witness launches into diatribes on more than one occasion, you may also ask the judge to instruct the witness to stop making speeches and to answer only what you have asked. Most witnesses will be very cowed by a judicial reprimand.

Remember, however, that judges have a good deal of discretion when it comes to the scope of witnesses' answers. Occasionally, even if you ask a question that calls for a yes or no answer, a judge may allow a brief explanation if the judge believes it is necessary to allow a witness to answer accurately.

3. Use Exhibits If They Are Helpful

If your adversary offered exhibits (such as reports, photographs or receipts) into evidence during direct examination, you may ask a witness to refer to those exhibits during your cross-examination. Once an exhibit is admitted into evidence it is the property of the court, not of the party who offered it. For example, assume that during an adverse witness's direct examination your adversary offers into evidence a photograph of his car to show the damage it sustained in an accident. You now want to use that photograph to call the judge's or jury's attention to the open bottle of beer shown on the front seat. On cross, you may show the photograph to the witness and ask about the object depicted on the front seat.

To do this, begin by retrieving the exhibit. Often, you will find it either in a shallow box on the counsel table or on the court clerk's desk. But it may be on the judge's bench, in which case you should ask the judge for "permission to have Exhibit 3." To show the exhibit to a witness, ask the judge for permission to approach the witness. (Check this procedure with the court clerk, or watch what the other attorney does. Some judges prefer for the bailiff to transport an exhibit from wherever it is to the witness while you remain at the podium or counsel table.) Then, ask the witness to refer to the exhibit and ask your question: "Ms. Spillenger, please look at Exhibit 3 and tell us if the object on the front seat depicted in that exhibit is an open bottle of beer."

Offering exhibits during cross-examination. Rules of evidence allow you to offer exhibits into evidence during cross-examination of adverse witnesses in the same way as you can during your testimony or direct examination of your witnesses. Whenever possible, however, offer exhibits into evidence only when you or your witnesses are testifying.

D. ELICITING HELPFUL EVIDENCE

Affirmative questioning (questioning to bring out evidence that supports your version of events) during cross-examination can be very effective. A witness called by your adversary may well have some information that helps you, and focusing on that helpful information may lead a judge or jury to conclude that the witness hasn't hurt you.

For example, consider an incident from the well-publicized 1993 federal court criminal prosecution of the four Los Angeles police officers who were charged with using illegal force to arrest Rodney King. One of the defendants called a Highway Patrol Officer, Melanie Singer, to testify that she was an eyewitness to the arrest and that King was acting in an aggressive, threatening manner towards the arresting officers. But on cross-examination by the prosecutor, Officer Singer cried on the stand as she testified that the defendant officers had kicked and struck King far too long and that she felt helpless to stop it. Without in any way attacking Officer Singer's credibility, the prosecution turned a defense witness into a witness who did not damage its case.

How can you elicit evidence on cross-examination that supports your own case? As with direct examination, start by looking at the facts you're trying to prove. (Remember, even as a defendant you may have facts that you are trying to prove. See Chapter 8, What to Prove at Trial: The Defendant's Perspective.) Then review the information you gathered before trial, whether through informal discussions, negotiation discussions or formal discovery, to identify information a witness has that supports those facts.

Let's take as an example a legal malpractice claim. Say you're suing a lawyer for negligently failing to advise your stepmother that in order for you to inherit all of the stepmother's property in accord with a will the lawyer had previously drafted, she had to change the will to specifically disinherit a child she gave birth to after the will was executed. You have presented all of your evidence and rested your case, and the lawyer's direct examination has just concluded. He testified that he prepared a will for your stepmother, that she came into the office to talk to him a couple of years after the will was executed, and that while she did talk casually about her relatives he is sure that she never said anything about having given birth to a child since signing her will.

You now have an opportunity to cross-examine the lawyer. From what you found out from the lawyer's answers to a brief set of interrogatories that you sent to him before trial, you know that estate planning is not the lawyer's specialty, and that he does about a will or two per year. Also, the lawyer has a paralegal (an assistant) whom he relies on to take down most of the information from will clients. This information does not impeach any testimony the lawyer gave on direct examination, but you want to elicit it during cross-examination to support your fact that the lawyer was careless. Your cross may go like this:

1 **You:**

Mr. Lawyer, preparing wills is not your legal specialty, is it?

2 **Witness (Defendant):**

Not my specialty, no.

3 **You:**

You probably don't do more than a will or two a year, right?

4 **Witness:**

Well, that's probably about right. But let me add that….

5 **You:**

Excuse me. Your Honor, the witness has answered the question. I object to further testimony.

6 **Judge:**

Yes, that's right. Objection sustained.

7   You:

My stepmother came to see you a couple of years after she signed the will you prepared for her, right?

8   Witness:

Yes, I've testified that she did.

9   You:

And you didn't conduct her interview by yourself, did you?

10   Witness:

Not entirely, no.

11   You:

You asked your paralegal assistant to get most of the information from her, right?

12   Witness:

Most of it, but of course I talked to her too.

13   You:

And a paralegal is not an attorney, right?

14   Witness:

That's true.

Transcript Analysis: This cross-examination does not directly attack the lawyer's direct testimony that the stepmother said nothing to him about a child born after the will was made. Instead, you concentrate on information about the lawyer's experience and client interview procedures that support your factual contention that the lawyer was careless.

All of your questions are leading, which gives the witness no opportunity to retell his own story.

And when the witness tries to explain an answer (No. 4), you quite properly and courteously stop his explanation by objecting that the witness has already answered your question. When the judge sustains your objection (No. 5), you promptly ask your next question. Since you stopped the lawyer quickly, you needn't ask the judge to strike any testimony from the record. (If the lawyer's answer to your questions contradict his interrogatory answers, you could impeach him with his contradictory interrogatory answers.)

You may also be able to base affirmative cross-examination on a witness's oral statement. For example, assume that you are seeking to regain custody of your children from your ex-spouse. Your ex-spouse calls one of your neighbors, Linda, as a witness to testify that you often have strangers staying overnight in your apartment. Another neighbor, Dick, has told you that in talking to Linda one day recently, Linda said a number of nice things about you—including that your apartment is always neat and clean and that she always feels comfortable asking you to watch her children for a few hours. On cross-examination of Linda you want to have her testify to this information because it is affirmative evidence for your custody. To do so, you might ask a series of questions such as:

- "Linda, whenever you've seen my apartment it's always been neat and clean, right?"

- "In the last year you've often asked me to watch your children for a few hours, correct?"

- "And you always feel comfortable asking me to watch your children, don't you?"

Here you do not impeach Linda's testimony that strangers often stay overnight at your apartment. Rather, you use Linda's oral statements to Dick as the basis of an affirmative cross-examination of Linda. (If Linda gives testimony that conflicts with what she told Dick, you may impeach her by later calling Dick as a witness.)

Note that these questions are within the scope of Linda's direct examination because they pertain to your fitness as a parent, the topic that Linda was asked about on direct.

E. IMPEACHING ADVERSE WITNESSES

Your second cross-examination goal is to impeach an adverse witness and give a judge or jury some basis for doubting the witness's credibility. Despite the incredible variety of events that give rise to litigation, there are really only a few legally-accepted impeachment methods that arise regularly. Most of them, such as raising the possibility that a witness is biased or prejudiced, will be familiar to you, because they are based on the same logic you rely on in everyday life to evaluate what you hear and see.

1. Bias in Favor of Your Adversary

"Bias" refers to a witness's emotional or financial interest in favor of your opponent. If you can show bias, you hope the judge or jury will doubt the credibility of the witness's testimony.

An emotional interest can arise from such sources as family loyalty and friendship. For example, if you can use cross-examination to establish that Sarah is testifying on behalf of her childhood friend Hilary, or that Adam is testifying on behalf of his cousin Kevin, the judge or jury may not

believe (or at least discount) Sarah's or Adam's testimony.

As you probably realize, a financial interest arises when a witness stands to gain financially if your adversary wins. For instance, one spouse or business partner may be testifying on behalf of the other in a situation where any financial gains resulting from the trial would be shared by both.

Whether the source of the bias is emotional or financial, the basis of impeachment is the same: the witness's interest in the outcome arguably casts doubt on the accuracy of the witness's testimony. Of course, the judge or jury may believe a witness despite his emotional or financial interest. But the possibility of bias will probably make the judge or jury more skeptical of the adverse witness's testimony.

Here's an example of how to impeach a witness on cross-examination based on bias. Assume that you are the homeowner in a breach of contract case, and have sued the building contractor you hired to do a remodeling job. You claim that he failed to complete the job and that he used substandard workmanship. On direct examination, Wilkins, one of the contractor's employees, testifies that you orally agreed to give the contractor two additional months to complete the work. Wilkins also testifies that a couple of weeks before this conversation you agreed to wait at home so a building inspector could sign off on the rough plumbing, and that when you failed to do so you caused a delay in the project. You dispute everything Wilkins says: you never agreed to a two-month extension, and the reason you did not wait for the building inspector is that neither Wilkins nor anyone else told you that the plumbing was supposed to be inspected. So in addition to testifying yourself on these points during your direct examination, you want to impeach Wilkins if you can.

When you took Wilkins' deposition before trial, you learned that he has had some discussions with the defendant about soon becoming a partner in the defendant's contracting business. Based on this information, you may cross-examine Wilkins in an effort to show that he has a potential financial interest in seeing the defendant win the case. You want the judge or jury to infer that since Wilkins has hopes of becoming the defendant's business partner, he both wants to remain on good terms with the defendant and to share ownership of a financially stable business. Here's how the cross-examination might go:

1 **You:**

Mr. Wilkins, you've worked for the defendant for about nine years, right?

2 **Witness:**

That's right.

3 **You:**

And you and the defendant have discussed your becoming a partner in the business, right?

4 **Witness:**

Well, there's nothing definite about that.

5 **You:**

But you hope to become a partner, don't you?

6 **Witness:**

We've talked about it, yes.

7 **You:**

That means you would put money into the business?

8 **Witness:**

Yes.

9 **You:**

So you want this business to be worth as much as possible in case you become a partner, right?

10 **Witness:**

I suppose so.

Transcript Analysis: In No. 4 Wilkins tries to downplay his potential interest in the business. However, in No. 5 you stick to your guns and ask if Wilkins has a long-term interest in the business. No. 5 is legally proper question; you have a right to press for an unequivocal answer. By contrast, you would be improperly argumentative if you asked this additional question: "And because you want the business to be worth as much as possible, you've lied on the stand, haven't you?" Such an attempt to put words in Wilkins' mouth is not a question, though if put in a less inflammatory way it is possibly material for your final argument. Note that your questions are leading and leave Wilkins no room to retell the story he told on direct examination.

Questioning to bring out bias can often be even shorter than this. Assume that instead of learning that Wilkins hopes to become a partner in the defendant's business, you've learned that Wilkins and the defendant are brothers. In that case, you might just use one question to show that Wilkins has an emotional stake in the outcome of the case:

1 **You:**

Mr. Wilkins, you're the defendant's brother, right?

2 **Witness:**

Yes.

Impeach using what you learned through discovery. By working backwards, you can see that if you want to impeach a witness as biased at trial, you should always try to find evidence of bias before trial, either through informal discussions with people who know a witness or through formal discovery tools such as written interrogatories and depositions, though the latter may be costly. Discovery tools are discussed in Chapter 4, Investigating Your Case.

---

2. Prejudice Against You

In legal terms, prejudice is the flip side of bias. Instead of showing that a witness is biased in favor of your adversary, you show that a witness might be prejudiced against you.

For example, assume that one of the witnesses who testifies against you in a traffic accident case is your former spouse, with whom you have argued bitterly concerning the custody of your children. If you bring out your former spouse's bitterness towards you during cross-examination, the judge or jury might disbelieve or at least partially discredit the former spouse's testimony.

To illustrate how this works, let's put the contractor's employee, Wilkins, back in the witness box. Now assume that you noticed that on a couple of occasions when he was working on your new addition, Wilkins appeared to have had too much to drink. You reported this fact to Wilkins' employer, the defendant. As a result of your complaint, Wilkins was suspended for two weeks without pay. In this situation, after Wilkins testifies, you may cross-examine to show that he is prejudiced against you:

1 **You:**

Mr. Wilkins, I made a complaint about you to your employer, didn't I?

2 **Witness:**

I remember that, yes.

3 **You:**

My complaint was that you had come to work having had too much to drink on a couple of occasions, right?

4 **Witness:**

That's what you said. But that's not the way it was.

5 **You:**

Your Honor, that last sentence is improper. I just asked him what my complaint was, I didn't ask him for his side of things.

6 **Judge:**

Yes, that's improper. I'll strike the second sentence.

If this is a jury trial, the judge might instruct the jury to disregard Wilkins' improper remark.

7 **You:**

So you know I made this complaint?

8 **Witness:**

Yes.

9 **You:**

And because of my complaint, you were suspended two weeks without pay?

10 **Witness:**

Yes, I was.

Transcript Analysis: Again, because all of your questions are leading, and because they all focus on the specific topic of prejudice, you give Wilkins no chance to retell his story. When Wilkins does try to throw in information not called for by your question (No. 4), you properly object. The judge strikes the improper testimony, meaning that the judge or jury must totally ignore that testimony when weighing the evidence and making a decision.

3. Prior Inconsistent Statements

One of the most widely used types of impeachment consists of proving that a witness's testimony at trial doesn't square with a statement the witness previously made. The theory behind this type of impeachment is that accurate tales do not change in the telling. Not surprisingly, lawyers call this impeachment with a prior inconsistent statement.

Use of this cross-examination tool does not depend on whether the witness made the previous statement under oath during a deposition, in a letter to her Aunt Agnes or while playing tennis with a friend. If any statement previously made by a witness is inconsistent with the witness's in-court testimony, the previous statement is admissible for impeachment.

a.   Oral Statements

Our old but long-suffering friend Wilkins can provide us with an example of this type of impeachment. Assume that on direct examination, Wilkins testified that serious problems with your house's foundation necessitated the contractor's demand for an additional $20,000 to complete the remodeling job. You want to impeach Wilkins with a statement that he made to another construction worker, Alice Johnson. According to Ms. Johnson, after inspecting the foundation Wilkins told her, "There's no problem with the foundation. It's in great condition." Your cross-examination bringing out Wilkins' prior statement may go as follows:

1 **You:**

Mr. Wilkins, you testified that the reason for the demand of an additional $20,000 to complete the remodeling job was that you discovered a serious problem with the foundation, right?

2 **Witness:**

That's correct.

3 **You:**

Another person working on my job was named Alice Johnson, is that right?

4 **Witness:**

Yes, Alice was working on your job some of the time.

5 **You:**

And just after inspecting the foundation, you told Ms. Johnson that it was in great condition, didn't you?

6 **Witness:**

I did say something like that.

Transcript Analysis: This concludes your impeachment. You contrast Wilkins' testimony (No. 1) with his inconsistent prior statement (No. 5). You hope that the inconsistency will lead the judge or jury to conclude that Wilkins is untrustworthy.

What can you do if Wilkins denies making the statement to Alice Johnson? During the cross-examination of Wilkins, there is nothing you can do. However, after your adversary finishes presenting evidence (rests), you typically have a chance to present additional testimony impeaching your adversary's witnesses, even from witnesses who have previously testified for you. Here, if Wilkins denies making the statement to Alice Johnson, you could eventually call her as a witness to testify that Wilkins told her that the foundation was in great shape.

b.   Written Statements

Now let's look at how you can cross-examine Wilkins if, instead of an oral statement, you have written evidence of a prior inconsistent statement. For example, assume again that during direct examination Wilkins testifies that there were serious problems with the foundation of your house. But during his deposition, Wilkins admitted that his inspection revealed that your house's foundation was in very good condition.

To impeach Wilkins with his deposition statement, which is now in the form of a written transcript, mark the deposition as an exhibit, ask the judge for permission to approach Wilkins, and when permission is granted hand the exhibit to him. (See Chapter 14, Exhibits.) Open the deposition transcript to the signature page and ask Wilkins to verify his signature. Then tell the judge and your adversary what page of the deposition the inconsistent statement appears on and read the prior inconsistent statement into the record. You do not need to give the witness a chance to deny making the prior statement or to explain why he has changed his story. The impeachment will go as follows:

1 **You:**

Mr. Wilkins, you testified that the reason for the demand of an additional $20,000 to complete the remodeling job was that you discovered a serious problem with the foundation, right?

2 **Witness:**

That's correct.

You mark the deposition as an exhibit, ask the judge for permission to approach the witness, and once permission is granted you hand the deposition to Wilkins.

3 **You:**

All right, looking at your deposition, Exhibit 4, please examine it and tell us if this is the sworn deposition you gave in this case?

4 **Witness:**

Yes, it is.

5 **You:**

The signature on the last page, that's your signature?

6 **Witness:**

Yes.

7 **You:**

Your Honor, I'm reading page 23, lines 13-20 of Mr. Wilkins' deposition. "Question: What was your initial task in connection with my remodeling job? Answer: To inspect the foundation. Question: And what did that inspection reveal? Answer: That the foundation was in very good condition."

Transcript Analysis: Once you establish that the exhibit is the witness's deposition, you can read into the record any portion of the deposition that is inconsistent with the witness's testimony. And if the witness has given other direct testimony that is inconsistent with his deposition testimony, you can again impeach him without having to re-identify the deposition.

4. Ability to Perceive

We have all seen movies in which the key eyewitness turns out to be legally blind, or someone who claims to overhear a crucial conversation is revealed to be almost deaf. In real life, chances are you will never be able to attack so decisively an adverse witness's ability to perceive.

But you may be able to cause a judge or juror to doubt a witness's ability to perceive what she claims to have seen or heard. Sometimes you will base your impeachment on adverse conditions in the outside world, such as when a witness claims to have overheard a whispered conversation while standing at a busy intersection. Other times, your best chance to impeach may be based on a witness's condition, such as when a nearsighted witness claims to have seen the color of a distant traffic light at dusk—or, if luck is really with you, ten minutes after leaving an optometrist's office where his eyes were dilated.

Let's go back to the negligence case involving your claim that you were crossing Main Street in a crosswalk when you were struck by a truck driven by Sarah Adams, a building contractor. Assume that Adams, the defendant, calls a witness named Kris Knaplund, who testifies that she was coming out of a nearby shop when the accident occurred. Knaplund further testifies that after you were struck by the truck you said, "Oh my God! Why didn't I use the crosswalk?" When you get a chance to testify later, you will deny making this statement. You will testify that what you really said was, "Oh my God! Why didn't you see me in the cross-walk?" But before that, during cross-examination of Knaplund you want to cast doubt on her ability to have overheard your statement accurately. Your cross-examination of Knaplund may go like this:

1 You:

Ms. Knaplund, you heard me say something after the accident?

2 Witness:

Yes.

3 You:

Isn't it true that what I really said was, "Oh my God! Why didn't you see me in the crosswalk?"

4 Witness:

No, that's not what I heard you say.

5 You:

You were just coming out of a shop when you heard me?

6 Witness:

That's right.

7 You:

The shop was a video game arcade?

8 Witness:

That's true.

9 You:

There were a number of noisy games being played at the time, right?

10 Witness:

Yes.

11 You:

Isn't it true that those machines and the people playing them are so loud that you have to talk extra loud to be heard inside the arcade?

12 Witness:

Well, they're noisy, that's true.

13 You:

And isn't the arcade about 75 feet away from where I was hit by the truck?

14 Witness:

I wouldn't know, I'm not too good at estimating distances.

Transcript Analysis: Here, you begin by asking Knaplund directly about your statement (No. 3). You do not expect her to suddenly admit that she made a mistake, but you have nothing to lose by having the judge or jury hear your side of things.

Then you mention some outside factors that may cast doubt on Knaplund's ability to accurately hear what you said: just coming out of a noisy video game arcade (Nos. 5-12) and being some distance away from the scene (No. 13). Your cross cannot prove that Knaplund was unable to hear your statement accurately. But together with your own testimony, your cross can lead the judge or jury to doubt Knaplund's credibility.

5. Implausible Testimony

All of us carry around beliefs about how people usually behave and events usually occur. When we are told something that is at odds with these beliefs, we tend to doubt what we are told; we find it implausible. For example, if Jones tells you that he walked three blocks at 2 a.m. to return an overdue library book, probably you would doubt him. Your own life experience suggests that people do not go out in the middle of the night to return a library book when the library is closed and the book would have to go into a drop box.

In the same way you should examine an adverse witness's story for its overall plausibility. Even if you have no other basis on which to try to impeach a witness, perhaps you can show that the witness's story is in some way implausible. This is far from an ironclad method of impeachment. What you consider implausible may seem quite normal to a judge or jury. A judge who grew up in a family of librarians, for example, might think it quite admirable to return a library book at 2 a.m.

To see how to conduct this type of cross-examination, return again to Knaplund's testimony in the negligence case (Subsection 4 above). Assume that Knaplund gave a statement to the investi-

gating police officer who came to the scene of the accident, but neglected to mention that just after being struck you said you should have been in the crosswalk. You consider this implausible; if she really had heard you say this, surely she would have reported it to prevent the truck driver from being unfairly held responsible for the accident. Your cross of Knaplund to emphasize the implausibility might go like this:

1 You:

Ms. Knaplund, you say that right after the accident I said "Oh my God! Why didn't I use the crosswalk?"

2 Witness:

Yes, that's what I heard.

3 You:

A few minutes later a police officer came to the scene, right?

4 Witness:

That's correct.

5 You:

The officer was in uniform, correct?

6 Witness:

Yes.

7 You:

You knew that he was there to investigate the accident, right?

8 Witness:

That's true.

9   You:

You wanted to make sure that the police officer got accurate information about what happened, right?

10   Witness:

I guess so.

11   You:

But you never told him that I said something about wishing I had been in the crosswalk?

12   Witness:

No, I didn't.

Transcript Analysis: In this excerpt, you use leading questions to suggest that Knaplund's failure to mention what she heard you say is implausible. You hope that the implausibility will lead the judge or jury to discredit Knaplund's testimony.

6.   Prior Convictions

In most court systems, you may impeach a witness by showing that the witness has been convicted of certain serious crimes. (For example, Federal Rule of Evidence 609 and California Evidence Code § 788 allow this.) However, in a civil case chances are that the witnesses you cross-examine will not have been convicted of a crime. Moreover, the rules are very strict and often confused as to what kinds of convictions are admissible. If you find out that an adverse witness has been convicted of a crime, consult your self-help law coach or do some legal research to determine whether the conviction is admissible in evidence.

When implying wrongdoing, be sure you are right. You cannot ask a witness about a criminal conviction or otherwise imply wrongdoing on the part of a witness unless you have what the law calls a "good faith basis" to believe that your charge is accurate. At the least, you need to be able to point to a reliable source of information that justifies your question.

For example, assume that you have no evidence that an eyewitness had been using drugs. Nevertheless you ask, "Had you been using any narcotic drugs just before you witnessed the accident?" If your adversary objects to the question, the judge may ask you to reveal your source. If you cannot identify a reliable source that the judge regards as a good faith basis for believing that the witness had used drugs, the judge will surely sustain the objection. And even allowing for your inexperience as a pro per litigant, a judge may restrict your right to ask further questions.

F.   BASE QUESTIONS ON EVIDENCE YOU CAN OFFER

One of the oldest cross-examination clichés is to "never ask a question that you don't know the answer to." This doesn't mean that you have to be 100% certain of how an adverse witness will answer your questions, because an adverse witness can always give an unexpected answer. What it does mean is that generally you should not ask a question unless you can offer evidence to contradict an unexpected answer. And this advice applies regardless of whether the information you seek on cross-examination supports your own fact or impeaches a witness.

Look back at some of the examples in this chapter. In one instance, you wanted to elicit helpful evidence from Linda that she has often asked you to take care of her children (Section D, above). Based on information you have from Dick, a friend of Linda's, you expect Linda to provide this evidence. But if Linda gives an unexpected answer, you can call Dick as a witness yourself to contradict her.

Similarly, in each of the impeachment illustrations you could contradict an unexpected answer because your cross-examination questions were based on evidence that you could produce in court. Thus, you could impeach Wilkins with his statement to Alice Johnson because if he gave an unexpected answer you could later call Johnson as a witness and ask her what Wilkins told her. In addition, you could impeach Wilkins with his deposition testimony because you could contradict an unexpected answer with the deposition transcript.

Without any way to contradict an unexpected answer, your cross-examination may amount to a foolish "fishing trip." Without your own source of evidence to fall back on, your firm belief that an adverse witness is either lying or mistaken does you no good. To see this, assume that you have solid information that Knaplund was just leaving a noisy video arcade when she supposedly heard your "crosswalk" statement. Unless you can produce the person who provided you with this information as a witness, cross-examining Knaplund about where she was when she heard the statement is risky. If she answers that, no, she wasn't leaving the arcade, but was standing outside the library, just ten feet from where you fell, you have no way to contradict her.

G. IF ONE OF YOUR WITNESSES IS IMPEACHED

If your adversary impeaches one of your witnesses, say with a prior inconsistent statement, talk to your witness during a recess (ask the judge for one, if necessary) or at lunch to see if she has a good explanation for the change of story. If your witness has an explanation that eliminates the negative impact of a prior inconsistent statement you can let her give it during redirect examination, which takes place immediately after cross-examination. (See Chapter 11, Direct Examination.)

For example, assume that in a case in which you are suing your employer for sexual harassment, Laura Rosas testifies for you on direct examination that she heard your employer tell you that you needed to date him if you expected a promotion. On cross-examination the employer's lawyer impeaches Rosas with a statement she previously made to an investigator from the Fair Employment Practices Department in which she said that she could not remember your employer ever asking you for a date. Talking to Rosas at the recess that immediately follows her cross-examination, you learn that the reason she made that statement was that your employer threatened to fire her if she gave any information to the investigator. By bringing out this explanation during your redirect examination of Rosas, you hope to convince the judge or jury that Rosas' testimony during direct examination is credible. Your redirect may go as follows:

 You:

Ms. Rosas, did you tell the Fair Employment Department investigator something different than you told the court today?

2 **Witness:**

Yes, I did.

3 **You:**

And why is that?

4 **Witness:**

Because the day before the investigator came to the office, our employer said that he would fire me if I said that he had done anything wrong.

5 **You:**

Then why are you willing to testify against him today?

6 **Witness:**

I'm in court and I'm going to tell the truth. If he fires me, I guess he's going to have another lawsuit on his hands.

Transcript Analysis: Note how your questions on redirect (especially Nos. 3 and 5) are open questions. Just as during direct examination, during redirect you cannot ask leading questions of your own witnesses. (See Chapter 11, Direct Examination, for a discussion of the different types of questions.)

H. PREPARING FOR CROSS-EXAMINATION

Before trial, make an outline that briefly summarizes the testimony you expect an adverse witness to give on direct examination. Then in separate sections, list additional evidence a witness can provide that supports your version of events and evidence that impeaches the witness. You may even want to write down specific questions in each section, because on cross-examination you are likely to be limiting your questions to only a few pieces of information. Finally, you may list any exhibits you plan to refer to or introduce during cross-examination, though probably you will only offer exhibits during your own testimony or direct examination of your own witnesses.

Make sure to update your trial notebook. Devote a separate section of your trial notebook to cross-examination, and make a separate Cross-examination Outline for each witness you will cross-examine. (See Chapter 17, Organizing a Trial Notebook)

Below is a form Cross-Examination Outline that you may want to use.

Cross-examination Outline

Witness:

Expected direct examination testimony:

Additional information that supports my
version of events (List specific questions):

Impeachment (List specific questions):

Exhibits that I will refer to or introduce:

ADDITIONAL RESOURCES
ON CROSS-EXAMINTAION

The Art of Cross-Examination, by Francis Wellman (Macmillan & Co.). Many lawyers regard this 1903 book as the classic cross-examination work. While some of Wellman's language is dated, the book reviews the most common bases of cross-examination and is filled with colorful examples drawn from actual cases, including Abraham Lincoln's famous "almanac" cross-examination. (Lincoln impeached a witness who claimed to have seen an incident by moonlight by producing an almanac showing that there had been no moon that night.)

Winning Strategies and Techniques for Civil Litigators, by James Lyons (ed.) (Practising Law Institute) is a briefer and more modern approach to cross-examination. One chapter of the book consists of the "10 rules of cross-examination" interestingly set forth by the late Irving Younger, a renowned speaker on trial techniques, in the form of a letter from the ancient Roman orator, Cicero; a second chapter consists of a modern lawyer's reply.

Trial Advocacy in a Nutshell, by Paul Bergman (West Publishing Co.) is an inexpensive review of trial techniques. Chapter 9 focuses on cross-examination and presents an approach for determining when you can contradict an unexpected answer.

Fundamentals of Trial Techniques, by Thomas Mauet (Little, Brown & Co.) reviews the common bases of cross-examination and provides numerous brief examples. ■

13

CLOSING ARGUMENT

Closing argument is your opportunity to tell the judge or jury why you should win. After repeatedly warning you not to argue when you deliver your opening statement, present evidence or cross-examine witnesses, we can finally say, "Go for it."

During the trial, your story is presented a piece at a time, through testimony and tangible evidence: You have some control over the evidence and the order in which it comes out, but no opportunity to tie it all together. Closing argument gives you the valuable chance to help the judge or jury fit the pieces together—and to convince them that the evidence presented at trial proves you should win.

Closing argument is also your chance to make a good last impression. But, contrary to *Perry Mason* films or scenes from *L.A. Law*, trials do not usually turn on dramatic closing arguments: Rather, most times, a case is won or lost because of the persuasiveness of the evidence presented. With that in mind, don't expect the judge or jurors to all nod their heads enthusiastically during your closing argument, and don't expect to (or feel you need to) give an award-winning performance. Just be yourself, and try to follow the guidelines below.

Don't be rude. You are allowed to "argue" during closing argument, but not in the same sense as that word is often used in private. In the courtroom context, permissible argument is telling the judge or jury how the evidence proves you should win. There are limits; don't yell, pound the table or call your opponent names. You'll get a reprimand from the judge and alienate the jury, too.

A. WHEN YOU DELIVER CLOSING ARGUMENT

Closing arguments follow the presentation of all the evidence. That means they come after both you and your adversary have put all your witnesses on the stand and conducted direct and cross-examinations. Usually the plaintiff gives closing argument first, then the defendant. The plaintiff can ask the judge to reserve (save) a small amount of time—for example, five minutes—for rebuttal argument, after the defendant's closing argument. This gives the plaintiff one last chance to try to refute the defendant's argument.

During jury trials, judges instruct jurors as to their legal responsibilities in deciding a case before closing arguments, others after closing arguments. If yours is a jury trial, whether your closing argument comes before or after the jury instructions, you may use them to prepare your argument and you may refer explicitly to the language of the instructions during your closing argument. (For more on locating jury instructions, see Chapter 22, Legal Research.)

B. PREPARE AND REHEARSE YOUR CLOSING ARGUMENT BEFORE TRIAL

In order to decide what evidence to look for when you first investigate your and your adversary's legal claims and defenses, it helps to know what facts you will eventually have to prove or disprove in court. And, to win your case, you must show the judge or jury how the evidence presented has actually proved or disproved those same facts. For this reason, some experts actually suggest you start writing the outline for your closing argument when you are in the very first stages of investigating your lawsuit. The good news is that you have already learned how to connect evidence to the legal elements you need to prove or disprove (some call this "marshaling evidence"), in Chapters 7 and 8. And if you look back to those chapters, you will see that the outlines you learned to do then are really the first drafts of your closing argument.

It is also important to rehearse the closing argument you've prepared before your trial, because you may not be allowed much time to prepare during trial. If your case is fairly complex, the judge may give you an hour or more, after you and your adversary have rested your cases, to review your closing argument. But in many cases, for example those where less than $50,000 is at stake, your whole trial may last only a couple of hours. In these cases, especially if the court has lots of other cases on its calendar, you may be asked to go forward right after the close of evidence, and the judge may push you to finish up quickly. Even if the judge is pressed for time you can likely get a five- to ten- minute recess to use the restroom. That is better than nothing; it may allow you to gather your thoughts and regain your composure.

C. HOW TO PUT TOGETHER A CLOSING ARGUMENT

To convince the judge or jury to rule in your favor, the most important thing you can do is show how the evidence supports your case. While you cannot be untruthful, you can and should emphasize those facts that are favorable to you and explain away facts that hurt you. In addition, you can say why your witnesses were believable and your opponent's were not. And finally, you can review key pieces of evidence in an organized, persuasive way that is easy to follow and leads to the conclusion that your case is a winner. If you are the plaintiff, that review will emphasize the evidence that establishes that you have met your legal burden of proof; if you are the defendant, it will show that the plaintiff has failed to meet the requisite burden.

The main headings in the outline of your closing argument will be similar to the subheadings in this part of this chapter: introductory comment about your pro per status, the legal and factual issues to be decided, evidence marshaling, the burden of proof and the result you want. You will weave into the evidence marshaling section of your argument the points you want to make about the believability of witnesses and exhibits. The core of your closing argument outline will be your list of the facts satisfying the legal elements, with the key evidence that proves or disproves them underneath each element—the same core outline you did in Chapter 7 (if you are the plaintiff) or Chapter 8 (if you are the defendant).

Pointers for effective deliveries. Section E of Chapter 10, Opening Statement, includes a variety of suggestions for effective courtroom speaking. You may want to refer to that section when preparing to deliver your closing argument.

1.   Make Introductory Comments

Some judges and jurors may respect and even be extra sympathetic towards you if you very briefly acknowledge that in representing yourself, you have tried your best and hope you have not made too many mistakes. But you probably don't want to make too big a deal about this. It could backfire if the judge or jury doesn't find you genuine or thinks you are deliberately playing on their sympathies. As an introductory remark to a judge, you may try saying something like:

Your Honor, you have heard all the evidence. You have heard about how my roof leaked so badly last winter that water fell onto the electric stove while I was cooking. As my friend, Jane Keith, testified, it was so bad that one time when she was making breakfast, a piece of the ceiling plaster fell into our omelet.

I know I am not as familiar with court procedures as my opponent, but I have tried my best. I hope I have shown you why I had to get out of that apartment and proven to you that my landlord breached his duty to keep the apartment habitable. Now, to review the key pieces of evidence.

In fact, in some simpler cases, where the whole trial lasts only an hour or two, the introductory remark may be almost enough for your entire argument, especially if you add a sentence stating how you want the judge to rule. For example:

Based on the evidence, I ask that you find that I did not breach my rental contract as the defendant contends, and that I do not owe the defendant any money for the rent since I left or any back rent for the money I withheld during those last months when the roof was leaking.

 Make closing argument to a judge shorter than to a jury. If you are arguing to a judge alone, you should prepare and deliver a much shorter closing argument than if you have a jury trial, for these reasons:

- Judges know the meaning of legal terms; you don't need to explain them.

- Judges are used to hearing testimony from witnesses, applying the law to various factual situations and following along at trials.

- Judges can stop and ask you questions if they don't understand something; jurors cannot.

If you're addressing a jury, your introductory remarks may be:

Ladies and gentlemen, I have tried to present evidence to you today showing that the negligent driving of the defendant, Ms. Adams, caused the serious and painful leg injuries that I told you about. I know I made some errors during the trial. Frankly, as a non-lawyer I have felt somewhat like a fish out of water. Unfortunately the high cost of hiring a lawyer left me no choice but to go it alone. Nonetheless....

And, if your opponent's attorney was particularly stuffy or aggressive toward you, you may find it effective to add:

Probably it's clear that I don't have years of legal experience like my opponent's highly skilled lawyer, Anna Turney.

2.   Identify the Issues to Be Resolved

You want to let the judge or jury know exactly which issues need to be determined—which questions of fact or law they must answer—in order to find for you. This is especially important in longer, more complex cases. To determine which factual and legal questions remain to be determined by the judge or jury, you have to look at three things:

- The elements of the plaintiff's claims. Remember, the plaintiff has to prove each element to win.

- Rulings the judge made during trial.

- Stipulations you made with your opponent. If you and your adversary agreed on an issue, the judge or jury doesn't need to rule on it.

Though you will want to keep it much shorter in a judge trial, narrowing the issues can be helpful to a judge or jury, since they may not remember exactly what has been cleared up. Saying what remains to be decided can help avoid confusion and prevent wasting time and energy on questions that have already been resolved.

The example below is based on the negligence case in which you are suing Sarah Adams, a building contractor, whose truck struck you as you crossed the street. In this version of the case, certain issues were resolved during trial, and you note that in your argument to the judge, as follows:

Your Honor, there are only two issues before you this afternoon: Whether Ms. Adams breached her duty to drive with due care, and whether her truck's hitting me caused my injuries. There is no question she owed me a duty; she stipulated that her truck struck me, so she owed a duty to me to use reasonable care. Also, there is no question about the amount of damages I suffered; the defendant stipulated that the doctor bills and employment records I introduced into evidence are accurate.

With a jury, you want to go into more detail:

Ladies and gentlemen, to prove the defendant was negligent and have you rule for me, I must establish all four of the legal elements of the negligence claim. Those are: one, that the defendant owed me, a pedestrian on a public street, the duty to drive carefully; two, that she breached that duty by driving carelessly; three, that her careless driving caused my injuries; and four, that I am out $100,000 because of money I had to pay for doctor bills, money I lost from being out of work, and money to compensate me for the pain I suffered from those injuries.

Element number 1 is not at issue. I was walking and she was driving on a public street, so she does not dispute that she has the duty that licensed drivers all have—to drive carefully. And element number 4, damages, has been resolved as well; the defendant stipulated that the doctor bills and work records I introduced into evidence were accurate, and that I in fact suffered a great deal of pain.

That leaves only two things for you to decide: element 2, whether or not Ms. Adams was driving carelessly and element 3, whether her truck's hitting me caused the injuries.

Starting with element number 2, did the defendant drive carelessly? Let's look at what the eyewitnesses who testified before you had to say about her driving. First, Cynthia White testified....

You can also use an exhibit to help show the judge or jury the issues to be decided. For example, if your case involves a dispute over a document like a contract, you may say:

We all admit the contract is valid, Your Honor. So this case really boils down to clause 2 [holding up the contract and pointing to the clause]. All it says is the defendant, Louis Coombs, agrees to repair my roof. You have to decide what that means. My position is that it means Mr. Coombs was required to use the quality of wood that experts, such as Ed Barr who testified in this case, say is used by other roofers in the community. But the defendant thinks he had every right to use cheap plywood, even though the roof fell in this past winter, just because this clause doesn't specify a certain type of wood....

3.   Marshal the Evidence for Each Element You Must Prove

Marshaling evidence means connecting it up to the legal element it helps to prove or disprove. The outlines you prepared in Chapters 7 and 8, which help you do this, will form the backbone of your closing argument. (You may want to skim those chapters again before reading on.) In those outlines of your legal claims (or those of your adversary), you listed facts that would be used to try to prove each element, and items of evidence that would be used to prove these facts.

Using the negligence case discussed above, here's an outline of what the plaintiff must prove:

1. **Duty:** The defendant owed me the duty to drive carefully.

2. **Breach of duty:** She breached that duty by driving carelessly.

3. **Causation:** Her careless driving caused my injuries.

4. **Damages:** I am out $100,000 because of those injuries.

Element 1:

The defendant owed me a duty to drive carefully.

Fact to prove Element 1:

Defendant is a licensed driver, driving down a public street. That creates a duty to me, as a pedestrian in the vicinity, to drive carefully.

Element 2:

Defendant breached that duty by driving carelessly.

Facts to prove Element 2:

• Defendant was looking down at her car phone instead of at the road, and she was distracted by the call.

Evidence to prove this fact:

• Cynthia White's testimony that defendant was holding a car phone receiver to her ear and looking down, instead of paying attention to the road.

• Defendant's car phone records showing a call around the time of the accident.

Element 3:

Her careless driving caused my injuries.

Facts to prove Element 3:

• I was injured when her truck hit me.

• If she'd been paying attention, she wouldn't have hit me.

<u>Evidence to prove these facts:</u>
- Doctor's bills and my own testimony
- Cynthia White's testimony

<u>Element 4:</u>

<u>I am out $100,000 because of those injuries.</u>

<u>Facts to prove Element 4:</u>
- I paid $50,000 to doctors, lost $15,000 for four months of work, and suffered great pain.

<u>Evidence to prove these facts:</u>
- Doctor's bills
- Employment records
- My testimony about pain and suffering

When preparing your closing argument outline, select the key evidence that supports your claims and the key evidence that refutes your opponent's claims, and tell the judge or jury explicitly how the evidence proves or disproves those claims.

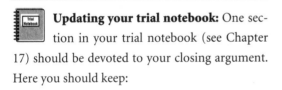 **Updating your trial notebook:** One section in your trial notebook (see Chapter 17) should be devoted to your closing argument. Here you should keep:

- an outline of your intended closing argument

- blank paper for notes, and

- exact quotes—for example, explicit language from jury instructions.

---

4. Discuss Credibility

When weighing evidence, the judge or jury evaluates its credibility. As you know, one thing you tried to show in direct examination was why your witnesses were believable, and one of your main cross-examination goals was to attack the credibility of your adversary's witnesses. But in those earlier phases of trial, all you could do was bring out the evidence that supported or attacked the witnesses' credibility. You cannot, until closing argument, specifically tell the judge or jury why particular evidence should be discredited (because the witness was biased) or bolstered (because the witness was reliable). This type of information is an important ingredient to give the judge or jury as they move into final evaluations of evidence before making a decision.

One reason for a witness appearing less or more credible to the judge or jury is a personal connection, or lack of one, to the parties. (See Chapter 12, Cross-Examination.) For example, your not knowing the eyewitness to your car accident before it occurred may make the witness believable; why lie for you if the witness didn't even know you? But if your opponent's chief eyewitness is his mother, the judge or jury may be more skeptical and conclude that she is biased in your adversary's favor.

There can be more than one reason why testimony is not credible. You will want to bring out these facts explicitly in closing argument. For example:

Your Honor, the witness, Ms. Speevack, said there were never any roaches in the defendant's apartments and that the roof had never leaked in the 20 years Mr. Shelley (the defendant) owned the property. But, Your Honor, let's remember that Ms. Speevack is Mr. Shelley's mother, and she quite understandably may see things in his favor.

What's more, she doesn't live in the building. And while she may have come around often to visit her son, she admitted on cross-examination that she did not conduct regular inspections of the apartments or talk to the tenants. As I testified, I don't ever remember her coming into my apartment....

People also lose credibility when they make statements that are inconsistent. Once you have brought out the inconsistencies during trial, you can use them in closing argument. Here's an example:

Ladies and gentlemen, Cynthia White said this morning that she could see the defendant's truck perfectly clearly, that traffic was light and nothing was in front of her, and that she saw exactly what happened. But during a deposition that took place only three months after the accident, Ms. White said, under penalty of perjury, that there was a bus in front of her in the left turn lane at the time of the accident. Now this accident did occur some three years ago. Clearly, memories fade, and Ms. White seems to have forgotten about a bus that she herself had said was right in front of her at the time. How faded are the other details that she now claims to remember perfectly?

Notice, in the previous example, you didn't accuse White of lying but of simply forgetting. That is often a better tactic than accusing people of lying on the witness stand (which amounts to perjury, punishable as a crime). Judges and juries are reluctant to assume a witnesses is deliberately lying. By calling a witness a liar in your closing argument, you risk that the judge or jury will discount your version of what happened altogether rather than believe that an otherwise sympathetic person lied. But it isn't difficult to believe a witness forgot or made a mistake, especially if the events the witness described happened a long time before. Forgetting is not a crime.

Every day we use our perceptions, experiences and even prejudices to decide whether or not we find someone believable. Obviously our prejudices are as different as we are. Nevertheless, it makes sense to try to put yourself in the position of judge or jury and try to determine which witness may seem the most credible. For example, a person who wears a business suit and speaks in an articulate way may appear more believable to certain judges or jurors than someone wearing sweat pants and a T-shirt who mumbles. Or, for instance, since some people don't believe anything used car salesmen say, if your key witness sells used cars for a living, you might try to bolster his credibility in your closing argument by saying:

Ladies and gentlemen, you may have heard people say that no one is as untrustworthy as a used car salesman. But remember, that is a stereotype, and in the case of Mr. Reback, a totally false stereotype. As you heard, Mr. Reback is just working at the car dealer to put himself through school. He has finished three years and has only one to go to complete a degree in chemical engineering. He doesn't have a relationship with either myself or the plaintiff; he stands to gain nothing from this case. He, like Cynthia White, just happened to be at the corner of Elm and Main when the accident occurred. Mr. Reback told you he saw the plaintiff run out from between two parked cars, not in the crosswalk as Ms. White testified....

You want to integrate points about a witness's credibility into your closing argument outline. The easiest way to do this is to put the point in right where you talk about that person's testimony. For instance, if you are the defendant, part of your outline might look like the one shown below:

Element 2:

Breach of duty to drive carefully

Fact Plaintiff will try to prove:

I was careless.

Evidence to disprove this fact:

Testimony of Mr. Reback

- Eyewitness.
- Testified he saw me driving carefully and
  not speeding.
- Saw plaintiff run out between from parked
  cars; Noticed Plaintiff NOT in crosswalk.

Reback is credible:

- "Used car salesman" is bad stereotype.
- Reback is in college; car sales is just part-
  time job, not career.
- nothing to gain from lying….

My testimony

Under penalty of perjury I said:

- I was careful.
- not distracted.
- I'm used to car phone calls….

5. Explain the Burden of Proof

Normally, the plaintiff has to prove each legal element of a claim by a measure lawyers call a "preponderance of the evidence." In other words, as the plaintiff you do not have to prove the evidence beyond a reasonable doubt (as does the prosecutor in a criminal trial), but just by something more than 50 percent.

Judges know these terms, so you don't need to explain them during a judge trial, though you may want to mention the burden of proof. For example, you might say simply:

Your Honor, I recognize that I have the burden of proof in this case. But given all the evidence I have put forward, as to each of the legal elements of negligence, it seems I have clearly met that burden….

To explain what this means to a jury or visualize it yourself, you may use the "scales of justice" metaphor. As the plaintiff, you can point out that if each side's evidence were piled on a scale, and the evidence tilts even a fraction of a feather weight toward you, then you have satisfied your burden. To make your explanation clear, you may want to hold your two hands in front of you as if each hand were one side of the scale and drop one hand ever so slightly lower.

Another way to explain the burden of proof to juries is to analogize it to a football field. If you are the plaintiff, you say:

Imagine I'm on a football field, ladies and gentlemen. Preponderance of the evidence does not mean I have to score a touchdown. I only have to make it past the 50-yard line.

You can never be certain if an explanation will go over well, but be cautious about images you think are universal. Some of your jurors may not know much about sports, for example, so if you use the football analogy, you may want to use the scale analogy, too. In one recent case, an attorney was reprimanded for using an analogy to batting averages while cross-examining a witness because the judge didn't know or like much about baseball.

If you are the defendant, emphasize that the plaintiff has the burden of proof—that it's not up to you to prove what did not happen, but up to the plaintiff to prove what did. Focus on the legal elements where the plaintiff was weakest, pointing out how he failed to prove them. Also, just as the plaintiff defines the legal term preponderance of the evidence for the jury, so too should you. But, in your comments, you will stress that if the jury does not believe there is more weight on the plaintiff's side of the scale—that is, if they feel the evidence weighs equally for both sides—they must find in your favor. For example:

Ladies and gentlemen, as the judge will instruct you, the plaintiff has to prove four things: one, that I owed a legal duty to him to drive with reasonable care; two, that I breached that duty by driving carelessly; three, that my careless driving caused his injuries; and finally four, that he was damaged because of those injuries. Number one, I admitted. That is an agreement we all make when we get our very first driver's licenses. And I do not dispute that the plaintiff's doctor bills show he was treated for injuries and spent the money he claims he spent.

But ladies and gentlemen, that is only two elements out of four. The plaintiff has failed to prove number two that I was driving carelessly, or number three that his injuries were caused by my truck hitting him. He has not proven them at all, let alone by a preponderance of the evidence, as he must in order for you to find for him.

The plaintiff told you that what the preponderance standard means. He said that meant if you weighed the evidence and the scale tipped in his favor, he would win. But if you believe that he has not proven any one of the elements—and I will point out the severe weaknesses in his evidence as to my driving and as to what actually caused his injury—then you must find in my favor. Also, the scales must tip. If after hearing all the evidence, you are not sure, you think that the evidence for both sides is more or less equal, then the plaintiff has failed to meet his legal burden of proof and you must find for me.

Now let's look at the evidence more closely….

After going through and showing why his evidence was weak and yours strong for each of the elements you dispute, you may conclude by saying:

At this point you may have some doubts. Part of you may think that the evidence shows I was careless, that Cynthia White is accurate when she says I was speeding. And part of you may believe I was driving fine and that the plaintiff caused the accident by running out in the middle of the street, as I and Mr. Reback testified. You also may not be sure what really caused plaintiff's injuries, the accident or a pre-existing condition.

It's human to have some doubts. We all do. Nevertheless, the law still makes your decision clear, ladies and gentlemen. As the judge will instruct you, the plaintiff must prove all these things to you by a preponderance of the evidence. That means you must be more than 50% sure. The plaintiff told you this means he doesn't have to score a touchdown. Well, he is right. But he does have to get past the 50-yard line— and he's already gotten tackled by a few big players. I mean there are a lot of holes in his evidence. The most important one is that he did not prove that I was careless. As the plaintiff, he bears the burden of proving each element of his case to you. And if you are not more than 50% sure that he's proven all four, you must find that I am not responsible for his $50,000 in doctor bills or other damages he has claimed.

6. Use Exhibits and Other Visual Aids

Visualizing the facts you or your adversary have put into evidence can help make your version of the story clearer for the judge or jury. For example, assume that you're the plaintiff in the negligence case mentioned earlier. During your direct examination of Cynthia White, you had her make a diagram of the accident scene at Elm and Main, where Ms. Adams's truck hit you. She marked the places where you, the truck, the parked cars and the children playing on the street were located. You introduced the marked diagram into evidence. (See Chapter 14, Exhibits.) It may be very helpful and effective for you to hold White's drawing up for the judge or jury when you are reviewing her testimony. For example, you may say:

Ladies and gentlemen, you may recall that when Cynthia White testified, she marked on this map [holding it up] *where all the key players in the accident were located.* [Pointing as you talk] *Here I was, here's where the defendant was and here— where these children were playing. You can see how easily the defendant might have been distracted by watching these children instead of the road....*

Visual aids can help your argument, but there are some potential negatives in using them. You may feel clumsy carrying a bulky chart into court (you are already carrying a trial notebook); you may not be a great artist and might be concerned that your chart looks sloppy; you may not know where to set up your prop so that it can be clearly seen.

Judges may exclude visual aids they find misleading, if they were not admitted into evidence during trial. For example, a map of Elm and Main streets that your witness marked during trial is fine and likely helpful. But a judge may exclude a diagram, not introduced in evidence during the trial, that you drew up the night before your closing argument, especially if the judge feels your drawing misrepresents the evidence. Or the judge may view your diagram as an attempt on your part to introduce new evidence, which you cannot do in your closing argument. You can argue only from what is already in the record. (See Section D, below.)

To decide whether to use a visual aid, think about what aspects of your case it will help explain and whether you can adequately explain them in words. For instance, to explain the legal concept of "preponderance of the evidence," you may do better orally explaining the analogy rather than drawing a football field with the yard lines clearly marked. The cons (bulky, judge may not allow it) may outweigh the pros (clear image of how much evidence it takes to meet the burden). But if your visual aid relates to specific factual evidence in your case and will help the judge or jury clarify a key point, it may help make your argument more concrete and believable.

7. Tell the Judge or Jury What You Want

One good way to finish your closing argument is by asking for an explicit result in the case. Even though some people feel awkward asking for money, it is important to let the judge or jury know exactly what you want them to decide. Otherwise, they might not know what to do. Here's an example:

Your Honor, you have heard all the evidence showing how flimsy the wood was that the defendant used to repair my roof. My family and I were terrified the night the roof caved in. It cost $10,000 to repair the structural damage to my home that was caused by the collapse. And I spent $20,000 more than I bargained for in the original contract just to get a solid roof over our heads—not to mention the countless hours it took to clean up the mess. Your Honor, please find that the defendant breached the contract by using the cheap plywood and order that he pay me the $30,000 I lost.

D. WHAT NOT TO DO IN CLOSING ARGUMENT

Now that you know what to include in your closing argument, here are some things to avoid.

1. Do Not State Your Opinion

The basic principle is that you must argue from the evidence and show why it is or is not convincing. You must not interject what you believe unless you have presented some proof of the facts behind that belief to the judge or jury. For example, *do not* say:

Ms. Adams claims that the call she got on her car phone before she hit me was not important. But look at her, she is shifty-eyed, and I just know she's a liar.

You should use facts that came out in trial that bolster a witness's credibility, but it is not appropriate to add your opinion about that witness's honesty or other good qualities. It doesn't matter to the judge that you like and trust your witnesses. *Don't say* something like:

I trust Ira; I've know him for years. If he says he saw me cross the street in the crosswalk, then that's exactly what happened.

And don't put your own credibility on the line except as to particular facts you testified about during the trial. To illustrate, you can say:

As I testified, I have been a building contractor in this community for 25 years. I value my reputation, and if I thought I was responsible for the plaintiff's roof falling in, I would have repaired it immediately. But that is not what caused the damage to his roof. As you heard from the inspector, the plaintiff let the large oak tree grow too close to the power lines, and during the storm....

But avoid saying something like:

I'm an honest man; I wouldn't have brought this to trial if I didn't think I had a good case.

"...but I digress."

2. Don't Argue from Evidence Unless It Was Presented at Trial

A key rule in making your closing argument is: Don't talk about evidence, even if it will help you win, unless it is in the trial record —either testified to orally or in a document that was admitted into evidence. This is not the time to sneak in something you forgot to cover during the trial.

Take good notes during trial. It can be difficult to remember exactly what was said during your trial. So pay close attention and try these techniques.

- Keep your trial notebook open, and check off issues on your outline that your adversary stipulates to (admits).

- Note bits of testimony that strike you as particularly helpful or damaging to your case. You can use them to support your case or try to explain them away, as necessary, during closing argument.

- Have a friend or relative come with you and take notes too, in case you miss something. Although you could order a transcript of the trial record from the court reporter, it will be quite expensive and probably can't be done quickly enough for you to use in your closing argument.

While you must not misstate facts or argue what is not in the record, you can rely on logical inferences to show the judge or jury how particular evidence relates to the elements you must prove to support your legal claims. For example, assume you are the plaintiff in the car accident case and evidence was

introduced that Ms. Adams got a call moments before she hit you. You can properly argue:

Ms. Adams got a call on her car phone moments before she hit me. She was talking to someone in her office about the fact that her company messed up. They missed an important inspection. She said the job was an important one, potentially worth a lot of money. I ask you, is it possible that Ms. Adams's attention was not on the road, but on the call she got when she hit me? People who have just received important news, especially news that is likely to cost them a lot of money, are often distracted, even upset by such news. When someone is distracted, she has a harder time concentrating on traffic....

Notice that while no evidence was presented that Adams was distracted, you are able to ask the judge or jury to draw the inference, based on their common knowledge, that people who receive important phone calls are involved in their conversations and less attentive to the road. Making such inferences is perfectly acceptable during closing argument, and important to make to help the judge or jury interpret the evidence in a way that is favorable to you.

E. REBUTTAL ARGUMENT

If you are the plaintiff, and you decide to reserve a portion of your closing argument for rebuttal argument, your rebuttal should briefly state why particular things the defendant said in closing argument were wrong or misleading; you should not rehash things you already said or make brand new points. If you do, your opponent may object, and the judge may rule them outside the scope of rebuttal.

F. OBJECTIONS DURING CLOSING

Either you or your adversary can object during the other's closing argument. If you do not follow the rules—for example, you argue facts that are not part of the record—your adversary may well object. Also, a more experienced opponent may try to use technical objections to throw you off balance. Even though it might look bad for a lawyer to bully a pro per, some do. If you get an objection to some point in your closing argument, think through what is being said, remain calm and stick up for yourself if you think the objection is wrong. (See Chapter 16, Making and Responding to Objections.) Or try rephrasing your statement. Here are two examples of how to handle an objection:

EXAMPLE 1

Plaintiff:

Therefore, Your Honor, since Ms. Adams admitted she got an important call on the car phone moments before she hit me….

Defendant:

Objection, Your Honor. There is no evidence in the record that the call was important.

Plaintiff:

Your Honor, may I rephrase my statement?

Judge:

You may.

Plaintiff:

Since Ms. Adams admitted that moments before she hit me she got a call on the car phone reporting a missed inspection….

EXAMPLE 2

Plaintiff:

Therefore, Your Honor, since Ms. Adams admitted she got an important call on the car phone moments before she hit me….

Defendant:

Objection, Your Honor. There is no evidence in the record that the call was important.

Judge:

Plaintiff?

Plaintiff:

There certainly is, Your Honor. The defendant made that statement in this courtroom last Tuesday when I was cross-examining her.

Judge:

Overruled. You may proceed.

Should you object to your opponent's argument? Object only if you really feel strongly that your adversary is misstating evidence or arguing about evidence that was not presented at trial, and that the argument is prejudicing your case. (See Chapter 16, Making and Responding to Objections.) It can be self-defeating to object at this stage, because judges often allow people a lot of leeway when making closing arguments.

G. SAMPLE CLOSING ARGUMENT AND OUTLINE

Now that you've gotten a sense of the various key parts of closing argument, let's take one all the way through. Below is a sample argument in a jury trial of the traffic accident case in which you have sued Sarah Adams for negligence. You were hit by Adams' truck as you crossed the street. Following that is a short analysis and sample outline of the argument. You will likely want to write out your intended argument in full (to the extent you can) before trial so that you can practice it and perhaps show it your legal coach. Then, you can summarize it in outline form to use during your actual argument.

1 *Good afternoon. The evidence has come to a close and the task of deciding whose story you believe is in your hands, ladies and gentlemen. I have presented my evidence as well as I could —despite the fact that I am clearly not at home in the courtroom like my talented opponent.*

2 *You have heard lots of facts today, and you are very familiar now with what happened to me. As the judge instructed you, there are four legal elements I must show in order to prove that Ms. Adams was negligent. First, that she owed a duty to me as a pedestrian on a public street to drive attentively and follow the rules of the road. Second, that she breached her duty by driving carelessly. Third, that my injuries were caused by her truck hitting me. And last, that I lost $15,000 because of work I had to miss; I paid $50,000 in doctor bills; and it is fair to award me $35,000 to compensate me for the terrible pain I suffered as a result of her carelessness.*

3 *Let's take a look back to some of the key testimony that proves each of those four elements. First off, the judge instructed you that Ms. Adams had a duty to me to drive with due*

and reasonable care. She admits this, so the first element is proven.

4 *Second, I must show that the defendant breached her duty of care to me by driving carelessly. This has also been proven. The evidence shows that the defendant was not driving safely. She let her mind and eyes wander, ladies and gentlemen, because she was distracted. What distracted her? A business call on her car phone, which the telephone bills you saw show happened just moments before she slammed into me. A business call that, as she herself told you, reported a missed inspection on a big job. Now, the defendant told you this did not distract her at all, that inspections are missed all the time. But she may be forgetting exactly how much money was at stake in this job. Her own business records show it was a ten million dollar deal. She told you that the missed inspection could have caused delays both on this job and other ones. Ms. Adams is an entrepreneur who owns her own business. She is the one who is financially responsible if jobs are missed. And how many delays can occur before her reputation and business suffer? Isn't it likely that this phone call upset her and caused her to drive carelessly?*

5 *You also heard from Cynthia White. She told you she was waiting for a bus at the Elm Street stop. She saw the whole thing. Ms. White is a school teacher. She didn't know me or the defendant. She has no reason to be anything less than truthful with you. And she had a perfect view of the whole scene from the bus stop. Yes she told the defendant at her deposition that a bus was in front of her in the left turn lane, but she also told you she could see* *the crosswalk fine since it was off to the side of where she was. She told you that I was in the crosswalk when the defendant hit me, and that she watched the defendant sit in her truck and wait for the police. After hitting me, she didn't even check to see that I was all right. Ms. White's testimony proves that I was in the crosswalk, and that the defendant was negligent for not stopping for me.*

6 *I have also proven elements 3 and 4. The defendant's truck hitting me caused my injuries, and I have suffered a great deal—in physical pain, money, and lost wages. As I testified, when I saw her truck coming at me, I tried to get out of the way. But she hit me. I felt my leg snap as I fell to the ground. Dr. Duncan testified he treated me that day for a broken leg. It took four months to heal, though as Dr. Duncan testified, my limp may never go away. During those months, I was in constant and excruciating pain. I had difficulty sleeping, and as I testified, I couldn't do even the most basic of household chores like taking out the trash. I spent most of my time in bed and seeing doctors. I showed you the doctor bills.*

7 *Now, the judge has given you some important instructions on how you should weigh the evidence you've heard. She said I must prove my case to you by a preponderance of the evidence. Let me tell you what that means. It does not mean I must prove my case beyond a reasonable doubt. That is only in criminal trials, like what you may have seen in the movies. A preponderance of the evidence only means that if you imagine weighing the evidence on a scale and my side weighs a tiny bit more than the defendant's, then I have met my*

burden. That is all it takes. You don't have to be absolutely certain.

8 *It is up to you, now. Deliberate fairly and honestly. Make the right decision, and hold the defendant responsible for the accident she caused. Please have her pay me back for the $50,000 I had to pay in doctor bills, the $15,000 I lost being out of work, and the $35,000 I have requested to compensate me for the painful injuries she caused me to suffer. Thank you.*

Transcript Analysis: This closing argument begins with some simple introductory comments, then moves right into the legal elements (No. 2). Noting that the jury is familiar with the evidence, you appropriately suggest that this closing argument will not simply rehash the evidence. Next, you are up front that you have to prove all four legal elements, and begin immediately to show how you have done so. You first set out the elements (No. 2), then go back and connect the evidence to each one (Nos. 3, 4, 5 and 6).

If this argument had been to a judge alone, you would have done well to skip No. 2 and go right into the next sections. (You would also skip No. 7, of course.) Before a judge, make your arguments short, cut out as much as possible your explanations of the law, and hit only the key facts that prove each element.

Beginning in No. 3, you go element by element, emphasizing the key evidence that proves each.

In No. 4, you say that the defendant "let her mind and eyes wander." Evidence was presented that her eyes wandered (White saw her on the car phone, looking down), but you really don't know where her mind was; only the defendant knows that. But it is proper to ask the jury to make an inference that because she was engaged in an important phone call, she was thinking about business rather than the road. The jurors, after all, are free to disagree.

Next comes some rebuttal of the defendant's testimony. Without saying she is a liar, you suggest that she may simply not remember the amount of money involved, and how upset or distracted she really was.

Then, White's key testimony is summarized, along with some facts that bolster her credibility, such as her being a teacher and not knowing either party before the accident. You explain away the apparent contradiction in statements about her view being unobstructed, and add that the defendant did not even come to see how you were, perhaps to make her look cold or insensitive.

Next (No. 6), you hit the elements of causation (leg snapped when truck hit you) and damages (the doctor bills and pain and suffering). And last, you discuss the burden of proof, stressing that the jury doesn't need to be absolutely certain, and asks for a specific result.

Here is one possible way you would make an outline for the sample closing argument above. As you read it, note how much of it could have been done before trial. There of course will be evidence you first learn about during trial, points your adversary emphasized that you want to try to contradict or explain away, and other odds and ends you need to fill in during or just after the evidence has been presented. For that reason, it's a good idea to leave some room in your outline to add such items in.

I. Introduction

- Evidence finished. Decision in your hands
- I tried but I'm not at home in the courtroom
- You know what happened

II. Legal Elements

I must prove all 4

(Introduce 1st, then repeat w/evidence)

1. Defendant (D) has duty to follow rules of road, drive carefully
2. She breached duty by driving carelessly
3. My injuries were caused by her truck hitting me
4. I was damaged (money on doctors, lost wages, pain and suffering) as a result of her carelessness

(Evidence clearly proves each element)

1. Duty:
   - Public street. D has Driver's license. D has duty to be careful
2. Defendant was not driving safely; breached duty of care
   - mind and eyes wandered
   - she was distracted by call on her car phone
   - call moments before hit (telephone bills)
   - big job/ missed inspection (defendant admitted)
   - said missed inspections are common—not believable. This was big job, lots of money at stake
   - D owns business; she's responsible, might hurt her reputation and business

Cynthia White testimony
- White is credible—teacher, didn't know us
- White waiting for bus; saw whole thing
- Perfect view of scene—Yes, she said in depo that her view was blocked—but she meant her view of the street. Bus was in front, accident to side. So her view of the accident was clear
- She saw me in cross walk when defendant hit me
- She watched defendant sit in cab of truck, wait for police, didn't even check if I was okay

3. Causation
- Her truck hit me
- When I saw her truck, I tried to get out of way, but couldn't
- Leg broke on impact; I felt it

4. Damages
- Pain, suffering, 4 months to heal
- You saw doctor bills at trial
- Lost work wages

III. Jury Instructions/Burden of proof

Judge said I must prove case by "preponderance of the evidence"
- That does not mean beyond a reasonable doubt like criminal cases

- Scales—tiny bit more on my side, I meet burden
- "You don't have to be absolutely certain."

IV. Results

- Up to you, now
"Hold the defendant responsible for the accident she caused"
- Make her pay $ 50,000 (doctor bills and costs), $ 35,000 (pain and suffering), $ 15,000 (lost work)

V. Thank you

RESOURCES ON CLOSING ARGUMENT

Trial Advocacy in a Nutshell, by Paul Bergman (2nd Ed., West Publishing Co.), an easy-to-read, helpful and inexpensive paperback about effective and persuasive trial techniques. Chapter 10 covers closing arguments.

The Trial Process: Law Tactics and Ethics, by J. Alexander Tanford (The Michie Co.), a textbook on trial practice which includes excerpts from many other leading books and dialogues of trial scenarios.

Art of Advocacy, by Lawrence J. Smith (Matthew Bender) includes an extensive separate volume filled with examples of actual closing arguments, titled *Summation.* ■

14

EXHIBITS

Exhibits are the tangible objects that you present to a judge or jury during trial to help establish your case. Typical exhibits include documents such as letters, contracts and receipts. Reports, such as those a child psychologist or a radiologist may prepare when testifying as an expert witness, are also exhibits. So too are photographs, X-rays and all other physical objects. For example, if you sue someone for injuries you received as a result of being struck by a badly-thrown boomerang, the boomerang can be an exhibit.

Under most circumstances you are under no legal obligation to offer exhibits into evidence. You can present your entire case through oral testimony from you and your witnesses. But you can dramatically add to the persuasiveness of your case in at least three ways by backing up testimony with exhibits:

- Just like the "show" part of "show and tell" in the first grade, tangible objects make your story more real and interesting.

- Exhibits have a longer shelf life than oral testimony. When it comes time to deliberate and arrive at a verdict, a judge or jury may forget oral testimony. But usually they have the opportunity to hold and examine an exhibit.

- A little like shy first graders, you and your witnesses may testify more confidently—and therefore more credibly—when holding and talking about tangible objects.

For an exhibit to officially become evidence that the judge or jury can consider when deciding your case, you must present it to the judge and demonstrate that it is authentic and trustworthy. You do this by offering (through your own testimony or that of your witnesses) what lawyers refer to as "foundational testimony." If the judge decides that your foundational testimony meets evidence rule requirements, the judge will formally admit the exhibit into evidence. This chapter describes and illustrates the process for handling exhibits during trial, and shows you how to elicit the necessary foundational testimony for many common types of exhibits.

A. ADMITTING EXHIBITS INTO EVIDENCE: AN OVERVIEW

The type of foundational evidence you need to offer to admit an exhibit into evidence varies greatly from one exhibit to another. Fortunately, the procedural steps are almost always the same. Here is an overview of those steps; you will read about each in more detail below.

Step 1: Mark your exhibit for identification and allow opposing counsel (or your adversary, if neither of you is represented by counsel) to examine it. (See Section B below.)

Step 2: Identify (authenticate) your exhibit by asking the judge for permission to approach the witness, handing the exhibit to the witness and asking the witness to state what the exhibit is. (In some courts your judge may ask you to hand the exhibit to the bailiff, who will then pass it along to the witness.) (See Section C below.)

Step 3: Personally testify to or elicit from a witness any legally required foundational evidence. (See Section D below.)

Step 4: Ask the judge to admit the exhibit into evidence.

💡 **You can offer exhibits into evidence during cross-examination.** While you will probably offer exhibits into evidence through your own testimony or that of your witnesses during direct examination, you can also offer an exhibit during cross-examination of an adverse witness. Apart from perhaps receiving more grudging responses to your questions, the process is identical.

As an alternative to this four-step process for admitting exhibits into evidence, ask your adversary before trial to stipulate (agree) to the admissibility of your exhibits. Stipulations to the admissibility of exhibits are common. Especially when the admissibility of exhibits is clear, attorneys (and pro pers) often stipulate to the admissibility of each other's exhibits.

If you and your adversary do reach a stipulation, put it in writing and sign it to prevent your adversary from suddenly denying the stipulation at trial, leaving you with no way to produce foundational evidence. A sample stipulation is shown below.

SAMPLE STIPULATION

STIPULATION

Plaintiff Jean Nolo and Defendant Sherry Mason hereby stipulate that the lease agreement dated March 12 and signed by each of them, consisting of three pages, may be admitted into ev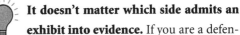idence in Nolo v. Mason, Superior Court

No. 11359.

Jean Nolo   Date: March 1, year

Jean Nolo, Plaintiff in Pro Per

Aaron Samuels   Date: March 1, year

Aaron Samuels
Attorney for Defendant

💡 **It doesn't matter which side admits an exhibit into evidence.** If you are a defendant, you may find that by the time it is your turn to present evidence the plaintiff has already offered an exhibit into evidence that you planned to offer. For example, if you are the tenant in a landlord-tenant case, the landlord may offer the lease and some canceled checks into evidence, two exhibits that you planned to offer. This won't affect your planned testimony.

Whether you or an adversary offers an exhibit into evidence, you may testify about the exhibit yourself, hand it to your witnesses and ask them questions about it, and make the same arguments about it that you would have made had you offered the exhibit into evidence. Perhaps you can even thank your adversary for offering the exhibit into evidence: it saves you the trouble of offering foundational testimony.

Then, either in a brief pre-trial conference or when you or your witness is about to refer to the exhibit, inform the judge that you've reached a stipulation as to its admissibility. In the example above, you would say something like, "Your Honor, the defendant and I stipulate that the lease agreement of March 12, signed by me and Ms. Mason and consisting of three pages, may be admitted into evidence." The judge will almost certainly grant your request, because it saves court time.

B. STEP 1: MARK YOUR EXHIBITS AND SHOW THEM TO YOUR ADVERSARY

Marking an exhibit for identification consists of tagging an exhibit with a number or letter, to distinguish it from others. You do not have to be testifying under oath when you mark an exhibit, so you can mark an exhibit either while you are presenting evidence yourself or while you are questioning a witness.

Traditionally, plaintiffs' exhibits are numbered, and defendants' exhibits are lettered. But like the former practice of attaching only feminine names to hurricanes, this traditional system has been dropped by many courts. Read your local court rules or check with the court clerk in advance to find out what marking procedure your judge likes to follow.

In some courts, the court clerk does the actual marking of exhibits. Or the clerk may ask you to mark all your exhibits before trial starts. But usually, you'll mark an exhibit for identification and let your adversary examine it the very first time

you or a witness refer to it. For instance, assume that you are the plaintiff in a breach of contract case. You have testified to the oral discussions leading up to the contract, and you now want to offer the contract itself into evidence. Before you do, you must get it marked for identification like this:

"Your Honor, I have here a two-page document. It is headed 'Agreement,' and dated December 8 of last year. I am showing it to defense counsel. May it be marked Plaintiff's Exhibit No. 1 for identification?"

 Keep calm as you move about the courtroom during the marking process. Going through the marking process while you are testifying personally can be something of a logistical challenge. You may have to move back and forth between the witness box, the clerk's desk, your adversary at counsel table and your file folder containing the exhibit. Do not panic; with the judge's guidance you will probably glide about the courtroom with the grace of Fred Astaire or Ginger Rogers.

When the judge gives you permission to mark the exhibit, you may write "Exh. 1" on the agreement itself with a pen. If an exhibit cannot be easily marked with a pen (for example, your exhibit is a boomerang or a hat), most court clerks provide small, gummed labels that you can attach to an exhibit and then mark. When you mark an exhibit, say no more than is necessary to identify it. For example, the statement above about the contract refers to objective characteristics of the exhibit: how many pages it consists of and its title and date. Do not try to gild the lily by turning the marking process into an argument. Never say anything like, "Your Honor, I want to mark this contract that proves that the defendant owes me $25,000."

Once an exhibit has been marked for identification, keep the record clear by mentioning its assigned number or letter whenever you talk about it in court. For example, when testifying on direct examination you might say, "The first time I saw the lease, Exhibit 1, was when…."

💡 **Make extra copies of written exhibits.** When you mark an exhibit before showing it to a witness, hand extra copies that you have made before trial to opposing counsel and the judge. This speeds up the foundational process, because a single piece of paper does not have to pass through four different pairs of hands. More importantly, you may impress the judge with the care you have put into your case, and the judge may give you the benefit of the doubt if a ruling on the admissibility of an exhibit could legitimately go either way.

C. STEP 2: IDENTIFY (AUTHENTICATE) YOUR EXHIBITS

The next step is for you or a witness to identify (authenticate) an exhibit. Do this by offering brief testimony that tells the judge what the exhibit is and shows its connection to the case.

By way of illustration, assume again that you are the plaintiff in a breach of contract case and that you have just finished marking the contract for identification as "Exhibit 1." You are now testifying. Hold the exhibit and identify it as follows: "Exhibit 1 is the contract that the defendant and I signed on December 8 of last year." This testimony identifies the exhibit as the actual document that you and the defendant signed.

You can often add impact to authentication testimony by referring to the basis of your identification. With the contract, for example, you (or your witness, of course) could testify that, "I know that Exhibit 1 is the contract I signed because when I signed it I noticed that the upper right-hand corner of the top page was torn, as you can see here."

YOU DON'T ALWAYS NEED THE REAL THING

If you don't know the whereabouts of the actual physical object involved in your case, consider substituting a "look-alike." When (as is often true) the precise appearance of the actual object is not significant, you can use a substitute that is similar in appearance if you make sure that everyone understands it is a substitute. (If however, the exhibit is a document, you may be required to produce the original or explain why you can't. See Section F, below.)

For example, assume that you are suing a defendant for carelessly throwing a boomerang in a shopping mall and striking you with it. You do not have the actual boomerang that struck you, but want to use an exhibit to add impact to your testimony. You know what the boomerang looked like and have gotten another one that is in all important respects identical to the one that struck you. To offer the substitute into evidence, simply identify it as "a boomerang that looks just like the one that hit me."

D. STEP 3: LAY A FOUNDATION

Once an exhibit is marked and identified, the judge can consider whether to admit it into evidence. Often, however, simply identifying an exhibit is not sufficient to admit it into evidence. In addition, you have to elicit testimony called "foundational evidence" that demonstrates that an exhibit meets evidence rules requirements. Not surprisingly, the process of eliciting this evidence is called "laying a foundation."

To complicate this task, foundational requirements are different for different types of exhibits. For example, the foundation needed to admit a business receipt is very different from the foundation needed to admit a photograph. And the foundation needed to admit a hospital record is different from either of them.

We do not have space in this book to describe the necessary foundation for every possible type of exhibit you may want to offer into evidence. We do, however, illustrate how to lay a foundation for many common types of exhibits. If we do not cover the type of exhibit you want to offer, consult one of the books listed at the end of this section for help.

 Consider other rules of evidence before deciding that an exhibit is admissible. Even if you lay a perfect foundation for an exhibit, other rules of evidence may bar the exhibit from being admitted into evidence. For example, you may provide foundational testimony for a letter, yet see the letter excluded because its contents are either irrelevant or inadmissible hearsay. Carefully study both this chapter and Chapter 15, Basic Rules of Evidence, before deciding that an exhibit is admissible.

---

1. When Identification Is Enough for Admissibility

Sometimes the testimony that identifies an exhibit also provides all the foundational evidence you need for the judge to admit it into evidence. Gen-erally, identification evidence alone is a sufficient foundation when an exhibit is a physical object rather than a document, and you or a witness can identify it on the basis of your personal knowledge.

For example, assume again that you are testifying about how you came to be struck by the carelessly thrown boomerang. After you were hit, you picked up the boomerang and ran after the defendant. He got away, but his hat with his name in it fell off and you picked it up. To illustrate and add impact to your oral testimony, you want to offer the boomerang and the hat into evidence. One at a time, you go through the process of marking both the boomerang and the hat for identification and showing each to opposing counsel. Next, you identify each of them with this testimony: "Exhibit 2 is the boomerang that hit me on the back of my head. Exhibit 3 is the hat that fell off the defendant's head when I chased him. I know these are the actual objects because after I was hit I picked up the boomerang and the hat and took them home with me."

In this situation, you have personal knowledge of both exhibits, and your identification evidence is the only foundation necessary for the judge to admit the boomerang and the hat into evidence. After giving the identification testimony above you would ask the judge to admit both exhibits into evidence in this manner:

1   You:

Your Honor, now I'd like to offer the boomerang, Exhibit 2, and the hat, Exhibit 3, into evidence.

2   Judge (To opposing counsel):

Any objection?

3   Opposing Counsel:

None, Your Honor.

4   Judge:

Very well. Exhibits 2 and 3 are admitted into evidence.

Once the judge admits the exhibits into evidence, both you and your adversary can testify or ask questions concerning either of them.

⚠️ **Exhibits stay in court.** When an exhibit is admitted into evidence it becomes court property until it is released, usually after the verdict. Do not walk out of the court with "your" boomerang and hat at the end of the day, thinking you'll bring it back in the morning. Otherwise you, the boomerang and the hat may end up spending the night together in the courthouse, courtesy of the bailiff.

---

2.   When an Exhibit May Have Been Tampered With

With most exhibits, such as a contract, a business record, a photograph or a boomerang, a witness with personal knowledge of the exhibit could likely readily detect any alterations in it. In such situa-tions, you do not have to account for an exhibit's whereabouts prior to trial. But with other kinds of exhibits, if your adversary objects, the judge may refuse to admit an exhibit into evidence until you show that you have kept it secure so that it has not been tampered with. Such a situation may arise if you offer a liquid, a food or drug or a similar perishable item into evidence.

For example, assume that you claim that your adversary was driving under the influence of alcohol. You want to admit into evidence the open bottle of liquid you found on the front seat of his car along with the testimony of a laboratory technician who tested the liquid and determined that it was vodka. In this situation, before you can get the bottle of vodka admitted into evidence you need to satisfy the judge that the liquid you had tested and are now offering into evidence is the same liquid you found in the car; lawyers call this "establishing a chain of custody."

To establish a chain of custody, both you and the laboratory technician must provide foundational testimony. You will need to testify to keeping the bottle and its contents in a secure place before and after it was tested, and then identify the bottle and its contents as the object that you delivered to the technician. The technician will have to identify the same bottle and contents as the one that she received from you, tested and then either returned to you or brought to court. The judge will not admit the exhibit into evidence until both of you have testified.

As you can see, establishing a chain of custody can be complex. If you seek to admit an important exhibit for which a chain of custody is necessary, refer to one of the evidence treatises listed at the end of this section or consult your self-help law coach if you are uncertain about how to do it.

3. Offering Foundations for Common Exhibits

This section examines the foundational requirements for the kinds of exhibits you are most likely to encounter as a pro per litigant.

a.   Photographs

As suggested by the old expression that "a picture is worth a thousand words," photographs often make stories more convincing. But because a photograph is one step removed from whatever physical objects it depicts, you must lay a foundation beyond marking and identifying a photograph before you can offer it into evidence. When, as is usually the case, a photograph depicts an object that you or one of your witnesses can identify from personal knowledge, such as the interior of an apartment or a damaged car, the foundation for the photograph is quite simple. You offer testimony that the photograph is a "fair and accurate representation" of whatever it depicts. For example, assume that you want to introduce into evidence a photograph of your living room, showing a portion of the ceiling that collapsed due to water damage. The witness who is testifying is a friend who has just concluded describing what the damaged portion of the ceiling looked like. You now offer foundational testimony for the photograph:

1 **You:**

Your Honor, I'm holding a photograph that has been marked Plaintiff's Exhibit 3 for identification and have shown it to defense counsel. May I approach the witness to show her the photograph?

2 **Judge:**

You may.

3 **You:**

Ms. Tobias, please look at the photograph, Exhibit 3, and tell me if you recognize what it shows.

4 **Witness:**

Yes, this looks like a picture of your living room ceiling, showing the part that collapsed.

5 **You:**

Does the photograph fairly and accurately depict the way the room looks since the ceiling collapsed?

6 **Witness:**

Yes, it does.

7 **You:**

Your Honor, I ask that the photograph be received in evidence.

8 **Judge:**

Any objection? Hearing none, it is received.

Here, the key foundational testimony comes in Nos. 5 and 6. By testifying from personal knowledge that the photograph fairly and accurately depicts what she saw, the witness links the photograph to the damaged ceiling. Technical details such as the kind of camera, lens and film used to take the photograph are unnecessary. Note that a witness does not have to be absolutely certain of what a photograph depicts for the photo to be admissible in evidence. A qualified response like "I'm pretty sure that's your ceiling" or "I'd say that's your ceiling" normally demonstrates sufficient personal knowledge for admissibility (see No. 4, above). On the other hand, if a witness says something like, "I'm guessing that's a picture of your ceiling," the judge will probably rule that the witness has not shown sufficient personal knowledge to admit the photo into evidence. If you are going to show a photo (or other exhibit) to a witness during trial, first show it to the witness during a pre-trial rehearsal to make sure that the witness recognizes what it depicts.

 More foundation is needed if a camera reveals what no witness saw. In very unusual circumstances, you may want to offer into evidence a photograph that depicts something that no witness actually saw. In one famous case, a photograph showed a stabbing taking place in the background; neither the photographer nor any other available witness had personally observed the stabbing. The photograph was admitted into evidence, but only after extensive foundational evidence about the camera, film type and other details. In the unlikely event that you want to offer a photo that depicts something that neither you nor one of your witnesses can identify from personal knowledge, consult an experienced trial lawyer.

Photographs don't have to be taken right away. As long as you or a witness can testify that a photograph fairly and accurately depicts a scene as it existed when relevant events took place, it does not matter how long after those events a photograph is taken. So if you suddenly realize days, weeks or even months after events took place that photographs will greatly help a judge or jury understand your version of events, don't worry. As long as the physical condition of whatever you want to photograph has remained largely unchanged, you can take a photograph of it and offer the photograph into evidence.

For instance, you might want to show a photograph to demonstrate that an accident occurred because the view of an intersection is obscured by a large leafy tree, or that in a car crash your vehicle was hit in the right rear, or that part of your living room ceiling collapsed after heavy rains. As long as you or your witness can testify that the photos fairly and accurately depict conditions as they existed when the events occurred, you can successfully offer into evidence a photo taken long after the incident in question took place.

b.   Diagrams

A diagram is an excellent way to illustrate some types of testimony. You and your witnesses may testify with far more clarity and confidence when you can point at and make markings on a visual representation of an event. You can efficiently use a diagram to help you or a witness explain such things as the path of a car before a collision, the floor plan of an apartment or where on your child's body you saw bruises when he came home after a weekend visit with your ex-spouse. Be creative. A diagram is your chance to develop an exhibit on your own; you are not limited to tangible objects that existed when events giving rise to your dispute took place.

While you or a witness can draw a diagram directly on a courtroom blackboard (if there is one), a diagram becomes an exhibit that you can offer into evidence only if you or a witness draw it on a sheet of paper. To do this, obtain a large sheet of paper and vividly colored marking pens so the diagram you create will be clear to the judge or jury. You can prepare an entire diagram before trial and later testify to what it depicts. Or you can prepare a skeleton diagram before trial and complete it while you or a witness testify. Either way, a diagram does not have to be drawn to exact scale; it is enough for admissibility that a diagram fairly approximates whatever it depicts.

For example, assume that you are the plaintiff in a negligence case. You call Cynthia White to testify that a car driven by the defendant Sarah Adams made a left turn in an intersection and struck you in a crosswalk. During your pre-trial rehearsal, you and White can prepare a skeleton diagram of the intersection that may look like the one shown below.

As White testifies, have her refer to the diagram. Begin by laying a foundation showing that the diagram fairly approximates the intersection where the accident took place. Based on this diagram, the testimony might look like this:

1 | **You:**

Your Honor, the bailiff has pinned a diagram to the easel. May it be marked Plaintiff's Exhibit 1 for identification?

2 | **Judge:**

It will be so marked.

3 | **You:**

Ms. White, looking at Exhibit 1, do you recognize what it depicts?

4 | **Witness:**

Yes, it is the intersection of Elm and Main Streets.

5 | **You:**

How do you know that?

6 | **Witness:**

Well, I know that intersection and I drew this diagram of it when I met with you last night.

7 | **You:**

Would you say it is a fair approximation of that intersection?

8 Witness:

Yes. Of course it's not exactly to scale.

9 You:

Can you explain the markings on the diagram?

10 Witness:

It shows that Elm is a north-south street; Main runs east-west. Each street has two lanes of traffic in each direction. There's a left-turn lane for traffic going east on Main to turn north on Elm. There are crosswalks between all the corners.

11 You:

The crosswalks are the parallel lines at all corners?

12 Witness:

Yes.

13 You:

I see you put an "X" on the northeast corner of the intersection. What does the "X" stand for?

14 Witness:

That's where you were standing when I first saw you.

15 You:

And what about these two boxes, one marked with a "V" and one with a "D?"

16 Witness:

The one with a "V" is my car; that's where I was waiting for the light to turn green so that

I could go south on Elm. The one with a "D" is the defendant's truck, at the place where I first saw it, going into the left-turn lane.

Transcript Analysis. This testimony lays the foundation to admit the diagram into evidence. Though it is not an exact depiction of the intersection, the diagram "fairly approximates" the scene of the accident (Nos. 7-8). Note that while No. 7 is a leading question asked on direct examination, judges generally allow leading questions to elicit foundational evidence. (See Chapter 11, Direct Examination, for a discussion of forms of questions and when each may be used.) The rest of the foundation simply explains the markings, giving you a chance to make White's testimony more vivid and real.

As a witness testifies, it is proper to ask the witness to make additional markings on the diagram. For example, assume that White testifies that the next time she saw you, you were in the crosswalk. To illustrate that testimony in a vivid way, ask her to walk over to the diagram and indicate your position:

23 You:

Where was I the next time you saw me?

24 Witness:

You were in the crosswalk.

25 You:

About how far from the curb?

26 Witness:

I'm not great at distances, I'd say about ten feet.

27 You:

Could you please mark "X-1" on the diagram to show where I was the next time you saw me?

28 Witness:

OK, right about here.

(The witness concludes her testimony about the diagram.)

55 You:

Your Honor, may the diagram be admitted into evidence?

56 Judge:

Any objection? All right, Exhibit 1 is admitted.

Transcript Analysis: You might have asked the judge to admit the diagram into evidence after No. 16, when the witness supplied foundational testimony for the skeleton diagram. But when you intend to ask a witness to make additional markings on a diagram (or when you personally will mark a diagram while testifying), it is proper to delay offering it into evidence until you are done.

Keep a diagram simple. When you use a diagram to illustrate a witness's story, include only major changes in location lest you have so many markings that the diagram becomes unintelligible. At all times a judge or juror should easily be able to follow what's going on. If you can, rehearse any drawing that you or a witness will make in court in front of an audience and ask for suggestions as to how you can improve your presentation.

---

c.   Letters and Faxes

To offer a letter or a fax transmission into evidence, you need to lay a foundation showing that the person or organization you claim wrote it actually did so. There are many ways to lay such a foundation. (See Federal Rule of Evidence 901.) For example, if you claim that Edelstein wrote a letter, here are some of the possibilities:

- Edelstein's own testimony that he wrote it

- the testimony of a witness who actually saw Edelstein write the letter

- if the letter is handwritten, the testimony of a witness who has personal knowledge of Edelstein's handwriting style

- if the letter is typed and signed, the testimony of a witness who is familiar with Edelstein's signature

- testimony that, based on the contents of the letter, it is unlikely that anyone other than Edelstein wrote it.

Here is a sample foundation for introducing a letter into evidence based on your personal familiarity with the writer's signature. Assume that you are involved in a breach of contract case, and you have testified that you talked to Edelstein about buying what he said was a valuable baseball card collection. You now want to offer into evidence a letter that you say was written by Edelstein and that contains what you claim are false statements about the collection. You are laying the foundation through your personal testimony:

1 You:

Two days later, I think it was on the 18th, I got this letter. May I mark it Exhibit 3?

2 **Judge:**

You may. What is the date?

3 **You:**

June 16.

4 **Judge:**

OK, a letter dated June 16 is marked Exhibit 3. Has defense counsel seen it?

5 **You:**

Yes, she has. This is the letter I received from Mr. Edelstein. I recognize the signature as Mr. Edelstein's because I've seen his signature on other letters that he sent me and we talked about. I'd like to offer Exhibit 3 into evidence.

6 **Judge:**

No objections? It is received.

By testifying from personal knowledge that you recognize the signature as Edelstein's, you lay an adequate foundation to admit the letter into evidence.

If the document you want to offer into evidence is a fax transmission, you may have no handwriting to identify. However, just as with an old-fashioned letter, you have to offer foundational testimony connecting the fax to the person or organization who you claim produced it. Again, you may do this in a variety of ways. For example, if you claim that the fax was sent by your adversary, before trial you may send a request for admission asking your adversary to admit that he sent it. (See Chapter 4, Investigating Your Case, for a discussion of requests for admission and other discovery devices.) In addition, you may testify that you had a conversation with or sent a fax of your own to the person

whom you claim sent the fax, and that the exhibit in court was sent in response to the conversation or your fax. Even a letterhead or similar logo on a fax is likely to be sufficient for a judge to admit it into evidence.

d. Business Records

(See also Computerized Business Records, in Subsection e below.)

As all of us know only too well, most business activities generate paperwork. For example, if you are a manufacturer who shipped merchandise to a customer who has refused to pay for it, included in your paperwork will be the record of the unpaid bill and your delivery document (receipt). If you are a landlord, you probably have a rent book showing when the tenants paid and did not pay the rent. And if you are a parent seeking additional payments from your ex-spouse to cover your child's large medical expenses, you have medical bills.

At trial, exhibits such as these are generally referred to as "business records." The term is very broad; almost any document produced by any kind of organization, including nonprofit corporations and community groups, is considered a business record. To have business records admitted into evidence, you must lay a foundation proving that they are likely to be accurate. The requirements are nearly identical in every state. (See, for example, Federal Rule of Evidence 803 (6), New York Code of Evidence § 803 (c)(5), California Evidence Code § 1271, and Texas Civil Rule of Evidence 803 (6).) All provide that your foundation has to show three things:

- Your document was made in the normal course of business.

- It was prepared around the time of the event to which it pertains.

- The way the business makes and keeps records suggests that the document is trustworthy.

BUSINESS RECORDS AND THE HEARSAY RULE

Chapter 15, Basic Rules of Evidence, explains the hearsay rule, which excludes many out-of-court statements, and some of the important exceptions to the rule that make some types of hearsay statements admissible. A business record is hearsay when it is offered to prove that the transaction recorded by the record occurred. But if your case relies on a business record, you can relax: One of the most important hearsay exceptions is the one making business records admissible upon a proper foundational showing.

For example, assume that you are a manufacturer of car stereos and that you delivered 100 radios to the defendant, a retailer who has refused to pay for them. You want to offer your company's unpaid invoice into evidence to prove that the defendant owes your company $10,000. If you are offering the invoice through your own testimony, your foundational evidence would look like this:

I have this Invoice No. 229 that has been marked as Exhibit 1 and shown to the defendant. Exhibit 1 is one of my company's invoices. It was prepared by my assistant manager, Steve Von Till; I recognize his initials in the lower right hand corner of the invoice. Our company's business practice is to prepare an invoice for every order we receive the same day we receive it. Unpaid invoices are kept in a separate file folder by number. All payments received go to our bookkeeper, who stamps "paid" on these invoices and puts them into a folder labeled "paid invoices." I took this invoice from the folder holding the unpaid bills, and it has not been stamped as paid. I ask for Exhibit 1 to be admitted into evidence.

This foundational evidence qualifies the invoice as an admissible business record. You did not prepare the invoice personally, but that is not necessary. Its trustworthiness comes from the routine practice of preparing and keeping invoices. You identify the invoice as a record of your business, establish that invoices are prepared right after orders are received and explain your record-keeping system. This foundation suggests that the fact that the invoice has not been stamped "paid" is a reliable indication that it was not paid. Thus, the judge should admit the invoice into evidence.

 Ask your adversary to stipulate to the admission of your business records. Business records are often admitted into evidence by stipulation. Your adversary may well stipulate to the admissibility of business records, because there is often no doubt of their accuracy. (See Section C, above, for a form of stipulation you might use.)

Records from someone else's business. You will have to lay much the same kind of foundation for a business record that comes from someone else's business. Absent a stipulation, you may need someone familiar with the records of the other business to come to court and lay the proper foundation. For instance, assume that you are a parent seeking an award of additional money from your ex-spouse to pay for large medical expenses that your child recently incurred. You want to offer into evidence the sheaf of hospital bills you have received. The bills are business records of the hospital. If your ex-spouse will not stipulate to their admissibility, to admit them into evidence you will need to lay a foundation showing how and when the bills are prepared and maintained in the hospital's regular course of business.

To do this it is necessary to serve a document available for free from the court clerk, called a subpoena duces tecum, on the hospital's Custodian of Records. A subpoena duces tecum orders someone from the hospital's record-keeping staff to come to court on the date specified in the subpoena (that's the subpoena part) and bring along a copy of the hospital's bills (that's the duces tecum part). Then you will call the hospital employee as a witness and question the employee about the hospital's record-keeping procedures. (See Chapter 11, Direct Examination, and Chapter 4, Investigating Your Case, for additional information about subpoenas.)

e. Computerized Business Records

Many businesses today store most of their records in computers. For example, if you are a manufacturer, employees probably regularly enter data into a computer reflecting merchandise delivered to and payments received from your customers. To prove at trial how much a customer owes, you will probably need to make a printout of the account and offer it as an exhibit.

Fortunately, evidence rules are flexible enough to permit admission of a business record consisting of a computer printout. As with any other business record, you will need to offer foundational evidence concerning how your business prepares and keeps records. Your foundation should include

 Your court may have faster ways to admit business records. To save businesses the time and expense of employees going to court, many states have adopted a shortcut procedure for business records known as the Uniform Photographic Copies of Business and Public Records as Evidence Act. If your state has adopted this law, a business can comply with your subpoena duces tecum asking for a business record by mailing records to the court along with an affidavit signed under penalty of perjury as to how the records are prepared and kept. The records are then admissible in evidence without your having to offer any further foundation.

Look in your state's evidence statutes to see if it has adopted this uniform act. As of this book's publication date, the Uniform Act has been adopted by the following states:

Alabama	New Hampshire
Arkansas	New Jersey
California	New York
Colorado	North Carolina
Connecticut	North Dakota
Georgia	Pennsylvania
Idaho	South Carolina
Iowa	South Dakota
Kansas	Utah
Kentucky	Vermont
Maine	Virgin Islands
Maryland	Virginia
Massachusetts	Washington
Michigan	West Virginia
Minnesota	Wisconsin
Nebraska	

information about your business's computer system. Don't worry, you will not need to call an expert witness to explain the scientific theory behind and the reliability of computers. Simply have a computer-literate employee explain how your records are entered and retrieved, and that the computer from which the record was retrieved was in good working order. As long as your business has routine and reliable procedures for using and maintaining its computers, and the particular record was maintained according to those procedures, you should have no difficulty admitting the record into evidence.

f.   Government Records

"Official records" is the legal system's label for reports and documents prepared by government officials and offices. For instance, if you are a tenant in a landlord-tenant case and you have your apartment inspected by a County Health Inspector, the inspector's report is an official record. Likewise, if a police officer investigates an accident, the police officer's report is an official record.

Because record-keeping by government offices is much like that of private businesses, the foundation you need to admit an official record into evidence is similar to that of business records. (See, for example, Federal Rule of Evidence 803(8), New York Evidence Code § 803(c)(7), California Evidence Code § 1280 and Texas Civil Rule of Evidence 803(8).) If anything, your judge will probably require less of a foundation for official records than for business records, based on a perception (reasonable or not) that official records are very likely to be accurate.

For example, assume that you are the defendant in an automobile accident case. To counter the plaintiff's claim that you drove on the wrong side of the road, you want to prove that your car left skid marks in your proper traffic lane. You know that soon after the accident, Officer Krupke arrived, examined the skid marks left by your car and later prepared a report as to the location and length of the skid marks. After calling the police department and inquiring how to subpoena an officer, you served a subpoena duces tecum on Officer Krupke by leaving it with the Watch Commander of Krupke's assigned police station. Krupke has come to court with the report, and you want the judge to admit this report into evidence as an official record. Your foundational evidence will look something like this:

1   You:

Officer Krupke, what is your occupation and assignment?

2   Krupke:

I'm a police officer for West Side City, assigned to routine traffic patrol.

3   You:

Did you investigate an accident in the 2100 block of Hillcrest Road on the afternoon of December 23?

4   Krupke:

Yes, I did.

5   You:

And what did you do?

6   Krupke:

After ascertaining that nobody was injured, I examined a set of skid marks that extended for approximately 50 feet behind the car you were in.

7 You:

Was there any reason you examined the skid marks?

8 Krupke:

It's routine investigation.

9 You:

Officer Krupke, did you prepare a report of your findings with regard to the skid marks following your investigation?

10 Krupke:

Yes, I did.

11 You:

When did you prepare it?

12 Krupke:

In line with department policy, I prepared the report before I went off duty, about three hours after I completed my investigation.

13 You:

How did you prepare that report?

14 Krupke:

From the notes about the skid marks that I made at the scene of the accident.

15 You:

Officer Krupke, the bailiff is handing you a document marked "Defendant's Exhibit C for Identification." Is this the report you prepared in this case?

16 Krupke:

Yes it is. This is my signature.

17 You:

Your Honor, I offer the report into evidence as an official record.

18 Judge:

Yes, I'll admit it.

Transcript Analysis: This excerpt demonstrates that Officer Krupke, a government official, prepared the skid mark report as part of his official, routine duties. It was prepared in timely fashion, just a few hours after his investigation. In Nos. 15-16, Krupke identifies the exhibit as the report that he prepared. Thus, you have met all requirements for admissibility.

RESEARCHING FOUNDATIONAL REQUIREMENTS

If you plan to offer an exhibit into evidence but are uncertain about the foundation you have to lay, you'll have to do some research. One book that you may find especially useful is *Evidentiary Foundations*, by Edward Imwinkelried (The Michie Co.). In a question-and-answer format, it illustrates foundational testimony for numerous kinds of exhibits.

Other books you may want to consult include:

McCormick on Evidence, by John Strong (ed.) (West Publishing Co.). This is a one-volume treatise widely referred to by lawyers and judges; Titles 8 and 9 review exhibits.

Evidence, by Ken Graham (Casenotes Publishing Co.). This is a paperback "outline," which is a quick, relatively inexpensive refresher aimed at law students. You will find this and other evidence outlines in most law book stores near law schools.

Researching evidence rules themselves is another way to find out about foundational requirements. The evidence rules governing trials in federal courts are found in the Federal Rules of Evidence. By way of example, Federal Rule 803 (6) lists the foundational requirements for business records, and Rule 901 lists foundations for authenticating documents. Many states have enacted the Federal Rules almost in their entirety and collected them in a separate volume of laws. In a few states, evidence rules may be harder to find because they are included in a more general collection of civil laws; in these states you may have to ask a law librarian to help you find evidence rules. (See Chapter 22, Legal Research.)

In addition to doing research, this is a good time to consult your self-help law coach, particularly if admission of an exhibit is crucial to your case. The brief time it should take an attorney to help you organize a sufficient foundation may be well worth the expense.

Finally, if you find yourself in the middle of trial uncertain about what you need to do to lay a foundation, do not be afraid to ask the judge for help. Ask to approach the bench, and say something like, "Your Honor, I've got this repair estimate that I want to introduce into evidence, but I'm not quite sure what to do." Some judges may even respond by asking questions themselves to develop the necessary foundation.

E. LETTING JURORS SEE YOUR EXHIBITS

If you review the mechanics for offering exhibits into evidence discussed above, you will realize that in a jury trial the jurors are frozen out of the process. An exhibit goes from your hand to the witness (sometimes via the bailiff) and then to the judge. Once an exhibit is admitted into evidence, the witness may give oral testimony concerning the exhibit, and then it is put in the custody of the court clerk.

Normally the judge allows the jurors to have all the exhibits with them when the case is complete and they deliberate. (See, for example, California Code of Civil Procedure § 612.) But that may be too late to influence them in your favor. If possible, you want to melt the jury freeze-out and allow the jurors to examine each exhibit as soon as the judge admits it into evidence.

Fortunately a procedure does exist for showing an exhibit to a jury at the time it is admitted into evidence. (In some courts, this is called "publishing an exhibit.") Immediately after an exhibit is admitted into evidence, ask the judge for permission to show the exhibit to the jurors. Say something like, "Your Honor, may I hand Exhibit C, the photograph [business record, letter, etc.] to the jurors?" The judge, who probably wants to keep the trial moving, may respond by asking you to justify your request. If so, you can do two things to encourage the judge to rule in your favor:

- Explain why seeing the exhibit during the testimony will help the jury understand your evidence. For example, you may point out, "I'm going to be testifying about the damage to my car, and seeing the photo now will help the jury follow my testimony."

- If feasible, make enough copies of an exhibit to give to each juror. That will save time that otherwise will be wasted if testimony has to

halt while a single page or photo wends its way amongst the jurors.

F. WHEN EXHIBITS ARE REQUIRED: THE "BEST EVIDENCE" RULE

In most situations, you are not required to offer an exhibit into evidence. That is, though it may lack the storytelling impact of an exhibit, oral testimony describing an object is often admissible without the need of a physical back-up. For example, when you testify that you were struck by a boomerang, you are not legally required to offer the boomerang into evidence. Similarly, you or a police officer may orally testify to the skid marks left after a car accident without offering the officer's police report into evidence.

"Your Honor, after the trial will it be possible to purchase items from the exhibit table?"

But when you want to offer testimony about the contents of documents such as letters, business records and photographs, a legal doctrine known as the "best evidence rule" restricts your right to rely on oral testimony. This rule is also known as the "original writing rule." (See Federal Rule of Evidence 1002, New York Evidence Code § 1002, California Evidence Code § 1500, Texas Civil Rule of Evidence 1002 and similar statutes in almost every state.) The rule states that you (or a witness) cannot orally testify to the contents of a document unless you produce the document in court or prove to the judge that you have a valid reason for being unable to do so.

Offer at least a copy whenever possible. Though you or a witness may be allowed to testify orally to the contents of a document, if you cannot produce an original try your best to locate and introduce into evidence a copy. To offer a copy of a document into evidence, follow the same foundational procedure as for any other exhibit, but make sure that you tell the judge that your document is a copy, not an original.

To see how the rule works, assume that you want to prove that Ihori wrote you a threatening note. Because of the best evidence rule, you cannot simply testify that, "I got a note from Ihori and this is what it said…." You have to produce the note itself in court. If you cannot do so, you should offer a copy of the note if you made one. If you do not have a copy, you can testify orally to what the note said if you lay a foundation showing the judge you have a valid excuse for not having the document. For example, you may testify that Ihori stole the note from you, or that it was accidentally thrown out by your six-year-old child. (This descending order of preferences for originals, then copies, then oral testimony might remind you of the old folk song: "If you haven't got a penny then a hay-penny will do; if you haven't got a hay-penny, then God bless you.")

G. OBJECTING TO YOUR ADVERSARY'S EXHIBITS

In addition to offering your own exhibits into evidence, you have the right to object to those your adversary tries to offer. (Of course, your adversary has the same right with respect to your exhibits.) An objection asks a judge to exclude (refuse to admit) an exhibit, which means that the judge or jury cannot consider the exhibit in reaching a verdict. (See Chapter 16, Making and Responding to Objections.)

If the admissibility of an exhibit is challenged, the judge may have to halt the trial and conduct a short "mini-trial" on the spot to decide whether an exhibit is admissible. During the mini-trial, you and your adversary can present whatever evidence you have pertaining to the adequacy of the foundation. After listening to the evidence, the judge decides whether or not to admit the disputed exhibit into evidence. The main trial then continues.

For example, assume you offer foundational evidence that a letter was written by Edelstein, your adversary. But Edelstein objects to admission of the letter into evidence and asks to offer foundational evidence of his own that he did not write it. The judge holds a short mini-trial, during which you offer your evidence supporting your contention that Edelstein wrote the letter, and Edelstein offers evidence that he did not. The judge's decision about admissibility of the letter concludes the mini-trial, and the main trial resumes at once with or without the letter in evidence.

 You can ask the judge to exclude the jury during the mini-trial. The judge can exclude or permit a jury to remain during a mini-trial. If you do not want the jurors listening to evidence about an exhibit that you hope the judge will exclude, ask the judge to exclude the jury during the mini-trial. However, do not ask to exclude a jury unless the danger of prejudice is very high; jurors resent being left out of things, and excluding them delays the trial.

Here are the most common reasons for objecting to the admissibility of an exhibit.

1. Insufficient Foundation

You can object to an adversary's exhibit on the ground that the adversary has not laid a sufficient foundation. For example, suppose that you are the tenant, Marjorie, in a landlord-tenant case. The owner calls the apartment manager as a witness and asks the manager to identify a photograph allegedly showing you throwing a rock through the manager's window. (You deny throwing the rock.) In response, the manager testifies, "That looks like Marjorie, but I really can't be sure." If the landlord attempts to offer the photo into evidence based on this foundation, ask the judge to exclude it on the ground that the manager lacks personal knowledge or that the foundation is insufficient.

You can also object by offering conflicting foundational evidence. For instance, assume that your adversary offers a computerized printout of a business record showing that you owe your adversary a lot of money. Your adversary offers evidence about her business's careful record-keeping procedures. However, your position is that the printout is wrong, and you have information from a former employee of your adversary's business who is willing to testify on your behalf about the business's sloppy record-keeping procedures that regularly get accounts mixed up.

You may object when the adversary offers the computer printout into evidence and ask the judge to listen to your evidence before making a decision about whether to admit the print-out. Saying something like, "Objection, Your Honor. Lack of foundation. I'd like to call a witness to show that the printout is not trustworthy." Your objection may require the judge to conduct a mini-trial in which the issue is the admissibility of the computer printout. If the testimony from the former employee convinces the judge that the adversary's printout is not trustworthy, the judge will exclude it from evidence. And because your adversary's whole case may be based on the contents of the printout, by excluding the printout you may win the whole trial!

You can attack the reliability of an exhibit after it is admitted into evidence. If your judge admits your adversary's exhibit into evidence over your objection, it means only that the exhibit is admissible in evidence, not that it is necessarily accurate. You can still offer your own evidence attacking the exhibit's reliability and argue (as part of your closing argument) that the exhibit is so untrustworthy that the judge or jury should not pay any attention to it when arriving at its decision.

2. Violations of Other Rules of Evidence

Even if an exhibit offered by your adversary satisfies all foundational requirements, you may still ask the judge to exclude it on the ground that it violates another rule of evidence, such as the hearsay rule or the rule of relevance. (See Chapter 15, Basic Rules of Evidence.) If you are uncertain about whether or not one of these other rules may bar an exhibit offered by your adversary, research the issue in a law library or talk to your self-help law coach. (See Chapter 22, Legal Research, and Chapter 21, Getting Help from Attorneys: Hiring a Legal Coach.)

The following examples may help you understand how to use evidence rules to object to your adversary's offered exhibits:

Example 1: Hearsay. To prove that your carelessness caused an accident, your adversary offers into evidence a letter written by a person named Julie Even saying that you ran a red light. Object and ask the judge to exclude the letter as hearsay. The letter is made inadmissible by the hearsay rule even though your adversary properly marks, identifies and lays a foundation showing that it was written by Even.

Example 2: Unfair prejudice. A judge can exclude relevant evidence as "unfairly prejudicial" if its legitimate impact is outweighed by the likelihood that it will inflame the emotions of the judge or jury against you. For example, assume that your adversary claims that you carelessly ran a red light and collided with his car. He wants to offer into evidence photos of your car, one of which prominently shows a bumper sticker with the name of a musical rock group that many people claim promotes violent antisocial behavior. You may object that the photograph showing the bumper sticker is unfairly prejudicial. On the one hand it has minimal relevance; your adversary has offered into evidence other photos of your car. On the other hand, it is likely to prejudice you in the eyes of the judge or jury as a fan of an outlaw rock group. The judge may decide to exclude the photo even though your adversary properly marks, identifies and lays a foundation for the photo as a fair and accurate representation of your car.

⚠️ **Only part of an exhibit may be admissible.** Whether you or your adversary offers an exhibit into evidence, be aware that only part of it may be admissible. For example, an admissible medical report may contain irrelevant material, or a police officer's report may contain the inadmissible hearsay statement of a bystander. In such situations, the improper matter must be "severed" from the exhibit. Depending on the type of exhibit and the extensiveness of the improper matter, severing may be accomplished by crossing it out, cutting it out with a scissors or preparing a new document without the improper matter.

H. ORGANIZING EXHIBITS FOR TRIAL

To be thorough, refer to your exhibits in at least two different portions of your trial notebook. (See Chapter 17, Organizing a Trial Notebook.)

First, remember that Chapter 11, Direct Examination, advised making outlines of your planned testimony and the direct examinations of your witnesses. Include in each outline of a witness's testimony a reference to any exhibit you plan to offer during the direct examination of that witness. For instance, assume that you want to offer a photograph of the intersection of Main and Elm Streets into evidence during your direct examination of Cynthia White. In your outline of her testimony, write down a simple reminder such as, "photo of intersection." Also, you may want to briefly note key foundational requirements: "Ask if the photo is 'fair and accurate representation' of the intersection." (Normally you offer exhibits when you and your witnesses testify. But if you plan to offer an exhibit during cross-examination of an adverse witness, note that fact in your cross-examination outline for that witness.)

It's also wise to keep a separate list of all of your exhibits in a separate section of your trial notebook. You can then check off the exhibits as each is admitted into evidence.

What about the exhibits themselves? Generally, keep all your exhibits together in the order in which you plan to introduce them into evidence so that you can easily lay your hands on them during trial. But usually it is unwise to keep them in your trial notebook because you should not make notebook holes in original documents. And some of your exhibits may be too bulky for a notebook—for example, a boomerang and a hat are not well suited to storage in a trial notebook. It is usually best to keep your exhibits in a folder or box, separate from your trial notebook. ■

15

BASIC RULES OF EVIDENCE

The preceding chapters have explained many important evidence rules that apply to specific parts of the trial process. For example, you know that:

- During your opening statement, you cannot argue. (Chapter 10, Opening Statements.)

- During direct examination you are generally limited to asking open and closed questions. During cross-examination, you may (and indeed should) ask leading questions. (Chapter 11, Direct Examination, and Chapter 12, Cross-Examination.)

- Exhibits are not admissible in evidence until you lay a proper foundation. For example, a photograph is not admissible unless a witness testifies that it is a fair and accurate representation of whatever it depicts. (Chapter 14, Exhibits.)

- You may use any kind of document to refresh a forgetful witness's recollection. But you must show the document to your adversary, who may offer it into evidence. (Chapter 11, Direct Examination.)

By contrast, the evidence rules described in this chapter apply to every aspect of trial. They regulate information regardless of whether you are testifying personally, asking questions of your witnesses or those of your adversary, offering an exhibit into evidence, or making your opening statement or final argument.

Unfortunately, some of these rules run counter to common sense. They sometimes prevent you from offering the types of evidence that you probably rely on in everyday life. All the more important that you read this chapter carefully when you prepare for trial. If, after reading it, you are still not sure about whether important evidence that you or your adversary plans to offer is admissible, consult one of the books listed at the end of the chapter or talk to your self-help law coach.

THE ROLE OF OBJECTIONS IN ENFORCING EVIDENCE RULES

Evidence rules are not self-enforcing. If one side offers legally improper evidence at trial, the evidence will normally be admitted, and can be considered by the judge or jury in arriving at a verdict, unless the other side objects. To keep out improper evidence, you must ask the judge to rule that the evidence is improper by making an objection and the judge must uphold (sustain) the objection and exclude the evidence. On occasion, if evidence is blatantly inadmissible, a judge will exclude evidence without waiting for an objection. Chapter 16, Making and Responding to Objections, explains the objections process.)

A. RELEVANCE

The most fundamental rule of evidence requires a logical connection between a piece of evidence you offer and the legal claim you are trying to prove or disprove. It's called the relevance rule. (See for example, Federal Rules of Evidence 401-402, California Evidence Code §§ 140 and 351; New York Code of Evidence §§ 401-402, and Texas Civil Rules of Evidence 401-402.)

To be relevant, evidence does not have to prove a certain point conclusively. Evidence is relevant if it makes a fact that a party is trying to prove a little more probable, or a party is trying to disprove a little less probable. For example, say you are attempting to prove that Melinda was speeding, and you offer evidence that at the time of the accident she was late for an important meeting. Your evidence is relevant. Melinda's being late by no means conclusively proves that she was speeding. But common sense tells you that sometimes people do speed when they are late for meetings. The evidence of lateness adds to the probability that Melinda was speeding.

Let's turn this example around, and assume that you are Melinda and you are attempting to prove that you were not speeding. You offer evidence that at the time your were driving you had a valuable crystal vase on the back seat of your car. This evidence too is relevant. Again, common sense suggests that people sometimes drive more

slowly when they are carrying expensive, breakable objects.

Judges have broad discretion to decide what evidence is relevant. Whether your judge deems particular evidence relevant or not is often a close call that depends on considerations such as the facts of a case, the importance of the issue to which the evidence pertains, other evidence already in the record and the need to keep a trial moving efficiently. On the theory that, like snowflakes, no two trials are ever the same, legal precedent (prior court decisions about relevance) has almost nothing to do with the determination of whether evidence is relevant.

"I don't give a damn what Judge Wapner said!"

⚠️ **Not all relevant evidence is admissible.** Evidence must be relevant to be admissible. But the converse is not true; relevant evidence is not always admissible. The rules you will read about in this chapter often exclude evidence even though it is relevant. For example, relevant evidence may be excluded because it is unfairly inflammatory, or hearsay.

Perhaps the best way to demonstrate the meaning of relevance is with a few more examples, some of which are favorites of law professors:

- Lipkis is on trial for murder. The prosecution offers the murder weapon into evidence. Lipkis objects that the gun is irrelevant, because a police officer found it precisely halfway between Lipkis and a person standing next to Lipkis at the murder scene. *Ruling:* The gun is relevant. True, the gun evidence does not distinguish between Lipkis and the other person as the possible murderer. Nevertheless, evidence that the gun was found somewhere near Lipkis adds to the probability that he committed the murder. Again, evidence does not have to be conclusive to be relevant.

- In a divorce case, you are seeking custody of your young child. You testify that you recently heard your ex-spouse verbally abusing your child when you arrived to pick up your child. Your ex-spouse calls Shelley to testify that the day before the trial, she engaged in a short experiment at your ex-spouse's request. She will testify that she stood at the same spot where you were standing when you testified you heard the verbal abuse, and that she was unable to hear a thing even though your ex-

spouse claims to have been yelling loudly. *Ruling:* Shelley's evidence is irrelevant. There is no logical connection between what two people can hear on two different occasions. Not only do people vary in their hearing ability, but also the external circumstances are likely to have been different. For example, it is unlikely that your ex-spouse used exactly the same tone of voice on both occasions or that background noise from cars and other people was the same.

- You have sued Jones, a co-worker, for assaulting you. You offer evidence that about a week before the assault, Jones told a third co-worker, I'm "going to get Nolo [you] the next chance I get." The defendant objects that the evidence is irrelevant, because people often make threats that they do not carry out. *Ruling:* Your evidence is relevant. Evidence that the defendant made a threat against you increases the probability that the defendant later assaulted you.

- The plaintiff has sued you for negligence, claiming that your speeding was the cause of an accident on 3rd Street. You deny that you were speeding or otherwise negligent. To help prove that you were going too fast, the plaintiff offers testimony that about a week earlier, you were seen speeding on 9th Street. *Ruling:* The plaintiff's evidence is irrelevant. There is no logical connection between how you drove at one time and location and how you drove at another time and location.

- You sue Universal Metals for fraud and breach of contract. You claim that Universal's personnel director, Sonny Ancher, induced you to leave another job by promising to hire you at an increase in salary, and that he later reneged. Universal denies that any employment offer was made to you. To show that Ancher did violate an agreement with you, you offer evidence that a week after you filed the suit against Universal, Universal fired Ancher. *Ruling*: The evidence that Universal fired Ancher is irrelevant. Because Universal's decision to fire Ancher could have been based on so many different factors, there is no logical connection between your claim and his firing.

How to object to irrelevant evidence. To ask the judge to keep out irrelevant evidence offered by your adversary, simply say, "Objection, Your Honor. Irrelevant." Do this as soon as you realize that your adversary's question seeks, or the adverse witness's answer refers to, irrelevant evidence. Do not make an argument as to why the evidence is irrelevant unless the judge asks you to do so. (See Chapter 16, Making and Responding to Objections.)

B. EXCLUDING RELEVANT BUT UNFAIRLY PREJUDICIAL EVIDENCE

If a judge believes that evidence offered has minimal relevance, which is outweighed by the risk that admitting the evidence will unfairly prejudice the other side, the judge can exclude the evidence. (See, for example, Federal Rule of Evidence 403, California Evidence Code § 352, New York Code of Evidence § 403, and Texas Civil Rule of Evidence 403.)

Evidence may be excluded as unfairly prejudicial when it is so likely to inflame the emotions of the judge or jury that the judge or jury will attach too much importance to it. For example, assume that you have been sued for fraud for supposedly intentionally concealing a dangerous condition in a house that you sold to the plaintiff, as a result of which the plaintiff suffered head injuries. Your defense is that no dangerous condition existed at the time of the sale. After testifying to her injuries, the plaintiff offers into evidence a series of photographs depicting her bloody head injuries before and during medical treatment. The photographs are of some relevance, because they support the plaintiff's testimony about the extent of her injuries. But their relevance is slight since they do nothing to answer the question of whether the dangerous condition existed at the time of sale. And there is a risk that the photographs will inflame the passions of the jury against you and cause the jury to rule in favor of the plaintiff no matter what the condition of the house. So if you object, the judge may conclude that the risk that the photographs will be unfairly prejudicial outweighs their relevance and exclude them from evidence.

As is true with many rules of evidence, your judge is more likely to exclude evidence as unfairly prejudicial when your case is being heard by a jury rather than by the judge sitting without a jury. Judges tend to think that while jurors are likely to be unduly influenced by prejudicial evidence, judges are able to sort the relevant wheat from the prejudicial chaff. Nevertheless, even in a judge trial you should make the objection if you think the situation warrants it. Even if the judge overrules (denies) it, your objection may remind the judge that your adversary's evidence carries a risk of unfair prejudice.

💡 **How to object to unfairly prejudicial evidence.** To ask a judge to exclude unfairly prejudicial evidence offered by your adversary, say, "Objection, Your Honor. The evidence is unfairly prejudicial." Object as soon as you realize that your adversary's question seeks, or the adverse witness's answer refers to, unfairly prejudicial evidence. Do not make an argument as to why the evidence is unfairly prejudicial unless the judge asks you to do so. (See Chapter 16, Making and Responding to Objections.)

If yours is a jury trial, also consider making a "motion in limine" to exclude unfairly prejudicial evidence before trial gets underway. (See Chapter 16, Section B.) The fact that you are a pro per litigant may work in your favor, because the judge should realize that you may be unable to prevent a jury from hearing unfairly prejudicial evidence if you have to wait to object until the evidence is offered at trial.

C. THE RULE AGAINST OPINIONS

If you are old enough to remember the character of Sgt. Joe Friday in the television show *Dragnet*, you may remember that he always asked witnesses for "Just the facts." Sgt. Friday's warning sums up the opinion rule: Parties and witnesses are supposed to testify to specific factual observations, not to opinions. It is up to the judge or jury to decide what conclusions to draw from those observations. (See Federal Rule of Evidence 701, California Evidence Code § 800, New York Code of Evidence § 701, and Texas Civil Rule of Evidence 701.)

Like the relevance rule, the opinion rule is impossible to define with precision. Your judge necessarily has wide discretion to decide what constitutes an improper opinion. To see why, let's take what may seem like a silly example. Ruth testifies, "I saw a car." Fact or opinion? It seems like a factual observation that would satisfy even Sgt. Friday. But if you stop to think about it, you will see that Ruth is giving an opinion. After all, she could have testified to greater factual detail: "I saw a large metal object with four round metallic objects covered with a black, rubbery material…" and left it to the judge or jury to conclude that what she saw was a car. But if a judge were to ban this kind of opinion, most types of information that people rely on every day to make sensible judgments would be forbidden, and a simple trial might last for weeks.

In practice, what the opinion rule really means is that witnesses can testify to opinions if these three things are true:

1. The witness has personal knowledge of the facts on which the opinion is based.

2. The opinion is of a common-sense type that people make every day.

3. The opinion does not consist of an unnecessary legal judgment that the judge or jury is supposed to make.

To illustrate, let's return to Ruth and the car. Ruth would probably not be allowed to testify that, "In my opinion, the blue car caused the accident." Even if she saw the events leading up to the accident, Ruth would be attempting to perform the job of the judge or jury. Also, a judgment of legal fault is not a common-sense, everyday opinion. It is reasonable to ask Ruth to testify to what she saw, and leave to the judge or jury the job of deciding who caused the accident.

Again, perhaps the best way to get a feel for the opinion rule is with concrete examples. A judge will normally allow a witness to give opinions such as the following:

- "When I saw him, Kebo was happy (or angry or sad)."

- "I watched Johnson for a half hour, and he seemed drunk."

- "Especially considering it was a rainy day, the car was going too fast."

- "In the couple of years that our families have been friends, Becky has always seemed more comfortable around her father than around her mother."

In each example, the opinions are likely to be admissible because they meet the three-part test set out above.

At the other extreme are a variety of opinions that witnesses cannot give because they combine observations with unnecessary legal judgments. A judge will probably not allow a witness to state opinions such as:

- "Philippe was driving carelessly."

- "It will be in Becky's best interests to live with her father."

- "Her former attorney committed legal malpractice."

- "I think the plaintiff should get a million dollars in damages."

In each example, it is reasonable to expect a witness to describe the behavior underlying the

opinion, and leave the legal judgment to the judge or jury.

⚠️ **Expert witnesses march to a different drummer.** Expert witnesses are allowed to state opinions even if those opinions make legal judgments and are not based on personal knowledge. For example, a trained family counselor can testify to an opinion that a father should be granted custody of a minor child. (See Chapter 18, Expert Witnesses.)

💡 **How to object to improper opinions.** To ask your judge to exclude an improper opinion offered by your adversary, say, "Objection Your Honor. The question calls for an improper opinion." Object as soon as you realize that your adversary's question seeks, or the adverse witness's answer refers to, an improper opinion. Do not make an argument as to why an opinion is improper unless the judge asks you to do so. (See Chapter 16, Making and Responding to Objections.)

Don't worry if the judge rules that the opinion you are testifying to or seeking from a witness is improper. You can almost always bring out the information you are after. You just need to testify, or elicit from a witness, the details on which the opinion was based. Consider this example in which you are questioning a woodsman:

1 **You:**

And what happened next?

2   **Witness:**

The wolf intended you to think that he was your grandma.

3   **Adversary:**

Object and move to strike the testimony as to the wolf's intent as an improper opinion.

4   **Judge:**

Yes, the witness lacks personal knowledge as to the wolf's actual intent. Objection sustained.

Transcript Analysis: Here your witness's opinion (No. 2) is ruled inadmissible. But the ruling does not prevent you from offering evidence about the wolf's intent. You can continue by asking the witness to describe the behavior leading him to form this opinion:

5   **You:**

Please tell us exactly what you saw.

6   **Witness:**

Okay. When I arrived outside the cottage I saw the wolf in bed dressed in a ladies' nightgown and cap, with the covers pulled all the way up to his chin.

7   **You:**

And what was the wolf doing?

8   **Witness:**

He was talking in a very soft voice, saying over and over how nice you were for coming to visit your dear sweet grandma.

9   **You:**

And then what happened?

10   **Witness:**

You said something about what big eyes your grandma had, and the wolf said in the same soft tone of voice that he had just gotten new contact lenses that made his eyes look a little funny.

11   **You:**

Yes, go on.

12   **Witness:**

….

Transcript Analysis: This brief series of questions seeks the factual information underlying the witness's improper opinion about the wolf's intent. In fact, compare the improper opinion (No. 2) with the factual information; doesn't the latter have more persuasive impact? Evidence rules aside, you are probably better off eliciting the details underlying the improper opinion.

D.   THE RULE AGAINST CHARACTER EVIDENCE

Character evidence is evidence of past behavior that suggests that a person has a propensity (a "trait of character") to behave in a certain way. In daily life, we commonly use what we know of people's past behavior to make judgments about their characters. For instance, we may think of a person as being careful, violent, honest or nasty. And once we form an opinion about a person's character, we are likely to project it onto their specific conduct. For example, once we conclude that a person has a propensity to drive carefully, we may reason that the person was probably driving carefully on a particular occasion.

But for a variety of reasons, evidence rules contain a strong policy forbidding character evidence in civil trials. (See Federal Rule of Evidence 404, California Evidence Code § 1101, New York Code of Evidence § 404, and Texas Civil Rule of Evidence 404.) One reason is simply to save time. Trials would be much too long if parties were allowed to fight not only about how specific events took place, but also about each other's character traits. Another reason is that character evidence is thought by our legal system to be of dubious value: people simply do not always behave in accordance with their character traits. And a third reason is that evidence of character itself may be untrustworthy: witnesses are not omniscient, and they may easily misjudge the character of you or your adversary.

Some examples may help you understand the type of information forbidden by the rule against character evidence:

- To prove that you were driving carefully before a traffic accident, you cannot ask a witness who has carpooled with you for 20 years to testify that in her opinion you are a safe driver. Similarly, you cannot offer evidence that you've never gotten a traffic ticket for a moving viola-

tion or that you've never before been involved in an accident. In each situation, you improperly ask the judge or jury to infer that because you have a propensity (a character trait) to drive safely, you were driving safely at the time of the accident involved in your trial.

- Although by way of introduction you are allowed to briefly question your witnesses about their personal backgrounds when conducting their direct examination (see Chapter 11, Direct Examination), generally you cannot ask about a witness's good deeds, community activities, awards and the like. As a judge is likely to view it, such evidence amounts to an improper attempt to prove that a witness is of upstanding moral character.

- To prove that a defendant assaulted you, you cannot offer evidence that the defendant has been involved in other fights. And you cannot call a witness, who knows the defendant well, to give an opinion that the defendant is violent. Again, such evidence improperly asks the judge or jury to infer that because the defendant has a propensity (a character trait) to be violent, the defendant assaulted you.

- Similarly, to prove that you struck the defendant only in self-defense, you cannot offer evidence that you have never instigated a fight or that in the opinion of a friend who knows you well, you are a peaceful person. This evidence, too, improperly asks the judge or jury to infer from evidence of your peaceful character that you were not the aggressor in the fight with the defendant.

- To prove that your landlord falsely promised to install a new central heating system in your apartment, you cannot offer evidence of a witness's opinion that your landlord is dishonest or that she has made false promises to others.

 How to object to improper character evidence. To object if your adversary tries to introduce favorable character evidence about himself or one of his witnesses, or unfavorable character evidence about you or one of your witnesses, say, "Objection, Your Honor. That's improper character evidence." Object as soon as you realize that your adversary's question seeks, or the adverse witness's answer refers to, improper character evidence, but do not make an argument as to why the evidence constitutes character evidence unless the judge asks you to do so. (See Chapter 16, Making and Responding to Objections.)

E. HEARSAY

This section explains the hearsay rule, which potentially comes into play whenever parties offer evidence of out-of-court statements, which are simply statements made outside the courtroom. Because the rule does not apply to many kinds of out-of-court statements, and because it is riddled with exceptions, out-of-court statements are often admissible in evidence. If an out-of-court statement is important evidence either for you or your adversary, study this section very carefully. If you are still not sure about the admissibility of an out-of-court statement, refer to the Resources listed at the end of the chapter or consult your self-help law coach.

 The hearsay rule applies to both oral and written out-of-court statements. Don't be fooled by the word hearsay. The rule potentially applies to all out-of-court statements, whether they are made orally or written down in a letter, business record or other document.

1. The Rule Against Hearsay

In our trial system, we do not think it fair to admit into evidence statements from witnesses who are not in court where they can be seen and cross-examined. Hence we have adopted the hearsay rule, which under certain circumstances forbids a witness from testifying, "He said...." or "She said...." (For example, see Federal Rule of Evidence 802, California Evidence Code § 1200, New York Code of Evidence § 802, and Texas Civil Rule of Evidence 802.)

For example, assume that you are defending yourself against a claim that you were speeding. The plaintiff calls Andrea as a witness against you. Andrea testifies, "A couple of days after the accident I talked to Mark, who saw the whole thing. He said that he saw Nolo [you] going at a speed of at least 75 m.p.h." The plaintiff offers Andrea's testimony about what Mark said to her to prove that you were speeding.

An objection to Andrea's testimony as hearsay should be quickly sustained by any judge. Our system of justice does not consider it fair for the plaintiff to use what Mark said as evidence against you. The reason is simple: Since Mark is not in court to testify personally, you cannot cross-examine him, and the judge or jury cannot observe his demeanor and credibility. Of course the judge or jury can observe Andrea, and you can cross-examine her. But that will do you little good. She is not claiming to have seen the accident; all she can do is repeat what Mark said.

The hearsay rule can also prevent witnesses from testifying to their own out-of-court statements. For example, assume that you are testifying on your own behalf in a case in which you are seeking to limit visitation with your child, Summer, by your ex-spouse. To prove that your ex-spouse has been neglecting Summer during weekend visits, you testify that, "Last weekend I said to my neighbor Mr. Binder that my ex-spouse always returns Summer to me with torn and dirty clothes." Your testimony as to what you said to your neighbor is inadmissible hearsay. To avoid the hearsay problem, testify to the incident itself (that Summer always arrives home with torn and dirty clothes), and do not testify to your out-of-court statement to your neighbor.

2. When Out-of-Court Statements Aren't Hearsay

Despite the hearsay rule, witnesses can often properly testify to out-of-court statements, because they are not always hearsay. Confused? Don't worry, so are many lawyers. The hearsay rule makes out-of-court statements improper only if they are offered for their truth. If an out-of-court statement is relevant regardless of whether or not it is true, the statement is "non-hearsay" and admissible.

When would you want to admit an out-of-court statement if no one cares if it's true? Let's look at some examples. First, assume that you are trying to prove that Bob was alive on March 5. As

evidence of this, you call Marisa as a witness to testify, "On March 6, I heard Bob say that all sports car drivers drive too fast." Here, you are not offering Marisa's testimony for the truth of Bob's statement, so there is no need to cross-examine Bob about the statement. Regardless of whether Bob's statement about sports car drivers is true or false, we know that people who say things on March 6 were alive on March 5. Thus, you are not offering Bob's statement for its truth, and it is fair to admit Marisa's testimony as non-hearsay.

Consider a more subtle example of a non-hearsay use of an out-of-court statement. Remember the negligence case involving the building contractor, Sarah Adams, who made a careless left turn and struck a pedestrian in a crosswalk. Assume that you're the pedestrian, and you have evidence that moments before she hit you, Adams got a call on her car phone from Holden, her assistant manager. In this phone call Holden told Adams, "There's a major problem on the Jennifer Drive job. It looks like it'll set us back a few weeks. You'd better get right over there." You can offer Holden's statement to Adams into evidence as non-hearsay to prove that Adams was not paying attention to the road. Apart from the truth of whether there was really a major problem on the Jennifer Drive job, Holden's making this statement to Adams is likely to have distracted and upset her and made it more likely that she would drive carelessly. Lawyers refer to this type of non-hearsay use as "effect on the hearer." Holden's statement is admissible as non-hearsay because of its possible effect on Adams, the hearer of the statement.

Here's another example of non-hearsay. You are involved in a child custody dispute with your ex-spouse. A neighbor of your ex-spouse tells you that when your child, 11-year-old Margaret, recently had an overnight visit with your ex-spouse, your ex-spouse screamed at her and said, "You are the worst little brat in the whole world. You deserve to be locked in your room for a week." You can properly call the neighbor as a witness to testify to your ex-spouse's statement. You are not offering the statement because you think it's true—that Margaret is the worst brat in the world who deserves to be locked in her room for a week. Instead, what your ex-spouse said is itself some evidence that your ex-spouse is a poor parent who should not have custody of Margaret. Thus, the neighbor's testimony is non-hearsay.

Consider a final example. Assume that Tobias sues you for assaulting him. You admit exchanging blows with Tobias, but claim that you acted in self-defense. To help prove that you did not assault Tobias, you will testify that about a week before your fight with Tobias, you got a letter from Pat in which Pat wrote, "Tobias beat up a friend of mine yesterday." You want to testify that this letter made you afraid of Tobias, and that therefore you would not have tried to assault him. Pat's letter is admissible as non-hearsay. You are not offering it as proof that Tobias in fact hit Pat's friend, but for its effect on the hearer (you). Since the person (you) whose demeanor the judge or jury needs to observe and who Tobias needs the opportunity to cross-examine is in court, it is fair for you to testify to the content of Pat's letter. Of course, Tobias can argue that Pat's letter made you want to get in the first blow. But this possibility affects how much credence (weight) the judge or jury attaches to Pat's letter, not the question of whether the letter has a valid non-hearsay use.

At this point, the difference between hearsay and non-hearsay may seem like a semantic distinction dreamed up by a gaggle of bored judges for the sole purpose of confusing you. But if you look back at the examples of non-hearsay, you will see that it really is fair to admit out-of-court statements when they are not offered for their truth. Only when an out-of-court statement is offered because the party offering it wants the judge or jury to believe it's true does the judge or jury need an opportunity to cross-examine the maker of the statement.

As you can see, you cannot tell merely by looking at an out-of-court statement whether or not it is hearsay. You have to know what the statement is offered to prove. If it is offered for its truth, it is hearsay and inadmissible in evidence—unless a hearsay exception applies. (See Section 3 below.) If it is offered for a relevant purpose other than its truth, it is non-hearsay and likely to be admissible. So whenever you want to offer evidence of what someone said out of court (whether the out-of-court statement is oral or written), always consider whether you can offer it for some purpose other than its truth.

How to object to hearsay. To object to a hearsay statement offered by your adversary, say something like, "Objection, Your Honor; hearsay." Make your objection as soon as you realize that your adversary's question seeks or the adverse witness's answer refers to hearsay evidence, but do not make an argument as to why the evidence constitutes hearsay unless the judge asks you to do so. (See Chapter 16, Making and Responding to Objections.)

3. Exceptions to the Hearsay Rule

Finding a relevant non-hearsay use for an out-of-court statement is one way of making it admissible. (See Section 2, above.) You can also successfully offer a hearsay statement into evidence (that is, you can offer it for its truth) if it qualifies under one of the many exceptions to the general rule barring hearsay. Usually, exceptions apply when statements have been made under conditions making them likely to be accurate.

This section briefly reviews the most commonly used of the at least 30-40 hearsay exceptions that are recognized by statutes and court opinions. (Some are so obscure that you could probably try cases for 25 years and not run up against them.) For the full panoply of common hearsay exceptions, see Federal Rules of Evidence 803-804, California Evidence Code §§ 1220-1350, New York Code of Evidence §§ 802-803, and Texas Civil Rules of Evidence 802-803, or the comparable rules in your state.

a. Admissions

An admission is legal jargon for any out-of-court statement made by your adversary that you offer into evidence. The key word here is "adversary"; you can't offer your own statements or those of others as admissions. Despite the label of admission, your adversary's statement does not have to amount to a confession of wrongdoing for you to admit it into evidence. As long as your adversary made a statement—orally, in writing, during a deposition or pulled behind a blimp during the Super Bowl—that is relevant to the dispute, you can offer it as an admission if you think it helps your case.

For example, assume that you are suing Citron, the previous owner of your house, for fraudulently concealing the fact that the house had a leaky roof. In a conversation before the sale, Citron told Abby, a real estate broker he had previously employed, "I've never done a thing about the leaky roof, so I'd better sell the house during the summer." You can offer Citron's out-of-court statement to Abby as an admission. For instance, you may conduct the following direct examination of Abby:

1 **You:**

Did you speak with Mr. Citron on February 22?

2 **Witness:**

Yes, I did.

3 **You:**

Was anyone else present at this conversation?

4 **Witness:**

No, just the two of us.

5 **You:**

Do you remember where the conversation took place?

6 **Witness:**

I remember it was in the backyard, because we were talking about how warm it was for April.

7 **You:**

What was the purpose of the conversation?

8 **Witness:**

The house had been on the market for some time, and my exclusive contract period to sell it had just expired. Mr. Citron asked me to come over and he told me that he was going to try to sell the house himself.

9   You:

Do you remember Mr. Citron saying anything about the condition of the house?

10   Witness:

I do.

11   You:

And what did he say?

12   Witness:

He said that he had never taken care of the leaky roof, so that he wanted to sell the house during the coming summer months.

13   You:

How did you respond?

14   Witness:

I told him that he had never told me about the leaky roof, and that what he was talking about was illegal. He just said that I should take care of my business and he'd take care of his.

Transcript Analysis: Abby's testimony in Nos. 12 and 14 about what Citron told her is hearsay, but admissible in evidence as Citron's admission. Because Citron is your adversary and you are offering into evidence a statement he made, the hearsay rule does not exclude it. Also, if you look back at No. 14, you will see that Abby testifies not only to what Citron told her, but also to what she told Citron. This is in line with the general rule of "completeness" that if statements made by one party to a conversation are admissible, then so are statements made by the other party.

 How to respond to your adversary's objection that an admission is improper hearsay. When you testify or ask a witness to testify to a hearsay statement that qualifies as an admission, your adversary may object that it is hearsay. (Your adversary may be attempting to harass you or may not realize that the statement is an admission.)

To respond, say something like, "Your Honor, I am offering the statement as Citron's admission." Or wait a moment before responding; the judge may recognize that the statement is an admission and overrule the objection immediately. (See Chapter 16, Making and Responding to Objections.)

ADMISSIONS BY CORPORATIONS AND OTHER ORGANIZATIONS

If your adversary is a corporation or similar organization, you can probably offer into evidence a statement made by an employee or other representative of the organization as an admission. For a judge to admit such a statement, you typically have to show either that the organization specifically authorized the employee to make the statement or, more simply, that the employee's statement relates to her job duties with the organization.

For example, assume that you suffer injuries as a result of slipping on a banana peel in a supermarket, and sue the supermarket. To prove that the supermarket carelessly allowed the dangerous condition (the banana peel on the floor) to exist, you seek to offer into evidence a statement by the store manager, who came up to you right after you slipped and said, "I'm really sorry. I asked someone to clean up this peel hours ago." The manager's statement is admissible as an admission of the defendant supermarket because the statement relates to the manager's job duties.

b.   Present Sense Impressions

A "present sense impression" is a statement that a person makes about an event while it is going on or right after it has taken place. The exception to the hearsay rule for present sense impressions is based on the theory that statements made about ongoing events are likely to be reliable. Offering present sense impressions into evidence is often a useful way of explaining to a judge or jury the meaning of conduct that may otherwise be ambiguous.

For example, assume that you are involved in a dispute with your landlord, Patrick, about substandard and illegal conditions in your apartment house. One day you ask Alison, who is doing some work in the apartment hallways, what she is doing. She replies, "Oh, Patrick asked me to remove the fire detection devices now that the inspection has taken place." Alison's statement explains what she is doing and is admissible as a present sense impression. Without the statement, you may have difficulty proving the significance of Alison's actions to the judge or jury.

The key to showing that hearsay statements qualify as present sense impressions is to show that they were made during or very shortly after an event. For instance, assume that you spoke with Alison three days after you saw her working in the hallway of your apartment house. You asked, "What were you doing the other day?" Alison replied, "I was removing the fire detection devices because we had already been inspected." Now Alison's statement probably does not qualify as a present sense impression because it was made three days after the event, not during or right afterwards.

Some states allow present sense impressions to be admitted into evidence as exceptions to the hearsay rule only if the event described by the statement was startling or exciting. (These statements are sometimes called "excited utterances.") The evidence rule drafters in these states believe that only when people are excited are they likely to blurt out the truth, and that otherwise a present sense impression may not be sufficiently reliable. For example, assume that you have evidence that Kevin opened a door and said, "Hi, Hilary. Nice to see you. Watch your step." Kevin's statement will probably not be admissible to prove that Hilary was at the door in states that require the events described by present sense impressions to be exciting, unless of course Hilary is a long-lost relative who owes Kevin $30,000.

 How to respond to an objection that a present sense impression is hearsay. When you testify or ask a witness to testify to a hearsay statement that qualifies for admission into evidence as a present sense impression, your adversary may object that it is hearsay. (Your adversary may be attempting to harass you, or may not realize that the statement qualifies as a present sense impression.)

To respond, say, "Your Honor, I am offering the statement as the witness's present sense impression." Or you may wait a moment before responding; the judge may recognize that the statement is admissible and overrule the objection immediately. (See Chapter 16, Making and Responding to Objections.)

c.   Declarations of State of Mind

Statements in which people describe their then-existing emotions, physical sensations, intents, plans and the like are admissible as exceptions to the hearsay rule. Called declarations of state of mind, evidence rule drafters believe that such statements are likely to be reliable.

In the colorful 19th century United States Supreme Court case that created this rule of evidence, there was a question of the identity of a corpse found at Cripple Creek, Colorado. One party to the lawsuit, trying to prove the body was that of a man named Walters, offered into evidence Walters' statement that, "Next week I'm going to go meet my friend Hillmon at Cripple Creek." The Court ruled that the statement was admissible as non-hearsay, reasoning that people's declarations about their future plans (their intentions) are generally reliable and should not be barred by the hearsay rule.

The state of mind exception has many applications. Here are some examples of statements that describe present thoughts or feelings and so qualify as declarations of state of mind:

- You are trying to prove that Joe's arm was broken. The fact that Joe said "Ouch! That really hurts!" when someone touched his arm is admissible. (Note that this statement would also qualify for admission as a present sense impression.)

- You are trying to prove that a salesperson made a false statement to induce you to buy a product. The fact that the salesperson told a friend, "I'll do anything to make a sale; I really need the money" is admissible.

- You are trying to prove that you didn't start a fight with Lenny. The fact that two days before the fight you wrote to a friend, "I'm scared to death of Lenny" is admissible.

 How to respond to an objection that a declaration of state of mind is hearsay. When you testify or ask a witness to testify to a hearsay statement that qualifies for admission into evidence as a declaration of state of mind, your adversary may object that it is hearsay. (Your adversary may be attempting to harass you, or may not realize that the statement qualifies under the state of mind exception.)

To respond, say, "Your Honor, I am offering the statement as a declaration of the witness's state of mind." Or you may wait a moment before responding; the judge may recognize that the statement is admissible and overrule the objection immediately. (See Chapter 16, Making and Responding to Objections.)

d.   Statements Made to a Medical Practitioner

Statements made to a medical practitioner for purposes of treatment or diagnosis are admissible as an exception to the hearsay rule. Again, the drafters of evidence rules think such statements are likely to be reliable. After all, most patients don't want the doctor taking out their gallbladder when it's their right knee that hurts!

Here are some examples:

- Some months after an automobile accident, you go to a doctor for treatment. You tell the doctor or doctor's assistant, "My back has been hurting for the last six months." Your statement is admissible under this hearsay exception. You, the doctor, the doctor's assistant or whoever else heard you say it can testify to your statement.

- You go to see a doctor not for treatment, but just so the doctor can diagnose your condition and testify as an expert witness on your behalf at trial. The statements you make to the doctor are still admissible under this exception, because it covers statements made for purposes of treatment or diagnosis.

This exception may not cover everything said to a medical practitioner. A judge might admit into evidence some of what you've said and exclude the rest. For instance, assume you tell a doctor, "My back has been hurting ever since that idiot the defendant ran a red light and hit me." Your statement about your back pain is admissible. But the doctor really does not have to know what you think of the defendant and the color of the light in order to treat or diagnose you, so that part of your statement will not be admitted into evidence; it is inadmissible hearsay.

How to respond to an objection that a medical declaration is hearsay. When you testify or ask a witness to testify to a hearsay statement that qualifies for admission into evidence as a declaration of a medical condition, your adversary may object that it is hearsay. (Your adversary may be attempting to harass you, or may not realize that the statement qualifies under the medical declarations exception.)

To respond, say, "Your Honor, I am offering the statement as a declaration made to a medical practitioner for the purpose of treatment (or diagnosis)." Or may wait a moment before responding; the judge may recognize that the statement is admissible and overrule the objection immediately. (See Chapter 16, Making and Responding to Objections.)

e.   Business and Government Records

Written records reflecting regular business and government activities are admissible as hearsay exceptions. You must, however, lay foundations showing that the records are reliable. (See Chapter 14, Exhibits.)

f.   Other Hearsay Exceptions

We have discussed only a few of the numerous hearsay exceptions. Some others carry colorful titles such as "dying declarations" and "ancient documents." Others carry no title at all; in some court systems, judges simply have discretion to admit into evidence hearsay statements that they consider trustworthy. Again, if either you or your opponent has important evidence that consists of an out-of-court statement, and you are uncertain about whether or not it is admissible, you should probably seek legal advice as to its admissibility.

4. Having Trouble? You're Not Alone

If you are feeling a bit perplexed, take heart from the fact that the sometimes subtle distinctions between inadmissible hearsay statements, admissible non-hearsay statements and statements that are admissible under an exception to the hearsay rule are often as much a mystery to lawyers as they may be to you. Do not automatically assume that if a lawyer for your adversary makes what you think is an improper hearsay objection, or offers what you think is improper hearsay evidence, that the lawyer understands the hearsay rule better than you do.

Remember that the touchstone of the hearsay rule is fairness. If you think it is fair for you to offer an out-of-court statement into evidence against your adversary, or unfair for your adversary to offer an out-of-court statement into evidence against you, consider offering or objecting to the statement even if you are not sure of the correct legal analysis. Whatever a state's specific evidence rules, an overall policy of modern evidence law is to depend on a judge's discretion to ensure a fair trial for both sides in which truth emerges. Especially in a judge trial, a judge may discount techni-

cal concerns and make a ruling based on the trustworthiness of an out-of-court statement.

 RESOURCES ON EVIDENCE

Wigmore on Evidence, by John Wigmore (Little Brown & Co.). This multi-volume treatise, which has been revised by other authors since Wigmore's death in 1943, has been termed the greatest treatise ever written on any legal subject. It masterfully explores the history of and policies behind most modern rules of evidence, and its updates have case citations from every state. You should probably refer to the treatise only if you already have a basic understanding of evidence principles.

McCormick on Evidence, by John Strong, ed. (West Publishing Co.). A one-volume evidence text widely referred to by lawyers and judges.

Weinstein's Evidence Manual, by Judge Jack Weinstein and Margaret Berger (Matthew Bender). A single-volume treatise based on the Federal Rules of Evidence. It sets forth and explains the text of each rule.

Evidence, by Ken Graham (Casenotes Publishing Co.); *Evidence,* by Steven Emanuel (Emanuel Law Outlines). These books are single-volume evidence outlines designed as quick refreshers for law students. They are usually available in law bookstores near law schools. ■

16

MAKING AND RESPONDING TO OBJECTIONS

An objection is a request to a judge to rule that an adversary's statement or offer of evidence is improper under the rules of evidence. If the judge grants the request (sustains the objection), the improper evidence or statement will be excluded. Neither the judge nor a jury may then consider it when arriving at its verdict. This chapter shows you how to make and respond to objections. It also includes a list of common objections, which you can take with you into the courtroom and refer to.

You can make an objection at any point during a trial. For example, you can object to a statement made by your adversary during his opening statement or closing argument, to a question asked by your adversary during direct or cross-examination, or to an adverse witness's answer.

Nonetheless, in general you will be wise to follow a practice of many experienced attorneys: Do not object just because you believe that a technical evidence rule violation has occurred. One reason is that even if a judge sustains your objection, often your adversary can get the evidence admitted anyway simply by rephrasing an improper question or answer. Also, as a pro per litigant you are likely to come off second best if you turn your trial into a war of objections against your adversary's lawyer. So unless you think that the evidence your adversary is attempting to offer is both important and should be excluded from evidence altogether, an objection may serve only to slow down your trial and incur the wrath of the judge or jury. Hollywood images notwithstanding, attorneys often manage to try entire cases with few or no objections.

> ⚠️ **Evidence rules are covered in other chapters.** This chapter focuses on the procedures for making and responding to objections. Please refer to other chapters for discussions of the evidence rules on which objections are based.

A. OBJECTIONS: AN OVERVIEW

Many people believe that a judge plays a role similar to that of a football referee—that is, making sure that the "game" of trial is played according to the rules, in this case rules of evidence. If so, it may seem strange to you that you have to object at all. After all, referees call penalties on their own whenever a rule is violated; they do not wait for one team to object to something the other team has done.

But at trial, it's your responsibility to object to important impermissible evidence or statements. If you fail to object, you give up (waive) the objection, and the judge or jury may consider the impermissible information along with the rest of the evidence in arriving at its verdict.

Unfortunately, this system really works well only when both sides are represented by skilled trial lawyers. It may be less satisfactory when one side is a pro per litigant who doesn't (and can't reasonably be expected to) have in-depth knowledge of evidence rules. Fortunately, many judges understand this unfairness and will exclude obviously improper evidence on their own. But others will not, perhaps believing that being at a disadvantage serves you right for not hiring a lawyer. (Of course, many lawyers aren't exactly experts on the rules of evidence, either.)

Typically, objections are made orally and refer to the rule of evidence that a party believes has been violated. For example, if your adversary asks a witness to testify to an out-of-court statement, you might say, "Objection, Your Honor. Hearsay."

Normally, a judge makes an immediate ruling in response to an objection. If the judge thinks that the objection is erroneous—that is, that the offered evidence or statement is proper—the judge will deny (overrule) the objection. If the judge thinks that the objection is correct, the judge will uphold (sustain) it.

B. OBJECTIONS MADE BEFORE TRIAL: MOTIONS IN LIMINE

A "motion in limine" (rhymes with "Jiminy") is Latin legal jargon for any objection you make before trial starts. You may choose to make a motion in limine when you believe that important evidence your adversary plans to offer during trial is not admissible. However, you needn't make a motion in limine; you always have the option of waiting until your adversary offers the evidence at trial and making your objection at that time.

Why bother to make a motion in limine if you can object during trial? Two good reasons. First, you can plan more effectively if you know before your trial starts whether a judge will allow your adversary to offer a particular item of important evidence.

Second, if you wait to object until your adversary offers evidence, the jury may well hear some or all of it before you can object. Even if the judge sustains your objection, excludes the evidence and instructs the jury to disregard it, some jurors may still be influenced by it. Far better to exclude evidence in advance. This explains why motions in limine are primarily made only in jury trials. In judge-tried cases, the judge will hear about the disputed evidence anyway in order to rule on its admissibility.

To make a motion in limine, typically all you have to do is notify your adversary and the court clerk, or the judge during a pre-trial conference, that you want to make a motion in limine. If the judge agrees to hear the motion (the judge might refuse and ask you to raise the point during trial), the judge will conduct a short hearing on your objection before trial starts. During the hearing, orally tell the judge what evidence the adversary plans to offer and why you think it's improper. Your adversary will, of course, have a chance to respond to your argument.

Check your local court rules. Carefully read your local court rules for procedures that you must follow to make a motion in limine. For example, you may have to give your adversary ten days' notice (perhaps in writing) of your intention to make a motion. (For general information on pre-trial motions, see Chapter 6, Pre-Trial Hearings and Motions.)

The judge may rule on your motion in limine on the spot, or may postpone a decision by asking you to renew your objection when the evidence is actually offered. By delaying a ruling, the judge has a chance to evaluate how important or prejudicial the evidence is. Nevertheless, even if the judge postpones a ruling your motion will not be wasted effort. The fact that you have brought the judge's attention to the problematic evidence early and in an organized way is likely to encourage the judge to think more seriously about excluding the evidence than if you first raise the point during trial.

Motions in limine made by attorneys are sometimes submitted in the form of written arguments that lawyers call briefs (though their long-winded complexity often makes them just the opposite). Like an oral motion, a brief identifies the evidence that the lawyer seeks to have excluded and the grounds for objection. In addition, a written brief may include references (citations) to supporting legal authorities such as statutes and cases.

You, too, may find it sensible to do a little research and to present a written brief in support of your motion in limine. The sample below illustrates what a simple written brief in support of a motion in limine may consist of. (As with other sample documents in this book, this one is for illustration only. The motion you might file could well look very different, depending on your state's law and rules of procedure.)

USING A MOTION IN LIMINE AFFIRMATIVELY

In theory, you can also use a motion in limine to ask a judge for an advance ruling that evidence you plan to offer is admissible. But generally you should not do this. The motion may act as a red flag that admissibility of the evidence is in doubt. Put the burden on your adversary to object if the adversary thinks it's warranted.

C. HOW TO MAKE OBJECTIONS DURING TRIAL

As with so many things in life, success at making objections depends not only on what you say but how and when you say it. Or in the words attributed to Albert Einstein, "God is in the details." Follow these procedures:

1. Stand Up

When you make or respond to objections, stand up as a sign of respect to the court. You can begin speaking as you rise.

2. Speak Only to the Judge

Always state your objection directly to the judge rather than to opposing counsel or your adversary. If you want to talk directly to your adversary, ask the judge for permission to go "off the record."

3. State Your Objection Succinctly

To object, it is normally sufficient to refer briefly to the reason (legal basis) for the objection. For example, you might say, "Objection, Your Honor. Hearsay," or "Objection, Your Honor, Irrelevant."

When you object to only a portion of a statement, a question or an answer, specify the portion

SAMPLE MOTION IN LIMINE

1 Fred Nolo
[Street Address]
2 [City, State, Zip Code]
[Phone Number]
3
Plaintiff in Pro Per
4
THE _____ COURT OF _____ COUNTY
5
STATE OF _____
6 Fred Nolo)
) CASE NO. 11359
7 Plaintiff,)
v.)
8) PLAINTIFF'S MOTION
Amy Binder,) IN LIMINE
9)
Defendant,)
10 _____)

11

12   Plaintiff Nolo submits this Motion in Limine for an order excluding from evidence Plaintiff's three-year-old

13 conviction for reckless driving.

14   STATEMENT OF THE CASE

15   Plaintiff Nolo has filed suit against Defendant Binder for careless driving resulting in both personal injuries

16 to Plaintiff and property damage to Plaintiff's car. Defendant claims that Plaintiff's careless driving caused the

17 accident. As part of the Defendant's proof that Plaintiff drove carelessly, Defendant has indicated that she

18 intends to offer into evidence a record of Plaintiff's three-year-old conviction for reckless driving.

19   ARGUMENT

20   Plaintiff's conviction can not properly be admitted into evidence. This is a civil case governed by the laws

21 of the State of California, and California Evidence Code § 1101 provides that character evidence is not

22 admissible in a civil case to prove conduct. Plaintiff's prior conviction would be character evidence, as its

23 only purpose is to prove that Plaintiff has a propensity to drive carelessly and therefore was driving

24 carelessly when Plaintiff collided with Defendant Binder. Therefore, the conviction should not be admitted

25 into evidence.

26 Respectfully submitted,

27 *Fred Nolo*
Fred Nolo, Plaintiff in Pro Per

28

to which you object. For example, if your adversary asks a proper question and the witness refers to an improper hearsay statement while answering, you may say something like, "Objection to the portion of the answer in which the witness referred to what Mr. Moore said as hearsay." (If the judge sustains your objection, you should also ask the judge to delete (strike) the improper testimony from the record. See Subsection 6, below.)

4. Object Promptly

If your adversary's question calls for improper evidence, object immediately after the question—before the answer if you can. If you wait until after the witness answers to object, the judge or jury may hear improper information. More importantly, the judge may refuse to sustain your objection because it is untimely, or because by waiting you are deemed to have waived the objection. Similarly, if a question is proper but an adverse witness throws improper evidence into the answer, object immediately after (or even during) the answer and before another question is asked.

 Don't be overly polite—interrupt to object when necessary. If an adverse witness's improper answer is longer than a sentence or two, you do not have to wait until the witness is done talking but can interrupt the answer to object to improper evidence. Try not to "talk over" the witness; the judge and especially the court reporter are likely to become quite testy if you and a witness are both talking at once. Instead, say "Excuse me" and perhaps hold up your hand to stop the witness in mid-answer, then make your objection.

Consider this example of a late objection during your adversary's direct examination of a witness:

1 **Adversary:**

What's the next thing that happened?

2 **Witness:**

Well, just like she had done many times before, Ms. Nolo [you] began drinking a bottle of beer.

3 **Adversary:**

How much beer did Ms. Nolo drink this time?

4 **You:**

Objection to the testimony that I had done this many times before. That's irrelevant.

This ground for objection is discussed in Chapter 15, Basic Rules of Evidence.

5 **Judge:**

I agree with your objection, Ms. Nolo. But you should have made that objection before counsel asked the next question. I'll overrule the objection as untimely.

Transcript Analysis: In this example, opposing counsel's question (No. 1) is proper, but the answer that introduces prior drinking (No. 2) refers to evidence that you think is improper. Your objection should have come immediately after the answer, before your adversary asked another question.

A judge has discretion about how rigidly to enforce the rule that you must object as soon as the ground for objection appears, and a more sympathetic judge may treat you more leniently. Consider this example:

1 **Adversary:**

What did the person standing next to you say?

2 **Witness:**

He said that the blue car ran the red light.

3 **You:**

Objection, hearsay.

This ground of objection is discussed in Chapter 15, Basic Rules of Evidence.

4 **Judge:**

Mr. Nolo, you really should have objected before the witness answered, as it was apparent that the question called for hearsay. But I'll overlook that this time and sustain the objection. The answer is stricken and I instruct the jury to disregard it.

5. Don't Argue the Merits of Your Objection

Do not include in your objection an argument about why the judge should sustain it. Here's an example of how *not* to object to a witness's answer:

Your Honor, I object to that entire answer as irrelevant. This is a case about what happened on April 24. The witness is talking about things that took place three months earlier, and that has nothing to do with what we're talking about now.

This is called arguing an objection, and it is improper. State an objection concisely: "Objec-

tion, irrelevant." A judge who wants an explanation will ask for one. In that case, an explanation like the one above would be proper.

6. Ask to Strike Improper Evidence

Ask the judge to strike any improper testimony given or statements made before your objection was made and sustained. By striking (removing) improper evidence or statements from the official record, the judge indicates that the evidence can't be considered by the judge or jury when arriving at a decision.

Requests to strike improper testimony are necessary because, as you've seen, it's not always possible to object before objectionable testimony is given. For example, if the opposing attorney asks a proper question, but the witness gives improper testimony while answering, you cannot possibly object until the improper testimony has already been given.

A judge who sustains your objection to testimony that has already been given may strike the answer without being asked (as in the second example in Subsection 3, above). However, if the judge neglects to do this, it's up to you to request that the improper testimony be stricken by saying something like, "Your Honor, I also move to strike the answer."

If there is a jury, you should also ask the judge to instruct the jury to disregard the stricken testimony. Unless the judge instructs the jury to disregard it, the jury can properly consider even stricken testimony when arriving at a decision.

💡 **You can't unring a bell.** Whenever possible, try to keep a jury from hearing improper evidence in the first place rather than rely on a jury's ability to follow a judge's instruction to disregard it. Just like telling someone not to think about pink elephants may cause him to think of nothing but, so a judge's instruction to disregard stricken evidence is easier said than done. Or as lawyers are fond of saying, you can't unring a bell. This human weakness is a primary reason to consider making a motion in limine before trial. (See Section B above.)

Here is an example of how to follow up an objection with a motion to strike:

1   Adversary:

After the blue car completed making the left turn, what happened?

2   Witness:

It started swerving back and forth, like the driver had had too much to drink.

3   You:

Objection to "too much to drink," Your Honor. Lack of personal knowledge and an improper opinion.

The first ground of objection is discussed in Chapter 11, Direct Examination and the second in Chapter 15, Basic Rules of Evidence.

4   Judge:

Objection sustained.

5   You:

I move to strike the testimony, and ask that you instruct the jury to disregard it.

6   Judge:

The motion to strike is granted. Jurors, the witness's remark about drinking was improper, and I instruct you to disregard it.

Transcript Analysis: Here, you properly specify the portion of the answer to which you object. (No. 3) At your request, the judge strikes that portion and instructs the jury to disregard it.

💡 **Don't thank a judge for sustaining your objection.** Like a baseball umpire calling a strike, a judge is doing her job, not doing you a favor, by sustaining your objection. Many toadying lawyers ignore this advice and thank the judge early and often; most judges hate it.

⚠️ **You may be unable to object to deposition testimony.** The judge may give your adversary permission to read a portion of a witness' deposition into the trial record. Often, you can only object to deposition testimony at trial if you objected to it during the deposition. See Chapter 4, Investigating Your Case.

7. Object Only When Absolutely Necessary

As mentioned at the beginning of this chapter, if evidence to which you object is unimportant, or if your adversary can get around your objection by simply rephrasing a question or an answer, your repeated objections may succeed only in depriving you of whatever empathy the judge or jury may feel towards you. Use this chapter to learn the mechanics of objecting, but remember that your goal is to object as infrequently as possible, especially in a judge trial.

D. HOW TO RESPOND TO YOUR ADVERSARY'S OBJECTIONS

Of course you are not the only one playing the game called trial. The opposing attorney (or your pro per adversary) can object to a statement you make, a question you ask or testimony you or one of your witnesses gives. That means you also need to understand how to respond to objections.

Abusive lawyering is less likely to occur during a judge trial. Compared to a jury trial, where judges tend to enforce evidence rules more strictly, in a judge trial a judge is less likely to put up with numerous technical objections. She even may regard repeated objections as interfering with her power to decide what evidence she will listen to. It's another reason why as a pro per litigant you are usually better off with a judge than a jury trial. (See Chapter 9, Selecting the Decision-Maker.)

HARASSMENT BY YOUR ADVERSARY'S LAWYER

As radio therapists remind us regularly, you can control only your own behavior. Your sensible reluctance to make objections may not be reciprocated by your adversary. Particularly in a jury trial, the adversary's attorney may try to take advantage of your "new kid in court" status by sending a barrage of objections your way, no doubt trying to intimidate you. If this happens, your best bet is to ask the judge for permission to approach the bench or to have a conference in chambers (the judge's office). Ask the judge for the court reporter to be present and to take down what's said so that the official record will show that you sought the judge's help. Tell the judge that the attorney is using the rules of evidence improperly to try to harass and intimidate you and to prevent your having a fair trial. Ask the judge to warn the attorney that repeatedly trying to invoke technicalities to thwart the larger purpose of achieving a fair trial won't be tolerated.

In addition, during your final argument, you may use your adversary's unfair tactics to try to gain the judge's or jury's understanding. Point out that while you are not familiar with all the technical rules of evidence, you have done your best to present your case fairly and honestly and, unlike your adversary, did not try to hide behind a smoke screen of objections.

---

1. Making a Counter-Argument

Rule No. 1 is: Don't immediately follow an adversary's objection by arguing why the judge should overrule it. Instead, wait for the judge to either make a ruling or ask you to respond. In most cases, a judge will rule without asking for your position. Here's an example of the procedure you should follow:

1   You:

And after you saw the two cars collide, what happened?

2   Witness:

I remember this person standing right next to me said, "My God, that red car went right through the stoplight."

3   Adversary:

Objection, hearsay.

4   Judge:

Ms. Nolo, any response?

5   You:

Yes, Your Honor. I think that what the witness heard this person say is admissible as a present sense impression made in response to a startling event. The person saw two cars collide, so that's an exciting event, and he made a statement about what he saw right away.

See Chapter 15, Basic Rules of Evidence, for a discussion of this evidence rule.

6   Judge:

All right, I'll overrule the objection and allow the testimony.

7   You:

Thank you, Your Honor.

8   Judge:

What's that, Ms. Nolo? Didn't you read the earlier section telling you not to thank the judge after a favorable ruling?

9   You:

Oh, right, sorry. I'll move on. Now, after….

Transcript Analysis: In this excerpt, you properly wait for the judge to ask you to respond (No. 4) before telling the judge why you think the evidence should be admitted (No. 5).

 If you believe that a judge's ruling is clearly wrong, ask the judge to reconsider. When a judge follows the typical practice of making a ruling without giving you a chance to respond to your adversary's objection, you may ask for an opportunity to change the judge's mind if you are confident that you have a sound legal reason for thinking that the judge wrongly sustained the adversary's objection. Since the judge has already made a ruling, you first have to ask the judge for permission to talk about it.

For example, if the judge has sustained your adversary's objection that your evidence is irrelevant, you may say something like, "Your Honor, might I speak briefly as to why I think the evidence is relevant?" If the judge denies permission, that ends the matter. You have no right to argue evidence rulings. If the judge grants permission, you may then try to persuade the judge to change the ruling. And unlike baseball umpires, judges sometimes do reverse their rulings when an argument sheds additional light on the purpose of evidence. Nevertheless, it's just plain dumb to repeatedly challenge a judge's rulings. Save your fire for when it really counts.

2. Laying a Better Foundation

When your adversary objects, it will probably often be on the ground that you have failed to lay a sufficient foundation for evidence to be admissible. (See Chapter 11, Direct Examination, and Chapter 14, Exhibits, for additional discussions of laying a foundation.) If the judge is uncertain about whether a foundation is sufficient or simply wants to hear more foundational testimony to see what you are driving at, the judge may delay a ruling on the objection and let you lay a further foundation.

For example, assume that after your adversary objects to the out-of-court statement about the red car going through the stoplight (No. 5 in Subsection 1, above), the following dialogue takes place:

6 **Judge:**

Well, you may be right that the statement qualifies as a present sense impression, Ms. Nolo. But before I make that ruling, I'd like to hear additional foundational testimony.

See Chapter 15, Basic Rules of Evidence, for more information about this hearsay exception.

7 **You:**

What would that be, Your Honor?

8 **Judge:**

Well, it's really not my job to tell you the rules. But as you're representing yourself I'll tell you that before I rule I want to be satisfied that the person's statement really was blurted out in the excitement of the moment, which this state requires for a present sense impression to be admissible. Can you ask some questions that might satisfy me about that?

9 **You:**

I'll try. Mr. Grady, how far away from you was this person standing?

10 **Witness:**

Oh, not more than a few feet. He was as close to the collision as I was.

11 **You:**

How long had he been standing there, if you know?

12 **Witness:**

Well, we both came out of the store the same time, so he'd been there the same amount of time as me, about 30 seconds.

13 **You:**

And how long after the cars collided did you hear him say that the red car ran the stoplight?

14 **Adversary:**

Objection, Your Honor, leading.

15 **Judge:**

Overruled. The witness has already testified to what the person said [see No. 2 in the previous section]; Ms. Nolo is simply seeking to establish the time framework. Please refrain from meaningless objections.

16 **Witness:**

I'd say just a second or two. It was right away.

17 **You:**

That's all the questions I can think of, Your Honor.

18 Judge:

Let me ask one or two. What tone of voice did this person use?

19 Witness:

He really shouted. He made my ears hurt.

20 Judge:

And where did he go after he said this?

21 Witness:

I'm not really sure. I ran over to see if the drivers were OK, and I didn't see him again.

22 Judge:

Well, the issue is a close one, but on balance I think that there's enough of a foundation to admit this as an exception to the hearsay rule on the ground that it qualifies as a present sense impression. The objection is overruled. Ms. Nolo, you may resume questioning.

There's no harm in asking. As we have emphasized throughout this book, a judge is a human being who, within the limits set by the adversary system, may be willing to help you cope with the nuances of technical evidentiary rules. So if you are not sure of what foundation the judge has in mind, do not be too embarrassed to ask. The judge, you hope, wants to have the benefit of considering all proper evidence before making a decision, and may suggest the kind of foundational testimony you need to elicit.

E. CHECKLIST OF COMMON OBJECTIONS

Making objections is obviously a demanding task. In about the same tiny interval that it takes the average cab driver to honk a horn when a light changes from red to green, you have to decide not only whether to object, but also what objection to make. The following checklist of common objections should help, especially if yours is a jury trial where it often makes sense to object to inadmissible evidence.

1. Objections to the Form of Questions

An objection to the form of a question—for example, on the ground that it is leading—asserts that a question is improper. However, an objection to form does not challenge the admissibility of the information the questioner is trying to elicit. So even if the judge sustains the objection, the questioner can ordinarily elicit the information simply by rephrasing the question.

Object with caution when it comes to form of question objections: do not make them unless a question is so poorly phrased that you are not sure of what the witness will say in response, or your adversary is attempting to browbeat a reluctant witness into giving your adversary's desired testimony.

Here are common objections to the form of a question:

a. "Objection; the question is vague [or ambiguous or unintelligible]."

You may object on this ground when you are unsure of what a question means. Questions should be clear enough so that you can reasonably determine in advance what information a witness is being asked to give.

If the judge sustains your adversary's objection that your question is vague or unintelligible, think about the specific information you are after and rephrase your question.

b. "Objection; the question is compound."

You can object on this ground when opposing counsel combines two questions into one, leaving you unsure about which part the witness will answer. For example, say your adversary asks a witness, "What time did he arrive and what did he do when he got there?" But again, especially if there is no jury and the question is not otherwise improper, you are probably better off not making this kind of technical objection.

If the judge sustains your adversary's objection that your question is compound, break up the single question into two different questions.

c. "Objection; the question calls for a narrative response."

You can object on this ground when opposing counsel's direct examination question asks a witness to narrate a series of events. (See Chapter 11, Direct Examination, for a discussion of narrative questions.) Also, if an adverse witness starts into a lengthy narrative response to a proper narrow question, stop the witness in mid-answer and state, "Objection. The witness is narrating."

If the judge sustains your adversary's objection that your question calls for a narrative response, ask a question with a more limited scope.

d. "Objection; the question is repetitive [has been asked and answered]."

An opposing attorney may try to take advantage of you by trying to hit the judge or jury over the head repeatedly with the same information. This is improper because it wastes time and artificially boosts the importance of evidence. You may object on this ground when opposing counsel persists in asking questions about information a witness has already given.

If the judge sustains your adversary's objection that your question has been asked and answered, move on to a new topic.

e. "Objection; counsel is misquoting the witness."

You may object on this ground when opposing counsel misstates testimony that has already been given. This problem typically arises during cross-examination, when the proper use of leading questions allows your adversary to refer to evidence in a question. (See Chapter 12, Cross-Examination.) For example, assume that a witness who testified for you stated that "the red car was going at least 60 m.p.h." On cross-examination, adverse counsel asks, "Now, you said that the red car was going

pretty fast, right?" This question misquotes the witness's actual testimony.

If the judge sustains your adversary's objection that your question misquotes a witness, rephrase your question if you are able to recall the witness's actual testimony. If you cannot recall the actual testimony and want to refer to it, you may ask the judge to ask the court reporter to read back the previous testimony. However, the judge may not grant your request, especially if considerable time has elapsed since the answer was given. A third possibility is not to refer to the previous testimony in your question, but to ask the witness to repeat what was said earlier.

f. "Objection; the question is leading."

Consider objecting on this ground when opposing counsel asks an improper leading question during direct examination, especially if the witness seems reluctant to give your adversary's desired answer unless verbally bullied into doing so. This can be an important objection, because under some circumstances your judge may not allow your adversary to rephrase so as to elicit the evidence with a proper question. If the judge believes that your adversary is overtly trying to put words in the witness's mouth, the judge may not only sustain your objection but also forbid any testimony on the same subject from that witness.

If the judge sustains your adversary's objection that your question is leading, rephrase it in a way that does not suggest your desired answer. Or if the judge allows you to respond to the objection, perhaps point out that your leading question is proper because the information you seek to elicit is background or preliminary. (See Chapter 11, Direct

Examination, for a discussion of when leading questions are proper during direct examination.)

g. "Objection; the question is argumentative."

You can object on this ground when opposing counsel cross-examines your witness in a hostile or angry way, or asks a question before you or your witness have completed the answer to a previous question. (In movies and TV shows, this practice is often referred to as "badgering the witness.")

For example, assume that opposing counsel asks you or your witness, "So you're willing to perjure yourself," or "You couldn't possibly have done what you've said you did, could you?" These questions do not ask a witness to provide evidence. Instead, they amount to your adversary making an argument in question form.

If the judge sustains your adversary's objection that your question is argumentative, rephrase the question so as to elicit evidence rather than to state your point of view.

h. "Objection; the question assumes facts not in evidence."

You can object on this ground when opposing counsel surreptitiously inserts new evidence into the record while asking for other information.

For example, assume that you are a tenant in an eviction case, and that there has been no evidence admitted about complaints from other tenants concerning your supposedly loud stereo. The landlord's attorney asks you this question: "Ms. Nolo, even after numerous other tenants complained to you about your loud stereo, didn't you say to the landlord that she had no right to tell you how to live your life?" Here, the question asks only about a

statement you may have made to the landlord. The material about other tenants' alleged complaints is improperly inserted into the trial without giving you a chance to deny that there were complaints. As you may guess, this ground of objection is more important in a jury than a judge trial since you can expect a judge to disregard this sort of unsubstantiated remark.

If the judge sustains your adversary's objection that your question assumes facts not in evidence, make the portion of the question that assumes facts into a separate question. If you were the landlord in the cross-examination sample above, for instance, you could properly have asked, "Didn't you receive complaints from other tenants about playing your stereo too loudly?"

2. Objections to the Content of Testimony

Unlike form objections, content objections assert your belief that the information opposing counsel seeks is inadmissible no matter what type of question is asked. Because most of these grounds for objection have already been discussed in earlier chapters we make only brief references to them here.

a. "Objection; lack of personal knowledge."

You may object on this ground when an adverse witness has not personally seen, heard or otherwise acquired first-hand information about what he is testifying about. Clues that a witness lacks personal knowledge are in introductory phrases like, "It later came to my attention that…," "I later found out that…," "I'd guess that what happened is…," and "My best estimate is…"

If the judge sustains your adversary's objection that your witness lacks personal knowledge, ask the judge for permission to ask additional questions to lay a foundation showing that the witness is testifying from personal knowledge. (See Chapter 11, Direct Examination, for a discussion of the requirement of personal knowledge.)

b. "Objection; speculation [or improper opinion]."

You can object on this ground when an adverse witness testifies to matters that are hypothetical, beyond her powers of observation or impermissible legal judgments. Often, a lack of personal knowledge objection is equally correct in these situations.

Here are some examples of improper speculative testimony:

- A witness testifies that "Nelson intended to mislead me into buying the defective car." Instead, the witness must testify to Nelson's words and deeds, leaving it to the judge or jury to determine what Nelson intended.

- A witness gives an improper opinion, such as, "If there had been any truth to the rumor, I would have known about it." In most circumstances, a witness can testify only to what did happen and what she does know.

- A witness testifies to a legal judgment such as, "Bryant was negligent." Again, a witness has to describe factual circumstances and leave it to the judge or jury to determine their legal consequences.

If the judge sustains your adversary's objection that your question is speculative or calls for an improper opinion, ask questions that elicit factual details about which the witness has personal knowledge. (For more examples and an explanation of the opinion rule, see Chapter 15, Basic Rules of Evidence.)

c. "Objection; hearsay."

Object on this ground when an adverse witness testifies to hearsay, which is an out-of-court statement offered for its truth.

If the judge sustains your adversary's objection that your question calls for hearsay, consider whether you can respond that the statement is admissible as an exception to the hearsay rule or as non-hearsay. (See Chapter 15, Basic Rules of Evidence, for a discussion of the hearsay rule, the exceptions to it and non-hearsay.)

d. "Objection; irrelevant."

Object on this ground when you believe that the adversary's evidence has no logical connection to the claims that either party is trying to prove or disprove.

If the judge sustains your adversary's objection that the information you seek is irrelevant, move on to a new topic. (See Chapter 15, Basic Rules of Evidence, for a discussion of the relevance rule.)

e. "Objection; the value (probative value) of this evidence is outweighed by the unfair prejudice it will cause."

Object on this ground when you recognize that the adversary's evidence is relevant, but think that its slight relevance is outweighed by the likelihood of unfair prejudice to you.

For example, assume that an adverse witness is describing your car as the one involved in an automobile accident. The witness is about to mention that among a number of things she remembers about your car, it had a bumper sticker identifying you as a fan of a rock group that many people believe promotes antisocial behavior. You may object on this ground to prevent the witness from mentioning the bumper sticker. It has slight relevance to prove the identity of your car, and is likely to cause you to suffer unfair prejudice.

Make a motion in limine. Unfairly prejudicial evidence typically consists of gruesome photographs, improper character evidence and the like. Often you will know or strongly suspect that your adversary plans to offer such evidence before trial, so in a jury trial you should strongly consider making a motion in limine. (See Section B, above.)

If the judge sustains your adversary's objection that the probative value of your evidence is outweighed by its likely prejudicial effect, move on to a new topic. (See Chapter 15, Basic Rules of Evidence, for a discussion of the unfair prejudice rule.)

f.   "Objection; lack of foundation."

Object on this ground when adverse counsel has failed to elicit a proper foundation for evidence. This is a catch-all objection, because all evidence, whether it is oral or written, must be supported by some type of foundation. For instance, if a witness lacks personal knowledge, or there is insufficient evidence to show that a business record is reliable or that a photograph fairly and accurately represents what a witness actually saw, you may object based on lack of foundation. This can also be an important objection, as your adversary may be unable to supply the missing foundational evidence. (See Chapter 11, Direct Examination, and Chapter 14, Exhibits, for a further discussion of foundational requirements.)

Because it is a catch-all, you may be uncertain about what's missing if the judge sustains your adversary's lack of foundation objection. If so, you may need to ask the judge for help. Say something like, "Your Honor, I'm not really sure what foundational evidence is missing. Might you or opposing counsel tell me what evidence I need to introduce to lay a proper foundation?" If the judge sympathetically accedes to your request, ask additional foundational questions. (Note that, as suggested above, you ask the judge to ask opposing counsel to tell you what foundation is missing; don't ask opposing counsel directly.)

g.   "Objection; cumulative."

Object on this ground when your adversary calls a number of witnesses to testify to the same point. For example, you may object if your adversary is a home buyer who bought a house from you, claims that you concealed the fact that it had a leaky roof, and attempts to call five witnesses to testify that on one particular day, the roof leaked.

If the judge sustains your adversary's objection that your evidence is cumulative, move on to a new topic. Alternatively, you might ask the adversary to stipulate (agree) that if your additional witness were called and sworn, they would all testify that, for example, "On September 22, the roof leaked."

h. "Objection: improper character evidence."

Object on this ground when your adversary offers character evidence. Character evidence suggests that you have a propensity to engage in conduct associated with a particular character trait, and it is almost never admissible in civil cases. (See Chapter 15, Basic Rules of Evidence, for a discussion of character evidence.)

If the judge sustains your adversary's objection that your question seeks improper character evidence, move on to a new topic.

RESOURCES ON OBJECTIONS

Transcript Exercises for Learning Evidence, by Paul Bergman (West Publishing Co.). This book consists of brief explanations of many of the rules of evidence and 19 sample transcripts in a variety of civil and criminal case examples. Various questions, answers and judicial rulings within the transcripts are numbered; your task is to decide the legal propriety of each numbered transcript portion. An appendix gives the correct responses.

Trial Advocacy in a Nutshell, by Paul Bergman (West Publishing Co.)

Fundamentals of Trial Techniques, by Thomas Mauet (Little, Brown & Co.)

Trial, by Roger Haydock and John Sonsteng (West Publishing Co.).

These books discuss trial advocacy generally, but have specific explanations and examples of the objections process.

COMMON OBJECTIONS

Objections to the Form of Questions

a. "Objection; the question is vague (or ambiguous or unintelligible)."

b. "Objection; the question is compound."

c. "Objection; the question calls for a narrative response."

d. "Objection; the question is repetitive (has been asked and answered)."

e. "Objection; counsel is misquoting the witness."

f. "Objection; the question is leading."

g. "Objection; the question is argumentative."

Objections to the Content of Testimony

a. "Objection; lack of personal knowledge."

b. "Objection; speculation (or improper opinion)."

c. "Objection; hearsay."

d. "Objection; irrelevant."

e. "Objection; the value (probative value) of this evidence is outweighed by the unfair prejudice it will cause."

f. "Objection; lack of foundation."

g. "Objection; cumulative."

Make a copy of the list of common objections. Place it in your trial notebook, so you can refer to it throughout trial. (See Chapter 17, Organizing a Trial Notebook.) ∎

17

ORGANIZING A
TRIAL NOTEBOOK

Organizing key documents and trial prepar-ation outlines into a trial notebook can help you present your case effectively and persuasively. At trial, you want to make sure that you introduce all your planned evidence and exhibits and that you tie them to the facts you are trying to prove or disprove. By making a trial notebook, you will have the documents that can help you do this close at hand throughout trial. For example, you can refer to a Direct Examination Outline when you question a witness and to your Closing Argument Outline when you present your final argument.

This chapter reviews the documents that you are likely to need in your trial notebook and suggests how to organize them efficiently.

A. SETTING UP YOUR NOTEBOOK

A typical trial notebook is an ordinary three-ring binder in which documents are grouped and sepa-rated by index tabs. Be sure to buy a set of index tabs that are easy to write on or otherwise customize, and lay in a good supply of blank three-hole paper. You may also want to have a three-hole punch handy in case you need to punch holes in documents you want to have in the notebook.

⚠ **Never punch holes in materials you will offer as evidence.** Never alter originals of documents that you plan to offer into evidence, and keep them in a manila envelope or accordion file separate from your trial notebook. (You may have to keep larger exhibits, such as a piece of defective machinery or an article of clothing, in a bag or a box.) However, you may place copies of each original in the notebook to give to the judge, opposing counsel and the jury.

Now let's look at what you should place into your trial notebook.

B. INDEX TAB 1: LEGAL PLEADINGS

The pleadings (the complaint and answer) should be in your notebook because they form the legal backdrop of the trial. Unless a judge allows you or your adversary to slightly change the theory set forth in a complaint or answer to match the evidence presented at trial (this is called "conform-ing a pleading according to proof"), the pleadings control such matters as what facts each party can prove or disprove and the relevance of evidence. You can punch holes in your copies of the pleadings because the originals will already be in the court's file.

Your judge may issue a Pre-Trial Order (which you, your adversary or the judge herself will prepare) following a conference with you and your adversary. (See Chapter 6, Pre-Trial Hearings and Motions.) A Pre-Trial Order is essentially a plan of trial that supersedes the pleadings and identifies the facts each party may prove or disprove as well as each party's witnesses and exhibits. (See Federal Rule of Civil Procedure 16.) If your judge does issue a Pre-Trial Order, include it in this section of your notebook.

 You probably don't need to include pre-trial motion documents in your notebook. Usually, issues that give rise to pre-trial motions are (other than motions in limine, see Chapter 16) disposed of before the start of trial. You will probably not have to refer to the pre-trial motion papers during trial, and so needn't include them in the notebook.

C. INDEX TAB 2: DISCOVERY MATERIALS

Discovery is the formal process parties use to uncover evidence before trial. As a pro per litigant, the discovery devices you are most likely to encounter are depositions, interrogatories and requests for admission. (See Chapter 3, Starting Your Case.)

If you use formal discovery procedures, you might want to punch the information you get and insert it as is into your notebook. In most cases, however, even a short deposition or a single set of answers to interrogatories is likely to be too un-

wieldy for you to refer to quickly in the middle of trial. Instead, make summaries of the important information in your adversary's responses and put the summaries in your notebook. Include in the summary a reference to the specific page or interrogatory number where the important information appears in the original.

For example, a portion of your summary of a deposition you took of a witness named Prager might look like the one shown below.

> ### Summary of Prager Deposition
>
> ....
>
> 9. Jack fell down and broke his crown and Jill came tumbling after. (P. 24, lines 11-22)
> 10. Jack waited two days before going to see a dentist to repair his broken crown. (P. 25, lines 25-28)

A portion of your summary of answers you received in response to the written interrogatories you sent out might look like this:

> ### Summary of Berkowitz Co. Answers to Interrogatories
>
> ....
>
> 5. The person at Berkowitz Co. who inspected the car stereos before they were shipped is Stella Ong. (Answer to Interrog. 4)
> 6. Ong's inspection consists of testing the AM/FM switch on each radio. (Answer to Interrog. 5)

If you prepare summaries, you can keep the original discovery documents in your case file. Then, if you need information from a discovery document during trial (perhaps to impeach a witness with a prior inconsistent statement; see Chapter 12, Cross-Examination), refer to the summary in your notebook to find the exact whereabouts of the information.

D. INDEX TAB 3: LEGAL CLAIM OUTLINE

Whether you are a plaintiff or a defendant, you should prepare a legal claim outline. (See Chapter 7, What You Need to Prove at Trial: The Plaintiff's Perspective, and Chapter 8, What You Need to Prove at Trial: The Defendant's Perspective.) This outline is not tied to the testimony of any single witness, but rather lists the elements of the claim you are seeking to prove or disprove, identifies the fact satisfying each element, and lists the important evidence from all your witnesses tending to prove or disprove each fact. As the outline organizes important evidence according to facts, you want it near at hand to serve as a roadmap to the testimony you bring out and the arguments you make.

E. INDEX TAB 4: OPENING STATEMENT OUTLINE

An opening statement outline summarizes the information you will present to the judge or jury during opening statement. (See Chapter 10, Opening Statements.) You do not want to read your opening statement to the judge or jury, but you can use the outline as a reminder when you speak.

F. INDEX TAB 5: DIRECT EXAMINATION OUTLINES

Direct examination outlines identify, by witness, the important evidence you plan to elicit, selected specific questions you plan to ask, and any exhibits you plan to offer. (See Chapter 11, Direct Examination.) While you don't want to script a witness's direct examination, you can refer to an outline during questioning to make sure you elicit the witness's story in chronological sequence and do not overlook evidence or exhibits.

For example, let's say you own a small shopping center and that you have brought suit to evict a tenant, The Broccoli Shop, owned by Elvin Goodman, for non-payment of rent. One witness you plan to call is your on-site property manager, Brice Catlin. A direct examination outline for Catlin is shown below.

Direct Examination Outline

Witness: Brice Catlin

Background Information:

Married with three children; has been manager of the shopping center for six years; responsible all matters related to leases, maintenance and security for the center.

Important Evidence:

- Broccoli Shop became a tenant about 15 months ago.

- Terms of lease: Rent due on 1st of each month; $1,500 per month.

- Six months ago—Broccoli Shop started paying rent two weeks late.

- April 14—last rent payment received from Goodman.
- May 1: No rent paid.
- May 3: Brice talks to Goodman and Goodman says he's busy opening another store but will pay rent within three days.
- May 8: Brice again talks to Goodman. He says bookkeeper was supposed to send check, he'll see to it immediately.
- No further contact with Goodman.
- May 23: Brice serves eviction notice on Goodman.

Important Questions:

- When I bring out the foundation for the lease, remember to ask Brice to ask him how he knows it's Goodman's signature on the lease (Brice saw him sign it.)
- Show that Rent Book is admissible as a business record.
  Be sure to ask what the rent book is, and about our business practice of what the bookkeeper uses the rent book for. Then ask, "Does the rent book indicate any payments from Mr. Goodman after April 14?" (No)

Exhibits:

- Lease Agreement will be Exhibit 1.
- Rent Book will be Exhibit 2.
- Eviction Notice will be Exhibit 3.

⚠ Make a more detailed outline for an expert witness. Your outline for an expert's direct examination can follow this format, but it should be far more detailed. For example, you should list the background information that qualifies the witness as an expert and identify not only the expert's opinion but also the reasons for it. (See Chapter 18, Expert Witnesses.)

G. INDEX TAB 6: CROSS-EXAMINATION OUTLINES

Cross-examination outlines identify, for each adverse witness, the witness's expected direct examination testimony, evidence you plan to elicit to support your version of events, evidence you plan to elicit that impeaches the witness and (occasionally) exhibits you plan to offer. (See Chapter 12, Cross-Examination.) Because you may want to be sure you ask leading questions that seek to elicit very specific information, you may write down your questions and read them to an adverse witness during cross-examination.

For example, let's say that you're a plaintiff in a negligence case. You claim that due to defendant Sarah Adams's careless driving, you were struck by her truck while you were in a crosswalk. Adams claims that she was driving carefully, and that she unavoidably struck you when you suddenly ran out from between two parked cars some distance away from the crosswalk. You are planning to cross-examine Kris Knaplund, who will testify for Adams that after the accident you said that you should have been in the crosswalk. Based on information you gathered before trial, the cross-examination outline you put in your trial notebook and use as the basis of your questioning of Knaplund might look like the one shown below.

Cross-Examination Outline

Witness: Kris Knaplund

Summary of expected testimony:

Knaplund will testify that she heard me say that I should have been in the crosswalk.

Additional information that supports my version of events: none

Questions I have for impeaching her:

- "Ms. Knaplund, isn't it true that you were coming out of a video game arcade when you heard me say something after the accident?"
- "The arcade was noisy, wasn't it?"
- "Several arcade games were being played near you?"
- "Those games are so loud that you have to talk extra loud to be heard inside the arcade, right?"
- "And where you were standing is about 75 feet away from where I was hit by the truck, right?"

H. INDEX TAB 7: CLOSING ARGUMENT OUTLINE

A closing argument outline summarizes the introductory remarks you plan to make, lists the elements and facts you seek to prove or disprove and important items of evidence, the burden of proof, the exact language of important jury instructions (in a jury trial) and the results you want the judge or jury to reach. (A sample outline is in Chapter 13,

Closing Argument.) As in opening statement, you do not want to read your argument to the judge or jury. However, referring to the outline from time to time as you speak will ensure that you do not overlook important evidence or arguments. You can also ask the judge for a few moments to review your outline before you make your argument.

I. INDEX TAB 8: JURY TRIAL DOCUMENTS

In a jury trial, you'll need a blank Jury Chart on which to write down information about prospective jurors as it emerges during voir dire questioning. You can review this information when deciding whether you will challenge any jurors. For use during the questioning process, you may also want a make a list of topics or, if your judge asks all the questions but allows you to submit questions you want asked, a list of specific questions. (See Chapter 9, Selecting the Decision-Maker.)

J. INDEX TAB 9: MISCELLANEOUS DOCUMENTS

Depending on the complexity of your case and your judgment concerning what documents may prove important, you may want to have a "Miscellaneous" section of your trial notebook where you put documents such as the following:

- A list of all the exhibits that you plan to introduce. Keep this list at the top of this section so that you can easily check off the items as the judge admits them into evidence. If you have made extra copies of exhibits to hand to opposing counsel, the judge or the jury, place them immediately beneath the list. If you have copies of numerous exhibits, you may want to have a separate section of your notebook tabbed something like, "Exhibit List and Copies of Exhibits."

• A copy of any rules of evidence that may be important if you or your adversary is likely to object to the admissibility of important evidence during trial, having the text of the controlling rule of evidence in front of you will strengthen your argument.

For example, assume that your trial is in federal court and you want to offer an important business record into evidence. Your adversary has indicated an intention to object to the exhibit as hearsay. (See Chapters 14, Exhibits, and 15, Basic Rules of Evidence.) You may want to make a copy of Federal Rule of Evidence 803 (6), which specifies the foundational requirements for business records, and put it in this section of your notebook.

 Have all evidence rules with you during trial. Your court system's rules of evidence should be available in a book which you can buy. If the rules are part of a larger collection of rules that is too expensive for you to buy, perhaps you can photocopy the section on evidence. Either way, you should have the evidence rules with you during trial. You should also make a copy of a rule that is likely to be the focus of argument and put it in your trial notebook.

• If you or your adversary submits a written "motion in limine" (a pre-trial request to the judge to exclude evidence), insert the motion and any written response into this section. (See Chapter 16, Making and Responding to Objections.) Especially if the judge has "reserved" (postponed) a ruling on the motion until the evidence is actually offered, having the written motion in front of you during trial can help you present a stronger argument.

• A copy of any written stipulations.

• A list of the names, addresses and phone and fax numbers of your self-help law coach (if you have one who has agreed to be on standby to help you during trial) and your witnesses. If your witnesses are late to court, you or the judge may want to contact them immediately, sometimes with the sheriff's help!

• A copy of the list of common objections. (See Chapter 16, Making and Responding to Objections.)

• The names and addresses of a few good restaurants within easy walking distance of the courthouse. ∎

18

EXPERT WITNESSES

xperts are witnesses who have acquired specialized knowledge through education, training or other experience. Experts testify to opinions about the legal significance of evidence that is beyond the everyday understanding of the average judge or jury, and give the reasons underlying those opinions. Experts commonly appear in trials; as daily affairs have become more complex, parties have increasingly had to turn to expert testimony to prove their claims.

If proving your claim or disproving your opponent's claim requires making a judge or jury understand the significance of scientific, specialized or technical information, you may have to hire an expert witness. However, an expert witness is likely to be very expensive. This chapter helps you recognize when you really need an expert witness, tells you how to find the right expert and explains how to work efficiently with and elicit testimony from an expert.

⚠️ **The final decision rests with the judge or jury.** A judge or juror is free to disregard an expert's opinion. Evidence rules make experts' opinions admissible in evidence; the rules do not make the opinions binding on judges and jurors. It's up to you to find an expert who is well-qualified and likely to be convincing.

A. WHO ARE EXPERT WITNESSES?

As you might expect, given the variety of situations that end up in court, a wide spectrum of professional people offer their services as expert witnesses. One recent legal journal contained expert witness advertisements not only by doctors, lawyers and accountants, but also by experts in alarm system failures, architectural engineering, tree growth problems, accident reconstruction, escalator maintenance, corporate histories, ladders and other household devices, railroad accidents, bicycles, skydiving and many other subjects.

A person does not need an advanced professional or scientific degree to qualify as an expert. As long as a subject is beyond the understanding of the average judge or juror, any person who has special knowledge, experience or skill in that subject can qualify as an expert. (See Federal Rule of Evidence 702.) For example, if your case involves the cause of rutabaga crop failure, a farmer who has grown rutabagas for many years would likely qualify as an expert. Or if your case involves defective house paint, an experienced painter may qualify as an expert. (See Section E below for a discussion of how to qualify a witness as an expert.)

B. DO YOU NEED AN EXPERT WITNESS?

One of the first things you must determine is whether the subject matter of the claim you are trying to prove (or, if you are a defendant, disprove) requires expert testimony. The test is this: If understanding the subject matter of a claim requires specialized knowledge that is beyond the everyday experience of the average judge or jury, you will need an expert.

For example, assume that you have sued an accountant for negligently (carelessly) preparing an analysis of a financial statement for you. To prevail, you must prove that the accountant's preparation fell below the professional standards to which accountants are held. The average judge or jury doesn't know what those standards are. So you'll need another accountant, in the role of an expert witness, to describe the professional standards governing accountants and to explain how the accountant you sued negligently deviated from those standards. The defendant is likely to counter with another accounting expert in an effort to show that professional standards were complied with.

Here are some other types of claims that would probably require expert testimony:

- To prove your claim that a new home you purchased was built on improperly compacted landfill, you need an expert in soil engineering.

- To prove your claim that injuries you suffered as the result of an accident are likely to be permanent, you need a medical expert.

- To prove your claim that a piece of jewelry sold to you as a valuable "flawless" diamond is actually an inexpensive imitation, you probably need an expert in gemology.

- To prove your claim that you were injured because a lawn mower you purchased was defectively manufactured, you probably need an expert in lawn mower design and safety.

- To prove your claim that a series of psychological tests administered to your child demonstrates that your ex-spouse is not taking proper care of the child, you probably need an expert in child psychology.

What each of these examples has in common is that the average judge or jury cannot evaluate the truth of the claim without an expert's help. You would have to hire an expert with the proper qualifications prior to trial, demonstrate to the judge that your witness is sufficiently qualified to give expert testimony and then elicit the expert's testimony so as to convince the judge or jury that your claim is true.

By contrast, let's look at a few examples where expert testimony is *not* necessary:

- You claim that your opponent drove negligently by driving 50 m.p.h. in a residential area.

- You claim that a landlord's failure to fix problems in your apartment rendered it uninhabitable and so excused your obligation to pay rent.

- You claim that a witness who testified against you should not be believed because he is biased and has made inconsistent statements.

- You claim that a developer intentionally made false statements about the number of home sites in a tract of land to induce you to purchase one of the sites.

In these types of situations, a judge would not permit you to use an expert witness because the subjects are within the understanding of the average judge or jury. The legal system expects and trusts judges and juries to decide the truth of such claims based on their common sense and everyday experiences.

If you are uncertain about whether the subject matter of the claim you are making requires expert testimony, consult one of the reference works listed at the end of the chapter. Also, you may want to seek the advice of a self-help law coach well before trial. If you need an expert, it will take time to find and hire the right one and for the expert to familiarize herself with your case so that she can testify clearly and persuasively.

JUDGES ARE NOT EXPERTS

A savvy or sympathetic judge cannot take the place of an expert witness, even if the judge is very knowledgeable about a subject ordinarily thought of as reserved for experts.

For example, assume that you will offer evidence of your medical condition. Based on the fact that your judge was a doctor before becoming a judge, you may think that you do not need a medical expert to testify about how your medical condition will affect your future activities. Or, you may be suing your former lawyer for legal malpractice for omitting an important clause from a contract. Based on the fact that your judge was recently a practicing lawyer in the same field, you may think it unnecessary to call a legal expert to testify that omission of the clause was legal malpractice.

Think again—the rule is that a judge's personal knowledge is no substitute for expert testimony. The law regards all judges as having no more than everyday knowledge regardless of their actual personal backgrounds. If the subject matter of your claim is beyond the understanding of the average judge or jury, you must produce a qualified expert witness no matter what your judge's background.

⚠ **You must notify your adversary and the court well before trial that you will call an expert witness.** Check your local court rules for deadlines for advising your adversary and the court that you intend to call an expert and disclosing the expert's identity. If you fail to meet the deadline, the judge may not permit your expert to testify. For example, in federal court your expert must be named before the judge makes the final pre-trial order. (See Federal Rule of Civil Procedure 16.)

C. SPECIAL RULES FOR EXPERT WITNESSES

The rules of evidence reward experts—who, after all, have pleased their parents by developing special skills and knowledge—by bestowing on them three general advantages not shared by lay (non-expert) witnesses.

1. Personal Knowledge Is Unnecessary for Experts

Unlike lay witnesses, experts are not required to testify from personal knowledge. (See Federal Rule of Evidence 703.) Evidence rules allow an expert to gain information second-hand and then give the judge or jury an opinion about the significance of that information. An expert's review of documents and discussions with you and other people can substitute for the expert's lack of personal knowledge about what actually happened. For example, even though a medical expert does not know how you got hurt and never treated you, evidence rules allow the expert to examine your medical records and testify that your injuries are permanent. Similarly, even though a legal expert has no first-hand knowledge about what took place between you and a lawyer who once represented you, evidence rules allow the expert to testify that you were the victim of legal malpractice based on the expert's analysis of the lawyer's actions.

2. Experts Can Give Opinions Forbidden to Non-Experts

Unlike ordinary witnesses, experts can provide opinions about the meaning of scientific, technical or specialized evidence, even if that opinion refers directly to the legal issue the judge or jury has to decide. (See Federal Rule of Evidence 704.)

For example, a lawyer who qualifies as an expert witness can testify that it is his opinion that the attorney you have sued for legal malpractice deviated from professional standards, even though this is exactly the issue the judge or jury has to decide. Similarly, a child psychologist expert can give an opinion that it would be in the best interests of your children for them to remain with you rather than go to live with your former spouse, and a medical expert can give an opinion that an injury will cause lifetime discomfort. In each instance, the expert can render an opinion based on specialized knowledge that an ordinary witness would be unable to give.

3. Experts Can Testify to Otherwise Inadmissible Evidence

Because experts do not have to testify from personal knowledge, to form their opinions they often rely on information in reports and on statements made to them by the party who hired them and others. As long as the information is of a type that other experts in the same field reasonably rely on, the expert can testify to that information even if it would not otherwise be admissible under the rules of evidence. (See Federal Rule of Evidence 703.)

SCIENTIFIC EVIDENCE

For many years, judges have admitted scientific evidence if the evidence was based on principles that were "generally accepted" by the scientific community.

In federal court, however, it is now up to judges to make sure that scientific evidence admitted at trial is not only relevant, but reliable. Under a 1993 U.S. Supreme Court ruling, judges cannot admit scientific evidence just because it is based on generally accepted scientific principles. Judges must make their own decisions about the scientific validity of evidence. *Daubert v. Merrell Dow Pharmaceuticals Inc.*, 113 S. Ct. 2786 (1993).

For example, assume that in a lawsuit against your ex-spouse, you have hired a child psychologist as an expert to testify that in the expert's opinion, you should have sole custody of your minor children. In arriving at this opinion, the expert may have spoken to the children's teachers, read evaluations prepared by school personnel and consulted books written by other child psychologists. Much of this information would not itself be admissible under the rules of evidence. For instance, the hearsay rule would normally bar the expert from testifying to the teacher's out-of-court statements and to statements in a book. (See Chapter 15, Basic Rules of Evidence.) But if experts in the field of child psychology reasonably rely on such information, your expert can refer to it while testifying.

In formulating this rule, the drafters of modern rules of evidence have shown uncharacteristic humility. They have reasoned that if courts need expert testimony to dispense justice, there is no sense telling experts what information they may or may not use to arrive at an opinion.

 Your own expert can tell the judge what experts in the same field rely on. How does a judge, who after all is not an expert, know whether information is "of a type reasonably relied upon by experts in the particular field?" From your expert, of course. So when your child psychologist expert testifies to the information on which his opinion is based, ask, "Mr. Expert, do child psychologists commonly rely on information from teachers and from books written by other child psychologists in forming their opinions?"

The rule that lets experts themselves determine what information they can rely on has common sense limits. A judge may rule that the expert's reliance on certain information is unreasonable no matter what the expert says, and forbid the expert from testifying to the information or relying on it in forming an opinion. For instance, assume that your child psychologist expert testifies that "in forming my opinion I consulted the children's astrological chart, and we child psychologists commonly rely on astrological readings." A judge would undoubtedly forbid the expert from testifying to or relying on such information.

D. FINDING AND HIRING AN EXPERT WITNESS

The expert you hire should have good credentials that your adversary cannot easily impugn, be knowledgeable about the specific subject matter of your case, be able to communicate what she knows in language that a judge or jury will understand, and employ a credible manner of testifying in response both to your friendly direct examination and your adversary's challenging cross-examination. This section describes how to find and hire such a person.

1. When to Look for an Expert

If you need an expert witness, the best time to hire one is well before trial, when you are still looking for evidence to prove your claim or disprove your opponent's claim. Your expert can help coach you as to what evidence to gather, and the expert will have time to conduct whatever tests or research are necessary to formulate a reliable opinion.

2. Paying an Expert

Expert witnesses can be and almost always are compensated for their testimony. In most states, statutes prohibit ordinary witnesses from being paid to testify, allowing them only a small fee as reimbursement for the expense of traveling to and from the courthouse. But the legal system regards an expert's specialized knowledge and training as a personal asset for which the expert can charge whatever the market will bear.

Most experts charge an hourly fee—often hundreds of dollars per hour—for time spent in reviewing a file, conducting necessary tests, preparing a written report, preparing for trial and testifying. The expert may also charge you for out-of-pocket expenses incurred for materials and travel. Win or lose, you have to pay the expert—usually up front.

The potential for profit has spawned an army of experts who peddle their services for substantial sums. Like buying the services of a roofer or a piano teacher, if you need to hire an expert witness you'll need to be a wise shopper. Make sure your fee arrangement is in writing. And if one expert quotes you a fee that you think is too high, look for one with good credentials who will provide the help you need for less.

THE LOSER'S OBLIGATION TO PAY EXPERT WITNESS FEES

The judge normally awards the winner of a lawsuit "costs of suit" in addition to any other relief to which the winning party is entitled. One of the costs that the judge may award is the fee paid to an expert witness. So keep written records of your expert's charges and, if you win the case, ask the judge to order your opponent to pay you those charges.

Of course, a judge's ability to order payment of expert witness fees is a double-edged sword. If your opponent uses an expert witness and you lose, your opponent will surely ask the judge to order you to pay. Be ready to give the judge reasons for denying your adversary's request or limiting how much you have to pay. These reasons might include:

- **Lack of necessity:** Argue that your adversary's claim could have been proved without an expert. You may also be able to argue that your adversary, knowing you were not represented by a lawyer, needlessly hired an expert just to run up costs and try to force you to give up your right to a trial.

- **Too many experts:** If your adversary called two or three experts who gave similar testimony, ask the court to award your adversary costs only for one expert. Most judges resent cumulative testimony, so you may prevail on this argument.

- **Excessive fees:** If your adversary's expert's fee is based on what you think is an excessive hourly rate, or if the expert put in an excessive number of hours (especially compared to the amount of money at stake in the lawsuit), ask the court to order payment of only a portion of the fee. One way you can demonstrate that a fee is excessive is to point out to the judge that the expert who testified (or offered to testify) for you charged a much lower fee.

3. Where to Look

If you need an expert, you can start by checking the listings and advertisements in magazines aimed at trial lawyers. For example, the magazine *Trial*, published monthly by the American Trial Lawyers Association and available in most law libraries, lists experts according to subject matter. Many state and county bar associations (lawyers' organizations) also publish magazines or newsletters in which local experts advertise their services. Universities and local branches of professional associations (for example, the American Medical Association) are also possible sources of expert witnesses.

Many experts list their services by specialty in national "expert witness registries."

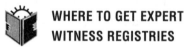 **WHERE TO GET EXPERT WITNESS REGISTRIES**

Expert Resources Inc.; 4700 N. Prospect Road, Peoria Heights, IL 61614, 309-688-4857, 800-383-4857; also local branches in many cities.

Legal Expert Network; 7904 Starburst Drive, Baltimore, MD 21208-3033, 410-653-5121, 800-597-5371; fax 410-484-9515. It will send the expert's credentials and receive payment only if you select one of its experts to review your case.

National Forensic Center; 800-526-5177. It annually publishes the *Forensic Services Directory*, a book of approximately 1400 pages listing experts by specialty all across the country. It costs $130 plus postage. The Center also publishes an annual *Guide to Expert Witness Fees*, which lists experts across the country according to their area of expertise and then divides them according to whether their fees are in the low, medium or high range. This year's *Guide* costs about $32.

4. How to Choose the Right Expert

The expert you hire must be able to render an opinion that backs your claim, and must be able to give convincing reasons in support of the opinion. When you do find an expert you are interested in hiring, here are some of the steps you can take to make sure you spend your money wisely.

When you contact a potential expert, ask for a "Curriculum Vitae" (VY-TAY) that includes the expert's personal background, education, job history, publications and honors. If you contact more than one expert, compare their CVs before deciding who to hire. Try to gauge whether a judge or jury will be impressed with your expert's credentials.

Ask for a list of cases (the more recent the better) in which the person has been hired as an expert and the names and phone numbers of the attorneys involved. Then check references to make sure the expert gets a good recommendation from cooperative attorneys and parties who hired the expert. If, however, a person has excellent credentials, do not automatically dismiss the person just because she or he has never before been hired as an expert. Everyone has to start somewhere.

Try to get as close a fit as possible between an expert's area of expertise and the facts of your case. For example, say you're involved in a legal malpractice case against the lawyer who failed to advise your stepmother that she had to change her will to accomplish her stated wish to disinherit a child born after the will was signed. You need a legal expert who will give an opinion that the estate planning lawyer's failure to give the advice constituted legal malpractice. Look for a lawyer who specializes in estate planning (will drafting and related matters) and is knowledgeable about the ethical rules of that aspect of legal practice. Do not hire as your expert a lawyer who has only general legal expertise.

Before you agree to hire an expert, make sure that the expert takes the time to analyze your legal position thoroughly before forming an opinion. (You may have to pay for the expert's time to conduct this analysis.) Give the expert whatever information the expert requests in order to formulate an opinion. You don't want to hire an expert who will jump at the chance to deliver whatever opinion you are willing to pay for. Nor do you want to invest time and money in an expert who is unwilling to render a favorable opinion.

Tell your expert the truth. Reveal all relevant information—good or bad— to your expert. Never try to hide bad information in order to get a favorable opinion from an expert. If you do and later at trial your adversary reveals the negative information to your expert, the embarrassed expert may change her opinion and do irreparable harm to your case.

If time, finances and number of potential experts permit, talk to more than one expert before hiring one. If the first expert you contact is unwilling to render a favorable opinion, of course you'll need to seek another opinion. Many areas of expertise involve judgment. Even if one expert disagrees with your position, a second expert may honestly make a favorable assessment.

But even if the first expert you talk to renders a favorable opinion, you may want to talk to others before deciding whom to hire. You want an expert who not only has a favorable opinion, but who is also knowledgeable, convincing and easy to work with. Remember that you will pay well for the expert's help, so there is absolutely no reason to be intimidated by the "expert" label. No matter how good an expert looks on paper, or no matter how solid the recommendations, your expert has to testify in a way that gives a judge or jury confidence in the correctness of the expert's opinions. If the expert cannot explain an opinion clearly and credibly to you, probably the expert will also be unconvincing in front of a judge or jury. It is your case, and you should hire only a person who is both well qualified and who can explain the meaning of evidence in clear, everyday terms.

Find out whether your expert has in the past represented more than one point of view. Generally you want to avoid experts whose opinion is the same in every case—for example, that doctors are negligent or that custody of children should be awarded to fathers. Your adversary is likely to bring this fact out at trial, leading a judge or jury to disbelieve your expert on the grounds of bias. Far better for your expert to testify that she testifies for different litigants and that her opinions reflect the unique circumstances of each case.

E. QUESTIONING YOUR EXPERT WITNESS AT TRIAL

There are two major phases of your expert's direct examination. First, you must elicit foundational testimony qualifying the witness as an expert. Then it's time to elicit testimony about the expert's opinion and the reasons justifying it.

1. Laying a Foundation

Before a witness can give expert testimony, you have to offer foundational evidence showing that the witness is qualified as an expert in the field to which the testimony relates. (For a refresher on the concept of evidentiary foundations, see Chapter 11, Direct Examination, and Chapter 14, Exhibits.) That means that you must begin the direct examination with questions about the expert witness's background. The idea is to demonstrate that the witness really does have specialized "knowledge, skill, experience, training or education" in the field of claimed expertise. Only after the judge rules that your witness qualifies as an expert can you go on to bring out the testimony that helps to prove your case.

 Make your expert seem as knowledgeable as possible. Though the purpose of foundational questions is to show that your witness possesses the necessary qualifications to give expert testimony, your questions have a secondary purpose. This is to show a judge or juror what an outstanding, credible expert your witness is. The more your expert comes across as a star, the more convincing the expert's testimony is likely to be.

So even if the judge tries to hurry you along, or your opponent offers to save time by stipulating (agreeing) that your witness is an expert, you should politely resist, especially if you are in a jury trial and your expert has a very distinguished background. For example, you might reply to the judge by saying something like, "I appreciate the offer to stipulate. I promise that I will not waste the court's time. But I need to bring out a few more facts about my expert's background to show the jury how well qualified he is."

Obviously the specific foundational questions you ask will depend on your witness's field of expertise. If your expert has testified previously, he should be able to tell you what topics to cover to bring out his qualifications to give expert testimony. Your foundational questions of an expert are likely to cover the following general topics:

- Education. This is particularly important for experts like doctors, lawyers and others who need advanced degrees to enter their profession. Ask about college and any graduate school degrees. It's also a good approach to ask about special courses the expert might have taken after completing formal training. For example, a tax attorney may just have completed a two-week course in "Tax Planning for Estate Planners," and a police officer expert may have taken a special Police Academy course in "Accident Reconstruction."

- Professional experience. For example, what is your expert lawyer's specialty, what does your expert doctor's practice consist of, or what is your expert farmer's experience with the growing of rutabagas? Your questions should allow your expert to describe whatever it is that constitutes her professional life or specialized knowledge, and the length of time she has been at it. Also elicit evidence about any licenses your expert holds, such as a doctor's license to practice Internal Medicine.

- Professional organizations of which the expert is a member. For example, a doctor may be a member of the American Medical Association and the College of Orthopedic Surgeons. If your expert is an elected officer of such an organization, or if she needed special qualifications to qualify for admittance to the organi-

zation, be sure to bring that out and have the expert explain what it means.

- Any courses taught by your expert, either in colleges or in special training courses.

- Any books or articles that your expert has written.

- How many times your expert has been previously qualified to give expert testimony.

To see how these factors combine into foundational testimony, let's go back to one of the sample cases used throughout this book: a legal malpractice claim against an attorney. You're suing the lawyer for failing to advise your stepmother that she needed to change her will in order to accomplish her stated wish to disinherit her child who was born after the will was signed. To prove that the defendant attorney committed malpractice, you may need to call another attorney as an expert witness to explain how the defendant's conduct violated professional standards. The foundational testimony that qualifies your witness to give expert testimony might go as follows:

1 **You:**

What is your name and occupation?

2 **Expert:**

My name is Anna Turney, and I am a lawyer and a part-time law teacher.

3 **You:**

How long have you been doing these things?

4 **Expert:**

I've been a lawyer for ten years, and a part-time law teacher for the last four years.

5   **You:**

What is your educational background?

6   **Expert:**

I graduated with a Bachelor of Arts degree from the University of Chicago 13 years ago, then went to law school at UCLA. I graduated with a law degree, known as a Doctor of Jurisprudence, ten years ago, passed the California Bar Exam and entered the practice of law.

7   **You:**

Are you licensed to practice law?

8   **Expert:**

Yes, I'm licensed by our State Bar. I'm also admitted to practice before the federal courts of our state.

9   **You:**

Can you briefly describe your practice experience?

10   **Expert:**

Yes, I began practice with Hoffman, Upham and Downey, a local law firm that specializes in estate planning. Five years ago I left the private practice of law to go to work for the Enforcement Division of the State Bar, which disciplines lawyers who violate the rules of the profession. I've been there ever since. I also teach a course in Professional Ethics every other semester at the Milwaukee Law School.

11   **You:**

Have you ever written about legal ethics?

12   **Expert:**

Yes, I've written three articles on ethical duties of lawyers. Two of these have been published in our state magazine for lawyers, the Bar Journal, and the other in a local county bar journal.

13   **You:**

How much of your work deals with professional standards for estate planning lawyers?

14   **Expert:**

Well, one of the articles that was published in the state Bar Journal dealt specifically with that topic, and because that was my practice specialty I regularly discuss the ethical responsibilities of estate planners in my Professional Ethics course. Working with the State Bar, I'd estimate that about 20% of the discipline cases that I investigate and prosecute involve estate planning lawyers.

15   **You:**

Can you give me any idea how many of these cases you handle in an average month?

16   **Expert:**

Well, if you mean estate planning discipline cases, I'd say about ten per month. This is about how many I investigate; of course I don't necessarily prosecute that many.

17   **You:**

Have you ever previously testified as an expert witness involving legal malpractice by an estate planning attorney?

18 Expert:

Yes, on two occasions within the last three years. In addition I was hired in connection with two other cases, but the cases settled before I testified.

19 You:

Your Honor, I request that Ms. Turney be accepted as an expert witness.

20 Judge:

Defense counsel, do you have any foundational questions you would like to ask the witness?

21 Adversary:

None, Your Honor.

22 Judge:

Very well, I rule that the witness is qualified to give expert testimony. Mr. Nolo, you may proceed with your questioning.

Transcript Analysis: This testimony establishes that the witness is qualified to give expert testimony in your legal malpractice case. Your witness

has five years of experience enforcing professional rules of conduct, teaches a course on Professional Ethics, and has written articles about lawyers' ethical duties (Nos. 10 and 12). Moreover, throughout her career she has been concerned with estate planning matters. In private practice she was an estate planning attorney (No. 10); both her articles and her teaching have focused on ethical rules in the estate planning contest (No. 14); and she regularly investigates and prosecutes disciplinary cases involving estate planners (No. 16). Finally, she has twice qualified as an expert witness in similar matters (No. 18).

Note that many of your foundational questions, especially Nos. 5, 9 and 13, ask the expert to provide a narrative of her background. These questions encourage the expert to describe her background fully in her own words, letting her display her expertise and bolster her credibility in the eyes of the judge or jury. As you may remember from Chapter 11, judges usually do not allow you to ask narrative questions during direct examination. But they often make an exception for experts because they trust experts to keep their answers within legal bounds.

 The adversary may be saving an attack for cross-examination. Your adversary's response in No. 21 indicates only that the adversary has no questions pertaining to Turney's qualifications as an expert. During cross-examination, your adversary may nevertheless attack Turney's credibility—for example, by showing that Turney always testifies on the side of plaintiffs who are suing their former attorneys.

2.   Eliciting the Expert's Testimony

Once your witness has qualified as an expert, you may elicit testimony in whatever way you decide. Unlike with ordinary witnesses, who usually describe events in chronological order, there is no standard format for expert testimony. Your main task is to bring out the expert's opinion and the reasons supporting that opinion in whatever way seems most credible. Remember, when testifying to the reasons for an opinion, the expert can refer to information that is not itself admissible in evidence.

Elicit the reasons for your expert's opinion. You aren't required to ask your expert the reasons for her opinion. (Rule 705 of the Federal Rules of Evidence and similar rules in most states.) But it is almost always far more convincing to elicit your expert's opinion and then ask for the reasons for that opinion.

When planning the direct examination, get help from your expert. Ask the expert to tell you all the reasons that support the expert's opinion. Then ask for the expert's advice as to how much of this information you should be sure to bring out during the expert's direct examination.

Here is an example of a format you may want to follow to elicit an expert's opinion and the reasons for it. Assume that you have already finished foundational questioning, and that the judge has ruled that your witness is qualified to give expert testimony. In the case of the legal expert in the legal malpractice case, your questioning would go as follows:

1   You:

Ms. Turney, do you have an opinion as to whether the defendant committed legal malpractice?

2   Expert:

Yes, Ms. Nolo, I do.

3   You:

And what is that opinion?

4   Expert:

My opinion is that the defendant breached the professional standard of care and committed legal malpractice.

5   You:

Can you please tell the judge how you arrived at this opinion?

Transcript Analysis: It is generally a good idea to ask the expert whether she has been able to arrive at an opinion (No. 1) before eliciting the opinion (No. 3). You can then go on to elicit the reasons underlying the opinion with a broad, narrative-type question (No. 5). Again, judges typically allow such questions of experts because they trust experts to stay on point.

The reasons supporting an expert's opinion will, of course, depend on the kind of expert a person is. An engineering expert may rely primarily on a stress test of a piece of metal, a medical expert on a physical examination of you and your medical history, an accident reconstruction expert on an inspection of the accident site and the condition of the cars, and a child psychology expert on the results of psychological testing and conversations with the child's parents, teachers and other counselors.

The following suggestions should help you max-imize the credibility of your expert's testimony.

- Ask the expert to explain her field of expertise. If the expert's field of expertise is likely to be unfamiliar to a judge or jury, ask the expert to briefly explain it. For instance, since many people know that a "radiologist" takes and interprets X-rays, you may not have to ask your expert radiologist a question like, "What is it that radiologists do?" But a judge or jury may not be familiar with more unusual fields of expertise such as "linguistics" or "ceramic coatings." Therefore, you might ask your linguistics expert questions such as, "What is linguistics?" and "What kinds of things do linguists do?"

- Ask the expert to explain any tests that were performed. Have the expert explain what the tests were, why they were administered, how they work and what the results mean. Any working models, charts, photographs, slides or other materials your expert can bring to court to illustrate how the tests were performed will almost certainly bolster the expert's credibility.

- Have the expert read from a treatise. If your expert consulted an authoritative textbook or treatise that supports the expert's opinion, consider asking the expert to read a clear, brief portion to the judge or jury. (See Federal Rule of Evidence 803 (18), which is a hearsay exception that allows an expert to read information from a reliable treatise to a judge or jury.) Before the expert does so, ask him why he consulted it and what makes it authoritative. Then, mark the book as an exhibit, have the expert testify that it is authoritative, and ask the expert to read the supportive portion to the judge or jury.

- Have the expert explain reports. If your expert prepared a written report before trial, have the expert explain how and when she prepared it. Then mark the report as an exhibit, have the witness authenticate it and offer it into evidence. (See Chapter 14, Exhibits.) This is especially important when an expert is a professional with an advanced degree, because the judge or jury will probably expect such an expert to document an opinion in writing.

- Have the expert describe discussions with others. If your expert based his opinion in part on statements from other people, ask him to describe who he talked to, why he consulted them, what they said and how their statements influenced his opinion. Ordinarily, testimony about the out-of-court statements of other people constitute inadmissible hearsay. (See Chapter 15, Basic Rules of Evidence.) But experts are allowed to refer to hearsay and other inadmissible evidence as long as it is of a type that experts in the particular field reasonably rely on.

- Have the expert use everyday language. Ask the expert to translate technical jargon into plain English. Almost every field of expertise has its own jargon, and experts tend to use it automatically without realizing that an ordinary judge or jury might not have the faintest idea what the expert is talking about. Up to a point this can sound like impressive "insider talk," but its impact will be lost if the judge or jury has no idea what it means. A good general rule is that if your expert had to explain a term to you, you should ask the expert to explain it to the judge or jury.

For example, a stock market expert might refer to "convertible subordinated debentures," a term that would baffle most judges or juries. Here's how you could ask your expert to explain this term:

1 **You:**

Ms. Expert, you used the term "convertible subordinated debenture." What exactly is a convertible subordinated debenture?

2 **Expert:**

A convertible subordinated debenture is a bond that a corporation issues to a person from whom it borrows money. The bond is paid back with interest or, if the lender chooses, is convertible into stock in the corporation, usually at a price set out in the bond. Obviously, the lender will take advantage of the convertible feature only if the price of the stock on the open market is higher than the price set out in the bond, so that the lender stands to make a profit by acquiring the stock.

3 **You:**

Thank you. Now let me ask you....

- Let the expert testify in her own words. You want the expert to impress the judge or jury with her expertise, so ask narrative and open

questions frequently. Broad questions allow experts to testify convincingly in their own words.

Make a direct examination outline.
Make an outline of the expert's testimony just as you do any other witness's testimony and include it in the Direct Examination section of your trial notebook. Include the important personal background information that qualifies the person as an expert, the expert's opinion, and the reasons supporting it. You might also want to include any specialized jargon that you want your expert to explain, as well as exhibits you plan to offer while the expert is testifying. (See Chapter 17, Organizing a Trial Notebook.)

---

3. Hypothetical Questions

Until evidence rules changed 20 years or so ago, experts almost always testified in response to hypothetical questions. Lawyers asked experts to assume that certain facts were true and then asked them to state what their opinion would be given those facts. Today, there is no need to use hypothetical questions to question experts, and we generally recommend against it. You can get trapped in a "Twilight Zone" between not putting enough information into a hypothetical to support your expert's opinion, and putting in so much information that the judge rules that you have improperly launched into your closing argument.

However, many attorneys (especially those whose legal education predated modern evidence rules) still use hypothetical questions, and they are still permitted. If your adversary uses a hypothetical question, make sure that the "assumed" facts in it accurately reflect testimony. If the facts are not accurate, you should object to the question. For example, if your adversary's hypothetical question misstates a witness's actual testimony, state your objection by saying that "The question is misleading because it does not accurately reflect the evidence before the court." (See Chapter 16, Making and Responding to Objections.)

F. CROSS-EXAMINING YOUR OPPONENT'S EXPERT WITNESS

If cross-examination of an expert were a pack of cigarettes, it would carry a warning label, "Caution. Cross-examining an expert witness may be hazardous to your health." The problem is that unless you have as much expertise in the subject area as the expert you are questioning, cross-examination is likely to give the opposing expert the chance to restate and even elaborate on her opinions.

In many cases, the smartest choice is to decline the invitation to cross-examine an expert witness. You can instead rely on your own expert as well as your other evidence to convince a judge or jury that your claims are accurate.

But if you cannot pay for your own expert testimony, and the judge refuses to appoint an expert, you may have no choice other than to try to undermine the adversary's expert's conclusions. In that situation, you may want to at least hire an expert for some pre-trial consultation. Tell your expert consultant what you expect the opponent's expert to say, and ask what areas of weakness you might probe during cross-examination. Even if

you come up with no more than four or five good questions, you may give the judge or jury some reason to question the expert's testimony.

Seek your consulting expert's help in wording your questions, and write down the questions exactly as you expect to ask them in your cross-examination outline. When you cross-examine an expert, the exact words you use are often more important than when you cross-examine ordinary witnesses.

If you do want to cross-examine your adversary's expert, here are some possible approaches. You may be able to use them during cross-examination without giving an adverse expert the opportunity to rehash all of his opinions.

- Demonstrate weaknesses in the expert's qualifications. Perhaps the expert testified impressively that he is a member of numerous professional organizations. If you show that any attorney, electrical engineer, accountant or other expert can join those organizations merely by paying a membership fee, the impressiveness may evaporate. For example, any lawyer willing to pay the required fee can join the American Bar Association—no special qualifications are required.

- Show that the expert lacks certain qualifications that she might be expected to have. For instance, medical experts are often "Board Certified" in particular medical specialties such as surgery or radiology, meaning that they have passed tests conducted by a national board of experts in their field. If you ask your adversary's medical expert if she is Board certified and the answer is no, you may undercut her credibility.

You may attack a qualified expert's background. You may attack an opposing expert's qualifications on cross-examination even though the judge has ruled that the witness is qualified to give expert testimony. Your questions are relevant to the credibility of the expert's opinions.

- Ask the witness about his fee. If you know from pre-trial discussions or answers to your formal discovery requests that your opponent's expert is receiving what the average judge or juror will think is a large fee, ask how much the expert is being paid. The judge or jury may conclude that the expert is slanting his testimony in favor of the hand that is feeding him.

- Show that the witness is biased. If you know that the expert always testifies on behalf of one position, ask the expert how often she testifies, and then how often she testifies for the same position. For example, assume that your opponent has called an expert legal witness to testify that your former lawyer, whom you have sued for legal malpractice, was not negligent. You may learn through discovery that this expert has testified in 20 other legal malpractice cases, and has always testified that there was no legal malpractice. When you bring out this background, you suggest that the expert is slanting her testimony (is biased) to favor an ideological position she favors rather than providing the truth.

- Contradict the expert with a reliable published opinion. If you know that the expert's opinion is at odds with a passage in a treatise or textbook that the expert regards as reliable, show the book to the expert, ask him to admit that experts in the same field generally regard that treatise or textbook as "authoritative," and then read into the record the conflicting opinion.

Cross-examining an expert based on a passage in a treatise that is at odds with an expert's opinion is a cheap way for you to introduce expert evidence favorable to your side. Although it requires you to find an authoritative book that takes a position at odds with that of an expert, this may not be so difficult if you have hired an expert to help you prepare for trial.

For example, assume that the adversary's expert, an economist, testifies that he can predict with reasonable accuracy the future rate of inflation by tracking the Consumer Price Index for the last five years. You have located a book that you are told is generally regarded as authoritative that says that "anyone who says that he can predict the rate of inflation is an idiot." On cross-examination, mark the book as an exhibit, show it to the expert and ask him to authenticate it as one that experts in the field regard as "generally authoritative," and then read the quoted language into the record.

You may also use widely respected books and articles to demonstrate that the information on which the expert's opinion is based is less than complete. For example, assume that an expert testifies that an important factor in his conclusion is "the results of test A," which he conducted. You have an authoritative treatise which states that "the best test is test B." By reading this conflicting passage into the record, you may lead the judge or jury to question the expert's methodology and by extension his opinion.

You can use formal discovery to prepare for the testimony of your adversary's expert witness. Federal Rule of Civil Procedure 26 (b)(4) is typical of rules that provide for pre-trial discovery of the identity of your adversary's expert and the expert's qualifications and opinions. Under this rule, you can send a written interrogatory (question) to your adversary asking if your adversary intends to call an expert witness and, if so, the expert's name and address. In a separate interrogatory, you can also ask your adversary to summarize the expert's likely testimony. Finally, if you need additional information you can take the expert's deposition. Doing so is likely to be costly, however. (For more information on depositions and interrogatories, see Chapter 4, Investigating Your Case.)

 Make a cross-examination outline. Include an outline of the evidence you expect to elicit from your adversary's expert in the Cross-Examination section of your trial notebook. This outline may be quite short. For example, you might limit it to the fee your adversary is paying for the expert's testimony and to reminders to probe for one or two weaknesses in the expert's qualifications. (See Chapter 17, Organizing a Trial Notebook.)

 REFERENCES ON EXPERT WITNESSES

Federal Rules of Evidence in a Nutshell, by Michael Graham (West Publishing Co.). A review of evidence principles organized according to the Federal Rules of Evidence, with an emphasis on their practical application.

Evidentiary Foundations, by Ed Imwinkelreid (Michie Co.). This book contains numerous sample foundational transcripts, including how to qualify an expert.

McCormick on Evidence, by John Strong, ed. (West Publishing Co.). A basic treatise on evidence, frequently used by judges and attorneys.

Weinstein's Evidence Manual, Student Edition, by Jack Weinstein and Margaret Berger (Matthew Bender). Also a well-regarded work organized according to the Federal Rules of Evidence.

Expert Witnesses and the Federal Rules of Evidence, by James McElhaney, 28 Mercer Law Review 463 (1977). This article was written shortly after the Federal Rules of Evidence were enacted, and it explains the provisions concerning expert witnesses. ■

19

WHEN YOUR TRIAL ENDS:
JUDGMENTS AND APPEALS

After both you and your adversary rest (have finished presenting) your cases and the trial ends, the judge or jury will render a verdict—make a final decision stating who wins and who loses. If your case is tried before a jury, the verdict will be read at the close of the case. But if your trial is before a judge alone, the judge may take the case "under submission" or "under advisement." That means the judge will think the matter over for anywhere from a day or two to several months and then let you know the final decision in writing.

Even when you find out the decision in your case, that may not be the last word. This chapter looks at three things that can happen after a verdict is rendered:

• The judge can overturn the jury verdict, in some circumstances.

• The decision can be appealed and reconsidered by a higher court at the request of a party).

• If you win the trial and your adversary doesn't appeal, you still have the sometimes time-consuming task of collecting your judgment—getting your adversary to pay you the money the judge or jury awarded you.

As you know, this book's primary focus is conducting your trial. It may be helpful for you to have an idea of what can face you after trial, however, as you make certain decisions along the way. This chapter is an overview, aimed at giving you a general picture of what you may encounter at and after the close of your trial; it is not a guide on how to actually make post-trial motions or appeal your case. Where possible, we have tried to refer you to other resources for further guidance on post-trial proceedings.

"After careful deliberation, Your Honor, we'd rather not get involved."

A. HOW FINAL DECISIONS ARE MADE AT THE END OF TRIAL

In many jury trials, the jury is just instructed to decide who wins and how much money that person is entitled to; the jury doesn't state the reasons for the decision. Some juries, however, are requested to return what is called a "special verdict." This means the jury makes a statement about particular facts it has found to be true, often in response to specific questions in the jury instructions. For example, in some states, each party to a personal injury action can be found partly responsible for the injury under a theory called "comparative negligence." In such states, a jury may be asked to make a special verdict in which it decides which party was responsible for what percentage of the harm.

Remember that jury verdicts in civil trials do not have to be unanimous. In most states, only three-fourths of the jurors have to agree in order to render a verdict. This means that if a jury panel consists of 12 jurors, 9 jurors must agree in order for there to be a verdict.

At the end of a judge trial, the judge may rule from the bench and orally declare a winner. Or a judge may rule later, in a document stating who won and how much the winner was awarded. Sometimes when a judge writes a decision, it is a one-liner, called a "Judgement," "Order" or "Final Order." A sample is shown below.

Other times, judges write longer opinions, which include the legal and factual reasons for their decisions. These documents are sometimes called "Opinions" or "Findings of Fact and Conclusions of Law." A judge can also state findings (legal and factual reasons for the decision) orally, from the bench.

The final decision or judgment in a case is often written up by the court's clerk. But sometimes, especially if the judge rules from the bench at the close of trial, the judge may ask you or your adversary to write up the findings and the judgment (who wins and what the loser is ordered to pay). The process is similar to the one sometimes followed with a court order on a pre-trial motion. (See Chapter 6, Pre-Trial Hearings and Motions.)

If the judge requests that you write up the decision or findings, ask the court clerk for a sample or form from another case. Ask also for an explanation of what document you should prepare and how you should prepare it, who must get copies and any other advice about the process. For example, in some courts, a party who prepares an order is expected to send a draft (sometimes called a proposed order) to the judge and the other party. Then, if the draft correctly reflects the judge's decision and there are no objections, the judge will sign the document.

Lawyers often jump at the opportunity to write the findings at the end of a case. Even though it takes work, the writer can sometimes interpret what the judge said in a way that is favorable to her client. Because appellate courts don't hear evidence themselves, if your case is appealed to a higher court, that court will rely on these findings to determine the facts the trial judge found to be true. And once a decision becomes part of the written record of the trial court, it is likely to take on a life of its own and be difficult to change.

For all these reasons, if you are asked to draft the judge's decision or specific findings, or if you are reviewing a document drafted by your adversary, pay attention to detail. And, if possible, have

SAMPLE JUDGMENT

```
 1   Sarah Adams
     [Address]
 2   [City, State, Zip Code]
     [Telephone]
 3

 4
     Defendant in Pro Per
 5

 6

 7

 8              IN THE _____ COURT OF _____ COUNTY

 9                          STATE OF _____

10

11   Nolo Pedestrian,                    )   CASE NO. 12345
                                         )
12                    Plaintiff,         )
                                         )
13        v.                             )   JUDGMENT
                                         )
14   Sarah Adams,                        )
                                         )
15                    Defendant.         )
                                         )
16   _____    )

17

18

19

20       Judgment for Defendant, Sara Adams.

21

22

23   _____        _____
     Date                            Victor Michaels, Judge
24

25

26

27

28
```

your self-help law coach or someone else whose legal savvy you trust read the document to see if it is open to interpretations you have not seen.

After the judgment is signed by the judge, it will be "entered"—which means it becomes part of the final, permanent court record. Only when a judgment is entered into the court records is it considered final. Understanding this is important because it is only when a judgment is final that you are able to appeal. Also, if you want to appeal, you may have to file a Notice of Appeal within a certain number of days after the judgment is entered. (See Section C2 below).

Make sure you are notified of the judgment. To be sure that you are properly notified when the judgment is entered in your case, ask the clerk whether you will receive a Notice of Entry of Judgment. You may want to also give the clerk a stamped self-addressed envelope in order to be sure you get a copy.

B. REQUESTING A NEW TRIAL OR CHANGE IN THE VERDICT

After a judge trial, the loser, be it you or your adversary, can ask the trial court judge to modify the judgment or vacate it (withdraw it altogether and order a new trial). Because you are asking the very judge who made a decision to change it, such a request is often unsuccessful—unless it asks merely to correct a typographical or mathematical error. But if you have a good reason to be unsatisfied with the judgment, such a motion may be worth a try, if only because it is generally simpler and less expensive to prepare, file and argue than an appeal.

1. Mathematical Errors in Judgments

One request that is usually successful is to modify the judgment if a party has found a mathematical error in the computation of the judgment amount. If you review the judgment and find such an error, ask if the clerk can fix it without any formal proceedings. If not, you may have to make a motion asking the court to change the judgment to reflect the correct amount. (For reference, see Federal Rule of Civil Procedure 60(a) on correcting clerical errors in federal court.)

If you do have to bring a motion, the judge will likely make a decision without a hearing, based on your and your adversary's prepared written papers. (See Chapter 6, Pre-Trial Hearings and Motions, for more on making motions.)

2. Other Reasons to Modify or Vacate Judgments

You can also ask the court to modify or vacate its judgment if you can show that the judge made errors of law or there was serious misconduct on the part of your adversary or the judge. (See Federal Rule of Civil Procedure 59, on requesting new trials and amendment of judgments in federal court, for reference.) Although unlikely, your written request (motion) could convince the judge to reconsider a decision, especially if you persuasively explain your reasons and clearly support them with citations to relevant, binding legal authorities. (See Chapter 22, Legal Research.)

Examples of the types of errors for which a court may change a judgment are:

- The judge excluded highly important, relevant and admissible evidence—for example, keeping out the computer records that were essential to your case as hearsay when they clearly fell within the business records exception as you argued at trial. (See Chapter 15, Basic Rules of Evidence.)

- The judge allowed your adversary to introduce highly prejudicial, irrelevant evidence despite your objections.

- Your adversary engaged in serious misconduct by making one-sided contact (ex parte) with the judge during trial, which prejudiced your case.

You can also request a new trial if after the judgment is entered you discover new and extremely helpful evidence which, for some very good reason, was not available at the time of trial. Not preparing because you were on vacation is not a good reason, but finding out your adversary lied about critical evidence during discovery would be. Another good reason is if something happens after the trial that you certainly would have wanted to introduce evidence about. For example, say you sue your roofer, Monica Doherty, for using inferior quality wood when repairing your roof. Two weeks after trial, five other houses on your block, also repaired by Doherty, collapse due to the same problem of inferior quality wood. You may be able to get a new trial to introduce this new evidence.

3. Overturning or Changing Jury Decisions

Judges have the power to overturn or modify a jury's verdict, but they rarely exercise it. You may, however, try to convince the judge to overturn the jury's verdict or change the amount of damages that the jury awarded. To do this, you make a written request (motion) for something called a judgment notwithstanding the verdict, often called

by the abbreviation "JNOV." (See Federal Rule of Civil Procedure 50(b), for reference.)

A motion for JNOV in effect says to the judge: No reasonable jury could reasonably have concluded what the jury in this case did. And because the jury verdict was so preposterous, you, as a judge of reason, should overturn their outrageous verdict— or at least change the ridiculously unfair amount of damages they awarded.

Here's an example of a situation where a judge might lower the amount of a jury's verdict. Assume that you are Sarah Adams, a building contractor who was sued by a pedestrian. The plaintiff alleged that you negligently struck him as he crossed the street. You defended yourself, but the plaintiff was represented by a lawyer.

The plaintiff, a fire fighter, was a community hero. Because of the injuries, he was confined to a desk job, unable to work on the front lines, and the jury clearly sympathized. Even though the jury found that you were only partly responsible for the injuries (the jury found that the plaintiff's own carelessness was a significant cause of the injuries), the jury still awarded the plaintiff a million dollars in damages.

You may be successful in arguing to the judge that the damages should be reduced because, however unfortunate his injuries are, the plaintiff is partly responsible for injuring himself.

Judges very rarely order new trials. A judge might order one if a juror admits some wrongdoing—for example, if one or more jurors say they did not follow the judge's instructions, were coerced to vote in a certain way and do not in their hearts and good consciences support the verdict or had one-sided contacts with your adversary outside of the courtroom during the trial, which prejudiced your case. Judges also order new trials in the event of a mistrial (a trial which ends before the full proceeding is completed because of some prejudicial conduct or error.)

If you decide to try making a post-trial motion to change the judgment or request a new trial, remember that it is not common to win. In all likelihood, you will have to appeal if you are not satisfied with the trial court judgment.

 RESEARCHING POST-TRIAL MOTIONS

To find information at a law library (see Chapter 22, Legal Research), ask the librarian to point you to reference books on "civil practice" in your state. Look for a section on post-trial motions or in the index under the following or a similar entry:

- Motion for a New Trial
- New Trial
- Judgment—Amendments to
- Judgment—Vacating.

C. APPEALS

If you lose your trial, you may have grounds for an appeal. Appeals, however, are often complex; you may be wise to have an attorney represent you even if you successfully conducted the trial.

While explaining the appeals process in detail is far beyond the scope of this book, here is a brief overview.

1. What Appellate Courts Do

An appeal is a request to a higher court to review and overturn the decision of a lower court. If it's

appealed, your trial court verdict will be reviewed by an appeals (appellate) court. Appeals of federal trial court (district court) decisions are heard by the U.S. Court of Appeals; in state court systems, appellate courts go by various names.

If either party is dissatisfied after the first appeal, that party can appeal to the highest court in the state or federal system, sometimes known as the court of last resort. For the federal courts, this is the United States Supreme Court; most states also call their highest court the state supreme court. These courts accept only a few of the appeals submitted to them. If they don't accept your appeal, you are stuck with the decision of the lower appeals court.

Appeals courts generally resist overruling trial judges on appeal. Normally, a higher court can overturn the decision of a lower court only if the lower court made a significant error of law.

The appellate court will not conduct a new trial or look at new evidence. Instead of putting witnesses on the stand and conducting a new trial for the appellate court, you will need to present a "brief"— a written argument setting out what mistakes the trial court made and the laws that support your positions. To write a brief, you will almost certainly have to look at how other courts have decided similar legal problems and apply their reasoning to your case. (More on researching case law in Chapter 22, Legal Research.)

The appellate court will review the official record (a transcript of the testimony plus exhibits) of the trial court, focusing on the legal errors you claim were made. It's up to you and your adversary to bring important portions of the trial transcript and exhibits to the appellate court's attention. Appellate courts will not scour the record of the trial court looking for injustices or mistakes that you neglect to identify.

2.   Filing a Notice of Appeal

There are strict time limits for filing appeals. You will probably have to file a paper called a "Notice of Appeal" very soon after you receive Notice of Entry of Final Judgment—often between 10 to 30 days. The Notice of Appeal notifies your adversary and the court of your intention to bring an appeal. Later, if you change your mind, you can withdraw your Notice of Appeal without penalty. But if you don't file it by the deadline, your right to appeal will likely be forever lost (waived).

You may have very little time to appeal. Even before your case is decided, find out the deadline for filing a Notice of Appeal. If you think you may possibly consider appealing, do not wait until the case is over; start work immediately. Usually a court clerk, your legal coach or a law librarian can show you the procedural rules on appeals in your court system. Also, check to be sure of when the court clerk will be sending the Notice of Entry of Judgment in case it gets delayed in the mail.

3.   The Appeals Process

Appealing a case involves preparing documents and making an oral argument before an appellate court. Appellate courts have their own sets of rules that differ from the rules in trial courts. This section outlines the basic process of an appeal. For further details, consult a book on appellate procedure for your court.

a.   Making and Preserving a Record

Because appellate courts do not hear evidence—they review the written record from the trial court—the trial record is all-important. The official trial record consists of:

- what is said and taken down by the court reporter during court proceedings
- exhibits that get admitted into evidence
- documents that are filed with the court.

Make a good record at trial. To make a complete record during trial, you must articulate clearly and make sure all the witnesses do as well. Also, if someone gestures or makes remarks that are not clear, clarify them "for the record."

For example, assume your witness in the faulty roof case, your neighbor Marla Kristy, testifies that her roof (repaired by Doherty Roofers, the same roofing company as the one that repaired your roof) also caved in during the heavy storms. As she is testifying, Ms. Kristy holds up a photograph of her collapsed roof (that you had previously marked as Exhibit A and asked the judge to accept into evidence). You ask, "Now, Ms. Kristy, how did you know that Doherty Roofers used inferior grade wood?" She replies, "I could see that the wood was a lighter color there [pointing to the left bottom corner of the photo where the roof fell in] than the rest of the roof." Unless you stop and say aloud, "Let the record reflect the witness is pointing to the left-bottom corner of the photograph of her house, Exhibit A," an appellate court will not necessarily know from reading the record that the witness was pointing to a photo.

b. Getting Necessary Documents

If you appeal, you will have to order a trial court transcript from the court reporter. (See Chapter 2, for more on court reporters). Transcripts are usually quite costly. But the court of appeal must have the official record from the lower court in order to review what happened at the trial court, and you must prepare and assemble that record for them. To do that, you may need to attach other documents to your appellate brief, such as:

- all or relevant parts of the trial court transcript, especially anything you refer to in your written papers

- copies of exhibits

- a copy of your Notice of Appeal (and Proof of Service of that Notice)

- a copy of the trial court's judgment.

c. Writing a Brief

Once you decide to appeal a case and file a Notice of Appeal, you will get a briefing schedule and hearing dates from the appellate court. To make sure you don't miss any deadlines, you may want to make a list of important dates, like the one shown below.

SAMPLE SCHEDULE

IMPORTANT DEADLINES

Event	Date
Judgment entered	_____
Deadline for filing Notice of Appeal	_____
Deadline for filing Appellant's Opening Brief	_____
Deadline for filing Respondent's Brief	_____
Deadline for filing Appellant's Reply Brief	_____
Oral Argument	_____

The person who brings an appeal (the "appellant" or "petitioner") usually files an opening brief, the other side (the "appellee" or "respondent") files a response, and then the appellant can file a response to that.

Appellate courts have extensive and often picky requirements for most every aspect of appellate practice; written briefs are no exception. The appellate rules often limit the number of pages, and specify the type of paper and binding, color of binding cover and size of print type. For that reason and because the law can be complex, drafting an appellate brief can be difficult even for an experienced attorney. You may have to do extensive legal research to effectively understand and make appropriate references to necessary statutes, court cases, administrative regulations and sometimes even your state or the federal constitution. (See Chapter 22, Legal Research.) It may be wise to hire a lawyer for your appeal.

RESOURCES ON APPEALS

For more information on appeals, an easy-to read inexpensive source is *Appellate Advocacy in a Nutshell*, by Alan D. Hornstein (West Publishing Co.). This book reviews the appellate process, appellate courts, and discusses the content of oral appellate arguments and written appellate briefs.

If you decide to write your own brief, ask a librarian for some references to appellate brief-writing resource books. One helpful resource is the *Handbook of Appellate Advocacy*, prepared by UCLA Moot Court Honors Program (West Publishing Co.). Though geared for law students writing briefs for hypothetical arguments (called moot court), this will give you an idea of what you must do.

d.   Making an Oral Argument

After the briefs are all in, you and your adversary may have the opportunity to appear before the appellate court to argue the appeal. It is common practice, however, for courts to decide many appeals on the papers alone. If you do appear in person you will normally have a limited amount of time—from two to five minutes in some state appellate courts, to 30 minutes in some federal courts, to make arguments about why you should be granted the appeal or your adversary denied the appeal. Because you and your adversary will have submitted your arguments in writing ahead of time, the appeals court will know what the issues are, and they may have specific questions for you or your adversary.

 Watch appellate court arguments before it's your turn. If you are going to argue before an appellate court, make an effort to observe that court in action before the date of your hearing. That is one of the best ways to find out what you are facing. Also, reference books you consulted for assistance writing your appellate brief may have helpful suggestions for oral argument.

---

4.   Should You Appeal?

In deciding whether to appeal your case, consider:

- The monetary costs—for filing fees, transcripts, and other fees, consulting a lawyer and missing work.

- The costs in time—doing legal research, writing a brief and preparing for oral argument.

- The emotional stress on you and your family.

- Your chances of succeeding.

You may also consider your desire for justice if you feel it was unfairly denied at trial. You may benefit psychologically by taking the case as far as you can because it's important to you to get fair treatment and respect. This may be especially true, for example, in lawsuits involving unlawful discrimination or similar civil rights claims. But before you appeal for these reasons, consider that you may feel far worse if you again lose after spending more time, money and energy to appeal.

Before committing yourself to taking an appeal, carefully review the procedural rules you'll need to follow and the paperwork you'll have to prepare. Next, draft a realistic timeline, estimating how long it will take, and a budget outlining how much it will cost. Then consult your legal coach to get an assessment of your chances for success. Armed with this information, you will be much better able to make a satisfying decision.

 Find an attorney who specializes in appeals. Ask the lawyer who serves as your coach about experience with appellate practice. An attorney who handles nothing but appeals may be better suited than a trial lawyer to evaluate your appeal prospects, and advise you or handle the appeal for you if you decide to proceed. Your present legal coach may be able to refer you to an appellate lawyer, or you can use the process outlined in Chapter 21, Getting Help from Attorneys: Hiring a Legal Coach, to find an appellate specialist.

5. If Your Adversary Appeals

Even if you win, remember that your adversary may appeal or may threaten to appeal. Don't party too hard quite yet, and whatever you do, don't throw out any of your files, papers or notes; you will need them if you do face an appeal.

Don't be intimidated if your adversary threatens to appeal. First off, if your adversary appeals but does not have valid grounds to bring an appeal, you may be able to request reimbursement for the attorneys' fees you incur defending yourself. Be aware that this also cuts the other way; if you file a frivolous appeal (one without validity), you may have to pay your adversary's fees. Second, an experienced attorney may cynically threaten to appeal to get you to settle for less money than the full amount of the judgment. And, third, it is common practice to file a notice of appeal to preserve the right to appeal even though no appeal may actually be filed.

If you receive a notice of appeal from your adversary, consult your legal coach, assess the pros and cons of continuing the process, and stand your ground unless there is a good reason to give in now. Remember, you won at trial, so the odds are strongly in your favor now.

D. COLLECTING AND PAYING JUDGMENTS

After the trial ends and you are notified of the court's decision, you will have to take specific actions in order to collect your judgment if you won, and to pay the judgment if you lost.

1. If You Won

Just because you win your trial, and the judge tells your adversary to pay you $50,000, doesn't mean the check will appear in your mailbox the next week. Unfortunately, enforcing or collecting a judgment (getting the dollars in your hands) can sometimes be as difficult, if not more difficult, than winning at trial. This is especially true if you won by default (your adversary did not appear in court and the judge ruled in your favor after you showed enough evidence to prove your claim).

⚠ **Your opponent can still stall.** Appeals and post-trial motions usually have the effect of putting a judgment on hold, sometimes called "staying" the judgment. If your opponent appeals or makes a post-trial motion, you will have to wait until it is resolved to collect your judgment.

It's important to understand that, generally, neither the judge nor the court clerk will help you collect a judgment. In some cases, however, you can ask the court to intervene. If your adversary intentionally disobeys the court's order—for example, by refusing to pay a judgment even though you have evidence that he clearly has sufficient funds to pay—you can bring a motion requesting the court to compel your adversary to come to court and explain why he or she is not complying with the court's order.

If the court concludes that the person deliberately disregarded the court's order, it is likely that the judge will find such a person in contempt of court (in violation of the court order) and impose sanctions, usually a monetary fine on top of the judgment. This often happens, for example, in family matters where a parent refuses to pay alimony or child support.

ENFORCING NON-MONETARY JUDGMENTS

If the court judgment ordered the losing party to do something other than pay you money, special rules apply when you try to enforce (get the loser to comply with) the judgment. For example, a judgment may require a losing party to fix your roof, reinstate your employment, not come near you (a restraining order) or not to build the second story that will block your view. These are all examples of what lawyers call "injunctive relief" as opposed to "monetary relief." Your best bet is to consult reference books on injunctive relief in your court system.

 For some basic information on injunctive relief, see *Injunctions in a Nutshell*, by John F. Dobbyn (West Publishing Co.), an inexpensive paperback which describes the different types of injunctions and the elements courts look at to grant and enforce them.

Common sense usually suggests you wait until the appeal period has ended before you push your adversary to pay the judgment. If you have still not been paid by a reasonable time after the deadline for filing a Notice of Appeal, you may begin the process of collecting your judgment.

First try writing a demand letter to your adversary. Sending a copy ("cc") to your self-help law coach and noting that at the bottom of your demand letter may provoke your adversary into responding. A sample is shown below.

SAMPLE DEMAND LETTER

Sally Adams
[address]
[city, state]

November 16, 19__

Re: *Nolo v. Adams*, Case No. _____

Dear Ms. Adams:

As you know, the court entered a judgment against you on May 27 in the sum of $80,000. It is November 16, and I still have not received payment from you. If you do not send the full payment to me within 2 weeks, I will have no choice but to begin enforcement proceedings against you.

Sincerely,

William Nolo

William Nolo

cc: Victor Rosenberg, Esq.

As with every document you send or receive in connection with your lawsuit, save a copy, mark the date and time you sent it and keep it organized along with other important papers relating to your case. If one demand letter doesn't work, you may want to follow it up with another sent registered mail, return receipt requested.

If you do not succeed by simply asking for your judgment, you will have to take steps to enforce it. If it's a money judgment, you will want to research and use one of the powerful legal remedies available to enforce judgments, such as attaching bank accounts, garnishing wages or requesting that the sheriff (or federal marshal, in federal cases) seize your adversary's assets.

RESOURCES ON ENFORCING JUDGMENTS

Telling you how to follow through on specific enforcement proceedings in your state is beyond the scope of this book, but information may be available from:

- The sheriff's or marshal's office where your opponent lives, does business or owns property.

- Your law library. (See Chapter 22, Legal Research.) It will have continuing education and practice books for lawyers that explain the steps necessary to collect judgments in your state. (Ask a librarian or look in the index under "collection of judgments," "judgments," "enforcement of judgments" or "debt collection.")

- Your legal coach or your coach's secretary or paralegal who may be able to put advice you and your hands on specific forms needed for enforcement proceedings.

- *Collect Your Court Judgment: 19 Ways to Get Paid When You Win a Lawsuit,* by Scott, Elias and Goldoftas (Nolo Press), an easy-to-use guide designed specifically for pro pers in California.

2. If You Lost

Even at this stage of the game, you still have some options. One, you can pay immediately and be finished with the whole matter. If you feel you did your best, had your day in court and lost after a relatively fair fight, it may be time to put the matter behind you.

Two, you can try to negotiate with your adversary. If you do not have the money to pay the judgment, for example, you might suggest that your opponent accept a lesser amount in exchange for a cashier's check payment in full now of that lesser amount. Your adversary may decide that it's more costly and time-consuming to fight with you and deal with a lengthy collections process than to accept less money now and be done with it all.

You could ask your adversary to accept a monthly payment plan, something workable within your budget. You may want to remind your adversary that he will not collect anything on the judgment if you are forced into filing for bankruptcy. An honest offer of a realistic payment plan will be appreciated much more, in the long run, than promising the full sum and not delivering.

If you and your adversary agree to settle the matter now for an amount or arrangement other than what was decided in court, be sure to get everything in writing. Your settlement agreement is in effect a new contract which, if breached, can give rise to another lawsuit for its breach.

Also, check your local rules to see if you are required to file any new agreements with the court. Since these settlements can change the terms of the judge's order (for example, less money for cash up front or a payment plan over time), they are sometimes called substituted judgments, because they substitute your agreement with the adversary for the court's judgment.

The court may order time payments. In some courts, if your adversary will not agree voluntarily to accept a payment plan from you, you have the right to go to court and ask the judge to order the other side to accept such payments.

Finally, you may not own any collectible assets; you may be what is called "judgment-proof." Generally, property that is necessary for basic living, such as food, clothing, and limited allowances for things like medical care, transportation and housing cannot be seized by creditors. It is said to be "exempt." This means your adversary cannot collect the shirt off your back to satisfy a judgment. ∎

20

REPRESENT YOURSELF IN DIVORCE COURT

I f you are getting divorced, need child support or alimony, seek a change in child custody, or want the court to protect you from an abusive spouse, chances are you will have to deal with a special court—increasingly known as family court. While family court proceedings are similar in many respects to the general civil court proceedings explained in the rest of this book, they also differ in some key areas. For example:

- Judges alone decide family law matters.

- Important issues are often resolved in short hearings, where you have but a few minutes to ask for specific outcomes and explain why you deserve them.

- Mediation—both voluntary and required—is used more frequently than in other courts.

- Judges tend to be paternalistic—they will commonly intervene if they believe that one of the parties isn't getting a fair deal. And if children are involved, judges often attempt to act more like the biblical Solomon than "the legal referee" described in other parts of this book. (See Sidebar below on Solomon's custody decision.)

- Unlike most other civil cases, family court cases often don't "end" for many more years. For example, divorced spouses may have to come back to family court even after a divorce is "final" to enforce or modify court custody or support orders.

➡ **Sections A and B provide background material.** If you have already filed for divorce and understand the key legal issues involved, please skip to Section C, below, where we deal with the specifics of the divorce process.

SOLOMON'S CUSTODY DECISION

As recounted in the Bible, Solomon, a king and judge, was approached by two women both claiming to be a child's mother. When Solomon proposed cutting the baby in half, so that each "mother" could get her half, one mother cried out No!—Rather than see the baby cut in half, she would let the other woman have it. Solomon determined that this woman, the one who would give up her own child rather than see it harmed, was the real mother and, accordingly, gave her the baby.

Today's fathers and mothers who end up in family court have much to learn from Solomon's wisdom. Just as was true of Solomon, most modern family court judges are highly sympathetic to the position of the parent who appears most concerned with the child's well-being. And these judges are far less sympathetic to a parent who places his or her own needs ahead of a child's or approaches the proceedings with a win-at-any-cost attitude. (More on this below.)

This chapter is designed to give readers facing family court hearings an idea of what to expect. The first two sections provide some background material designed to be especially helpful to people who know little about family law and divorce procedures. The next several sections explain in more detail about how divorce cases get filed and processed through the courts. The final section alerts readers to the most common traps for the unwary self-help litigant in divorce court and suggests ways to avoid them.

NOLO RESOURCES TO HELP YOU THROUGH YOUR DIVORCE

Throughout this chapter we suggest additional resources that may be helpful if you are doing your own divorce. Here are the ones published by Nolo Press. Some are national in scope, while others are limited to a particular state.

Nolo's Pocket Guide to Family Law, by Robin Leonard and Stephen Elias (Nolo Press), is a comprehensive reference book that answers questions on all aspects of family law, including divorce, custody, child and spousal support and more.

Divorce and Money: How to Make the Best Financial Decisions During Divorce, by Violet Woodhouse & Victoria F. Collins with M.C. Blakeman (Nolo Press), guides you through the process of divorce and helps you decide key financial issues, such as dividing real estate, investments, taxes and debt, setting alimony and child support and negotiating a settlement.

Child Custody: Building Parenting Agreements That Work, by Mimi Lyster (Nolo Press), presents a step-by-step method of creating workable agreements regarding child custody and visitation rights, and sets out a variety of solutions for each issue.

How to Mediate Your Dispute, by Peter Lovenheim (Nolo Press), shows you how to choose a mediator, prepare your case and go through the mediation process, and includes an extensive chapter on mediating divorce and child custody disputes.

Money Troubles: Legal Strategies to Cope with Your Debts, by Robin Leonard (Nolo Press), explains bankruptcy and non-bankruptcy alternatives for resolving financial difficulties and helps you decide which type of bankruptcy may be best for your situation.

Domestic Violence and Abuse: How to Stop it!, by Cheryl Anne Woodard (Nolo Press), a complete kit for stopping domestic violence, includes all forms and instructions that you need for a restraining order and provides step-by-step advice.

A. FORMULATE A DIVORCE GAME PLAN

Each year a million and a half American couples file for divorce. In a number of states, both spouses represent themselves in more than half of all divorces; in over 80%, at least one spouse does. These statistics underline a fundamental point: doing your own divorce is feasible. But that is not the same thing as saying it's easy. Nor does it mean that people representing themselves in divorce proceedings always get what they want or need from the court.

Before starting your own divorce case, you should gather enough information to be able to:

- file the right papers in the right court

- appear in court (or where allowed, process papers by mail) to get these papers approved by the judge, and

- have the resulting court orders (granting a divorce and awarding child custody and support, for example) officially entered in the court record.

To do this paperwork in an informed manner—so that you will fully understand your legal rights and attain the objectives you desire and are entitled to—you will need to:

- learn some basic legal terminology

- understand and possibly research the divorce laws in your state

- have a clear, realistic picture of your own needs and wants

- have as clear and realistic a picture as possible of your spouse's needs and wants

- understand what the family court is legally authorized to do.

What this amounts to is that you need to create a family court "game plan." This is important for a couple of reasons. First, by going into the divorce process with a clear, well-informed plan, you have a better shot at getting what you want from the court and saving yourself time, money and stress. (See Section A3, below, "Do Some Pre-Divorce Planning.") Second, by having a tight plan you will be prepared to promptly take corrective action if a critical step is missed by you, your spouse or the court.

1. Research Your State's Rules

Family courts follow state laws. While broadly similar throughout America, laws can differ in important ways from state to state. For instance:

- Each state has its own requirements for how long you must live in the state before filing for divorce. (Six months is typical.)

- Many, but not all, states make you wait for a period between when the divorce is preliminarily granted by the court and when it becomes final. (Three to six months is common.)

- Each state sets legal requirements for getting a divorce. In some, to get a no-fault divorce you and your spouse must agree to divorce, or you must actually separate for some continuous period of time, such as one year. But in many others, all it takes is a statement by one spouse that the marriage suffers from irreconcilable differences. In these states it is of no legal consequence that the other spouse may disagree.

- Each state has its own rules about how much child support should be paid and when alimony (spousal support) is appropriate.

- Each state has its own rules that define marital property and how it should be divided (some states use "community property" rules, while most states use a system called "equitable distribution"—see Section B2 below for definitions of this jargon.)

In addition, every state and county (and sometimes even individual courts) have different procedural rules governing the divorce process. Procedural rules govern what facts and claims (allegations) you must include in your divorce papers, what hearings are required before a divorce (or a temporary custody, support or restraining order) can be granted and how trials are conducted. Although the paperwork to get a divorce is similar in every state, not one state's rules or forms will work in another state without significant modification.

Fortunately, there are some good starting places for getting the information you'll need. *Nolo's Pocket Guide to Family Law* is a particularly efficient one, since it provides an introduction to the divorce rules of every state. And Nolo Press publishes self-help divorce books in California, Texas and Oregon. In addition, self-help divorce books from other publishers are available in most other states. However, chances are that you will have to supplement those books with additional information from a law library, Internet site or lawyer. (See Chapter 21, The Legal Coach, for more on finding a lawyer, and Chapter 22, Legal Research, for information on using a law library or getting information off the Internet.)

2. Legal Coaches

As discussed in Chapter 21, some lawyers are willing to advise you without handling your whole divorce. If you find such a lawyer, it may well be worth getting at least an hour or two of advice as early as possible in your case. Often, after asking you a series of basic questions, an experienced family lawyer should be able to tell you:

- whether you are eligible to file for divorce in your state or county (or whether you'll have to wait and if so how long)

- whether you have the correct forms (and possibly whether you have correctly completed them), or at least where you can obtain the correct forms and get help in completing them

- a "reality check" on what a judge has the power to decide and on how likely you are to achieve the result you desire and, possibly, give you a

lawyer's sense of whether you have a relatively simple case (that you could realistically handle on your own) or one that is likely to prove much more complicated, and

- how long the process is likely to take.

It can be tough to find a good legal coach. Unfortunately, many lawyers are not willing to advise divorce self-help litigants in a piece-meal fashion (possibly because they fear a later malpractice suit if things don't go well). And others who pretend they are open to legal coaching will primarily be interested in trying to get you to hire them to handle the entire case. We believe many more lawyers will be open to coaching in the future. In the meantime, if you absolutely can't find a lawyer sincerely open to coaching you, but need more information, consider meeting with a family lawyer for a consultation, so you can ask as many questions as possible. We don't suggest that readers should attempt to take advantage of lawyers— some of whom offer the first hour of advice free. Better to pay for the lawyer's time (or if it's free, to keep an open mind as to whether you may ultimately decide to hire the lawyer). If you receive free help but don't ultimately hire the lawyer, it is a good idea to write a polite thank-you letter explaining that although you've decided to represent yourself, you will recommend the lawyer to others in the future. That way, if your case turns dicey and you really do need help, the lawyer is far more likely to return your phone call.

---

3. Get Help If Your Spouse Is Playing Nasty

While a majority of divorces—especially those involving short marriages and modest amounts of property—can often be done on a self-help basis, it can be of critical importance to get competent help if your spouse does (or seriously threatens to do) any of the following:

- physically abuses, mentally harasses or otherwise hurts you or your kids

- takes your kids away from you without a court order

- cancels health insurance for you or your kids

- hides or sells your marital property, or

- denies your right to live in the family home without a court order.

Fortunately, if you are a victim of one of these types of domestic abuse, you should be able to get help and a referral to a lawyer from a battered women's shelter (mostly women suffer such abuse) or a domestic violence support group. Not only is it likely that a lawyer recommended by such an organization will be at least reasonably sensitive to your needs, but also the lawyer may offer to help you for free or a reduced fee if you cannot afford to pay more.

ASSISTANCE FOR DOMESTIC ABUSE VICTIMS

To get a good idea of how to protect yourself, one good resource is *Domestic Violence and Abuse: How to Stop it!,* by Cheryl Anne Woodard (Nolo Press 1996), which shows you how to get a domestic violence restraining order in California. People outside California will need to verify that the laws and practices in their states are similar (they mostly are), but anyone facing domestic abuse will find the book generally informative.

For emergency assistance in your area, look in your local or area phone book under the headings social services, rape crisis, domestic violence, victim services and mental health services to locate local helping groups. You may also get help from your local sheriff, courthouse or prosecutor's office (ask to speak to a specialist in domestic violence).

If you have difficulty finding local help through one of these methods, try one of the following organizations:

- National Battered Women's Hotline 800-799-SAFE (7233)

- National Victim Center at 800-FYI-CALL or online at http://www.nvc.org/fdir/assist.htm

- The National Organization for Victim Assistance (NOVA) in Washington, D.C., at 202-232-6682 (24 hrs.) or by e-mail at nova@access.digex.net. NOVA also lists toll-free "800" phone numbers for victim assistance nationwide online, at http://www.access.digex.net/~nova/resource.htm

---

4. If Necessary, Get a Temporary Restraining Order ("TRO")

Often, dealing with a spouse who engages in abusive conduct involves two steps:

- First and most important, if you fear for your or your children's safety, get out of harm's way;

- Second, go to court to obtain a "temporary restraining order." Often called a "TRO" or "protective order," a restraining order is a piece of paper signed by a judge ordering the person doing (or allegedly doing) the illegal or threatening behavior to stop. Judges may issue restraining orders before, during or after divorce proceedings.

A judge may also use a restraining order to tell a spouse to:

- Stay away from you or your kids, or visit them only in certain places, at certain times or under supervision (sometimes called "a monitored visit"),

- Move out of the family home,

- Not sell, mortgage or otherwise "encumber" (use as collateral or security for a debt) marital property, or

- Not cancel medical, life or other insurance.

Once a restraining order is issued, courts expect it to be followed. If a party nevertheless does something a restraining order prohibits (or does not do what it requires), a judge may follow up by issuing an arrest warrant. The police will then attempt to find and bring the violator into court, where the judge may reprimand, fine or even jail that person for "contempt of court" (disobeying a court order). In addition, although police should assist any spouse in trouble, regardless of whether she has a restraining order, law enforcement personnel often respond more quickly (and do so without questioning the victim) when a person needing help has a restraining order.

Usually hearings for restraining orders occur only after the responding spouse receives a notice of your motion (petition) and a time is set for him to appear and have his say. However, it is sometimes possible to obtain a restraining order without giving your spouse the advance written notice usually required by court rules. This single party ("ex-parte" in legal lingo) procedure is typically reserved for true emergencies, for example, where you have good reason to fear your spouse may hurt you or abduct your kids. Even so, some courts require at least some attempt to notify your spouse of your request for a restraining order (12- to 24-hour advance notice by telephone is common), while others dispense with the notice requirement altogether.

Any ruling or order a judge issues at a single party (ex-parte) hearing is called an emergency or "ex-parte order." This type of order is usually issued only for a short period so that the other spouse can be given a prompt opportunity to respond and be heard in court.

In the following dialogue, Mae Jules will ask Judge Duncan for an ex-parte temporary restraining order. Just as the clerk is getting ready to call a scheduled custody hearing, Mae runs into the courtroom, accompanied by a volunteer from the Southside Women's Shelter. The two women approach the bailiff. Mae tells the bailiff that she called the court clerk earlier in the day and was told to come in to request a TRO. The bailiff gives Mae and her supporter permission to approach the courtroom clerk's desk, which is located in front and below the judge's bench.

Clerk (C) to Mae:

What do you want?

Petitioner Mae Jules (P):

I called this morning. Someone in the clerk's office downstairs said I should just come to this courtroom. I want a restraining order against my—

C (In a loud whisper to the judge):

Oh yeah, this is the ex-parte request the clerk's office alerted us to on your voicemail. I called her back and told her to come in after lunch. (To Mae) You have your paperwork?

P (Nods):

Yes, here.

C:

Please hand them to the bailiff to give to Judge Duncan.

Procedural Note: Just above, note how the clerk asks rather brusquely, "What do you want?" and then whispers to the judge so that all can hear. Though surely not the most tactful approach, such behavior is typical of many courtrooms and likely not meant to be rude. Clerks are busy and trying to keep things moving. And, ex-parte hearings—even those where a divorcing spouse faces a truly scary situation—must be squeezed into an already over-loaded calendar. So try not to let comments of court personnel throw you off balance. Just move on, and answer questions as calmly and thoroughly as possible.

Mae hands the bailiff a copy of her forms. Judge Duncan takes a quick look and says softly to the clerk, "This is as good a time as any. I'll take it in

chambers." The clerk then announces to the people in the courtroom, "We will be taking a ten-minute recess." To Mae, Judge Duncan says, not unkindly, "Follow me." Mae and the judge go to the judge's office (called "chambers") behind the courtroom. The judge sits behind her desk and motions to Mae to sit on a couch near the bookshelf. Their discussion goes as follows.

J:

Let me take a minute to look over these papers. (After a few moments the judge says,) You obviously want a restraining order against your husband. Let's see what your affidavit says your main reason is. (The judge reads from Mae's sworn statement)

Repeatedly over the past few months my husband has threatened to kill me if I divorce him. I have marked the dates and exact language he used on the attached calendar pages. I've asked him to move out, but he won't. I am really scared for my life, I want him out and I want him to stay away from me. I also don't want him to be able to see the kids alone, at least not until he calms down. I'm afraid he will either kidnap them, or maybe even hurt them. He has directly threatened to take them from me, and he has hit me in front of them. I've also marked those occasions on the attached calendar. I fear he may hit them if he takes them alone and they say anything he doesn't like.

J:

Fine, your written statement is very clear. Now I need to ask, do you have any evidence to back what you say?

P:

Excuse me, Your Honor. I am not sure what you mean.

J:

Do you have any witnesses who can testify about your husband's past abuse of you, photos of a black eye or anything like that, or other proof, such as a medical report?

P:

Yes. I'm gathering them. My babysitter is willing to sign a statement that she once saw my husband hit me in front of the kids, and she's also heard him yell really nasty things at the children. And the counselor I saw at the woman's shelter, who I brought with me today, saw my bruises last week.

J:

O.K., but you did not notify your husband of this hearing?

P:

That's correct. I did not notify him because I was in a big hurry and because I was afraid he would hurt me for getting the courts involved.

J:

O.K., I'm going to try to call him right now. Do you know his work number? (Mae gives the judge her husband's work number and the judge tries but cannot not reach him.) All right, what I'm going to do, based on your affidavit and our discussion, is to issue a temporary restraining order stating that your husband must at all times stay over 100 yards away from you and the children. My clerk will also set a hearing date, as soon as possible, probably later this week, during which your husband will have the opportunity to come in and have his say. At that time, you will want to present your proof, such as a written declaration of the babysitter or, better yet, have her come to court. Also, I will listen to anything the counselor from

the women's shelter has to say, so please ask her to attend. The purpose of this hearing is for me to decide if the temporary restraining order should be made permanent and if it is necessary to set up a procedure for your husband to see the kids with formal supervision.

P:

Thank you, Your Honor. What about the kids?

J:

I will also order him to temporarily refrain from visiting the children until he comes into court for a hearing. After that, I may also order a home evaluation by the Children's Protection Agency. Then I will decide to grant unsupervised or supervised visitation, as the circumstances warrant.

P:

Thank you.

J:

You must also give notice of the hearing on whether to extend the temporary restraining order to your husband. Talk to the Clerk's Office, or the woman's shelter, if you need help.

Procedural Notes: Mae does several important things in her presentation set out above:

- She asks the judge to explain terms she doesn't understand rather than trying to answer when it's not clear;

- Her papers say clearly what she wants and she provides back-up documentation; and

- She sticks to the facts. Judges don't want to hear spouses name call or attack each other, unless what is said specifically relates to why the person needs a restraining order. Note that Mae wrote in her papers that she fears her husband might attack her or the children if she files for divorce—certainly a relevant and specific "fact," properly brought to the judge's attention.

Although most judges recognize that it can be difficult to "prepare" when asking for a restraining order in an emotionally charged and physically dangerous situation, judges are nevertheless more apt to grant relief to those people who clearly explain and, if possible, document what happened. Notice that in Mae's conversation with the judge, even though she had not yet written down the statements of the babysitter and counselor, she clearly tells the judge who these people are and exactly what they will be able to testify to. In addition, the fact that Mae had kept or reconstructed a record of when she was hit is obviously of interest to the judge.

Different judges have different styles. Some will act as Judge Duncan did, by hearing all TRO requests informally in chambers, while others may conduct the hearing in the courtroom. In addition, some judges will immediately try to contact the opposing spouse by phone, as Judge Duncan did, while others will simply grant an emergency order good for a few days. At the same time a prompt court hearing is scheduled to allow the other spouse to respond.

5.   Do Some Pre-Divorce Planning

Before you file for divorce, or if possible even before you separate, it's wise to gather key financial information, which you will almost surely need later. To do this, you will usually need to:

- make a list of everything you and your spouse own (assets) and owe (debts)

- do a current monthly budget of your income and expenses, and if possible a second budget projecting income and expenses after separation

- gather copies of important financial documents such as bank records, lists of investments, including retirement plans, and joint tax returns for the several years prior to separation.

The book *Divorce and Money,* cited in the resource box near the beginning of this chapter, can help you with these and other tasks. For example, at separation it is often wise to close joint bank and credit accounts, opening new ones in your name alone.

Parents who want to increase their chances of being granted joint or shared custody, or at least generous visitation rights, in a future court hearing sensibly plan ahead by polishing their "parenting resume." For example, a parent who has been less active in parenting, but wants to play a bigger role in the future, might take a parenting class or develop a better "track record" of participating in parenting tasks such as taking children to the doctor, participating in religious training, or involving themselves in school or after school-activities, such as attending PTA meetings, coaching a sports team or leading a scout troop.

6.   Become Familiar with How Mediation Can Help You

One reason for the increase in self-help divorces is that separating spouses understand that they can sensibly make most divorce-related decisions without turning them over to a judge. Some couples negotiate entirely on their own, while many others turn to mediation as an excellent place to work out disagreements.

Divorce mediation involves the parties sitting down with a mediator—a neutral third party. (More on mediation generally in Chapter 5, Settlement.) The idea is for the spouses to work through an orderly process designed to help them find mutually agreeable solutions to important questions, such as who will get what custody and visitation rights and how marital property will be divided. Divorcing spouses can participate in mediation by jointly choosing and paying for a private mediator and attending one or more mediation sessions. Or, if they live in one of the approximately 35 states that offer or require court-sponsored mediation for issues related to child custody and visitation, they may be eligible for free mediation assistance.

Solving problems through mediation is fundamentally different from fighting over them in court. For starters, mediation is less formal, taking place in an office or conference room and dispensing with the strict rules of evidence and procedure used in the courtroom. Instead, spouses speak for themselves in ordinary English. Where spouses want and can afford to have lawyers involved, the lawyers may attend mediation sessions, but typically only to give advice to their client and not to address the mediator directly.

The crux of the mediation process is that parties are encouraged to work together to resolve their

disputes. Mediators try to help spouses do this by getting each to articulate his or her true needs, as opposed to exaggerated demands. Mediation is a huge contrast to how disputes are settled in court, where a judge (often listening almost exclusively to their lawyers) imposes a decision on the parties, usually creating a "winner" and a "loser."

Couples who make their own agreements, with or without a mediator's help, usually file them or bring them to court. Often, by agreement of the parties, one spouse appears in court (with the other not contesting), and the judge confirms the couple's' decisions, unless they are grossly unfair to one spouse or do not adequately provide for the couple's children.

RESOURCES ON DIVORCE MEDIATION

Before engaging in mediation, it helps to know how it works. Start by looking at one or more of these excellent resources.

How to Mediate Your Dispute: Finding a Solution Quickly and Cheaply Outside the Courtroom, by Peter Lovenheim (Nolo Press), an excellent resource for people who want to understand the mediation process and resolve their disputes, including an extensive chapter setting forth strategies for mediating divorce and child custody disputes.

Child Custody: Building Parenting Agreements That Work, by Mimi Lyster (Nolo Press), an informative resource for people who wish to negotiate joint-parenting issues, with or without the help of a mediator. This book identifies all of the major issues typically involved in figuring out custody and visitation and sets out a variety of solutions for each issue (many of which have been identified by the author in the course of actual mediations).

The Complete Guide to Mediation: The Cutting-Edge Approach to Family Law Practice, by Forrest S. Mosten (ABA), a detailed exploration of the lawyer's role in mediation. As well as providing useful information and resources, this book will help readers learn what qualities and services they may want to seek in a mediator and/or lawyer if they hire one.

The Divorce Mediation Handbook: Everything You Need to Know, by Paula James (Jossey-Bass), an informative book written by a divorce mediator and family lawyer, including chapters on choosing a mediator, pros and cons of mediation, conferring with attorneys, the mediation process, protecting children and dividing financial assets.

Once you understand how divorce mediation can help you and your spouse, you may want to find a private mediator in your community. For a referral, contact any local community-based mediation program (sometimes called "justice center"), your family court, or a local bar association. Or contact:

—Conflict Resolution Center, Inc., 2205 E. Carson Street, Pittsburgh, PA 15203, (412) 481-5559, fax (412)481-5601, e-mail: crcii@igc.apc.org

—Academy of Family Mediators, 4 Militia Drive, Lexington, MA 02173, (617) 674-2663, fax (617) 674-2690, e-mail: afmoffice@igc.apc.org

—Society of Professionals in Dispute Resolution, 815 15th Street, N.W., Ste. 530, Washington, D.C. 20005, (202) 783-7277, fax (202) 783-7281.

—MEDIATE.COM, a mediation referral website on the Internet, at http://www.mediate.com

Or try looking in the phone book under "mediation" or "divorce assistance."

B. THE BASICS OF FAMILY LAW EXPLAINED

In addition to coping with emotional issues, divorcing couples almost always face one or more big decisions regarding property division, child custody, visitation and child and/or spousal support. In order to make educated decisions, mediate or engage in a court battle in any of these areas, you must know what the law provides. The information below will give you some legal background about key family law issues to help you get started in your research into your own state's laws.

➡️ **Section B explains several legal issues in detail.** Go on to Section C if you feel comfortably grounded in the basics of divorce law or if legal issues are not a big deal in your case (perhaps because you have no children and have already divided your property).

1. The Legal Divorce

Marriages typically end in death or divorce (see Sidebar for other endings).

ENDING A MARRIAGE BY LEGAL SEPARATION OR ANNULMENT

Some couples want to end their relationship but stay legally married for religious or financial reasons. For example, a spouse who is ill may want to stay married to continue using the other spouse's health insurance. Such couples may obtain what's called "a legal separation," which keeps the marriage intact but allows the family court to make orders dividing property and awarding custody and support. Other couples may seek a legal decree called an "annulment" or "nullity of marriage" that says, in effect, the marriage never existed. Annulments are usually only awarded when the marriage was induced by fraud or because of an unknown physical or mental condition that made the marriage unviable at the outset.

---

a. No-fault divorce

Practically every state now allows divorce on a "no-fault" basis (New York and a couple of other states are exceptions), although in a few states no-fault divorces are available only to couples who meet certain qualifications (for example, have been separated for at least one year). This means that if either or both spouses want a divorce, they can get it on the basis of "incompatibility" or "irreconcilable differences," with no legal battle over who was at fault for the breakdown of the marriage. In short, if there is to be a dispute, it will be about property, spousal support and/or child-related issues, not about whether the divorce itself should be granted.

b. Fault-based divorces

Before the advent of the no-fault divorce, state laws required that to get a divorce, one spouse typically had to prove that the other was insane, in prison for an extended period, or legally at fault for the breakdown of the marriage. Such laws commonly found "at fault" a spouse who:

- committed adultery

- inflicted emotional or physical pain on the other spouse

- deserted the other spouse (left the family home without consent for some prescribed amount of time).

If severe mistreatment (for example, committing adultery) was established, judges had the power to favor an innocent spouse over an at-fault spouse in dividing property. Although, as mentioned, most states no longer consider fault in deciding whether to allow a divorce or how to divide property, some states still consider fault in determining the amount (if any) of spousal or child support to award, and the extent of custody or visitation rights.

c. Uncontested divorces

Depending on a couple's practical situation (for example, do they have kids and lots of property?) and the attitudes of one or both spouses, divorce proceedings can be almost as easy as getting a driver's license, or they can be long, painful and complex. For the "easy" cases, where spouses agree on all major decisions (typically in shorter marriages with no kids and relatively small amounts of property or debt), many states now offer streamlined divorce requirements. Under these simplified procedures, an uncontested divorce may even be handled all by mail. Even where the person who files the initial divorce papers (the petitioner) has to make a court appearance, little more is involved than briefly confirming that the information she entered in the divorce papers (typically called the "petition" or "complaint") is correct. In Section D we explain in more detail how a typical uncontested divorce proceeds.

d.   Contested divorces

A divorce becomes contested if, after one spouse files a divorce petition, the other spouse files papers (usually called a "response" or "answer") opposing one or more of the first spouse's requests. In short, the court is put on notice that the spouses are not in full agreement about what should happen in the divorce.

Divorces tend to be contested when some or all of the following factors are present:

- emotions are running high

- valuable property is involved

- there are minor children and one or both spouses has strong doubts about the ability of the other spouse to be a good parent

- the spouses disagree about the amount of post-divorce support for the children or a non-breadwinner spouse.

Contested divorces may involve many pretrial procedures and court appearances. These are explained in more detail in Section E, below.

CONTESTED DIVORCES CAN TURN INTO UNCONTESTED DIVORCES

Fortunately, many divorces that start out contested later become uncontested—thereby avoiding the need for a court battle. This typically occurs when the parties reach agreement through negotiation or with the help of a mediator. But for the purposes of the self-represented divorce litigant, one thing about the contested divorce process is clear. If a divorce starts out contested, it will almost always be procedurally much more complicated than if all disputes are resolved before the first papers are filed.

Whether contested or uncontested, a divorce technically comes to an end when a court's final judgment or divorce decree is signed and entered into the court record and the time to appeal passes. But unlike many other civil proceedings (and, from the standpoint of self-help divorce litigants, very important), even after a divorce ends spouses may often be able to come back into court and relitigate some key issues. Most often, this is to seek a modification in the divorce judgment's provisions regarding child support or child custody and visitation, but occasionally the issue of spousal support can also be relitigated. Modifications are discussed in more detail in Section F.

2.   Property and Debt Division

Unless spouses have already divided debts and property, as is common when there is a long delay between separation and divorce, spouses need to make decisions about who will own what items of property and who will pay which debts. As part of thinking about how to do this, it is wise to understand your state's basic legal rules. You want to do this so you can determine:

- what property belongs to each spouse separately (usually called "separate property"), and

- what property the two of you own together (often called "marital property" or, in some states, "community property").

In many marriages where spouses don't own or owe a great deal, doing this is mercifully simple. But complications commonly arise when lots of property is involved. For example, deciding who owns a family business, real estate, an investment portfolio or even pensions can often be tricky.

But again, taking the time to understand who legally owns what can be crucial, since it will allow you to:

- in negotiation, make a clearer presentation of facts to support why you should get the property you want;

- in mediation, be able to make proposals that are clearly reasonable and not risk sabotaging the process by making clearly unreasonable demands; and

- in court, ask the judge for what you are entitled to, without annoying her with overreaching demands.

The final reason why you need to understand property law may strike you as odd. If, in an effort to get your divorce over with, you want to allow your spouse to keep more than he or she is entitled to under law (perhaps to minimize conflict, keep relations amicable and/or just get on with your life), you may have to justify your decision to a judge. If you are able to persuade the judge that you are making an educated decision, the judge is much more apt to grant your request on the spot than if the judge feels you are "selling yourself short" out of ignorance. Some judges who feel a self-represented spouse is getting seriously shortchanged will even require the spouse to consult with an attorney before proceeding further.

If you incurred a debt, you're still on the hook. A divorce judgment may and usually does divide both property and debts. But when it comes to debts there is an important catch. Regardless of whether the court assigns a certain debt to your spouse to pay, if you were responsible for paying the debt when it was incurred (for example, your spouse purchased a TV with your joint credit card), the creditor still has the legal right to go after you if your spouse violates the court order and doesn't pay. You, of course, have the legal right to rely on the divorce court's order and seek reimbursement from your spouse, but doing this won't help much if your spouse has disappeared or doesn't have money or other property to give you.

FINDING YOUR STATE'S PROPERTY DIVISION RULES

Chapter 22, Legal Research, will help you find the key property or debt division rules for your state. But before heading into the big thicket of legal research, it will help if you clearly understand basic rules. To accomplish this, take a look at one or more of the following resources:

Nolo's Pocket Guide to Family and Divorce Law, by Robin Leonard and Stephen Elias (Nolo Press), includes a chapter on property and debts. This book also contains much solid information on divorce, child support, domestic violence, mediation and other key family law issues.

Divorce and Money: How to Make the Best Financial Decisions During Divorce, by Violet Woodhouse & Victoria F. Collins with M.C. Blakeman (Nolo Press), will help you to understand the value of your house, investments, pensions and other property and debts. This book also capably deals with the many tax issues that accompany divorce.

Practical Divorce Solutions, by Ed Sherman (Nolo Press), includes numerous suggestions for constructive ways to work out property division agreements (some even as simple as flipping a coin).

DIVORCE AND BANKRUPTCY

Divorces all too often coincide with money troubles. As a result, many divorcing couples also find themselves considering bankruptcy. If this describes you and your spouse, you will want to learn about how federal bankruptcy laws and your state's divorce laws interact. For example, although most debts are "discharged" or wiped out in a Chapter 7 bankruptcy, this is not true for child or spousal support debts, which, because they are "non-dischargeable," still must be paid after bankruptcy. One reason it is important to know this is to avoid agreeing to a divorce decree that doesn't clearly identify spousal support, thereby raising the possibility that it might be discharged in a later bankruptcy. To start your research, consult one or more of these references:

Divorce and Money: How to Make the Best Financial Decisions During Divorce, cited in above resource box, which includes a section explaining the different types of bankruptcies and the basic interaction between bankruptcy and divorce.

Money Troubles: Legal Strategies to Cope with Your Debts, by Robin Leonard (Nolo Press), explains bankruptcy and non-bankruptcy alternatives for resolving financial difficulties and helps you decide which type of bankruptcy may be best for your situation.

How to File for Bankruptcy, by Stephen Elias, Albin Renauer and Robin Leonard (Nolo Press), helps you decide whether or not filing for bankruptcy makes sense and provides step-by-step instructions ands all the forms necessary to file.

3. Spousal Support (Alimony)

Spousal support (also called "alimony" or "maintenance") is money one spouse pays to the other following a divorce or separation. Once awarded routinely, spousal support is now typically ordered only in certain situations including:

- long marriages—especially where one spouse pursued a successful career while the other raised children

- where one spouse's earning power is significantly higher than the other's, or

- where one spouse is ill or disabled and without significant financial resources and the other has a decent job or other income.

HOW MUCH MONEY WILL YOU HAVE TO PAY?

In most states, judges determine how much, if any, spousal support to award, referring to published financial schedules (guidelines), unless the spouses signed a valid prenuptial (also called "antenuptial") agreement establishing the amount in advance. You should be able to locate these financial schedules in a law library, the court clerk's office or by consulting a lawyer. In addition, judges have discretion to consider factors such as:

- the length of the marriage,

- each spouse's earning power,

- each spouse's age, health, financial needs and the standard to which each is accustomed to living,

- the payer spouse's ability to pay and the recipient spouse's ability to become self-supporting, and

- how much property each party will receive under the property division.

When spousal support is awarded, one spouse is usually ordered to make monthly installment payments to the other for a set number of years (though in some cases judges order one lump sum payment). If the marriage lasted for many years, the payer spouse may have to pay spousal support indefinitely, or at least until the recipient spouse gets remarried.

 Tax considerations are important when spouses are trying to negotiate spousal support. Spousal support is tax deductible to the payer spouse and taxable to the recipient spouse. (For more information on divorce-related tax issues, see *Divorce and Money,* mentioned in the resource box near the beginning of this chapter, and the IRS's free Publications 503, Tax Information on Selling Your Home; 504, Tax Information for Divorced or Separated Individuals; and 523, Child and Dependent Care Expenses.)

---

4. Child Custody and Visitation

Parenting after a divorce obviously involves making many important decisions. Who will physically take care of the children, where and when? Who will decide whether and what type of education and medical treatment they get? Who will pay for which of the children's needs?

DETAILED PARENTING AGREEMENTS OFTEN WORK BEST

Court orders dealing with child custody are very brief, often stating no more than who has custody during what time intervals. When spouses get along well, following this approach of leaving details vague is usually not a problem. But experts have found that where tensions between the spouses are running high, everyone is usually better off creating a detailed written parenting plan. The idea is that disagreements have less opportunity to fester when both parents and children know exactly what to expect. For example, a detailed agreement might specify the exact time a spouse must pick up and drop off a child. And especially if the couple is attempting joint physical custody, it would list which holidays and birthdays kids will spend with each parent. It might also include a clear delineation of what, if any, visitation rights will be given to grandparents and other significant adults. An additional advantage of spelling out details is that if a dispute arises, the couple (and, if necessary, a judge) can look to the agreement to help resolve it.

As with dividing property, many divorcing couples work out their own parenting agreements. For couples who can do this, the family court may only get involved to approve the couple's agreement. But for those who cannot agree, or where one spouse does not abide by an agreement or court order, a couple may make repeated trips to family court to ask a judge to fine tune their child rearing decision making.

RESOURCES ON CHILD CUSTODY

Child Custody: Building Parenting Agreements That Work, by Mimi E. Lyster (Nolo Press), identifies the important issues that divorcing parents are likely to face and suggests practical solutions for each. The book also explains how to negotiate a comprehensive parenting agreement and how mediation can help if negotiations break down. A number of useful forms and worksheets are included.

Child Custody Made Simple: Understanding the Laws of Child Custody and Child Support, by Webster Watnik (Single Parent Press), provides a good overview of the laws governing child custody decisions.

The term "custody" doesn't just refer to whether minor children will live primarily at Mom's house or Dad's house. In addition to physical control over the children, custody governs which parent has the legal authority to make critical parenting decisions, such as what school kids will attend and what religion they will be taught. Up until 25 years ago, judges almost always awarded the mother custody and the father visitation rights. The current trend is more often towards "joint" or "shared" custody arrangements. Although mothers still get primary physical custody more often than fathers, joint custody means decision-making authority is shared.

When judges decide custody and visitation issues, they try to determine what arrangement is in the "best interests of child," considering factors such as:

- the age and sex of the child, and the child's relationship with the parent, stepparents and/or siblings. Not surprisingly, judges try to keep siblings together.

- the fitness (including mental and physical health) of each parent—including any history of verbal or physical abuse and alcohol or drug problems. In addition, most judges will carefully consider who is really the primary caretaker, who is the more nurturing parent and possibly who has better judgment.

- the familiarity of the children with an existing family home, school or community. (Courts seek to disrupt kids' lives as little as possible), and

- the child's preference (if a child is 10 to 12 years old or older, this is a far more important consideration than it is for younger children).

5. Child Support

Child support is money that one parent (usually the noncustodial parent or the parent with the higher income) pays to the other parent (usually the custodial parent or the parent with the lower income). The trend toward joint custody arrangements sometimes makes it less clear which parent (if either) will have to pay child support.

Federal law requires every state to publish written guidelines for how child support is calculated in that state, often called child support "formulas" or "schedules." Typically these guidelines are based on a combination of each parent's ability to pay, which parent has physical custody most of the time and the needs of the children. Guidelines are important, even for couples who make their own child support agreements, since judges probably won't approve an agreement unless it provides at least the minimum amount of child support set forth in that state's schedules. In short, finding out how much child support you should receive or will have to pay under your state's guidelines is another example of key legal information you should get early on in the divorce process—either by doing the legal research or asking the clerk of your family court.

Child support orders issued by the court typically specify how many years the payer spouse has to pay child support. If no time period is specified, payments usually continue until the child reaches 18 years old (or, in a few states, through college). Child support payments may not be claimed as tax deductions by the payer spouse, nor are they considered taxable income to the payee spouse. But as with other aspects of divorce, there are significant tax ramifications to the paying of child support and custody—for instance, who may claim the child as a dependent. If there is no written agreement on this issue, the general rule is that the custodial parent gets to claim the child as a dependent. However, if a non-custodial parent pays for more than 50% of the child's support and can produce a written waiver of exemption from the custodial parent, he can claim the exemption instead.

⚠ **Child support survives bankruptcy.** Neither child support arrears (support owed for past periods of time), nor future child support obligations may be discharged (cancelled) in a bankruptcy proceeding. This means that if a person owing child support is unable to pay it (for example, she loses her job), she will be smart to ask the family court for an order at least temporarily reducing her support obligation instead of letting it pile up and thereby creating a debt that must eventually be paid off.

WHAT HAPPENS IF CHILD SUPPORT ISN'T PAID?

All states have an easy method for garnishing wages if a wage earner fails to meet his child support obligation. In fact, in many states child support is automatically paid out of a person's wages before he even gets his paycheck. However, if the person owing support is not employed or is self-employed, there may be collection problems if payment isn't made voluntarily. When this occurs, the person owed support can ask for a court hearing (often with the help of the district attorney's child support enforcement division) to request that the judge enforce it. Often this means the judge will first verbally order the non-paying spouse to mend his ways and if that doesn't work, hold him in contempt of court (and issue a fine or even a jail sentence).

C. FILING FOR DIVORCE

From a formal legal point of view, divorce proceedings begin when one spouse files a document called a "complaint" or "petition," depending on the state. The person who files this document (called the plaintiff or petitioner) then arranges to have it served on (delivered to) the other spouse (called the defendant or respondent).

1. Creating a Divorce Petition or Complaint

Though states vary as to exactly what language you must include in a divorce petition (or complaint), most require:

1) A statement of facts (often called "allegations")—including a statement that one or both spouses reside within the state, dates of the marriage and separation, names and birth dates of any minor children and lists of property owned and debts owed;

2) The grounds for divorce—often a short sentence saying that the couple no longer wants to be married because they have "irreconcilable differences." Here the exact terminology differs from state to state; for example, in Hawaii and several other states, the spouses must say their marriage is "irretrievably broken." But the requirements are usually the same in the states that allow no-fault divorces—the petitioning spouse states that the spouses can no longer live together and want to end

their marriage. In the few states where fault is still taken into account in some divorces (see Section B1b above), the petitioning spouse will typically describe the "wrong" (such as desertion, mental cruelty or adultery) committed as the grounds for divorce; and

3) A statement describing what the petitioner or plaintiff wants, usually appearing near the end of the petition and sometimes called the "prayer."

The prayer typically will include a request that:

- the marriage end

- the marital property and debts be divided

- the petitioning spouse be awarded custody of any minor children (or both spouses be awarded "joint custody")

- assuming that the petitioning spouse will have primary physical custody, he or she be awarded a specified monthly sum for child support

- if appropriate, spousal support be awarded (see Section B3 above)

- if desired, the wife's former name be restored, and

- if the petitioning spouse has a lower income, the other spouse pay all attorney fees and court costs.

In some states, a petitioner must type or neatly print all of this information in narrative form. Other states use pre-printed forms; the petitioner need only check the appropriate box and insert requested information in specified blanks.

Below are three examples of the first pages of various states' complaints.

PETITION FOR DISSOLUTION OF MARRIAGE—CALIFORNIA

ATTORNEY OR PARTY WITHOUT ATTORNEY *(Name and Mailing Address)* :   TELEPHONE NO.:   *FOR COURT USE ONLY*

ATTORNEY FOR *(Name)* :

SUPERIOR COURT OF CALIFORNIA, COUNTY OF

STREET ADDRESS:

MAILING ADDRESS:

CITY AND ZIP CODE:

BRANCH NAME:

MARRIAGE OF

PETITIONER:

RESPONDENT:

CASE NUMBER:

PETITION FOR

☐ **Dissolution of Marriage**   ☐ **And Declaration Under Uniform**
☐ **Legal Separation**   **Child Custody Jurisdiction Act**
☐ **Nullity of Marriage**

1. RESIDENCE (Dissolution only) ☐ Petitioner ☐ Respondent has been a resident of this state for at least six months and of this county for at least three months immediately preceding the filing of this Petition for Dissolution of Marriage.

2. STATISTICAL FACTS
   a. Date of marriage: c. Period between marriage and separation
   b. Date of separation: Years: Months:

3. DECLARATION REGARDING MINOR CHILDREN OF THIS MARRIAGE FOR WHOM SUPPORT MAY BE ORDERED OR WHO MAY BE SUBJECT TO CUSTODY OR VISITATION ORDERS
   a. ☐ There are no minor children.   b. ☐ The minor children are:

Child's name	Birthdate	Age	Sex

   c. IF THERE ARE MINOR CHILDREN, COMPLETE EITHER (1) OR (2)
      (1) ☐ Each child named in 3b is currently living with ☐ petitioner ☐ respondent
          in the following county *(specify)* :
          During the last five years each child has lived in no state other than California and with no person other than petitioner or respondent or both. Petitioner has not participated in any capacity in any litigation or proceeding in any state concerning custody of any minor child of this marriage. Petitioner has no information of any pending custody proceeding or of any person not a party to this proceeding who has physical custody or claims to have custody or visitation rights concerning any minor child of this marriage.
      (2) ☐ A completed Declaration Under Uniform Child Custody Jurisdiction Act is attached.

4. ☐ **Petitioner requests** confirmation as separate assets and obligations the items listed
      ☐ in Attachment 4 ☐ below:

Item	Confirm to

NOTICE: Any party required to pay child support must pay interest on overdue amounts at the ''legal'' rate, which is currently 10 percent. This can be a large added amount.

(Continued on reverse)

Form Adopted by Rule 1281
Judicial Council of California
1281 [Rev. January 1, 1995]

PETITION
(Family Law)

Family Code, §§ 2330, 3409
Calif. Rules of Court, rule 1215

PETITION FOR DISSOLUTION OF MARRIAGE—OREGON

1	
2	
3	
4	
5	
6	
7	IN THE CIRCUIT COURT OF THE STATE OF OREGON
8	FOR THE COUNTY OF _____

In the Matter of the Marriage of   )
)
_____)   No. _____
Petitioner   )
and   )
)
_____)   PETITION FOR DISSOLUTION
)   OF MARRIAGE
Respondent   )

1.

I request a dissolution of the marriage because irreconcilable differences between the husband and wife have caused the irremediable breakdown of the marriage.

2.

No domestic relations suit or support petition involving this marriage is pending in this state or any other state.

3.

a. ☐ I am a resident of Oregon and have been continuously for the past six months before filing this petition.

b. ☐ My spouse is a resident of Oregon and has been continuously for the past six months before filing this petition.

Page 1- PETITION FOR DISSOLUTION OF MARRIAGE

PETITION FOR DIVORCE—TEXAS

Cause No. _____

IN THE MATTER OF THE MARRIAGE OF:

_____ , Petitioner

and

_____ , Respondent

IN THE CIRCUIT COURT

OF _____ COUNTY

_____ JUDICIAL DISTRICT

ORIGINAL PETITION FOR DIVORCE

This suit is brought by _____

Petitioner, Soc.Sec.#. _____, Drivers License # _____

age _____,who resides at _____

Respondent is _____

Soc.Sec.No._____, Drivers License #_____ age _____,

who resides at _____

I. RESIDENCY:

Petitioner has been a domiciliary of the state of Texas for the preceding six months and a resident of the county in which this petition is filed for the preceding ninety days.

. . . .Respondent is a domiciliary of the State of Texas.

. . . .Long Arm: Respondent is a nonresident of Texas.

Page 1 of _____

NON-LAWYER HELP IS USUALLY AVAILABLE FOR DIVORCE PAPERWORK

In addition to other resources identified in this book, legal typing services (often called independent paralegals) can be a huge help to people filing their own divorce. These small business people who operate in many states help self-helpers prepare divorce papers for a reasonable fee (often in the range of $100-$250). Because typing services are not owned or ooіéated by lawyers, their personnel may not give you legal advice. But because they are very familiar with the paperwork involved in the typical divorce (many are former legal secretaries), they can make your job much easier. But remember it's your divorce and therefore your responsibility to carefully check any advice or information you receive from a typing service.

2. Filing and Serving the Petition or Complaint

Once the required divorce forms are completed, filing and serving them usually involves the following:

- The filled-in forms (with the appropriate number of copies) are taken or mailed to the appropriate Clerk's Office in the county where one of the parties lives. In some states this is the main trial court where many other types of lawsuits are handled, while in others it is a separate family court.

- The filing fee is paid (often from $25-$150, depending on the state).

- The clerk hands (or mails back to) the filing spouse a stamped ("conformed") copy. The conformed copy will typically have a case number (sometimes called a "cause" number) on the front page. All other documents filed with

the court as part of the divorce proceedings should have that same number.

- The documents are "served" on (delivered to) the non-filing spouse. Each state has its own technical service rules and these should be checked (with a clerk, law coach or through legal research) before service is made. It is important to complete this step correctly since it is serving your papers on your spouse that gives the family court authority (jurisdiction) to decide your case. (See Chapter 3, Section D2 and Chapter 4, Section B5 for general service requirements.)

What happens next depends, most importantly, on whether the divorce is contested or uncontested. Procedurally, this will turn on whether the non-filing spouse files responsive papers. Your state's divorce law requirements will also play a part in determining your next steps.

If you and your spouse have reached agreement on all the important issues that affect your divorce—or your spouse is simply no longer in the picture and everything has already been taken care of—your divorce is uncontested and you can proceed to Section D.

- If you don't know whether or not your divorce is likely to be contested, reread Section B above, and depending on what you conclude, proceed to Section D (uncontested) or Section E (contested).

- If you file for divorce now without reaching agreement with your spouse as to all major issues, your divorce will be contested unless your spouse decides not to respond in court. For now, you should assume that the divorce will be contested and proceed to Section E.

D. HOW UNCONTESTED DIVORCES WORK

The vast majority of divorces in the United States are uncontested.

1. Why Divorces Are Uncontested

Perhaps the most common reason why a divorce is uncontested is that there is nothing to fight about— no minor children, no valuable property, few debts and no alimony. Another reason why so many divorces are uncontested is that after spouses separate, they often live separately for a long period of time (several years is common) before one of them decides to make it official by filing for divorce. During this separation period, passions have time to cool and the spouses work out agreements on all significant issues, such as child custody and support and the division of property. Still another reason for uncontested divorces is the increasing use of mediation to help divorcing spouses resolve disputes (see Section A6 for more on mediation).

2. Typical Uncontested Divorce Procedure

Whatever the reason for uncontested divorces, the fact that there is no fight means they are usually very simple to handle in court. Here are the steps to be taken in most states:

Step 1: As mentioned in Section C above, one of the spouses (the plaintiff or petitioner) files a document called a petition or complaint with the court containing required facts. In some states, both spouses can file one petition as co-petitioners.

Step 2: When one spouse files, the divorce petition is delivered to (served on) the other spouse. If the other spouse is cooperative and willing to acknowledge receiving the papers, then this process can be quite informal (first-class mail or personal delivery by the filing spouse). If the other spouse does not cooperate, a process server must formally serve the papers on the other spouse. When a spouse can't be located, paper service can often be accomplished by publication.

Step 3: Typically, the other spouse does not file responsive papers with the court. If responsive papers are filed, they do not identify any areas of disagreement.

Step 4: If responsive papers are filed and there are some areas of disagreement, the spouses (or if they are represented, their lawyers) engage in informal negotiation, or use mediation, to quickly resolve them before the case goes any further.

Step 5: Once spouses reach agreement—with or without a mediator—they put their agreement in writing and file it with the court.

Step 6: Once the court is informed that the divorce is (or has become) uncontested, it either 1) issues a divorce decree on the basis of written documents, with no court hearing required, or 2) schedules a hearing before the judge with one or both spouses attending. A sample dialogue of a hearing on an uncontested divorce petition is set out below.

Step 7: In some states the divorce is effective immediately; in others there is a waiting period before it becomes final.

3. A Sample Uncontested Divorce Hearing

Here we set out a transcript of a hypothetical un-contested divorce hearing. In this hearing, both spouses are present. But if no responsive papers are filed, it is also possible (likely in some states) that only the petitioning spouse will be in court. In this hypothetical case, the parties originally disagreed about property division, but managed to reach agreement and put it into a formal document called a marital settlement agreement that they filed with the court before the hearing. In cases where there is little or no property or one spouse is missing, there will be no written agreement of this type.

! **Research Your Own Court's Procedures.** Please understand that because the facts of any particular case and the rules and customs of each court will differ, this transcript is only an illustration. As we stress throughout this chapter, to effectively handle your own case, you should do additional research and preparation, including, if possible, sitting in on similar hearings in front of the judge who will hear your case. Fortunately, finding out who this is likely to be will often be easy, since many family courts assign all family court cases to one or a few judges.)

Uncontested divorce hearing

Entering the packed, noisy courtroom, we wait for Judge Jackie Equitable to take the bench as people constantly come in and out. In last-minute confer-ences with their clients and each other, lawyers hauling big briefcases huddle with their clients in the spectators' seats or chat with each other near the front of the courtroom. When the judge enters, the clerk or bailiff will often ask everyone to stand—at which point things quiet down. After the bailiff or perhaps the judge herself says, "Be seated," the low buzzing of whispers will continue. Judge Equitable spends a few minutes sipping coffee and looking through a stack of papers. The judge's clerk, sitting at a desk either in front or to the side of the judge's bench, also sifts through stacks of files, stapling and marking documents. Occasionally the clerk hands a file to the judge, making a few whispered remarks. (See Chapter 2, The Courthouse and the Court-room, for more on the layout of a courtroom.) Finally, after what seems like a long time but is probably only a few minutes, the clerk calls, "Supe-rior Court, now in session. The Honorable Jackie Equitable presiding. Come to order." To the judge, the clerk whispers, "First up, Peter Parto v. Rita Parto—uncontested."

Clerk:

Next case, Parto.

Judge (J):

Are the parties present and ready to proceed?

Petitioner (P) (standing):

I am.

Respondent (R) (standing):

I am also.

J:

Please approach the bench. (Peter and Rita get up from their seats in the spectator section of the court-room and walk up to the judge's slightly elevated bench.)

Procedural Note: In this hearing, the judge requests that the parties stand before the bench. Although many judges handle uncontested proceedings this way, in other courtrooms, proceedings are more formal, with the judge asking the petitioning party, in this case Peter, to present the case from the witness box.

J (nodding toward Peter):

You are?

P:

Peter Parto, and I am the petitioner in this case.

J (nodding toward Rita):

And you are the Respondent, Rita Parto?

R:

Yes, Your Honor.

J:

Are all the facts stated in this petition and the response true?

P:

Yes, Your Honor.

R:

Yes.

J:

And, at the time this petition was filed, you both had resided in this state for six months?

P:

Yes.

R:

Yes.

J: (Nodding to Peter Parto):

You were married on December 7, 1995, and separated on July 4 of this year?

P & R:

Yes.

J:

During the course of your marriage unreconcilable differences developed, leading to the breakdown of the marriage, and there's no hope you'll get back together?

P:

That's right.

R:

Yes.

J:

Do you have children?

P & R:

No.

J (flipping through papers):

I see here you have filed a marital settlement agreement with regard to property division, which you both have signed. Petitioner, is this your true and correct signature?

P:

Yes.

J:

And have you signed voluntarily?

P:

Yes.

J:

Respondent, is this your true and correct signature?

R:

Yes, and I signed voluntarily also.

J (After glancing at the agreement):

You are aware that under the laws of this state, your property probably would be divided somewhat differently than you have agreed in this writing?

R & P:

Yes.

J:

And you both wish that this agreement be made part of the proposed dissolution decree you have submitted?

R & P:

Yes.

Procedural Notes: Note just above that the judge questioned the parties' decision to make a different property division than the 50-50 division called for under that state's law. Though this judge did not pursue the matter beyond verifying that the parties are aware of a difference, many family law judges would question the parties further. Specifically, in this type of situation the judge might encourage the party who agreed to take less than what he would be entitled to under law to rethink this issue or even to see a lawyer before the case proceeds further. Occasionally, a judge might even try to unilaterally decide to divide the property as he or she sees fit regardless of what the parties say they want. If this occurs, one or both parties may want to ask that the case be delayed so that legal advice can be obtained.

J:

Do either of you have anything further to say at this time?

R:

Yes, Your Honor. I would request that the court's order also restore my former name, Rita Singla.

J:

So ordered. The proposed order for dissolution of marriage is granted.

Clerk:

Next case.

Procedural Note: Except for Rita's affirmatively asking for her name to be changed, most of what occurred in the dialogue above was the judge asking all questions necessary to qualify the parties for a divorce and the parties answering "yes" or "no." However, as noted above, if this case were heard in another courtroom, it might have proceeded very differently. For instance, the judge might have said little more than, "You may proceed." At that point, the petitioner must make an oral presentation that includes all key information the judge needs to hear in order to grant a divorce.

For instance, if Peter Parto were in such a court as a self-help litigant on a default divorce, he might begin by saying something like, "Good morning, Your Honor. Rita Parto and I were married on December 7, 1995, and we separated on July 4 of this year. We have not lived together as husband and wife since that time. I am seeking a divorce because we have reached irreconcilable differences that have destroyed all that was good in our marriage and has led to its irretrievable breakdown. Therefore, I am here today to request a divorce."

FIND A SELF-HELP DIVORCE BOOK FOR YOUR STATE

Self-help divorce books published in virtually every state explain exactly what a petitioner must say to qualify for a divorce. Since you can't count on a judge to be as helpful as Judge Equitable, you will want to obtain this information and practice your presentation.

The following books show you how to handle your own divorce without a lawyer, including sorting out debts, taxes, division of property, child support, child custody and visitation and provides forms required to get a divorce in the respective states.

Do Your Own Divorce in Oregon, by Robin Smith (Nolo Press),

How to Do Your Own Divorce in California, by Ed Sherman (Nolo Press), and

How to Do Your Own Divorce in Texas, by Ed Sherman (Nolo Press).

E. WHAT HAPPENS IN A CONTESTED DIVORCE

If an uncontested divorce is usually simple, a contested divorce can be nightmarishly complex. Not only are the court procedures necessary to resolve any contested dispute often complicated, time consuming and, if lawyers are involved, expensive, but divorce cases are also further complicated by the fact that the parties are often trying to use the courts to punish each other.

What follows is a brief outline of the typical procedures experienced in a contested divorce case. But remember, all states have their own slightly different laws and procedures. This means that if you are involved in a contested divorce case without legal help, you will need to do additional legal research. In addition, you will want to master the information about representing yourself in a contested court action discussed in the body of this book.

1. Getting a Lawyer

The first big question in a contested divorce is whether to hire a lawyer. As we stress in Section A6, divorcing parties are almost always better off if they mediate their disputes rather than fight them out in the courtroom. However, if feelings are running extremely high, there is a history of abuse or one spouse is far more powerful or knowledgable about business affairs than the other, mediation may not be advisable, at least at first. What then? The traditional solution is to turn to the legal profession.

If one spouse hires a lawyer, the other spouse may also feel the need to hire one. Once two lawyers are in on a case, there is no longer self-representation and the divorce is obviously beyond the scope of this book. But it is also possible for one spouse to hire a lawyer (typically the spouse who files the divorce) and the other spouse continue to self-represent.

2. Filing a Divorce Petition or Complaint

One of the spouses (the plaintiff or petitioner) files a document called a petition or complaint with the court (see Section C, above, for what is typically contained in a divorce petition).

3. Serving the Petition or Complaint

Where one spouse is filing, the divorce petition is delivered to (served on) the other spouse. See Section C, above, for how this is typically done.

4. Filing a Response

The spouse served with the papers prepares a written response (usually called an answer) to clearly set out what that spouse wants the judge to do and how this differs from what the petitioner (called a plaintiff in some states) is asking for.

5. Obtaining Temporary Orders

If your spouse moves out and leaves you with not enough money to provide food and shelter for your kids, you can go to court for a temporary order before the divorce is completed—or in some instances, even before the initial divorce pleading (complaint or petition) is filed. Especially where the trust level between the spouses is low, one or both of the spouses will typically want the court to immediately intervene and issue certain types of temporary orders that will be in effect pending the final divorce decree. If physical abuse has occurred or is feared or a spouse has threatened to abscond with the children, a temporary restraining order can be sought, as described in Section A4 of this chapter. But even if this type of emergency relief isn't necessary, a spouse may want the court to:

- temporarily establish who has custody of the children and when the other parent may visit

- temporarily require child or spousal support payments

- issue orders freezing or preventing the sale of assets, or

- award temporary possession of the family home or car to one of the spouses.

Unless an emergency order has been obtained (again, see Section A4, above), the actual process of getting a temporary order, including the paperwork you must complete and file and preparation for the hearing, is similar to that involved in other motions (requests for court orders). To succeed, you must typically prepare, file and have served on your spouse:

- An application (request) for an Order to Show Cause (OSC) and the OSC itself. An Order to Show Cause is a legal form or short typed legal document that sets out what you are asking for—in this case a temporary or-ßr—and tells (orders) your spouse to come to court at a specific time and explain (show cause) why the court should not grant your request.

- A supporting declaration—a written statement under penalty of perjury by you that sets forth facts necessary to legally justify the issuance of the temporary order. Although a temporary order may be issued on the basis of your declaration alone, you are also entitled to submit declarations of other people who have first-hand knowledge of the facts. (More on declarations in Chapter 6, Pre-Trial Hearings and Motions.)

- A proposed temporary order granting you the relief requested in your application (it's "proposed" because the court hasn't signed it yet).

- A proof of service—a document that provides the court with the sworn statement of a process server or other proof that your spouse has been properly served with the papers described just above. (See sample proof of service in Chapter

3, Starting Your Case.) If you haven't filed this proof of service by the time of the court hearing, the hearing will likely be postponed.

Your next step is to attend the court hearing to determine whether the temporary order should be granted (this is often called an "order to show cause hearing"). The judge may listen to testimony from you, your spouse and possibly other witnesses, or may only accept written evidence, such as medical bills, rent receipts, expense budgets or declarations submitted by you or persons with knowledge of the facts. Either way, the judge will:

- review your requests (or those of your spouse if he or she is requesting the order) and the underlying facts,

- possibly ask you some questions, and

- ask your spouse for his or her side of the story (if your spouse is present).

Then the judge will likely make a ruling, usually either issuing the requested temporary order, denying your request or continuing the hearing to another day. If, as discussed in Section A4 of this chapter, you previously obtained an emergency restraining order without your spouse being present (an ex-parte order), the judge may simply continue that order in effect or modify it slightly.

When you request a temporary order, make sure to cover all key details, since the order may remain in effect for a year or two (depending on how long it takes to complete the divorce procedure). Although a judge can modify or terminate the order if circumstances change, it is no fun to have to return to court.

Here is a sample dialogue of a hearing on an OSC for an order setting Temporary Child Custo-dy and Visitation. Mark Daniels has come to court to request temporary custody of his son. During the course of the hearing, visitation issues also come up when Mark accuses his spouse of not allowing him to see their son. Responding to Mark's concerns, the judge also makes a temporary ruling on when visits will occur.

Clerk:

Next case, Daniels.

Judge (J):

Is Mr. Daniels present?

Mark Daniels (MD):

Yes, Your Honor.

Judge (J):

Ms. Daniels?

Diane Daniels (DD):

Also here, Your Honor.

J:

You may be seated. (Mark and Diane walk to and take seats at the respective counsel tables. See Chapter 2, The Courthouse and the Courtroom, for an explanation of where litigants sit. Shuffling through papers, the judge continues,) Mr. Daniels, let's see, you want custody of your son?

MD:

Yes, my wife Diane and I are trying to work out our divorce. We have been going to mediation, and we've decided most of the property issues. But the mediator told us it could be awhile before we finish, and even longer before the divorce is final. I want custody of our boy, at least for the present, while we're trying to work things out.

J:

Go on.

MD:

My son Roger is now living with his mother, who asked me to leave the house months ago—which I did. But she is not letting me see him regularly. (Shaking his head, Mark adds) She's so damn difficult—

J:

Watch your language in my courtroom, Mr. Daniels. And please stick to the facts.

MD:

Excuse me, Your Honor. It's just that, every time I go to pick Roger up, he's hungry. I've spoken with my wife's daycare provider, and she says Diane brings little Roger in at 7 a.m. and doesn't pick him up until after 6 pm. I work freelance, mostly from home. I could spend much more time with him. He wouldn't need to be in daycare more than six hours a day if I had him. I feel this neglect has been going on long enough. I have to step in and do something now. I can't wait while we hash things out in mediation. Who knows if we'll ever agree. Also, my wife says she has been "busy" lately, so the past few mediation sessions have been delayed. Meanwhile, my son's most precious years are rushing by. I am here today asking for you to grant me primary custody of Roger—at least until we can work out an agreement that's fair to both of us.

J (to Diane):

Do you have anything to say?

DD:

Yes, yes, Your Honor. I sure do. Diane stands and gathers some papers in front of her. I'm just astounded at Mark's claims. It's absurd for him to say Roger goes hungry.

J:

Mrs. Daniels, it will help me if you will state the facts and keep the value judgments to yourself.

DD:

I'll do my best, Your Honor. The point is, Mark never fed Roger when he lived with us. I've always been the one who took care of all Roger's physical needs. He's a growing healthy boy, and I'm responsible for that. And, Roger probably does say he's hungry when Mark picks him up because he knows his father will buy him ice cream or some other junk food, which I don't usually allow. As to the daycare, forgive me if I say I'm in shock. First off, Mark and I picked the daycare provider together. He knows it's a good place. Second, I need to work long days to provide for Roger and pay the entire mortgage, now, on my own. I'm working extra to try to keep Roger and me in a home fit for a child—backyard, friendly neighbors, the whole package. Also, it is true Mark works "freelance," but his idea that he has a regular six-hour workday with plenty of time for Roger just isn't accurate. What he really has are long periods when he's not doing much, then crunches when ten projects hit at once and he works round the clock. What will he do with Roger then? Call me.

J:

Is it true that you are not letting him visit your son regularly?

DD:

Well, no. Not really. There have been a few times lately when I've said Mark can't take Roger. But that was because he didn't tell me ahead of time, or because Roger was involved in something else at the time—like taking a nap. One time I said no, Mark had shown up unexpectedly when we had planned to visit Roger's grandmother. Another time I'd bought tickets for the circus before he asked to visit with Roger. Mark cannot just come over to play whenever he feels like it; he doesn't live with us anymore. He's got to make arrangements with me in advance and stick to his promises.

J:

Mr. Daniels, do you have any proof other than your own testimony that Diane Daniels is not adequately caring for your son?

MD:

Proof?

J:

Yes. Medical records? Testimony of other witnesses who also believe he is not being properly fed?

MD:

No, your Honor. But I know I can do better for the child. I will be there more for him—

J:

Without documentation, and based on the fact that Roger is currently living in the family home he is used to, I am denying your custody request, Mr. Daniels. Temporarily, and until this court enters an order stating otherwise, Ms. Diane Daniels will have primary custody over Roger Daniels, and Mark Daniels will have the following visitation rights. Mr. Daniels

will take the boy every other weekend—beginning this coming Friday, January 15. He will come to your house, Ms. Daniels, and pick Roger up at 6 p.m. every other Friday evening, and return him to your home by 7 p.m. the following Sunday. You will have Roger ready to go, and will not refuse Mr. Daniels the right to have Roger for those weekends. As for you two, Mr. and Ms. Daniels, I strongly urge you to go back to your mediator ASAP to work out a custody arrangement that both of you can live with—but more important, one that puts Roger's interests to stay close to both of you without lots of tension first and foremost. Mr. Daniels, if you continue to truly believe your wife is not properly caring for your son, get some evidence together and file it with my clerk.

6. Engaging in Discovery/Disclosure

As with other civil actions, family law cases provide a means for the parties to obtain information from each other through such formal legal tools such as depositions, interrogatories, requests for admission and subpoenas. (See Chapter 4, Investigating Your Case, for more on discovery.) In addition, many states automatically require divorcing couples to exchange disclosure statements designed to detail their income, property and debts, as well as their knowledge about property-related transactions made during the marriage that may affect the rights of the other spouse in the divorce.

7. Home Investigations

If child custody and visitation issues are in dispute, you or your spouse may have to undergo a court-ordered home study or investigation, in which a counselor checks out your parenting situation and submits a written report for the court.

8. Pre-trial Hearings

One or more pretrial hearings may be necessary when one party feels the other is not abiding by proper procedures (for instance, one party may ask the court to enforce a discovery request the other side has failed to comply with).

9. Informal Negotiation

As the divorce proceeds, offers and counteroffers are likely to fly back and forth between the spouses regarding one or more issues. For example, one spouse might propose to keep the house and several investments in exchange for the other gaining full ownership of a small family-owned business. This type of informal negotiating can be emotionally draining, as it requires the spouses to pay constant attention to a process that frequently causes one or both of them a fair amount of pain.

10. Mediation

Frequently, courts encourage divorcing spouses to mediate their differences rather than submit them to the court for settlement. In many states, if the spouses can't agree on child custody or visitation issues, the court will require them to participate in court-ordered mediation. (See Section A6 for more on mediation.)

11. Settlement Conference

Depending on the state and sometimes the individual court, sometime during the divorce process the court will order a settlement conference to be held at which the judge will meet with the spouses and try to narrow contested issues and look for areas of agreement. Judges can quite forcefully urge compromise in these settlement conferences and, in situations in which one party refuses to go along, may even indicate how they plan to rule on a particular issue if the parties don't settle it first. Sometimes, the judge's intended ruling is seen as being in neither spouse's best interest and therefore encourages settlement, occasionally as late as the day of the trial.

12. Trial

Although most divorce-related disputes are settled before trial, occasionally a formal court trial is held. However, especially in divorce cases, many courts are experimenting with informal procedures in which one or both of the parties are self-represented. Still, most information in Chapters 8-17 of this book applies.

13. Judgment

A marriage eventually ends when the judge issues a decree or judgment of divorce. In some states the judgment or decree is final on the date it is issued, while in others (where it is often called an "interlocutory decree") it is not final until a period of time passes during which the divorcing spouses have the opportunity to change their minds.

⚠ **You may have to prepare the final decree.** In many states, after the judge orally issues a divorce decree it is up to the parties to prepare the necessary paperwork to ensure that the decree is written and entered into the court's docket. A self-help divorce book designed for use in your state should show you how.

14. Appeals

If a contested trial is held, either or both parties can appeal. Normally, appeals succeed only if the trial judge has made a clear legal mistake (for example, ordered child support in an amount below the minimum allowed in your state). Appeals claiming the judge made a poor decision based on the facts of the case (for example, ordered one spouse to have primary child custody over the objection of the other) are almost never successful.

F. MODIFICATION OF SUPPORT, CUSTODY AND VISITATION

Though provisions regarding the care and support of children of the marriage are usually written into court orders (or marital settlement agreements), they are not set in stone. If circumstances change significantly, you may go back to the judge and ask that the support, custody or visitation order be modified (changed) or enforced in one or more of its particulars. For example, divorced people may go back into court and request that child support may be modified if:

- either parent's income decreases substantially (for example, a parent loses his job)

- either parent's financial needs substantially increase (for instance, if either has a baby)

- either parent receives a large inheritance or gift, thereby either increasing their ability to provide support or decreasing their need to receive it

- a change occurs in one parent's life that bears on his ability to care for the children

- the needs of the children change (for example, a teenager may want to go to school near Dad's, rather than Mom's, house)

Some courts handle modification requests in public court just like other motions. Other judges handle such requests—as well as requests to change or enforce support payments—informally in chambers (the judge's office).

In the following dialogue, Molly Patricks, who recently lost her job, wants her former husband to pay more child support based on her reduced income. Molly filed with the family court and paid the sheriff's office to serve (deliver to her ex-husband) an Order to Show Cause (OSC) ordering her ex-husband to appear in court if he wished to say why the court should not modify the child and spousal support payments (see Section E above for more on OSCs). The Order to Show Cause contained the date, time and location of the court hearing along with Molly's supporting documentation, which consisted of an income and expense declaration.

Judge Wilbur Washington (J):

Patricks?

Molly Patricks (M):

Present, Your Honor.

J:

Is the respondent present?

M:

No.

J:

Do you expect him to be here today?

M:

I have no idea. It's already 10:30 a.m.; my papers say the hearing will be in this courtroom at 9 a.m.

J:

Indeed. (The judge flips through a file, mumbling, Proof of service, OSC, checking to see the paperwork is in order.) Ms. Patricks, I see your modification request here is based on the fact that you lost your job?

M:

Yes.

J:

Do you have a letter from your employer verifying that you no longer work there?

M:

No, Your Honor, but I have here a pay stub which indicates it is final payment for the last period.

Procedural Note: Molly did not have the exact document the judge was requesting, so she wisely admits as much. But she also sensibly tells the judge she has other evidence that establishes the same point.

J:

Hand it to the bailiff, please.

(Molly hands the pay stub to the bailiff, who hands it to Judge Washington.)

J:

And are you looking for another job?

M:

Yes. Actively. I have clippings here from want ads for positions I have applied to, including a list of the

salaries offered. Unfortunately, all pay less than what I made at my former job. I hope to find another job soon, but I am not sure how long it will take, and I'm pretty sure that even when I do the pay will be significantly less, since several companies in my industry, like the one I worked for, are relocating out of state where wages are lower.

J:

And your declaration here estimating the Respondent's income is based on what facts?

M:

What he was making at the time we divorced, two years ago, as he entered on his income statement. Plus I added a small cost of living increase, which I am sure he has received. I didn't put anything in for a real raise, which I'm pretty sure he's also gotten since then.

J:

O.K, I'm just going to run some numbers. (The judge does some work at a laptop computer on his desk while everyone waits. After a few minutes he looks up and says,) Respondent having been duly notified and not appearing to contest the OSC, modification from $___ monthly to $____ monthly is hereby granted.

Procedural Note: The last bit of legal gobbledigook translates into English as follows: "The father was given proper notice of this hearing. He didn't show up or file any responsive papers and therefore I'm going to assume he doesn't want to argue over the request to increase child support and in any event the request is reasonable in light of our state's support guidelines. Therefore I'll give Ms. Patricks what she has requested." ■

21

GETTING HELP FROM ATTORNEYS:
HIRING A LEGAL COACH

Even though you are determined to prepare and try your own case, consulting a lawyer along the way can be a big help. When a lawyer advises you on how to conduct your own case but does not actually represent you, the lawyer is serving as what we call a "legal coach." Instead of turning your case over to the lawyer, you pay—by the hour, usually—for limited help and advice. This arrangement can be an affordable way to get the help you need.

This chapter reviews some of the situations where a legal coach can help out and explains how to find and get the most out of your coach.

A. WHY CONSULT A LAWYER?

Even though you are representing yourself, a legal coach can help you in several important ways.

1. To Confirm That You Have a Good Claim or Defense

Not every wrong amounts to a valid legal claim that is worth pursuing in court. For instance, if a home appliance breaks, explodes and burns your hand, causing injuries that are painful and require a doctor's treatment, you likely have a good case against the product's manufacturer, the store where you purchased the product and possibly other defendants. If, however, the home appliance breaks after its warranty has expired and doesn't do any damage to anyone or anything, you may be inconvenienced but not have grounds to bring a lawsuit.

The process of preparing, filing and serving a complaint takes time and money. (Chapter 3, Starting Your Case.) And if you file a frivolous lawsuit

(one without valid grounds), you may be penalized by having to pay the other side's costs. For these reasons, you may want to consult a lawyer before you go to the trouble.

For example, say you want to sue a lawyer who drafted your stepmother's will because the lawyer failed to advise her to change her will to reflect her stated desire to disinherit a child born after the will was signed. Your stepmother told you, before she died, that she wanted all her money and property to go to you; because of the lawyer's bad advice, you will have to split it. You began investigating by talking to your stepmother's friends and other relatives to see if they ever heard her say what she really wanted. You assembled letters she wrote you saying that she wanted you to have everything. And you read the will. But you are not sure you understand the language in the will, what responsibilities the lawyer had to your stepmother or whether you could actually prove the lawyer did anything wrong. You may want a legal coach to help you determine whether you have a good case.

2. To Find Out the Law That Applies in Your Case

To determine what evidence to look for and eventually present in court, you must know what substantive law applies to your case. It may be relatively easy to determine what law applies to your case, especially after you have read this whole book.

For example, say you are suing the driver of a truck who hit you because she was driving carelessly. You know from Chapter 7, What You Need to Prove at Trial, and Chapter 22, Legal Research, that the general area of the law that governs your case is called "tort law" (personal injuries), and the particular legal theory that likely governs your case is called negligence. You even know (from Chapter 7) what the standard elements of a claim for negligence are.

But it is still likely to be more difficult for you, the non-expert, than for an experienced attorney to identify applicable law.

 Ask to use your legal coach's law library. Your legal coach may be able to tell you fairly easily about the laws that govern your case. If your coach doesn't know right off, a law clerk or paralegal who works with your coach may be able to do the research (at a lower rate than the lawyer) or show you what books to look in. If you need a place to do research, you may want to use your coach's library. That way you can verify that you are finding and correctly applying relevant laws.

3. To Assist with Preparing Documents

Your legal coach may be able to help you make sure any legal document you prepare is correct, logical and persuasive. A legal coach can help you draft or respond to the initial pleadings (the complaint or answer) or proofread pleadings you have prepared. If these documents are not properly prepared, you may unintentionally waive (give up) important legal rights. For example, if you are the defendant and fail to state some types of "affirmative defenses" (reasons why you are not legally responsible for the wrongs the plaintiff alleged in the complaint) in your answer, you may not be able to raise them later at the trial. (See Chapter 3, Starting Your Case.)

 A coach won't sign or be responsible for your documents. A lawyer acting as your legal coach, not your attorney, will not sign your legal documents but simply help you prepare them. You will sign all papers you file with the court in your own name. The caption (heading) on your legal documents will state your name, address and phone number, and that you are representing yourself. (See sample pleadings in Chapter 3, Starting Your Case.)

You may also wish to ask your coach to go over any pre-trial motions or discovery documents, such as interrogatories (written questions), which you want to send to your adversary. (See Chapter 4 for information on discovery.) Or you may want assistance responding to your adversary's motion for summary judgment. (See Chapter 6, Pre-Trial Hearings and Motions.)

Your coach may also be a big help if the judge asks you to write some legal document—for example, if she asks you to "brief" a question (write a persuasive argument about a legal issue) or draft a court order or factual or legal findings.

Ask your coach for sample forms. If you have to prepare a pleading or other legal document, ask your coach to see a sample of a pleading she filed in a similar case so that you can see what it's supposed to look like. Once a document has been filed in court, it is almost always public record and therefore no longer confidential. You can also consult a form book. (See Chapter 22, Legal Research.) Reviewing a sample before preparing your own draft will give you a good place to start, and your coach can edit what you did instead of starting from scratch.

4. To File and Serve Your Legal Documents

In addition to helping you draft documents, your coach, or assistants in her office such as paralegals or legal secretaries, may be able to help you put those documents together in the right format. Legal documents often have to be written up in certain ways—sometimes even on a specific kind of paper—and filed and served according to detailed rules. (See Chapter 3, Starting Your Case.) Your legal coach may be able to assist you a great deal by typing court documents into final form and filing and serving them on your opponent for you.

5. To Answer Questions Along the Way

Ultimately, what to say and do at trial will be your judgment call. But preparing and trying a case necessarily involves maneuvering within a complex and impersonal system. You not only need to understand legal rules, but also to plug them into a winning strategy—a strategy you'll typically have to fine-tune as your adversary reacts to your actions. It can help you a lot to run your general plans by an experienced lawyer. You may also come to particular points of confusion where some expert legal advice can save you much time and frustration. For example, you may want assistance planning a deposition (see Chapter 3, Starting Your Case), subpoenaing documents (see Chapter 11, Direct Examination) or deciding whether to accept a settlement proposal from your opponent (see Chapter 5, Settlement).

It may be especially helpful to have your coach review your outlines of what you expect to testify to and what you plan to ask witnesses on direct and cross-examination. (See Chapters 11 and 12, Direct Examination and Cross-Examination.) Your coach may spot areas where you reveal information you are better off keeping to yourself or questions that are likely to get you into trouble. For example, your proposed questions might give a hostile witness too much of a chance to expand upon testimony that might damage your case. And asking your adversary's expert witness certain questions would allow the expert to repeat harmful information.

Legal Help Lines. A fairly new type of legal service now provides answers to some legal questions by phone. Two such services are Telelawyer at 800-835-3529 or 900-370-7000 (which is charged to your phone bill) and the California Divorce Help Line at 800-359-7004.

6. To Be "On Call" During Trial

It may help to have a knowledgeable attorney who is familiar with your case available for last-minute consulting in case something happens at trial that throws you for a loop. If your coach agrees to be available by phone, you can ask the judge for a five-minute recess, even during the middle of trial if necessary, and make a quick call for advice. For example, say at trial, your adversary, Marie Driscoll, calls all the witnesses you expected her to. Then, unexpectedly, she calls Dr. Dean Duncan to the stand. Since she never told you that she was going to call the doctor as a witness, you have not had time to investigate him, conduct appropriate discovery or prepare cross-examination. A quick phone call to your coach may calm you down and give you some options. Your coach may remind you that Ms. Driscoll violated court rules by failing to mention, during the pre-trial conference, that she planned to call Dr. Duncan. (Federal Rule of Civil Procedure 16 (c)(5) and similar state court rules.)

Your coach may recommend that you go back into the courtroom and request that the judge either refuse to allow Dr. Duncan to testify altogether, or grant a continuance and have the doctor testify later so that you have time to prepare a cross-examination. Your request would be based on Ms. Driscoll's failure to reveal her intention to call the doctor at your pre-trial conference. Your coach may also tell you if the judge allows Dr. Duncan to testify despite the surprise, you should state your objections clearly for the record to preserve your right to appeal in case his testimony seriously damages your case.

7. To Take Over If Things Get Out of Control

You may know right now that there is no way you can afford to hire a lawyer and that you will try your whole case from start to finish no matter what. But, although you want to save as much as possible on legal fees by handling the case yourself, don't rule out hiring a lawyer to take over if you really need help and can afford it. If you have consulted a legal coach from time to time in preparing for trial, that lawyer may be in a good position to step in for you if feel you are unable to continue representing yourself.

8. To Handle an Appeal

Even if you represent yourself at the trial, you may want to hire an attorney if you or your adversary appeals the case. Appeals can be complicated, and you want to be sure that the legal principles you rely on and the procedures you follow are correct. (See Chapter 19, When Your Trial Ends: Judgments and Appeals.)

B. WILL LAWYERS AGREE TO BE COACHES?

Some will and others won't. Lots of lawyers agree that the legal system has become overly costly and complicated, and they are opening up to new approaches. They understand and are sympathetic to the fact that the average person can no longer afford to pay for full service representation in many lawsuits, especially since lawyers' fees can run upwards of $25,000 in even fairly uncomplicated trials.

Many lawyers also need work. Some may view legal coaching as a good way to develop future business. By providing helpful consultations on cases that are routine or involve small dollar amounts, a lawyer can generate referrals for full-service representation on bigger, more complex matters that you (or your friends or family) face in the future. Some lawyers may even view helping pro pers as combining the concept of pro bono work (free services provided for the public good or public assistance) with earning a modest fee.

But many lawyers won't go for the legal coach arrangement. Some simply don't want to get involved in what they see as the messy world of self-representation. Others will claim that their malpractice insurance won't allow them to or that they don't want to risk being legally liable if you make a mistake.

The bottom line, however, is that lawyers can and do sell advice by the hour without being responsible for every use to which their counsel is put. And with close to one million lawyers in the United States, you are likely to find more receptivity to the self-help law coach approach than you would think—especially if you help by educating a lawyer about what the relationship entails.

C. HOW TO FIND AND SELECT A QUALIFIED LEGAL COACH

Finding a good legal coach isn't impossible, but it is likely to require some searching. You want a lawyer with trial experience and familiarity with the legal issues involved in your case. You also want someone you are comfortable with—someone who understands, respects and agrees to perform the role

of legal coach. Use the techniques suggested below to select several qualified people, and then interview the possible choices before making your final selection.

1. Obtain Referrals

To develop a pool of potential legal coaches to interview, try the following sources of lawyer referrals.

a. Your Friends and Family

Many people find lawyers—especially those who handle routine matters such as small business contracts disputes or family law—by asking friends or relatives about lawyers they have been happy with. Law practice is increasingly specialized, though, so a fine attorney who handled your friend's divorce may not be able to help coach you through a lawsuit against your former employer for wrongful termination. But, since lawyers tend to know lots of other lawyers and know of their reputations, even if the lawyer you are referred to can't help, she may be able to recommend someone else who can. Tell the first lawyer the name of the friend who referred you, that your friend felt the lawyer did a superb job and that you would appreciate a referral to a lawyer who specializes in your type of case.

b. Small Businesses

Business people almost always know and work with lawyers. And, a small business person savvy enough to run a good business is likely to work with a trustworthy lawyer. So one good strategy for finding a legal coach is simply to call a company whose work relates to the type of problem you have or a local business with similar operations to your own (if you are a business person), and ask for the names of the lawyers they use.

c.   Legal and Other Community Organizations

Try writing or calling a local legal aid center (non-profit law office that usually handles cases for lower income people), the local chapter of a national legal organization such as the ACLU, or a community organization focusing on the issues in your case, like a tenants' rights group (for landlord-tenant disputes) or a women's organization (for sex discrimination cases). Ask to speak with an attorney or paralegal and ask for a referral. Explain that you intend to represent yourself but that you need assistance from a lawyer.

People who work in these organizations may know of lawyers in the community who have good reputations. And chances are that lawyers who are involved in or supportive of such organizations will be sympathetic to your situation.

You may qualify for free legal help. Some organizations represent clients who either meet certain financial hardship requirements or whose cases focus on large policy issues. If either is your situation, you may be able to get direct representation, free of charge. (Chapter 1, Going It Alone, Section B, discusses sources of free legal help.)

d.   Paralegals

Independent paralegals, non-lawyers who help people complete and file court papers but do not give legal advice, frequently refer clients to lawyers and get feedback on the lawyers' work. They are typically listed in the Yellow Pages under "Paralegals" or "Typing Services." You can also call the National Association of Independent Paralegals at 800-542-0034 for lawyer referrals.

e.   Bar Association Referral Services

Many local bar associations have lawyer referral services. For a few dollars or sometimes without charge, you will be referred to a lawyer, who will give you an initial consultation for a reduced fee or free of charge. Unfortunately, bar associations usually provide minimal screening for lawyers they list. In many areas, any local lawyer who has joined the association (paid the required dues) will be listed.

Despite the obvious weakness of an uncritical referral system, it can be a starting point. And you can check the names you get with referrals from friends, family and local businesses, look up the referred lawyers' qualifications in a legal directory such as the *Martindale-Hubbell Law Directory* (discussed below), or phone a legal organization to see if an attorney or paralegal can confirm the referral.

2.   Investigate Qualifications

Lawyers aren't hard to find—but you're not looking for just any lawyer. You want someone who is philosophically amenable to the legal coach role, and you want someone who has actual litigation experience, as well as work experience in areas similar to your case. Just because someone is a lawyer does not mean she has experience with your type of case or can adequately help coach you to try your case in court. Beginning lawyers and even law students may be able to research the law, but many

FINDING A LAWYER: AN EXAMPLE

You are a homeowner who bought a house from Colleen Larky, who told you that the roof was in very good condition. You have just discovered that she lied. The roof, patched in several hard-to-see places, must be replaced before the winter. And your neighbor, Craig Jamner, just told you that he is planning to build a guest house on part of your garden near his house, which he claims belongs to him. Craig said that he had allowed Colleen to plant rosebushes there while he wasn't using the land, but that she knew he would eventually want it back. You want a lawyer to tell you whether you would have a good lawsuit against Colleen for misrepresenting these important facts, and to serve as a legal coach to help you prepare and try the case if you decide to.

To find some initial referrals, you ask friends and family. All you come up with is that your uncle Pat was very happy with a lawyer who recently wrote his will. You call the lawyer and say you were referred by Pat. You explain (briefly) what your case involves and that you understand that this area is not the lawyer's specialty. And you politely ask for the name of one or more good lawyers in your community who regularly handle property disputes. You get two names.

Then, you phone several businesses in your area: a title insurance company, a real estate brokerage firm and a lumber yard, and ask who they use. The title insurance company says "None of your business," but the other two supply you with names of lawyers they recommend.

Then you look in *Martindale-Hubbell*, a nationwide directory of lawyers, under your city's listing. You find one attorney who has written an article on property law and belongs to the local real estate lawyers' groups, and two more who are part of the real estate group.

One lawyer on your list was referred by two of your sources. It is sensible to start your interviews with that lawyer.

of them have no more experience trying a case in court than you do. Even among very experienced attorneys, many rarely handle trials. Some, such as those who advise on tax and other business matters, may never have set foot in a courtroom even after practicing law for decades.

Law is rapidly becoming a field dominated by specialists. Wrongful job terminations, medical malpractice and sexual harassment are just a few of the areas that usually require a specialist. Sometimes you can tell if an attorney has special expertise in a particular substantive area of law by checking the attorney's professional background, the associations to which he belongs or the articles he has written. To find out such information, consult a set of reference volumes called the *Martindale-Hubbell Law Directory,* which is available in most law libraries. It lists law firms by state and city. Each firm lists and gives a brief biological sketch of its lawyers.

In addition, you can call ahead and ask for an attorney's professional resume (curriculum vitae or "cv") and articles the attorney has written, if any. The law firm may also have a brochure describing its practice. Many lawyers will give you names of clients—after, of course, getting permission from those clients—so that you can talk to people who have used the lawyer's services. Naturally, you'll get the names of satisfied customers. But you can still learn a lot by asking them about how the attorney handled their cases.

Perhaps the most important qualities you should look for are matters of personality—those you can find out only by interviewing someone yourself. A lawyer who is patient and caring may be more helpful to you than the most experienced trial lawyer in the country.

3. Interview Prospective Legal Coaches

When you've narrowed your list to a few possibilities, call the recommended lawyers' offices. Briefly explain the facts of your case, say why you think it is a good case and state your reasons for representing yourself. If the lawyer isn't open to coaching or doesn't handle your type of case, you needn't waste your time even scheduling an appointment.

If after your interview you find the lawyer to be a promising candidate, you will probably want to discuss further what exactly you expect of the coach relationship and assure the lawyer that you are sincere and hard-working.

 Don't expect something for nothing.
When calling for an appointment, be sure to ask how much the initial interview will cost. Nothing starts a relationship off worse than being slapped with a bill you did not expect. Many lawyers do give initial consultations for free or for minimal fees. But don't expect this. Since you are asking for an unconventional relationship, one where you will be paying for isolated services rather than full representation, the lawyer is not likely to do as much work (or earn as big a fee) in your case. It may be fair to have you pay for all consultations, even the first interview.

---

a. Ask About Fees

You'll want to ask about cost—from the initial interview forward. It obviously defeats your purpose if you have to spend more to consult a legal coach than to hire a lawyer to handle your entire case.

Typically, lawyers use hourly, fixed or contingency fee arrangements. Most likely, someone serving as your legal coach will charge you by the hour.

Hourly rates for lawyers who do personal legal services work typically run from $100 to $250 per hour. Certain experts and big firm lawyers charge even more. It is important to find out exactly how the lawyer will calculate the bill. For example, some lawyers who charge by the hour bill in minimum increments of 15 minutes (quarter hour), and others bill in increments of six minutes (tenth of an hour). That means that a five-minute phone conversation, for which you are billed the minimum amount, could cost you different amounts, depending on how the lawyer figures the bill.

Although getting good value for your money is key, this doesn't mean always looking for the lowest hourly fee. You can often benefit by hiring a more experienced attorney, even if her hourly rates are high, since she may take less time to review and advise you on particulars of your case.

Many lawyers routinely ask clients to pay a "retainer"—a deposit or advance fee—which is kept in a trust account and used as services are provided. Your legal coach may ask for a retainer in order to see that you are serious and have the money to pay. However, you shouldn't be expected to come up with a large amount of money, since you do not plan on running up high legal bills. A fee of more than $500 is excessive, especially before you know whether the legal coach relationship is really working out.

Choose a coach you are comfortable with. Offering piecemeal (sometimes called "unbundled") legal services as a self-help legal coach is a fairly new approach for lawyers. It may not be clear from the first consultation how much you can do on your own and how much help you will need as your case proceeds. You and the lawyer you choose may have to decide together what the fairest approach is for you to pay for the lawyer's services. For this reason and many of the others stated above, be sure to choose a lawyer whom you feel comfortable enough with to frankly discuss fee arrangements and other thorny issues.

OTHER KINDS OF FEE ARRANGEMENTS

Contingency Fees. When representing people in a personal injury cases, lawyers often take a percentage of the final judgment—often one-third, but varying depending on factors such as whether a case settles before trial—as their fees. Since you will try your own case, you will probably not use a contingency fee arrangement. If your coach suggests one, do not agree to give too high a percentage, since you will really be doing all the work.

Fixed Fees. A fixed fee is a set fee for a particular project. For example, a lawyer may charge $500 to write your will. It is unlikely that an attorney will suggest a fixed fee to coach you through your whole case, because the lawyer will have little idea of the amount of work involved. But the lawyer may suggest fixed fees for particular services along the way. For example, you may find a lawyer willing to charge you no more than a specific sum of money to review and edit your complaint or help you respond to your opponent's interrogatories.

b.   Ask About Accessibility

The self-help legal coach arrangement likely won't work for you unless the lawyer promptly answers your questions by returning phone calls and responding to letters. Because this is something many busy lawyers are notoriously weak at, it may be helpful at the outset to sketch a time frame, noting when your case was filed and the likely trial date (if you know it). That way, you and the lawyer can assess with more accuracy the kind of time your case will need, and the lawyer can determine whether or not she has enough time to devote to coaching you.

If you talk to other clients, among your first questions should be whether the lawyer returns phone calls promptly and is generally easy to reach.

Ask when and how to contact the lawyer. The lawyer you choose as a legal coach is probably busy with many other cases. You are likely to have a much more effective working relationship and save yourself time and aggravation if you are sensitive to the lawyer's time constraints. For instance, some attorneys may find it helpful if, as much as possible, you call before 9 a.m. or after 5 p.m. when they are not likely to be in the middle of other cases.

c.   Say What You Want

Let the attorney know that you intend to work hard to put together your case, but that you want help to keep you on the right track. Be as specific as you can. Explain, for instance, that you want the attorney's help with locating the law that governs your case, consulting with you as to your trial plans and strategies and, if possible, being available by phone or fax during your trial in case you need help pulling yourself out of a legal hole.

You may even show the lawyer this book and particularly this chapter, or at least let the lawyer know you have a book to consult for guidance.

4.   Put Your Agreement in Writing

The lawyer may reasonably request that you sign an agreement that makes it clear that the lawyer is merely advising you, that you are making your own decisions and are responsible for the results in the case. It may also be to your benefit to have an agreement so that the terms don't change in the middle of the relationship. And in some states, certain fee agreements are required by law to be in writing. For example, California requires a written agreement whenever a lawyer and client expect legal fees to exceed $1,000, or if the client agrees to a contingency fee.

A sample agreement, which you and your legal coach may adapt to your own circumstances, is shown below.

Pay your bills on time. However your legal coach charges, be sure to pay your bills on time. You will likely get much more prompt and polite service in return if you do.

D.   KEEPING LAWYER BILLS DOWN

A legal coach relationship with a competent, supportive lawyer will likely be well worth the expense. But there are certain approaches you can use to keep the bills down and get the most for your money.

1.   Prepare Before You Talk to Your Coach

Prepare for all sessions, including the initial interview and phone calls, by sending or bringing the attorney copies of all key background documents, such as the contract if you have a contract dispute. Preparation will make you speak more concisely— and remember, time really is money when you're paying by the hour. Preparation will also help ensure that you don't forget to mention important details.

2.   List Your Questions Before You Meet

Whenever possible, put your questions in writing and mail, fax or deliver them to your coach before meetings, even if they are phone meetings. That way the lawyer can find answers if he doesn't know them off the top of his head without having to call you back and charge for a separate phone conference. This also helps focus the meeting so there is less of a chance of digressing into (and having to pay to discuss) unrelated topics.

3.   Consolidate Your Questions

Because hourly charges are divided up into parts of an hour, you may be charged for more time than you actually spend. For example, if your legal coach bills in 15-minute intervals and you only talk for five minutes, you may still be charged for the whole 15. If that is your coach's practice, it

SAMPLE LEGAL COACH AGREEMENT

LEGAL COACH AGREEMENT

William Nolo, a pro per litigant ("Nolo"), and Anna Turney, an attorney in the state of

_____ ("Lawyer"), agree as follows:

Lawyer will serve as Nolo's legal coach to advise Nolo on the negligence action he has filed against Sarah Adams.

1.   Nolo is representing himself in the Nolo v. Adams case. Lawyer is not representing Nolo, but merely advising Nolo on an as-needed basis if and when Nolo seeks Lawyer's advice.

2.   Nolo takes all responsibility for decisions made in litigating the case and for all results that stem from the case.

3.   Lawyer will keep all communications made by Nolo to Lawyer in connection with this case confidential.

4.   Nolo will pay for Lawyer's advice at the rate of $_____ per hour. This advice may include but is not limited to matters such as helping Nolo research the legal issues involved in his case, reviewing pleadings that Nolo has prepared or received in connection with the case and assisting Nolo in developing and implementing a litigation strategy.

5.   Nolo may also arrange, through Lawyer, for assistance from Lawyer's office personnel, such as a paralegal at the rates of $ ___ per hour and a legal secretary at the rate of $ ___ per hour.

6.   Nolo will pay Lawyer a $300 retainer. Lawyer will bill Nolo monthly.

7.   Nolo will have reasonable access to Lawyer's office services, as needed, including the conference room and library.

William Nolo
_____
William Nolo

March 24, year
_____
Date

Anna Turney
_____
Anna Turney

March 24, year
_____
Date

pays to gather your questions and ask them all at once, rather than calling every time you have a question.

4. Beware of Other Costs

Whatever the formal fee arrangement, always verify if there will be any incidental fees, such as photocopy and fax charges. If there are, you may be able to find ways to cut them down. For example, if you learn the law office charges $3 or more for each page it faxes, and you live nearby, pick up a document instead of having it faxed to you. And request generally that unless papers are urgent, your legal coach use regular mail, not fax. Make extra copies of documents so the lawyer doesn't have to do it. Often lawyers charge more than the local copy shop since they charge for the time it takes to make copies.

 Carefully review lawyer bills. Read your bill. Lawyers make mistakes, and your charges may be wrong. For example, a ".1" (six minutes) may be transposed into a "1." (one hour) when the data is entered into the billing system. That's $200 instead of $20 if your lawyer charges $200 per hour.

5. Try to Answer Questions on Your Own

Remember that you are hiring a legal coach, not a full-service lawyer. That means doing as much as you can by yourself and only turning to the coach when you are really stuck. By reading this book all the way through and consulting a nearby law library, you can answer many of your questions on your own. And those you cannot answer completely you can often narrow down.

RESOURCES ON LAWYER-CLIENT DEALINGS

Finding the Right Lawyer, by Jay Foonberg (ABA), a detailed guide to finding and hiring a lawyer, from the ABA Section of Law Practice Management.

Mad at Your Lawyer? by Tanya Starnes (Nolo Press), presents techniques for extricating yourself from a relationship that isn't working. ■

22

LEGAL RESEARCH

In law, as in life, there is always more information to be had, and for a variety of reasons you may want to do some legal research into matters not covered by this book. But if your case is relatively straightforward, you may not need to conduct extensive legal research in order to effectively represent yourself in trial.

The purpose of this chapter is to introduce you to some basic legal research tools and give you practical suggestions for getting information from commonly available resources. The chapter is not a comprehensive guide to conducting legal research. If you want a thorough explanation of the legal system, legal authorities and how to use a law library, consult two excellent Nolo Press resources, both of which are relatively inexpensive and also usually available in most law libraries:

- *Legal Research: How to Find and Understand the Law,* by Stephen Elias and Susan Levinkind, an easy-to-read book that provides step-by-step instruction on how to find legal information.

- *Legal Research Made Easy,* a 2H hour video tape, hosted by Robert Berring, an experienced law librarian and legal research professor, that clearly explains what resources to use and how to go about efficiently researching a legal problem.

- *Legal Research for Beginners,* by Sonja Larsen and John Bourdeau (Barrons), a general legal research guide with emphasis on computerized research methods.

A. WHAT YOU MAY WANT TO RESEARCH

Normally, the information you may want to research in order to try your own case in court will fall into three areas:

- substantive law, governing your and your opponent's legal claims and defenses.

- rules of evidence, and

- rules of civil procedure.

1. The Substantive Law of Your Case

"Substantive" law is the term for rules that govern the heart of your dispute, like particular laws about a contract or tort (civil wrong or personal injury) lawsuit. The term "substantive" law is used in contrast to "procedural" law, which deals with the rules that govern how your case moves through the court system and is tried.

Substantive law can be classified into certain discrete subjects—for example, contracts, torts, wills, property, tax, immigration and bankruptcy. But keep in mind that your case may involve more than one subject.

For example, if you are involved in a divorce and child custody battle, naturally you'll need to deal with "family laws" covering divorce, alimony, child custody, child support and division of marital property. But in dividing your property, you may also deal with federal and state tax laws and state property laws.

The same is true if your case deals with a car accident. You claim that your adversary was negligent in that he made an unsafe lane change and sideswiped your car. To find laws relating to what lane a car must be in when making a turn, you will look at your state's traffic laws (perhaps grouped together in a section, title, chapter or code under "Vehicle" or "Traffic"). Laws relating to the standard elements of a negligence claim may be in state laws under a general "Civil" category, perhaps grouped under the heading "negligence" or "torts"and supplemented by the decisions of judges (case law).

State or Federal Law. Both state and the federal governments enact laws that may affect your case. Some areas of law are unique to the federal system, such as bankruptcy, copyright and patent. Other areas of law are typically state court subjects—for example torts (personal injury), contracts, family law (divorce, child custody, guardianship) and wills. Your case may involve both federal and state laws. For instance, divorce cases may involve state family law and federal income tax law, and claims of civil rights violations may be made under federal and state civil rights laws.

a. Elements of the Claims in Your Case

Probably your most important substantive research task is to learn the legal elements of each of the legal claims (sometimes called "causes of action") or defenses in your case. (See Chapter 7, What You Need to Prove at Trial: The Plaintiff's Perspective, and Chapter 8, What You Need to Prove at Trial: The Defendant's Perspective.) You need to know these elements to prepare for trial, present relevant evidence during trial and make persuasive legal arguments to the judge or jury at the close of trial.

One good place to look for lists of elements is standard jury instructions (instructions the judge reads to the jury at the close of trial). These instruc-

tions identify the elements that a jury has to find in order for a plaintiff to win a particular legal claim. Judges use the same elements in deciding cases without a jury.

RESOURCES ON JURY INSTRUCTIONS

Many states have books that set out complete jury instructions for common kinds of lawsuits. For example, federal jury instructions are published in a book called *Modern Federal Jury Instructions,* by Leonard Sand (Matthew Bender). Michigan has a book called *Michigan Standard Jury Instructions,* Civil Committee on Standard Jury Instruction (Institute of Continuing Legal Education). New York has *New York Pattern Jury Instructions, Civil*, Committee on Pattern Jury Instructions (Lawyers Co-Operative Publishing Co.). And in California, there's the *California Jury Instructions, Civil: Book of Approved Jury Instructions (BAJI),* Committee on Standard Jury Instructions (West Publishing Co.). Ask a law librarian where to find the published jury instructions in your state.

b. Understanding the Elements

Once you've found the elements of each of the claims in your case, you've got to figure out what they mean. So you may need to do some more research to find out more about particular elements of your legal claim. For example, assume that you bring a breach of contract action against a painter who agreed to paint your roof, then stopped midway through the job. You want to recover both the deposit you gave the painter originally and the difference between the amount of money you were going to pay this painter and the sum you ended up having to pay another painter to complete the job. You know (from Chapter 7) that a claim for breach of contract usually consists of four elements:

1. **Formation:** You and the defendant had a legally binding contract.

2. **Performance:** You performed as required under the contract.

3. **Breach:** The defendant failed to perform as required under the contract.

4. **Damages:** The defendant's failure to perform caused you economic loss.

But you may need to do some legal research to find out what the abstract legal jargon of the elements means in English. For instance, what constitutes a legally binding contract, the first element? What if you had only spoken with the painter, and neither of you had anything in writing? When he walked off the job, he was angry and said something like "I'm outta here. Just try to sue me; we don't even have a contract. You'll never be able to prove anything."

One question you may ask is, "Can an oral contract be valid?" For the answer, you may first try asking a reliable resource person, such as your legal coach, or you can go to a law library and look up the answer. Ask a law librarian to direct you to some resources about oral contracts. You may consult a treatise (reference book) about contract law, such as *Contracts Law in a Nutshell,* by Gordon Schaber and Claude Rohwer (2d Ed., West Publishing Co.), or a legal encyclopedia. (See Section B, below, for more on reference books.) You will find that you do not need a written contract or other document to form a valid contract for painting a house; an oral contract is sufficient as long as it can be proved. (Of course, you may have more trouble proving the terms of an oral contract than a written contract.)

2. Evidence Rules

After you understand the substantive law affecting your case, you will want to be sure you are up to speed on evidence rules. These rules govern how you and your adversary present your own testimony and that of witnesses, the exhibits you and your adversary refer to and what you both attempt to introduce into evidence.

Chapter 15, Basic Rules of Evidence, explains the most frequently encountered rules of evidence and refers to particular Federal Rules of Evidence. The Federal Rules are good starting places for research because they have been adopted or used as a guideline in over half the states. But you may want to read a particular rule of evidence in your state or find out how courts in your state have interpreted some aspect of a particular rule of evidence. Ask a law librarian to show you where to find the evidence rules for your state, or where the library keeps the Federal Rules of Evidence if your case is in federal court.

3. Procedural Rules

Procedural rules govern the process of conducting litigation before, during and after trial. Rules of civil procedure control such things as how many days you have to answer your adversary's complaint, the deadline for requesting a jury trial, how many interrogatories you can ask the other side during discovery and dozens more details of litigation.

Procedural rules for civil cases may be grouped together in a particular chapter, title or section of general state laws under the heading called "Civil Procedure." Some states have conveniently separated books of rules called "codes." In those, you will find a separate "code of civil procedure." In other states, you will likely have to use the general index to the statutes to find the rules you need. In the federal court system, they are in the Federal Rules of Civil Procedure. Before you begin looking around, you may want to ask a law librarian how to find the rules of civil procedure that apply to your case.

Local court rules also affect procedure, and they can be critical to effectively trying your case. Local rules can govern many details—for instance, how many copies of legal documents you must submit or the type of paper you must use. These sound like picky little details, and they are. But they are details that you must follow. Even different counties within the same state can have different rules—for example, one area's local rules may allow ten days to reply to a motion, another's two weeks. So as early on as possible in the process, go to the court clerk or law clerk where your case is pending (or the courthouse law library), and ask for a copy of all local rules of court.

B. SOURCES OF INFORMATION

Many people faced with a legal research task are tempted to begin by poring over stacks of books. For the novice, this too frequently results in floundering for hours through material that doesn't relate to your case. Fortunately, there are better ways to get the information you need. One, simply enough, is to just ask someone; another is to consult a book that explains and organizes the substantive law. Finally, you may want to look up the law itself—a piece of legislation or the written decision of a court. This section discusses all these sources of information.

1. People

You may not always get a right answer or even an answer at all, but you can often get quick and helpful information by asking someone who regularly deals with legal documents. The most likely candidates for help with your case are court clerks, law librarians and your legal coach.

a.   Court Clerks

Clerks at the court where your case is pending can sometimes be very helpful, especially when it comes to procedural details. For example, court clerks can help you greatly by locating for you or telling you where to obtain copies of documents such as:

- local court rules
- state or federal court rules
- legal forms (pleadings, motions or court orders), or
- jury instructions.

You may, however, encounter resistance or even outright hostility from court clerks, some of whom view pro pers as people who will waste their and the court's time. For example, a clerk may refuse to answer your questions, saying something like, "I'm not allowed to give legal advice." But asking how to get forms and copies of court rules is not seeking legal advice. Being polite and expressing how much you appreciate the help may make the difference between getting assistance from clerks and not. You have nothing to lose by asking.

b.   Law Librarians

All sorts of legal information, including legal forms, reference books explaining particular areas of law, rules of evidence and procedure, court cases, statutes and more are available at law libraries. Law librarians, who usually have extensive legal training, can be most helpful in pointing you to these and other resources.

Do not ask or expect a law librarian to do your research for you, and don't ask for legal advice. They can't and won't provide these services. But they will help you find what you need and, often, how to use the research tools you've found.

FINDING A LAW LIBRARY

In some states, finding a well-stocked law library that is open to the public is no problem; at least one library will be at a principal courthouse in every metropolitan area. But in other states, courthouse libraries are nonexistent or inadequate, and the only decent law libraries open to the public are located at a publicly funded law school. Some private law schools also open their law libraries to the public, at least for limited hours.

For simple legal research tasks, a public library can be a fine place to start. The main branch of your public library may have a small but helpful legal section where you can find your state's statutes as well as county and local ordinances. Another possibility is to ask for permission to use your legal coach's law office library.

---

c.   Your Self-Help Legal Coach

Consulting a lawyer doesn't mean you have to hire the lawyer to handle the whole case for you. As discussed in Chapter 21, you can hire a lawyer to be your advisor or "coach," to help you prepare and try your case, on an as-needed basis. And one of the first and most important areas a legal coach can help you with is advising you where to locate laws, legal forms, court cases and other information that is relevant to your case.

2. Books and Other Publications About the Law

Books that summarize and explain court cases, statutes and other rules of law can be your most important legal research tools. They are a good place to start your research because they can help you get a picture of where you are going, maybe give you an answer or at least point you to a resource where you will find an answer. By streamlining your research, they can cut down on time and frustration.

⚠ **Publications about the law are not the last word.** If you find a useful explanation in an encyclopedia, treatise or article, keep in mind that the conclusions expressed are not the law itself but the analysis of the authors, and a judge does not have to follow what they say. Also, the author may be mistaken or information in the article may be outdated. If you want to use the laws that the author cites to support your position, look them up yourself.

a. Legal Dictionaries

Law, just like any other specialized aspect of our society, has its own jargon. When you are representing yourself it is very important for you to become fluent (or at least comfortable) with a lot of new terms. You probably have already increased your legal vocabulary a great deal by reading and consulting the Glossary in this book, but a good legal dictionary will be most helpful.

Obviously, you need to look up words you don't know. But it can even pay to look up words you think you know, since they may have different connotations in a legal context. Take "discovery." To non-lawyers, a discovery is a "find," as in "Columbus discovered America." But in law, discovery is the pre-trial process of gathering information, usually from your opponent. Another example is "hearsay," an important word you need to understand. Non-lawyers typically define hearsay as unsubstantiated talk or rumors. For example, someone said, "Loretta told me there were going to be mass layoffs next month, but I don't believe her; it's just hearsay." In legal language, hearsay means, "an out-of-court statement offered in court for the truth of that statement." It's similar to the non-legal meaning, but not identical. (Chapter 15, Basic Rules of Evidence, explains the hearsay rule.)

 READABLE DICTIONARIES

Traditionally, many lawyers refer to *Black's Law Dictionary*, but several published more recently are easier to understand:

Law Dictionary, by Stephen Gifis (Barrons).

Dictionary of Legal Terms: A Simplified Guide to the Language of Law, by Stephen Gifis (Barrons).

Law Dictionary for Non-Lawyers, by Daniel Oran (West Publishing Co.).

Legal Thesaurus-Dictionary, by William Statsky (West Publishing Co.).

Dictionary of American Legal Usage, by David Melinkoff (West Publishing Co.)

Family Law Dictionary, by Stephen Elias and Robin Leonard (Nolo Press). Explains family law terms in plain English.

Ballentine's Law Dictionary, by Jack Handler (Lawyers Cooperative Publishing).

b.   Treatises on Particular Subjects

Treatises have been written on almost every conceivable legal subject. They summarize whole areas of law, and can be one of the most useful research tools. But since the great majority are written for lawyers or law students, you may have to wade through a lot of legal jargon to get valuable information. Ask your law librarian or legal coach to recommend a treatise about the area your case involves—for example, torts or contracts.

"Nutshells," published by the West Publishing Company, are paperback treatises written in more down-to-earth language. Nutshells cover a wide range of legal subjects including trial advocacy, civil rights, community property, constitutional law, environmental law, worker's compensation and employee protection laws and lots more. To find out if there is a Nutshell for the subject you are interested in, check the first few pages in any Nutshell book for a list, in alphabetical order, of all the other Nutshell books. Also listed are West Publishing's major law textbooks and "hornbooks" (longer, usually hardbound treatises).

Only a few publishers, such as Nolo Press, gear their books especially toward non-lawyers. Nolo Press publishes books on a very wide variety of subjects including landlord-tenant law, wills, divorce, bankruptcy, tax, buying and selling property, sexual harassment and many more. Look at the back pages of any Nolo book for a list of all Nolo Press books and software.

Also, Southern Illinois University Press publishes a series of books edited by the American Civil Liberties Union (ACLU). These explain many civil rights—for example, the rights of crime victims, employees, gay people, Native Americans and women, and the right to government information.

c.   Form Books

Form books are collections of model legal documents. Most include fill-in-the-blank documents, which you can copy and complete. Form books can help you enormously when you have to prepare any legal paperwork such as initial pleadings (complaint and answer) and discovery tools such as interrogatories, pre-trial motions and stipulations. With a form in front of you, you don't have to reinvent the wheel, although you'll probably have to change the model forms a bit to fit the circumstances of your case.

Form books also usually explain the procedural background for each form. They can provide helpful explanations of the laws you will have to follow and instructions for completing the forms, and they refer you to other resources should you need further information.

Some states provide their own fill-in-the-blank forms that you must use for specific purposes. These are available for small sums of money at local courts. Ask the court clerk, a law librarian or your legal coach to assist you in locating either a book of forms or court approved forms.

A list of form books can be found in *Legal Research: How to Find and Understand the Law,* by Stephen Elias and Susan Levinkind (Nolo Press).

d.   Legal Encyclopedias

Legal encyclopedias, like regular encyclopedias, contain detailed explanations of various topics, organized alphabetically by topic. There is a detailed index at the end of the last volume, which you can look at to find the topic you want. Encyclopedias can give you a great deal of general background information about a particular subject and often refer you to state and federal statutes and cases. That makes them a good place to start if you just want to get a general understanding of the legal principles that govern your dispute.

NATIONAL AND STATE-SPECIFIC ENCYCLOPEDIAS

The two main national law encyclopedias are *American Jurisprudence* (Am. Jur.) and *Corpus Juris.* They include broadly based discussions on the laws of all 50 states. Both are now in their second series, so you'll find cites to "Am. Jur. 2d." and "C.J.S." (Corpus Juris Secundum). Many of the larger states have their own encyclopedias as well. Here are a few examples:

- *Pennsylvania Law Encyclopedia*

- *New York Jurisprudence 2d*

- *Encyclopedia of Georgia Law*

- *Florida Jurisprudence*

- *California Jurisprudence 3d* .

Check a law library to find an legal encyclopedia for your state.

e. Journals and Law Reviews

Many legal organizations publish journals (magazines) that contain articles covering current legal issues. For example, in a journal published by a state bar association, you may find a review of recent changes in your court's local rules or an analysis of a recent court opinion.

Law schools also produce journals, called "law reviews," which consist of scholarly articles written by law students, law professors and practicing attorneys. While law reviews are notorious for their complex and confusing language, they sometimes cover timely topics and can provide leads on where to find relevant state or federal laws.

To locate relevant articles, you can use the *Index to Legal Periodicals,* the *Current Law Index,* or a computerized index called LEGALTRAC, found in many law libraries.

f. Lawyers' Practice Guides

Books written for practicing lawyers can be helpful resources for finding instructions, practical suggestions and forms for specific areas of state and federal law practice.

These publications, sometimes called continuing legal education (CLE), cover a huge variety of subjects, such as negligence, copyright, bankruptcy, mechanic's liens, tax law and many more. There are also specific guides on pre-trial, trial and post-trial tactics, such as practice guides on pre-trial motions, discovery, direct and cross-examination, opening statement, closing argument, appeals and more. They are available in many states, and some publishers gear their materials specifically toward lawyers in particular states. For example, the Practising Law Institute (PLI) gears some materials toward New York lawyers, and the Rutter Group and Continuing Education of the Bar (CEB) toward California lawyers. Check a law library near you.

STATE STATUTES ON THE INTERNET

You may be able to find your state's laws on the Internet. Some states provide an entire set of up-to-date statutes, while others have only recently enacted laws or older statutes. Fewer than half the states do not have their statutes online. Check your state's Web site:

Alaska
www.touchngo.com/lglcntr/akstats/statutes.htm

Arizona
www.azleg.state.az.us/ars/ars.htm

California
www.leginfo.ca.gov/calaw.html

Arkansas
www.uark.edu/~govninfo/PAGES/WAIS-SEARCH/acts.cgi

Colorado
crs.aescon.com/

Connecticut
www.cslnet.ctstateu.edu/statutes/index.htm

Florida
www.scri.fsu.edu/fla-leg/statutes/

Idaho
www.idwr.state.id.us/idstat/TOC/idstTOC.html

Indiana
www.law.indiana.edu/codes/in/incode.html

Iowa
www2.legis.state.ia.us/Code.html

Michigan
www.icle.org/leg-sums/leglist.htm

Minnesota
www.leg.state.mn.us/leg/statutes.htm

Mississippi
www.mscode.com

Missouri
www.house.state.mo.us/homestat.htm

Montana
www.nfoweb.com/folio.pgi/MTCODE/doc?

Nebraska
unicam1.lcs.state.ne.us/folio.pgi/statutes.nfo?

Nevada
www.leg.state.nv.us/law1.htm

New Jersey
www.njleg.state.nj.us/folio.pgi/STATUTES.NFO?

New York
assembly.state.ny.us/ALIS/laws.html

Oklahoma
www.onenet.net/oklegal/statutes.basic.html

Oregon
www.efn.org/%7Ebobl/index4.html

South Carolina
www.lpitr.state.sc.us/newlaws.htm

Utah
www.le.state.ut.us/~code/code.htm

Vermont
www.leg.state.vt.us/statutes/statutes.htm

Virginia
leg1.state.va.us/000/src.htm

Washington
leginfo.leg.wa.gov/www/rcw.htmn

Wisconsin
www.legis.state.wi.us/constats.html

Wyoming
legisweb.state.wy.us/titles/statutes.htm

3. The Law Itself

The law itself consists of constitutional provisions, statutes, court cases, ordinances and administrative regulations.

 COMPUTERIZED RESEARCH

Most legal sources that you can look up in law books are also now available "on-line" on computers. But generally speaking, if you are new to legal research, it's better to research with books.

Two major systems, Lexis and Westlaw, maintain on-line databases of court cases, statutes, legal articles and a host of other resources (nationwide and even some worldwide). Users are usually charged for the amount of time spent on-line, which can get quite expensive, especially if you are not familiar with the system. There are some computerized systems that are free to users in public law libraries, such as the LEGALTRAC and INFOTRAC guides to legal periodicals. For more information on computerized research, ask a law librarian or consult *Legal Research: How to Find and Understand the Law,* by Stephen Elias and Susan Levinkind (Nolo Press).

a. State and Federal Legislation

Legislation is rules enacted by federal and state legislatures. These rules are sometimes called statutes, acts or, simply, laws. State statutes are grouped by subject matter. Most sets of statutes take up many volumes, but they are divided into "codes," "chapters" or "titles," which are in turn divided in sections and subsections. Federal laws are published in the "United States Code."

As are some other statute books, the U.S. Code is divided into titles and sections. Each statute has a particular number, called a citation or cite. Once you've found a citation to a statute, for example, from a treatise or article, you can easily find the statute. For example, an encyclopedia mentions a statute called the Civil Rights Act of 1964 and gives the citation, 42 U.S.C.A. sections 2000 a-h. To find this statute, look in Title 42 in the United States Code Annotated (U.S.C.A.) and then find the volume of that title containing section 2000, subsections a through h.

Statute books typically include a subject index in the last volume, where you can look for references to relevant laws. When using an index, try to think of several possible headings for the subject you are looking for. To do this, review headings in a treatise or encyclopedia or ask a librarian. If you don't find anything under the first logical heading, keep searching, or look in a legal dictionary to find related words or phrases. For example, if you don't know the name or citation to the federal law that forbids racial discrimination, you might first look in the index under "Civil Rights." If that doesn't work, you might try "Discrimination" or "Racial discrimination."

Legal subjects overlap, so you may find what you need under more than one heading. For example, a law regarding an exception to the hearsay rule may be listed under "evidence," "hearsay," "hearsay rule, exceptions to" and under the specific name of the exception itself—for instance, "business records."

When you look up statutes, try to use an "annotated" version of the statute books. Annotated versions contain the actual language of an official statute, along with short summaries of the significant court cases (including their legal citation for easy reference; see below) that have discussed each statute, and references to other resource books and articles.

Once you have found a relevant statute, here are some suggestions for reading and making sense of it:

- Make sure you understand all the terms. Refer to a legal dictionary to look up words in the statute. In longer statutes, the first parts often define terms used in other parts of the law.

- Always check to see if the law is current. Laws are often revised and sometimes repealed (removed from the books). So, after you find a statute in the main section of your state's hardbound statute book, be sure to look in the paper-bound supplement or update, called a "pocket part" usually located inside the back cover of the book. Pocket parts contain the changes that have been made to a law or its wording since the publication of the hardbound volume. Some pocket parts are also annotated with references—for example, citations to recent cases discussing a statute.

b.   Local Ordinances

Cities and counties pass a wide variety of ordinances—rules which, subject to state and federal laws, have the force and effect of law. They can have a great impact on your daily life and business. Among other things, they can affect:

- parking and driving

- health and safety standards in rental properties

- new building requirements, and

- zoning (restrictions on how land can be used).

THE NUMBERING SYSTEM FOR REPORTERS

Case reporters are published in numbered volumes. After a series accumulates years of numbered volumes, the publisher starts over with another series. So, you may find a cite to 2d or 3d series. For example, *York v. Story,* 324 F.2d 450 (1963) is at volume 324 of the Federal Reporter, second series, beginning on page 450.

In addition to the full text of the court's opinions, reporters include "headnotes," short summaries of the legal issues in a case. Headnotes are numbered in the order in which the issues are discussed in a case. They can be quite useful, both for a quick look at what a case is about and as a table of contents to help you locate issues that interest you.

Headnotes are not written by the judge who wrote the opinion, but by the editors of the reporter. They can be inaccurate and are not "law," so don't quote them to support for your position when making an argument to a judge. You must rely on the decision of the court itself.

Once court cases are published, they are usually not removed from the books even if later courts conclude that the decision is no longer correct. Thus, you always need to check that a case you rely on is still "good law," meaning that it has not been "overruled" by a later case. A series of case histories called *Shepard's Citations for Cases* reports the status of published cases. Ask a law librarian how to use *Shepard's* to verify that any case you intend to rely on is still good law. *Shepard's* can also help you find more recent cases that discuss (but don't overrule) the case you're interested in.

WHAT RULES JUDGES MUST FOLLOW

Sometimes it can be confusing to know which of the rules you may find in your research the judge will have to follow. Primary authorities (statutes, cases, administrative regulations and local rules and ordinances) can be "mandatory," which means that a court has to follow them. But they can also be just "persuasive," which means a court can consider them but does not have to follow them. For example, a state court in New York may find it helpful and convincing that a California court recently decided the same legal question now before the New York court. But the New York court does not have to follow the California court's decision.

A judge must, however, follow the decisions of higher courts in the same state. For example, a Los Angeles trial judge must follow a decision of the California Supreme Court (the highest state court in California), but a trial judge in Alabama doesn't have to.

When researching cases, it is best to find an appellate court case from your own state (or from your Circuit in the federal court system); that way the case is binding on your trial judge. But if all you can find is an out-of-state case that is nonetheless right on point and very helpful to your case, you may try to convince your judge that it's reasoning is persuasive.

Similar rules apply to statutes. Statutes are mandatory if they were enacted by the legislature in the state where your case will be tried.

Local governments vary as to how they organize and publish their ordinances, so you may have to check with a law librarian to find what you need. Public libraries often have local ordinances, too. Sometimes you can obtain copies of local ordi-

nances from a city office, such as a police or motor vehicles departments for traffic concerns or a planning department for zoning and building rules. If you know the specific subject of the ordinance you are looking for, you can probably get a copy by just calling the City or County Clerk's Office, or the City or County Attorney. They will usually send you a copy, free or for a small photocopying fee.

LAW SITES ON THE INTERNET

Nolo Press' Website (www.nolo.com) is a great place to start when looking for legal information on the Web. The site features Nolo's Legal Encyclopedia, a collection of articles and frequently asked questions (FAQs) on dozens of topics, including employment rights, consumer and insurance issues, real estate problems, debt and credit pickles and family and neighbor disputes. In addition, you may find some of the following sites helpful as you begin to get acquainted with your field of research:

http://www.law.emory.edu/FOCAL
Electronic Reference Desk—this site provides an index of laws by topic and includes links to both federal and state sites.

http://law.house.gov
U.S. House Internet Law Library—this is a general topical site, good for getting started.

http://www.law.cornell.edu
Legal Information Institute—this site provides a multitude of information, including links to state resources.

http://www.law.indiana.edu/law/v-lib/lawindex.html
The World Wide Web Virtual Library—this site provides legal resources by topic and has a vast list of links to other legal sites.

c.   Court Cases

In cases that come before appellate courts, appellate judges review the record and decisions of trial courts. They interpret the meaning of statutes, constitutional provisions and other court cases, making what's known as "common law" (judge-made law). Sometimes, appellate courts write decisions (called opinions, case law or cases), in which they summarize the facts that the trial judge or jury found to be true and set forth the appellate court judges' legal reasoning and "holding" (decision).

Appellate court cases are collected and published in hardbound volumes called "reporters," "reports" or "case reports." There are many separate reporters for different courts and geographical areas. For example, a case from the New York Court of Appeals may be published in a series of state reporters called *New York Appeals* and also in a regional reporter series called the *Northeastern Reporter,* which includes cases from several states. Federal cases are published according to the court that decided them. For example, decisions by the U.S. Courts of Appeal are collected in the *Federal Reporter.* At present in its second series, this is called the *Federal Reporter, Second Series* (F.2d).

Recent cases, not yet included in a hardbound reporter, are located in softbound supplements. And cases decided in the last few days or weeks may often only be available from the appellate court itself or a computer reporting service. If you want to look up a new case you just read about in the newspaper, for example, ask the librarian to assist you; it won't yet be in the hardbound books.

Cases, like statutes, have citations that let you look them up easily. Let's say you want to read the famous school desegregation case *Brown v. Board of Education.* Consulting an encyclopedia or legal dictionary, you learn its citation is 347 U.S. 483 (1954). The first number means the case is located in volume 347. The letters in the middle (U.S.) are the abbreviation for *United States Reports,* the case reporter series where the *Brown* case is published. The last number tells you the case begins at page 483. The names reflect the parties to the lawsuit, and the date at the end is when the United States Supreme Court decided the case.

d.   State Constitutions and the U.S. Constitution

The U.S. Constitution is the supreme law of the land, which means all local, state and federal laws must comply with it. State constitutions have the same authority over state laws, but state constitutions must also comply with the U.S. Constitution. Courts decide whether or not laws comply with constitutional provisions. Courts also interpret what constitutional provisions mean, just like they interpret statutes.

The research you do is not likely to involve constitutional law. Most of what you need will be found in reference materials, statutes and court cases. Because constitutional law is often complex, if your case involves a constitutional issue—for example, if you want to challenge a law that you feel is unconstitutional—you probably should consult a lawyer for assistance.

e.   Administrative Regulations

Administrative regulations ("regs") are enacted by federal, state and local agencies. For example, the federal Equal Employment Opportunity Commission, a state Veterans' Board, and a local school board probably all make their own rules. Administrative laws govern agencies' policies and procedures, such as how they conduct hearings and why they grant or withhold benefits.

You'll need to research agency regulations if you are presenting your case at a hearing before an administrative agency. Although the hearing may resemble a trial, in reality it is quite different. For example, most agencies do not follow the rules of evidence, and you have no right to a jury. Lawyers may be excluded, and you may not be able to subpoena witnesses or documents or even have witnesses testify. Some hearings are not open to the public.

C. RESOLVING LEGAL RESEARCH PROBLEMS

Now that you have a general sense of the types of legal research tools available to you, keep this three-step process in mind as you look for the answer to a legal question:

1. Try to find a resource person who can give you an answer or direct you to the place where you can find it.

2. Look for reference materials that explain and summarize the area of law your question involves. These may be able to guide you to the law itself.

3. When looking at the law itself, try to find pertinent statutes first. Then look for court decisions that clarify and interpret the statutes. ■

GLOSSARY

This glossary, which defines many of the terms that appear in this book, is intended for quick reference. A list of recommended legal dictionaries is in Chapter 22, Legal Research, Section B.

Action

Another word for a lawsuit. ("I began this negligence action last fall after the defendant, Ms. Adams, struck me while I was crossing the street at Elm and Main.")

Admission

An out-of-court statement by your adversary which you offer into evidence as an exception to the hearsay rule.

Affidavit

A written statement of facts made under oath. (See also, "Declaration.")

Affirmative defense

A claim made by a defendant in an answer that acts as a bar to a claim in a complaint. One common affirmative defense is that the plaintiff should not win because the "statute of limitations" (time limit within which to sue) has passed.

Alimony (also "spousal support" or "maintenance")

Money that one spouse pays to support the other (usually but not always monthly) following a divorce or separation.

Allegation

A statement by a party in a pleading saying what that party's position is and what that party intends to prove.

Annulment (also called a "nullity of marriage")

A legal decree that says, in effect, the marriage never existed.

Answer

A defendant's response to a plaintiff's complaint. It often both denies allegations made by the plaintiff and asserts affirmative defenses.

Appeal

A request to a higher court to review the legal decisions made by a lower court.

Appellant

The party who brings an appeal to an appellate court.

Appellate court

A higher court that reviews the decision of a lower court. ("The appellate court reviewed and overturned the decision of the trial court.")

Appellee

The party who responds to an appeal brought by an appellant.

Arbitration

A procedure for resolving disputes by an impartial third party (the "arbitrator") without a formal, court trial.

Argument

A persuasive presentation of the law and facts of a case or particular issue within a case to the judge or jury.

At issue memorandum

A document that states that all parties have been served, that the parties disagree (or are "at issue") over one or more points to be resolved at trial, and how much time the parties estimate will be required for trial.

Authenticate

Identify. You "authenticate" an exhibit by offering testimony that tells the judge what the exhibit is and its connection to the case.

Bailiff

A court official, classified as a peace officer and often dressed in uniform. The bailiff performs a wide variety of duties, such as maintaining order in the courtroom, escorting witnesses in and out of court and handing exhibits to witnesses who are testifying.

Battery

A legal claim of an uninvited touching. If someone hits you, you may have a claim of battery against that person.

Bench

The seat where a judge sits in the courtroom during a trial or hearing. Sometimes the word "bench" is used in place of the word "judge"—for example, someone might say she wants a "bench trial," meaning a trial by a judge without a jury.

Best evidence rule

A rule that restricts a witness from orally testifying to the contents of a document unless the document is produced in court, or it is proved to the judge that there is a valid reason why it can't be produced.

Breach

A failure or violation of a legal obligation.

Breach of contract

A legal claim that one party failed to perform as required under a valid agreement with the other party. ("The roofer breached our contract by using substandard supplies when he repaired my roof.")

Brief

A legal document written by a party to convince a judge of the correctness of the party's position on one or more issues in the case.

Burden of proof

The requirement that a party convince the judge or jury that his or her claim is correct. In most civil cases, the burden is a "preponderance of the evidence," which means something more that 50%.

Business records exception

An exception to the hearsay rule, which allows a business document to be admitted into evidence if a proper foundation is laid to show it is reliable.

Caption

A heading on all pleadings submitted to the court. It states basic information such as the parties' names, court and case number.

Case

Lawsuit. "Case" also refers to a written decision by a judge, found in books called case reporters or reporters. A party's case or "case-in-chief" also refers to the evidence that party submits in support of her position.

Case number (also called "cause" number)

Number assigned by the clerk's office to identify a particular case. Often the case number is stamped or printed on the front (or "caption") page of the initial pleading when it is first filed. That same case number should appear on the front page of all other documents filed as part of the case.

Cause of action

See "Legal claim."

Challenge for cause

A way to get a juror dismissed from your case in which you state a reason why the juror is objectionable.

Chambers (also called "judge's chambers")

A judge's private office, often located adjacent to the judge's courtroom.

Child custody

Physical control over the children and legal authority to make critical parenting decisions.

Child support

Money that one parent (usually the noncustodial parent or the parent with the higher income) pays to the other parent (usually the custodial parent or the parent with the lower income).

Child support formulas

Written guidelines (may be called "schedules")-typically based on a combination of the parents' ability to pay and the needs of the children-which set forth how child support is calculated in each state.

Citizenship

Allegiance to the government of the United States and to the state in which a person resides.

Circumstantial evidence

Evidence that proves a fact by means of an inference. For example, from the evidence that a person was seen running away from the scene of a crime, a judge or jury may infer that the person committed the crime.

Civil

Noncriminal. Civil lawsuits are generally between two private parties; criminal actions involve government enforcement of the criminal laws.

Claim

See "Legal claim."

Claim for relief

See "Legal claim."

Clear and convincing evidence

The burden of proof in a few types of civil cases, such as cases involving fraud. "Clear and convincing" is a higher standard than "preponderance of the evidence," the standard typical in most civil cases, but not as high as "beyond a reasonable doubt," the standard in criminal cases.

Clerk's Office

The administrative office in a courthouse where legal documents are filed, stored and made available to the public.

Closing Argument (final argument)

A persuasive presentation of your side of the case to the judge or jury at the conclusion of the evidence.

Common law

Judge-made law, resulting from appellate court decisions. Common law is often contrasted with "statutory law," which is enacted by legislatures.

Community property

A method used by about ten states to define property acquired during marriage and to divide property and debts upon divorce.

Compensatory damages

Money that is meant to compensate or make up for the losses the plaintiff suffered.

Complaint

The initial pleading, setting out the plaintiff's legal claims, which starts a lawsuit. Sometimes called a petition.

Concurrent jurisdiction

When two courts (often one state and one federal) both have power to hear a case.

Conformed copy

Copy of a document filed with the court that bears the court's stamp and date.

Consideration

Something of value which is given in exchange for a promise in order to form a legally binding contract.

Contempt of court

Behavior, in or outside of court, that obstructs court administration, violates or resists a court order or otherwise disrupts or shows disregard for the administration of justice. It is punishable by fine or imprisonment.

Contested divorce

A divorce is contested if, after one spouse files for divorce, the other spouse opposes some aspect of what the moving spouse requests in his or her initial pleading.

Contingent fee

A method of compensating a lawyer for legal services in which the lawyer receives a percentage of the money a client is awarded at the close of a trial or by a settlement.

Continuance

A delay. A party who wants the court to postpone a deadline requests a continuance.

Contract

A legally valid agreement to do or not to do something, such as an employment contract or contract of sale for real estate.

Costs (also, "costs of suit" or "court costs")

Expenses of trial other than attorneys' fees, such as fees and costs for filing legal documents, witness travel, court reporters and expert witnesses. Sometimes, the party who wins a lawsuit can recover costs from the opposing party.

Counsel

Attorneys or lawyers (also called counselors). To counsel means to advise.

Counterclaim

A legal claim by a defendant against a plaintiff.

Court clerk

A court employee who assists a judge with the many administrative tasks of moving cases through the court system. For example, the court clerk may prepare and maintain the judge's calendar, retrieve case files from the main Clerk's Office, administer oaths to witnesses during trial and prepare orders and judgments.

Court reporter

A person who records every word that is said during official court proceedings and depositions, and sometimes prepares a written transcript of those proceedings.

Cross-claim (also called a "cross-complaint")

A claim filed against a third party who was not a party to the original lawsuit.

Cross-examination

A party's opportunity to ask questions of her adversary's witnesses, including the adversary if he or she testified on direct examination.

Damages

Money sought by a party who has suffered some legal wrong.

Declaration

A signed statement of facts personally known to the "declarant," the person signing the statement.

Default

A party's failure to do what is required—for example, a defendant's failure to respond to the complaint.

Default judgment

A court order for judgment against the defendant to pay the amount requested by the plaintiff, because the defendant failed to answer and defend against a properly filed lawsuit.

Defendant

A party who is being sued. Sometimes called a respondent.

Demurrer

Another name, used in some court systems, for a motion to dismiss a complaint for failure to state a legally valid claim.

Deponent

A person whose deposition is being taken.

Deposition

A discovery (formal pre-trial investigation) tool in which a party (or her lawyer) asks a series of oral questions of another party or witness. The questions are answered under oath and taken down by a court reporter.

Directed verdict

A ruling by a judge, typically at the close of the plaintiff's evidence in a jury trial, which awards judgment to the defendant.

Direct examination

The initial questioning of a witness by the party who called that witness.

Discovery

Formal investigation that parties conduct before trial in order to obtain information from each other about the case to prepare for settlement or trial. The primary discovery tools in most cases are depositions and interrogatories.

Dismiss a case

When a judge dismisses a case, the judge essentially throws the case out of court, so that moving party must refile initial pleading papers.

Diversity jurisdiction

Federal court jurisdiction based on the parties to a lawsuit being citizens of different states.

Divorce

The legal ending of a marriage.

Divorce papers

Initial pleadings (typically called a "petition" or "complaint") filed with the court to start divorce proceedings.

Docket

The term is used in two ways:
1. A formal record of all the legal documents that have been filed and court proceedings and orders in a particular case.
2. A calendar or list of all the proceedings on a court's agenda.

Elements ("legal elements")

Component parts of legal claims. To win, a plaintiff must prove all elements of a claim.

Emergency order

An emergency procedure (reserved for urgent cases such as where you fear your spouse will hurt you or abduct your children) whereby a party may sometimes obtain a court order without giving the other party the advance written notice usually required by court rules.

Encumber property

To mortgage or otherwise use property as collateral or security for a debt.

Equitable distribution

A method the majority of states follow to distribute marital property equitably (fairly) upon divorce.

Equitable relief

A court order that a party perform an act (such as cut down a tree), rather than (or in addition to) pay money damages.

Evidence

Information presented to a judge or jury, including testimony of witnesses and documents.

Excited utterance

An out-of-court statement made about a startling event while the speaker is experiencing that event. Such statements are admissible in evidence under an exception to the hearsay rule.

Exhibit

A tangible object that a party presents to the judge or jury during trial to help establish his or her case.

Ex parte

One-sided. A contact with the judge by one party outside the presence of the other party is considered an "ex-parte contact" and is generally forbidden.

Expert witness

A person who testifies based on his or her special knowledge or training.

Fair market value

The price an item would get if sold today (as opposed to the original purchase price), such as a home, business, artwork or jewelry.

Family courts

Civil courts that typically have jurisdiction over matters such as divorce, child support and custody, spousal support, paternity and domestic abuse.

Fast track

A system certain courts have adopted to help streamline the administration and litigation of lawsuits.

Fault-based divorce

Laws requiring that a spouse filing for divorce prove the other spouse was legally at fault for the breakdown of the marriage-for example, alleging the other spouse committed adultery or left the family home.

Federal question jurisdiction

Federal court jurisdiction based on federal rules and statutes.

Former name

Maiden name.

Forum non conveniens

A claim that a case has been filed in an inconvenient court and should for that reason be moved to a different court.

Forum shopping

Trying to have a case heard in an advantageous court.

Foundation

A basis for the admission of testimony or exhibits into evidence.

Fraud

Intentional deception causing legal injury.

Freeze

To close, as in to freeze joint accounts and open new ones alone following a separation or divorce.

Frivolous motion

A motion that is made without legally valid grounds, such as a motion that is designed to harass an opponent or delay proceedings.

Full Faith and Credit

A constitutional requirement that court judgments (and other official rules) of one state be honored by all other states.

Hearsay

An out-of-court statement offered in court to prove the truth of what that statement asserts.

Hostile witness ("adverse witness")

A witness so hostile to the party who called him that the party can ask the witness leading questions.

Impanel ("empanel")

The act of assembling a panel of prospective jurors for jury selection.

Impeach

Discredit. To impeach a witness' credibility is to cast doubt on that person's believability.

Inadmissible

When evidence offered by a party is ruled inadmissible by the judge, it is not allowed to become a part of the court record.

Injunction or injunctive relief

A form of equitable relief, such as an order that the defendant stay away from the plaintiff.

In rem jurisdiction

A court's power to decide issues concerning property located in the court's geographical area.

Interrogatories

A set of written questions submitted by one party to another party to answer under oath as part of the pre-trial investigation of a lawsuit.

Irreconcilable differences

Terminology spouses must use in some states to say they feel certain they cannot get back together and want a divorce. (The exact term differs from state to state; for example, some say "irretrievably broken," but the idea is the same.)

Irrelevant

Not related to. Evidence that is irrelevant to the claims at issue in a lawsuit is not admissible in trial.

Joint (or "shared") custody

An arrangement whereby both parents share either or both the physical custody of the children (living with them some or all of the time) and the legal authority to make parenting decisions.

Judge

A public officer who presides over court hearings and trials.

Judge pro tem

A temporary or substitute judge, often a lawyer, who temporarily fills in for a regular judge. Parties can refuse to have their case heard by a judge pro tem.

Judgment

A final court ruling resolving the claims at issue in a lawsuit and determining the rights and obligations of the parties.

Judgment notwithstanding the verdict (JNOV)

A decision by the judge to overturn a jury's verdict because, as a matter of law, the jury's decision was unreasonable. This procedure is like a directed verdict but comes at the end of the case.

Judgment proof

A party who doesn't have money or other property to pay a court judgment is considered "judgment proof."

Judicial arbitration or mediation

Court-ordered alternative dispute resolution following the filing of a complaint and answer.

Jurisdiction

The scope of a court's authority. Often the term refers to the geographic area where a court has power.

Juror

A person selected to serve on a jury.

Jury

A group of people selected to apply the law, as given by the judge, to the facts jurors find true, to decide the outcome of a case.

Jury instructions

Legal rules given by the judge to the jury.

Jury selection

See "Voir dire."

Law clerk

An assistant to a judge, typically a recent law school graduate, who helps the judge with things like researching the issues and drafting court opinions or decisions.

Lawsuit

A legal case initiated in court.

Leading question

A question asked of a witness at trial that suggests the answer. It's really just a statement phrased as a question.

Legal claim (also called "claim for relief" or "cause of action")

A statement of the legal wrong (such as negligence or breach of contract) for which the plaintiff seeks legal relief.

Legal separation

A legal decree which keeps a marriage intact but allows the family court to make orders separating property and awarding custody and support.

Litigant

A party to a lawsuit.

Litigation

The process of resolving a dispute by a lawsuit in court.

Litigator

An attorney whose practice involves handling lawsuits.

Local rules

Rules adopted by specific courts or specific regions regulating case administration and litigation. Local rules sometimes modify state and federal rules, and it is critical to understand them to effectively present a case in court.

Magistrate

A court official who acts as a judge in certain (often lower level) court proceedings.

Malicious prosecution

A claim that a lawsuit was filed without sufficient justification or for an improper purpose.

Malpractice

Professional negligence; the failure to use the type of care a professional should reasonably use in a given situation.

Marital property

Most property acquired by a couple during marriage. (Marital property may be "community property" in states which use that system of property classification).

Marshal

A law officer who is empowered to enforce certain court rulings and orders. The federal government has U.S. Marshals, and some states have marshals, similar to sheriffs.

Mediation

An out-of-court dispute resolution procedure where parties use a neutral, third party (a mediator) to help them come to an agreement or settlement.

Memorandum of Points and Authorities

A document that cites (refers to) legal authorities such as statutes and court cases, and explains how those authorities support the position advocated by the party who wrote the memorandum.

Minimum contacts

Sufficient connections to a state to give jurisdiction to the courts of that state.

Mistrial

A trial that the judge ends before the full proceeding has been completed because a prejudicial error or wrong has occurred.

Modifications

Changes a court makes to previous court orders.

Monitored visit

Court requirement that a parent (or other related adult) only visit his or her children under supervision, sometimes also only in certain places or at certain times.

Motion

A request to the court for an order or ruling. Some motions are made orally, others in writing. Depending on the ruling sought, a motion can be made before, during or after trial.

Motion for a Continuance

See "Continuance."

Motion for Summary Judgment

See "Summary Judgment."

Motion in limine

A request for a court order excluding irrelevant or prejudicial evidence, typically made before a jury trial.

Movant

The party making or bringing a motion.

Moving Party

See "Movant."

Negligence

A legal claim that alleges a failure to use "ordinary and reasonable care" in a given situation.

No-fault divorce

Most states now allow divorce if either or both spouses want a divorce, on the basis of incompatibility, with no legal battle over who was at fault for the breakdown of the marriage.

Non-dischargeable debts

Debts such as child and spousal support, that are not wiped out by a bankruptcy.

Nonsuit (sometimes called "dismissal")

The court's dismissal of a lawsuit that a plaintiff began but did not follow through with.

Notice

Notification. To give someone notice of a hearing date is to let them know when and where it will take place and other basic information they need.

Notice of Motion

A document that notifies an adversary about when and where a hearing on a motion will be held, what the reason for the motion is and what supporting documentation will be relied on in making the motion.

Objection

A party's request, made during trial, asking the court to prevent certain testimony or exhibits submitted by the other side from being admitted into evidence.

Offer of judgment

A written settlement offer that can impose costs on a party who refuses it.

Opening Statement

A statement made by an attorney or pro per at the beginning of a trial (before the evidence is introduced) to preview the evidence and set the stage for the trial.

Order

A ruling or decision by a court. A court order can be made orally or in writing.

Order to Show Cause (OSC)

An Order to Show Cause is a legal document that sets forth the legal relief one party is asking for and tells the other party to come to court at a specific time and explain why the court should not grant the moving party's requests.

Overrule

Deny. When the judge overrules an objection the judge denies the objection, and the evidence objected to is allowed.

Pain and suffering

Inconvenience and discomfort resulting from injuries for which damages can be sought in a lawsuit.

Party

A person or entity who has brought a lawsuit, or one who is defending against or responding to a lawsuit.

Paternity

A court action to recognize a man as the legal father of a child.

Percipient witness

A witness who perceived the facts she testifies about. A percipient witness is an ordinary witness. (Compare an expert witness who, because of special knowledge or training, may testify about things she did not actually observe.)

Peremptory challenge

An opportunity for a party to challenge (dismiss or excuse) a potential juror during jury selection without having to give a reason. Each party gets a limited number of peremptory challenges.

Perjury

The crime of lying while under oath—while testifying during trial, in a sworn affidavit or in a deposition or interrogatories.

Personal jurisdiction

A court's power over a party to a lawsuit.

Personal property

All property that isn't real estate ("real property").

Petitioner

A person who brings a petition (in some court systems, another word for complaint) before the court.

Plaintiff

The person who initiates a lawsuit. Sometimes called a "petitioner."

Pleadings

Legal documents filed in court that set forth the legal claims and defenses of the parties to a lawsuit

Points and Authorities

See "Memorandum of Points and Authorities."

Prayer for relief

The concluding portion of a complaint, where the plaintiff specifies what she wants from the court.

Prejudice

Bias or discrimination.

Prejudicial error

A wrong that occurs during trial that seriously impairs a party's ability to have a fair trial.

Prenuptial (or "antenuptial") agreement

An agreement establishing in advance the amount a spouse will have to pay in the event the couple later divorce.

Preponderance of the evidence

The burden of proof in most civil actions (amounting to something more that 50%).

Present sense impression

A statement made about an event while, or just after, the event occurs. Such statements are admissible in evidence under an exception to the hearsay rule.

Pre-trial conference

A meeting of the parties, before trial, in order to resolve and narrow the disputed issues, identify undisputed facts and sometimes try to settle the case. Pre-trial conferences may be conducted by a judge in court or the parties themselves out of court.

Pre-trial memorandum

A document prepared before a pre-trial conference in which a party identifies undisputed and disputed facts, legal issues, witnesses expected to testify and other basic information to facilitate the pre-trial conference. Some courts require parties to meet and prepare this document together (then called a "joint pre-trial memorandum").

Pre-trial motion

A request to the court made before trial for an order or ruling. Typical pre-trial motions include a motion for continuance, motion to dismiss for failure to state a claim, motion for default judgment and motion for summary judgment.

Pre-trial order

A document prepared after a pre-trial conference and signed by the judge. It sets out the agreed upon facts and those remaining factual and legal issues to be resolved at trial, the anticipated witness list, exhibits the parties will introduce and other decisions made during the pre-trial conference.

Privileged

Confidential. Information that is confidential because of a particular legal rule, such as information revealed during a private doctor-patient examination or lawyer-client meeting, is said to be privileged.

Privileges

Legal rules and principles that keep certain information confidential and out of court or discovery. Some common privileges include communications made to a spouse, doctor, lawyer, psychotherapist or member of the clergy.

Probative

Tending to prove or disprove some contested issue. This term is usually used to describe evidence.

Pro bono

Legal services performed pro bono are done for free or a reduced fee. (Comes from the Latin meaning "for the good.")

Procedural law

Laws or rules that govern how a case is administered and tried in court. (Contrast rules of "substantive law," which define the rights and duties of parties.)

Process server

A person who is legally authorized to serve (deliver) legal papers to a party in the case, such as a sheriff.

Promissory note

A written agreement by a borrower of money to repay a loan at a definite time.

Proof of service

A document, often attached to a pleading, motion or brief, that states who such papers were served on and how and when the service was made. A proof of service must often be filed with the court.

Pro per

Someone who represents him or herself in court without a lawyer.

Proposed order

Your draft of a court order which you may present to the court along with your request for the order you seek. (It's "proposed" because the court hasn't signed it yet.)

Pro se

Same as "Pro per."

Protective order

A ruling by the court that limits or disallows a party's discovery requests. A party might seek a protective order, for example, if the other side's interrogatories ask for confidential, privileged information. The protective order would allow the party not to answer the objectionable questions.

Punitive damages

Damages meant to punish the person who committed a wrong, not simply to compensate the person who was wronged. Punitive damages are allowed only in certain circumstances—for example, when the defendant's conduct is shown to have been malicious.

Real property

Land or real estate (house, condo), as opposed to "personal property" such as money, cars and stereos.

Rebuttal evidence

Evidence offered to contradict evidence presented by the adversary.

Recess

A break in a hearing or trial.

Record

The official written transcript of court proceedings and depositions. When something goes "on the record," it appears in the official transcript. If some aspect of the case is "off the record," such as a brief procedural question at the judge's bench, it will not appear in the official transcript.

Recross examination

Additional cross-examination of witnesses called by an adversary on redirect examination.

Redact

To delete or cover up part of a document because it refers to inadmissible evidence.

Redirect examination

Additional direct examination of a witness by the party who called that witness. It takes place just after that witness has been cross-examined by the adversary.

Release

The abandonment of a claim against a party, often in exchange for a promise or offer by the other party.

Relevancy

A connection or applicability to the issues in the case. Relevant evidence is evidence that helps to prove or disprove some fact in connection with the case.

Relief

The benefit, compensation or redress sought in connection with a legal claim.

Remedy

The relief a party seeks in a case. Remedies for a typical tort (personal injury) claim, for example, are compensatory damages and monetary relief for pain and suffering.

Reply

A plaintiff's answer or responsive pleading to a defendant's counterclaim.

Request for Admission (Request to Admit)

A discovery tool in which a party asks an adversary to admit that certain facts are true. If the adversary admits the facts or fails to respond in a timely manner, they will be deemed true for the purposes of trial.

Request for Production of Documents (Request to Produce)

A discovery tool in which a party asks an adversary to produce (deliver or make available) specific documents.

Residency

Living in a particular state with the intention of remaining there.

Residency requirement for divorce

Each state has its own requirements for how long you must live in the state before filing for divorce, but six months is typical.

Respondent

The name for the defendant (responding party) in cases where the plaintiff is called a "petitioner." Also, the party who responds to an appeal (the appellee) is often called a respondent.

Response (or responsive pleading)

A general term for a legal document in which a party responds to an adversary's pleading, motion or brief.

Restraining order (also called a "protective order" or a "TRO")

A court order to stop certain illegal or threatening behavior. A restraining order may also require a person stay away from a spouse or children, move out of a family home, or refrain from selling property or canceling insurance.

Sanctions

Penalties, often fines, imposed by a judge for improper conduct during litigation.

Separate property

Certain property that a married person may keep separately to spend, give or will away without the consent of the other spouse.

Service of process

The delivery of legal documents, such as initial pleadings, to an opposing party.

Settlement conference

A meeting of the parties, with or without the judge present, to discuss settlement of a lawsuit. Many courts require the parties to have at least one settlement conference, called a mandatory settlement conference (MSC), before trial.

Small claims courts

Courts with informal procedures, often limited to cases involving a maximum of $5,000.

Statutes

Laws enacted by legislatures.

Statute of frauds

A law requiring certain contracts to be in writing—for example, contracts to buy or sell real property. Most other contracts can be oral.

Statute of limitations

The legal time limit in which a lawsuit can be filed for a particular legal claim.

Stipulation

An agreement between parties. For example, you and your adversary may stipulate (agree) to the admissibility of certain testimony or an exhibit.

Strike

Delete testimony from the official court record.

Subject matter jurisdiction

The power of a court to hear certain kinds of cases.

Subpoena (subpena)

A court order compelling someone to appear in court.

Subpoena duces tecum

A court order compelling someone to appear in court and bring along with them certain tangible objects or documents.

Substantive law

Rules defining the rights and duties of parties (as opposed to procedural laws, which govern the litigation process).

Summary judgment

A final decision by the judge resolving the claims in a lawsuit before trial, based on affidavits and written evidence. A summary judgment is issued when the parties have no issues of fact to litigate, only legal questions.

Summons

A notice, typically served along with a complaint, informing the defendant that a lawsuit has been initiated and notifying the defendant of where and when he or she must respond.

Supporting declarations

Written statements under oath setting out facts that justify the issuance of a court order.

Sustain

Uphold. When a judge sustains an objection, it is upheld, and the evidence objected to is not allowed in.

Tentative ruling

A preliminary decision of a judge in a hearing or trial, based on the papers submitted and typically issued sometime before the scheduled court proceeding.

Testify

To give testimony under oath.

Testimony

Evidence given by a witness under oath, in court or in a deposition.

Tort

A legal claim of civil wrong (other than a breach of contract), often referred to as a personal injury.

Transcript

A written record of a court proceeding or deposition.

Treatise

A legal reference book, usually covering an entire legal subject.

Trial

The in-court examination and resolution of issues between litigants.

Trial notebook

A notebook or binder set up to help you organize your case.

Uncontested divorce

A divorce is uncontested if both parties want the divorce and have agreed upon questions of property division, support and/or custody. Simplified court procedures are available for uncontested divorces.

Venue

The geographic area in which a court has authority to hear a case.

Verdict

The jury's final decision in a lawsuit.

Verified pleadings

Pleadings signed under oath.

Voir dire

The process of questioning and selecting a jury.

Waiting period

A period of time that many states require spouses wait between when a divorce is granted by the court and when it becomes final-often three to six months.

Witness

A person who testifies in court. ■

INDEX

C

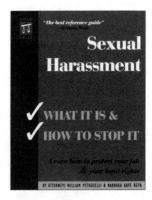

Your comments make a big difference in the development and revision of Nolo books and software. Please take a few minutes and register your Nolo product—and your comments—with us. Not only will your input make a difference, you'll receive special offers available only to registered owners of Nolo products on our newest books and software. Register now by:

PHONE
1-800-992-6656

FAX
1-800-645-0895

EMAIL
cs@nolo.com

or **MAIL** us
this registration card

REMEMBER:
Little publishers have big ears. We really listen to you.

- - - - - - - - - - - - - - - fold here - - - - - - - - - - - - - - -

REGISTRATION CARD

NAME	DATE
ADDRESS	

CITY	STATE	ZIP
PHONE	E-MAIL	

WHERE DID YOU HEAR ABOUT THIS PRODUCT?

WHERE DID YOU PURCHASE THIS PRODUCT?

DID YOU CONSULT A LAWYER? (PLEASE CIRCLE ONE)   YES   NO   NOT APPLICABLE

DID YOU FIND THIS BOOK HELPFUL?   (VERY)   5   4   3   2   1   (NOT AT ALL)

COMMENTS

WAS IT EASY TO USE?   (VERY EASY)   5   4   3   2   1   (VERY DIFFICULT)

DO YOU OWN A COMPUTER? IF SO, WHICH FORMAT? (PLEASE CIRCLE ONE)   WINDOWS   DOS   MAC

❑ If you do not wish to receive mailings from these companies, please check this box.

❑ You can quote me in future Nolo.com promotional materials. Daytime phone number _____

RYC 2.0

NOLO IN THE NEWS

"Nolo helps lay people perform legal tasks without the aid—or fees—of lawyers."
—USA TODAY

Nolo books are ..."written in plain language, free of legal mumbo jumbo, and spiced with witty personal observations."
—ASSOCIATED PRESS

"...Nolo publications...guide people simply through the how, when, where and why of law."
—WASHINGTON POST

"Increasingly, people who are not lawyers are performing tasks usually regarded as legal work... And consumers, using books like Nolo's, do routine legal work themselves."
—NEW YORK TIMES

"...All of [Nolo's] books are easy-to-understand, are updated regularly, provide pull-out forms...and are often quite moving in their sense of compassion for the struggles of the lay reader."
—SAN FRANCISCO CHRONICLE

fold here

- -

nolo.com
950 Parker Street
Berkeley, CA 94710-9867

Attn: | **RYC 2.0** |

DETROIT COLLEGE OF LAW